A THEATERGOER'S GUIDE TO
Shakespeare

A THEATERGOER'S GUIDE TO
Shakespeare

*Here will be found a careful survey of plots to the many
plays, together with helpful comments on their abundant
themes, characters, and puzzles, all written in plain
though not inelegant English, and intended to enhance
the gentle reader's enjoyment of a performance.*

ROBERT THOMAS FALLON

Ivan R. Dee

CHICAGO

A THEATERGOER'S GUIDE TO SHAKESPEARE. Copyright © 2001 by Robert
Thomas Fallon. All rights reserved, including the right to reproduce this book or
portions thereof in any form. For information, address: Ivan R. Dee, Publisher,
1332 North Halsted Street, Chicago 60622. Manufactured in the United States of
America and printed on acid-free paper.

Library of Congress Cataloging-in-Publication Data:
Fallon, Robert Thomas.
    A theatergoer's guide to Shakespeare / Robert Thomas Fallon.
       p. cm.
    Includes bibliographical references and index.
    ISBN 1-56663-508-x (acid-free paper)
    1. Shakespeare, William, 1564–1616—Stories, plots, etc.   2. Shakespeare,
William, 1564–1616—Outlines, syllabi, etc.   3. Shakespeare, William,
1564–1616—Handbooks, manuals, etc.   I. Title.
PR2987 .F35 2001
822.3'3—dc21   00-057018

Acknowledgments

I AM MOST GRATEFUL for the encouragement and advice of a host of family, friends, and colleagues, whom I have pressed into service to test the style and content of these pages. Prominent among family and friends are Marygrace Buckwalter, Elizabeth Fallon, and my daughter, Frances Schuster. Colleagues include the distinguished scholars James A. Butler, Kevin Harty, and William Kerrigan. As a group, they have urged me on and kept me from error and obscurity in this endeavor. I am especially grateful to Ivan R. Dee for his seasoned counsel and for his careful editing of the book.

I owe a special debt to a unique group of "the Bard's" ardent admirers, the Shakspere Society of Philadelphia, with the name spelled as it was at their first meeting in 1851. This venerable body, composed of bankers, accountants, doctors, lawyers, librarians, musicians, stockbrokers, independent entrepreneurs, and a scattering of academics, ranging in age from their thirties to their nineties, meets every other week from October to April to pursue their fascination with Shakespeare under the guidance for many years of the distinguished scholar Roland M. Frye. I was privileged to join the Society some time ago and owe many of my insights to the experience its members bring to the plays from worlds outside my own.

Contents

THE HISTORIES

Prologue

Piece out our imperfections with your thoughts.
—*Henry V*

THIS IS A BOOK for those whose first encounter with the plays of William Shakespeare, either on stage or in study, proved puzzling. It is for those as well who find them equally difficult in later encounters as students, as teachers offering a play for the first time, or as theatergoers drawn yet again to a performance. Shakespeare is never easy, yet each year millions flock to festivals devoted to his works in every corner of the globe, from Shanghai to Oslo, from Ojai, California, to Round Top, Texas, and Allentown, Pennsylvania, in New York, Atlanta, London, and, of course, in Stratford-on-Avon, where he was born and his bones now rest. Shakespeare's popularity persists despite the daunting surface of his text—the language, the poetry, and the allusions to the culture of his time—and most of those who read or watch a play find themselves at times wondering what in the world is going on. This book is intended to demystify that surface, so that the reader can follow the action with ease and savor the beauty and wisdom of the lines.

This is not a work of literary scholarship. It has arisen out of a love for Shakespeare nourished by teaching him for twenty-five years, an experience that has left me attuned to the difficulties encountered by those coming upon a play for the first time. During these years I have read extensively about these works, watched them performed, and talked about them with mounting pleasure. It is that pleasure I seek to share.

I address each play from a particular point of view—Hamlet's "mystery," Othello's passion, innocence in *The Tempest,* warfare in *Henry V,* and so on. Shakespeare's works are subject to a wide range of interpretation, however, so it goes without saying that mine is not the only way to confront the plays. In adopting a particular approach, I seek only to provide a measure of unity to the discussion, to highlight the dramatic qualities of the plays, and to offer readers a place to stand in coming to terms with them, so that they can arrive at their own evaluation of a performance.

The playgoer is likely to see a work performed in modern or any period dress; staged with an all-male or all-female cast; produced out of doors or in; slanted to favor some popular cause; or presented in its original Elizabethan setting, as Shakespeare would have conceived it. The possibilities are infinite, to be explored by any creative director, for the plays are infinite in their interpretation and appeal. Whether a stage or screen production succeeds, however, depends on its fidelity to the vision and poetry of the original. Some productions are ludicrous, some brilliant in their insight, but all depend for their success on Shakespeare's broad understanding of humanity. Those that depart from that vision regularly fail as theater. These surveys are therefore meant to prepare an audience for a variety of interpretations, to acquaint them sufficiently with the essential shape of a play so as to enhance their appreciation of any performance. In instances where alternate staging is a matter of great interest, as in a *Hamlet* or a *Henry V,* I call attention to those most frequently offered.

Since the intent of this book is to heighten the enjoyment of a performance, extended chapters are devoted to those plays most frequently staged, and only brief summaries to those performed less often. This more cursory treatment is not meant to imply that these plays should be dismissed. Their poetry, if more muted, has moments of astonishing power, and they feature characters that, though thinly drawn, blossom forth as consummate dramatic figures in Shakespeare's greater works— the tormented hero, the hidden villain, the wise fool, the demented lover, the doomed maiden, the madman.

It borders on an act of folly, of course, to characterize some of these plays as "Less Frequently Staged," since everyone has a favorite, often the one most recently seen. But a survey of the many festivals devoted to Shakespeare's works throughout the world reveals that theater producers, at least, find that some of them do not work as well as others on stage. The *Henry VI* trilogy, for example, is virtually never produced, and then only by companies that make an effort to stage the entire canon of thirty-seven plays over a period of years. So in the interest of offering a manageable book, we shall spend the bulk of our time with those plays that seem to work best, that is, those that keep filling theaters.

These appraisals may seem at times overly detailed, touching on matters that do not necessarily capture one's immediate attention during a performance. In the swift shuttle of dialogue, Shakespeare touches on common human experiences, loading the lines with sentiments that register on the pulse. It all happens too fast, however, for us to sort things out at the time—we can only watch and listen as the playwright strikes familiar chords in the imagination, prompting flashes of recognition that these are indeed the ways of a flawed humanity. Poetry is like music, and its words like the notes of a sonata, each individually struck but melding into others to produce a musical pattern, or melody. We examine the notes and phrases of music at leisure so as to comprehend the pattern, and in reading a play we can also pause over individual lines, as we do here on occasion, to enhance our understanding and enrich the experience of seeing it again on stage.

SOME NOTES ON THE TEXT

Since this is not a work of scholarship, I avoid as much as possible the specialized language of scholars and people of the theater. Some of their technical words and phrases, however, will prove helpful to the enjoyment of a performance. When this is the case, they appear *italicized* when first encountered in each chapter, indicating that a brief discussion of the term appears in the appendix, "Words and Phrases."

Further, readers will not find the kinds of footnotes that appear in scholarly works or editions of the plays. A few are scattered throughout the pages, but only on occasions when a source is essential or I can add an interesting sidelight.

Bold-face numbers in the text refer to the act and scene in which the action occurs. Thus, **2.4** is Act Two, scene 4.

A THEATERGOER'S GUIDE TO
Shakespeare

The Tragedies

As flies to wanton boys are we to th'gods
They kill us for their sport.
—*King Lear*

So oft it chances in particular men,
That from some vicious mole of nature in them,
. . . these men,
Carrying I say the stamp of one defect,
Shall in the general censure take corruption
From that particular fault.
—*Hamlet*

TRAGEDY

❧

THE WORDS "tragic" and "tragedy" will appear in this discussion frequently enough to raise a question as to what they mean. Probably the most useful definition for those who wonder why Shakespeare's plays work so well on the stage was written 2,500 years ago by the Greek philosopher Aristotle. The ancient Greeks were great playgoers, so much so that they held festivals in which prizes were awarded for the best group of plays produced; and they must have sat through scores of productions during the weeks of the contest. Aristotle examined the prizewinners to discover if they had features in common that contributed to their success, and he described his findings in a brief work, *Of Poetics*, which is so packed with insight that it is thought to be a set of notes he prepared for a series of lectures. Generations of scholars have expanded on those notes, speculating on just what he might have said in the lectures themselves.

The question of the *Poetics*—why do some plays work and others fail?—is not an easy one to answer. Every year artists who have toiled in the theater for decades troop to Broadway to mount plays that all who are concerned with the enterprise—the producer, playwright, director, and actors alike—are convinced will have a long run to enthusiastic critical acclaim, only to find that they must close after three performances for lack of an audience. Famous Hollywood producers pour millions into films, confident of their appeal, and are dismayed when the public stays away in droves while some unknown director fills theaters with a film made on a shoestring. It's a mystery, really, and always has been. Aristotle tried to unravel it by dissecting the prizewinners to determine why they worked.

Aristotle's explanation of what makes a play work is somewhat out of favor today. It is said, among other things, that he laid too heavy an emphasis on plot—and so indeed he did. But it is his few incisive paragraphs on character that are so valuable to our appreciation of Shakespeare's tragedies; and it is to those paragraphs that we turn, seeking some firm ground on which to stand in our encounters with the puzzling figures of these plays.

Aristotle begins by making distinctions, in the manner of philosophers of any age: A tragedy is a play in which the chief figure, or tragic hero, experiences a change from good fortune to bad; in a comedy the change is from bad to good. The tragic hero, he observes, must be an important person in the community, a king, a queen, a prince, or a famous warrior, a man or woman of substance and responsibility, because that figure experiences a fall, and any fall is more moving if it comes from a great height. It is evident that a figure who tumbles to death from the top of the Empire State Building will have a more dramatic impact than one who trips over a curb.

You will notice immediately that this quality does not always apply in the modern theater, which is filled with highly effective plays about the tragedy of the common man. Willy Loman, in Arthur Miller's *Death of a Salesman,* is not an important man except to his family, and the play opens upon him at the low point of his life; yet it is a highly effective tragedy. So Aristotle's observations must be taken with some caution—but they are useful. He is simply reporting on plays he has seen; and he observes that the most successful of them are about men and women in high places.

A corollary to this quality is his further observation that the tragic figure is famous as well, from one of the houses or families with which the audience is already familiar through knowledge of their history or mythology. Again, this quality need not necessarily apply to the modern stage, but it does bring up an important point: the Greek audience already knew what was to happen before the play began. This tends to rule out surprise endings, but it introduces into the action the element of *dramatic irony,* an essential effect of any successful play, comedy or tragedy. To illustrate: Aristotle's favorite work was Sophocles' *Oedipus the King,* the story of a famous man who, with every good intention, embarks on a determined effort to find out who his parents were. The Greek audience, familiar with the myth, were aware that unknown to Oedipus he has murdered his father and married his mother. Hence, when he says, "I must unlock the secret of my birth!" the audience becomes emotionally engaged in unfolding events.

This tragic hero, Aristotle tells us, should not be absolutely evil, since the death of such a figure, being only just, would fail to move the audience; nor should the figure be absolutely good, for his death would violate our concept of right and wrong, evoking not a tragic sense but a feeling of outrage. According to these guidelines, it would be impossible to mount a tragedy based on the lives of either Adolf Hitler, whose death we would feel was richly deserved, or of Jesus Christ, whose crucifixion was a gross miscarriage of justice. The figure must be, rather, an essentially good person, but one who suffers from an "error or frailty" in character—a person, in brief, much like ourselves. Moreover, the downfall of the tragic hero must come as a consequence of that same "error or frailty" in character, traditionally referred to as a "tragic flaw." Thus it may be said that Lear is rash, Macbeth ambitious, Othello passionate, and Hamlet melancholy, each possessed of emotions which we acknowledge in ourselves from time to time, but which these characters manifest to a degree fatal to themselves and those about them. Only thus can we recognize them as profoundly human and be moved by their fate. The tragic hero, in brief, illuminates everyday human choices by raising them to the level of life-or-death decisions, dramatizing the ordinary so that we may see significance in the common events of our lives.

Central to Aristotle's critique is the idea that something happens in the breasts of the audience as they watch events unfold on the stage. He suggests that we are moved by certain emotions, and he singles out pity and fear as the principal effects of tragedy. At certain points in the action these emotions, he says, having been aroused in the audience, are released, that is, either purged or purified. The Greeks called such a response a *catharsis,* an experience not unlike the release of grief through tears, or tension through laughter. All successful plays, he finds, include such moments, and if nothing of this sort occurs, the work fails to please. The skillful playwright will elicit this response, again, by placing before us the actions of a recognizable human being, one essentially good, indeed noble in nature, but possessed of an "error or frailty" in character that sets in motion a tragic chain of events. Such figures arouse pity in us,

Aristotle explains, because they are flawed human beings; and they excite fear because we acknowledge ourselves subject to the same flaw, one fully capable of growing to an excess of ambition like Macbeth's or of passion like Othello's. Pity and fear may occur at different intervals in the play, but Aristotle seems to imply that they are most effective when they come simultaneously. Commenting on the phenomenon, one scholar asks the reader to imagine walking down a narrow, dimly lit corridor and seeing a pitiable figure approach from the other end, one hobbling on crippled legs, gasping for breath, and dressed in ragged remnants of discarded clothes, and to further imagine drawing near the figure only to discover oneself facing a mirror.

Oddly, the great tragedies that reflect the qualities Aristotle has described do not leave an audience despairing. They depict the human condition as one in which the tragic hero struggles against all the flaws and follies of his nature and, even though he falls victim to them, achieves a kind of triumph in the end. Shakespeare achieves this effect in his closing scenes by restoring the hero momentarily to his former stature, reminding us briefly of the height from which he has fallen—as with Othello, or Lear, or even the villainous Macbeth. Although the curtain may fall on a stage strewn with the dead, leaving an audience stunned with a sense of loss, they depart the theater aware as well that the terrible events they have witnessed somehow affirm the inherent nobility of the human spirit.

KING LEAR

&

EARLY IN THIS CENTURY the distinguished scholar A. C. Bradley observed that "*King Lear* is too huge for the stage," a remark that can be taken in a number of ways.* *King Lear* is a long play, but Bradley surely had other matters in mind. He reflected a sentiment widely held that there was simply too much in it for one person to assimilate in a single evening's sitting, packed as it is with lines that illuminate so many complexities of the human condition—a father's relationship with sons and daughters; the specter of old age; questions of justice, nature, loyalty, and wisdom; the thirst for power; the role of the gods in human affairs; and the varieties of love. In truth, there is so much in the play that the viewer may emerge from a performance close to exhaustion, and many have found the final scene too much to bear.

Lear is the tale of an old and powerful monarch who is intent upon laying down the burdens of the crown. He divides his kingdom between two elder daughters, Goneril and Regan, and rashly disinherits his youngest, Cordelia, the only one of the three who truly loves him. He proposes to retain the dignity and trappings of the throne, however; and when his heartless daughters seek to strip him of his retinue, he rages at them and is finally driven mad by their ingratitude. Cordelia, married to the king of France, returns to England with an army to rescue him. Lear, exhausted by his suffering but eventually returned to sanity, is reunited

---

*Frank Kermode, ed., *King Lear, A Casebook* (London: Macmillan, 1969), p. 83. Bradley's remark echoes the judgment of Charles Lamb, who a century earlier had written that "Lear is essentially impossible to represent on a stage." *The Complete Works and Letters of Charles Lamb* (New York: Random House, 1935), p. 299.

with his loving daughter; but in the ensuing battle the French are defeated and the two are taken prisoner. The elder sisters die in a feud over
the English commander, the treacherous Edmund, who himself dies at
the hand of his brother, Edgar, but not before confessing that he has ordered the execution of Lear and Cordelia. The rescuers are too late to save
her and Lear dies, grieving at her death.*

1.1   The play opens, as do many of Shakespeare's, with a conversation between minor figures, as the Earl of Gloucester introduces his bastard son, Edmund, to the Earl of Kent. Gloucester chuckles rather
callously at the pleasure he had in conceiving Edmund, while noting that
he has yet another son who is legitimate and hence more highly favored.
We know Gloucester immediately as a blunt-spoken, earthy man, somewhat insensitive to the feelings of others. This brief exchange introduces
us to the subplot of the play, a sequence of events running parallel to the
main plot, which for a time is quite separate from the principal action. It
also introduces one of the important *themes* of the play, the relationship
between fathers and their children.

This theme is taken up immediately by Lear, who enters and announces his intent to divide his kingdom among his three daughters.
(There are no mothers in *King Lear*. Shakespeare takes up that relationship in *Hamlet* and *Coriolanus*.) An Elizabethan audience would sense
from the start that Lear's decision is unwise, creating the potential for
civil warfare, which had played such a destructive role in the history of
their country. Lear justifies his decision by declaring that he has grown
old and weary of the burdens of office. He wants to "shake all cares and
business from our age" but at the same time "retain / The name and
th'addition to a king," including a retinue of a hundred knights, which
his heirs are to support during his monthly visits with one or the other of
them. In brief, he wants to unburden himself of all the responsibilities of
kingship while keeping the honor and advantage of the position, a design

---

*Readers will find modern adaptations of *King Lear* of great interest, including
Akira Kurosawa's film *Ran,* which interprets the play in terms of the ancient Japanese
samurai tradition, with three sons rather than daughters, and Jane Smiley's splendid *A
Thousand Acres,* a Pulitzer Prize–winning novel that situates the action in a Midwestern
farming community.

that introduces the question, and the theme, of the effect of his advanced years upon his judgment.

The impression of flawed judgment is enhanced by Lear's desire to stage a court ceremony in which each daughter is to declare her love for him, presumably out of gratitude for his gifts. This is not to be a contest, since he has already divided the kingdom; it is rather to be a public spectacle to satisfy his vanity and demonstrate his authority over his daughters, an authority that ironically he is in the very act of surrendering, though it would appear that he is unaware he is doing so. Under the circumstances, will he believe their forced professions of devotion? It would appear he does, which only deepens our doubts about his judgment. The two older daughters dutifully pledge their love with embarrassing hyperbole, which seems to delight the king; but Cordelia, the youngest and obviously Lear's favorite, refuses to take part in her father's charade: "Now, our joy / And though our last, not least . . . Speak." "Nothing, my lord." "Nothing?" "Nothing." "Nothing will come of nothing, speak again." Enraged by her refusal, Lear disinherits Cordelia. When the king of France embraces her without dowry, her father shuts her out of his life—"we / Have no such daughter"—and banishes the loyal Earl of Kent for daring to defend her.

The effectiveness of the scene depends upon the contrast between Cordelia and her sisters. They appear as older, more haughty in bearing and severe in dress, to emphasize the superficiality of the speeches, while she, youthful and vulnerable, appears the more sincere in her sentiments, a daughter who truly loves her father but cannot, she says, heave her heart into her throat. The contrast lends emphasis to Lear's folly. Some commentaries find Cordelia insensitive and overly moralistic in her unwillingness to go along with an old man's willful fantasies, but she comes across as one who will not demean her love for her father by joining in his frivolous game of words. The audience emerges from the scene with only disgust for Lear; and we find ourselves reluctantly agreeing with the judgment of the distasteful sisters: "'Tis the infirmity of his age; yet he hath ever but slenderly known himself," and "The best and soundest of his time hath been but rash."

1.2 In the following scene between Gloucester and his sons, we encounter another painful image of fathers blind to the nature of their children. We are introduced, also, to one of Shakespeare's villains. If we wondered about Edmund's reaction to his father's insensitive remarks in the opening scene, his *soliloquy* reveals that he did not take kindly to them.

Edmund does not seem to dislike his father or his brother—he is, quite simply, ambitious. As the "natural" son of Gloucester, he worships nature, whose laws in his mind stand in contrast to those of society, the "plague of custom" that deprives him of inheritance. It seems to him only "natural" that he should employ his wits to remedy an injustice imposed by that "custom." "Now, gods, stand up for bastards!" he declares, defining his creed. Two new themes are introduced in the speech, the conflict between the forces of nature and the strictures of society, and the role of the gods in human affairs, both of which will be explored as well in future scenes.

Edmund is indeed evil, but Shakespeare does not dwell here on what makes him so (we must look to *Macbeth* for the spectacle of its growth in the human spirit), nor does he elaborate on Edmund's motives, though jealousy is strongly implied. Shakespeare's villains frequently announce their intentions from the outset, as do Iago and Richard III as well, creating situations rich in *dramatic irony* so that the audience may watch with fascination as they manipulate unsuspecting victims. In one sense, for Shakespeare evil simply exists, possessing an inner imperative of its own, one which for the wicked fully justifies the suffering they cause the innocent. In a larger sense, evil is a kind of nemesis, imposing a rough justice on those whose human flaws precipitate follies that would otherwise go unpunished. These villains are not without their charm, however, and we cannot dismiss a certain fascination with the bastard Edmund as he pursues his schemes to secure the lands of "Legitimate Edgar."

Edmund, feigning reluctance, shows his father a letter, persuading him that it was written by his favored brother. In it the "legitimate" son is said to be plotting his father's murder so as to inherit the earl's title. Gloucester responds with an unthinking abruptness that echoes Lear's sudden rage at Cordelia's refusal to speak—"Abhorred villain! Unnatural, detested, brutish villain!" He inquires no further into what must seem an uncharacteristic disloyalty on the part of a son whom he was assured loved him. Edmund offers to draw his brother into a conversation that the earl can overhear, so as to confirm Edgar's treachery.

Gloucester, already upset by Lear's actions, is doubly distressed now.

He identifies his own troubles with those of Lear—"there's son against father . . . there's father against child"—and finds the cause in forces beyond his control: "these late eclipses in the sun and moon portend no good to us." Left alone on stage, Edmund dismisses his father's superstition, revealing himself very much a man of the world—practical, rational, and unfeeling. It is "the excellent foppery of the world," he scoffs, to attribute our misfortunes to the movement of heavenly bodies when the true cause is "often the surfeits of our own behavior." Shakespeare's villains are not without wisdom, but their philosophy, so modern sounding, seems always to lead to their own destruction. When Edgar approaches, Edmund persuades him that his father is displeased with him and warns that he should arm himself.

Gloucester's response to the fabricated evidence of Edgar's treachery is as rash as Lear's to his seemingly unloving daughter. This very blindness of both to the nature of their children, and of themselves, leaves them vulnerable to the forces of evil.

1.3–4   Some time passes between scenes, and we find ourselves at the castle of Goneril, where Lear is favoring his daughter with a visit. She complains that he is overbearing and that his "knights grow riotous." She instructs her steward, Oswald, to show less respect for the "idle old man" and his retinue.

Lear is old, "four score and upward," as he tells us later, and it is tempting to attribute his follies to "the infirmity of his age," as Regan has earlier suggested. But while Shakespeare certainly calls upon Lear's advanced years to engage our sympathies in later scenes, it is not to his purpose to depict him as an addled old man. This play is to be a tragedy, and the story of a man full of years, one who has lived a rich and active life and finally succumbs to the end that awaits us all, does not arouse a tragic sense. We do not feel the same deep pity at the death of an old man as we might of the young, or of one at the height of his powers. If age is Lear's flaw, his fate is out of his hands, subject only to the cruel laws of nature rather than to his own willful arrogance. Hence Shakespeare takes pains to emphasize that Lear is still vigorous. However old, he is full of life and still savors of its pleasures, a man in whom its vital juices yet flow in abundance. He returns from an active day of hunting, surrounded by his energetic knights, calls loudly for his dinner and his Fool, and banters wittily with the disguised Kent. In his demeanor he comes across clearly as a man in full control of his physical and mental faculties, with years of rich life before him. He will change in the play, of course, as forces of his own making work to rob him of those years.

The staging of this scene is important, since the "hundred knights" of Lear's retinue are a central issue of later episodes, his daughters claiming them to be unruly and riotous and he that they are "men of choice and rarest parts." If they enter as a boisterous and disorderly band of ruffians, there may be something to say for Goneril and Regan, who must put up with them. If the knights are courteous and respectful of their hosts, on the other hand, the daughters' ingratitude is the more glaring. Something of their quality may be seen in Kent. First, he is intensely loyal to Lear, far beyond the traditional fealty owed by a medieval noble to his king, so loyal that he risks death to return in disguise and reenter his service (we are asked to *suspend our disbelief* that no one sees through the disguise). It tells us something, also, of the character of Lear that he can engage the devotion of such a man. No ordinary king can inspire the devotion of followers who "would fain call [him] master." Second, Kent *is* unruly, tripping up his hostess's servant, Oswald, whom he insults as "a base football player" when the man is simply following his lady's orders to demonstrate a "weary negligence" toward her father.

Character is everything here. Kent is a direct, impulsive, plainspoken counselor, who earlier had been so impolitic as to challenge Lear in his wrath: "What wouldst thou do, old man? . . . I'll tell thee thou dost evil." Oswald is often played as a stereotypical figure of fun on the Elizabethan stage, the court fop, an effete, dim-witted character who appears dressed in all the elaborate finery of contemporary fashion, with perfumed lace trim and an enormous hat which he sweeps off in performing ridiculously exaggerated bows. As we shall see, in Shakespeare's plays the appearance of such a figure frequently prompts arch comments about his dress and behavior, which go right over his head. Some productions avoid the caricature and present Oswald simply as an obedient servant, leaving it to a perceptive audience to recognize that in his encounters with Kent, Shakespeare is placing before us two different perspectives on loyalty to a master.

Lear's confrontation with Goneril introduces in quick succession several themes which future action will play out: Lear's knowledge of himself—"Who is it that can tell me who I am?"; his impending madness—"O Lear, Lear, Lear! / Beat at this gate that let thy folly in /And thy dear judgment out!"; his growing realization that he has been unjust to his youngest daughter—"O most small fault, / How ugly didst thou in Cordelia show"; the rash intensity of his reaction to Goneril's ingratitude—"Degenerate bastard," "Detested kite"—and his famous curse "that she may feel / How sharper than a serpent's tooth it is / To have a thankless child"; his blindness to the nature of his children—"I have another daughter"; and his pathetic ignorance of his political weakness—"Thou shalt find / That I'll resume the shape which thou didst think / I have cast off forever."

An audience cannot be consciously aware of all that is going on in the scene; the pace is much too swift and the lines too packed with passion for us to pause and contemplate what is happening. It is only in examining the action at leisure, as we do here, that we begin to comprehend Shakespeare's accomplishment. In the clash between father and daughter he pulls our sympathies this way and that as we respond intuitively to a conflict of emotions—loyalty, regret, anger, fear, disappointment, and love.

This scene also introduces the Fool. A jester was a familiar figure in medieval and Renaissance courts. His function was to entertain, which he did by singing songs and engaging in witty exchanges with courtiers in attendance. He delighted in riddles and word play, often in barbed remarks at the expense of his audience. Although given wide license in his antics, he walked a fine line. Lear threatens his Fool with the whip when he seems to come too close to the bone, and it may be that he has at times felt its sting. Lear's Fool, then, can talk to the king in ways others would not dare. In his quips, his songs, and his riddles, he often takes on the character of a *chorus,* both shaping and reflecting the audience's response to events, saying things that we would like to, were we given the chance. He calls the king himself a Fool for surrendering his kingdom to his daughters, since "all thy other titles thou hast given away; that thou wast born with"; and he chides Lear for making "thy daughters thy mothers— for then thou gav'st them the rod and put'st down thine own breeches." The Fool confirms what we suspected, that the division of the kingdom was unwise.

Just how unwise it was becomes evident with the entrance of an angry Goneril, who scolds her father for the unruliness of his "insolent retinue." Lear responds with bitter sarcasm but in his mockery articulates a major theme of the play: "Are you our daughter?" he asks archly, and then, "Does any here know me? This is not Lear. . . . Who is it that can tell me who I am?" The balance of the play may be said to answer that last question, as the turbulent scenes to follow slowly unfold to Lear who he is, and we watch the effect this harsh knowledge has upon him.

1.5 Lear responds to Goneril's rejection with a message to Regan, announcing a visit. The Fool persists with his riddles, but Lear is only half listening, his mind and spirit distracted by other matters: his injustice to Cordelia—"I did her wrong"; the "monster Ingratitude" of Goneril; and a growing awareness of his own tenuous grasp on sanity— "O, let me not be mad, not mad, sweet heaven!" The sage Fool judges well his condition: "Thou should'st not have been old before thou hadst been wise."

2.1 We return momentarily to the subplot. Edmund tightens the trap laid for Edgar, urging him to flee and luring him into a mock duel, effectively preventing a confrontation between brother and father that might unravel his plot. He persuades his father that Edgar attempted to implicate him in a scheme to murder the earl, and on being refused, drew his sword on him. Gloucester orders Edgar apprehended and slain. Like Lear, he denounces his child—"I never got him"—and promises Edmund, a "loyal and natural boy," that he will inherit his title and lands.

Regan and her husband Cornwall arrive at Gloucester's castle, having left their own to avoid Lear's visit. Cornwall, as Gloucester's overlord, requires hospitality of him, lending emphasis to the earl's divided loyalties, the conflicting claims of his obligation under the law to his liege lord and his natural loyalty to the old king. In his dilemma we are reminded ironically of Edmund's defiance of "the plague of custom" and his adherence to nature as his goddess, rather than to human law.

2.2–3 In the next scene Kent encounters Oswald, who is carrying a message from Goneril to Regan. We may well sympathize with the plight of the bewildered Oswald. He is going about his lady's business when he meets a complete stranger—he clearly does not remember Kent—who assaults him, first verbally and then with blows, for no reason he is aware of. Again, however, if Oswald is played as a thoroughly distasteful character, such sympathies might not arise. Kent, the most loyal of Lear's followers, matches his master in a tendency toward sudden anger and rashness. Cornwall appears to separate the two and after some discussion of the qualities of a loyal retainer, places Kent in the stocks. This is a serious step, the first overt act in the play to challenge Lear's status. Kent, as a messenger of the king, is performing his duties under the traditional protection of the monarch's power; by placing him in the stocks, Cornwall makes it clear that he no longer need concern himself with Lear's power.

To this point in the play, we have seen nothing to indicate that the elder sisters are anything more than rather cold and unpleasant women, exasperated, perhaps justifiably, with their father's behavior. Now Shakespeare begins to reveal the true nature beneath their outward show of concern for the proprieties. When Cornwall orders Kent stocked until noon, Regan scoffs maliciously, "Till noon? Till night, my lord, and all night too."

Kent, left alone, reveals that he has a letter from Cordelia. In the next short scene Edgar, in an effort to elude his father's order for his death or capture, disguises himself as a madman, a "Tom o'Bedlam," so that now, as he says, "Edgar I nothing am."

2.4   At the opening of the next tumultuous scene, Lear comes upon Kent in the stocks and cannot believe that Cornwall would dare do such a thing. The sight is a brutal revelation of the king's diminished status, which he refuses to acknowledge. He storms off to confront his daughter and son-in-law, only to discover that they refuse to see him, pleading illness and exhaustion. He storms back, raging at their disrespect in language familiar to us by now: "Vengeance! plague! death! confusion!" In the midst of his anger he pauses momentarily, as if gaining control over his passion, and finds an excuse for their refusal: "No, but not yet; may be he is not well." But the sight of Kent incenses him anew, as he searches frantically for an explanation other than the one staring him in the face—he is no longer a king.

Cornwall and Regan finally appear and Kent is released, though Lear's perfunctory response shows him less concerned with the suffering of his servant than the affront to his status—"O, are you free? / Some other time for that." He now submits to a self-imposed humiliation. Goneril has insisted that he reduce his train to fifty knights, but he dismisses her with withering insults, turning to Regan whom he is confident will accept his hundred. She replies by insisting that he come with but twenty-five, whereupon he turns back to Goneril—whom he had just moments before condemned as "a boil, / A plague-sore"—and he does so because her offer of fifty is "twice" Regan's love. Goneril in turn insists that he come with none, precipitating his final outburst; and in his anguish he is newly aware of his uncertain hold on sanity, "O Fool, I shall go mad!" The encounter is packed with Lear's impassioned invective against Goneril, and against both daughters. In the end, language fails him; it cannot bear the weight of his rage, nor can his imagination conceive of a revenge to match the anguish of his sudden sense of helplessness.

It is a grueling scene, one subjecting the audience to a complex mix of emotional responses to Lear—disgust, embarrassment, awe, sympathy. His invective against Goneril for cutting his retinue in half violates every sense of the natural bond between father and daughter. His fawning addresses to Regan, which we know are in vain, are an embarrassment, as is his feeble attempt to play one daughter off against the other. His measurement of love, in the first scene as the flow of honeyed words, here in numbers of knights, is pathetic. But the image of those relentless daughters, impassive to his distress, moves us to pity for the old man, valiantly struggling to retain his dignity and sanity in the face of those seeking to reduce him from a king to a "nothing," as they dwell on his age and urge him "being weak, [to] seem so." Finally, we sit in awe at his impassioned refusal to submit, admiring his scorn toward the inevitable—"age is unnecessary"—and his obdurate refusal to accept the equally inevitable decay of his standing in the kingdom. Lear, raging beyond reason, rushes into the gathering storm. We can now take full measure of his daughters' cold inhumanity as they close the castle gates upon their distraught father, leaving him to the mercy of the unkind elements.

3.1 The vagaries of nature is a theme of the play, and it enters now with a vengeance. This first short scene of Act Three serves two functions, one of which may be understood best in terms of the limitations of the Elizabethan *stage.* Shakespeare sought to reproduce the effects of a raging storm for an audience watching the play in a theater open to the skies in the clear light of day. The storm scene is central to *King Lear,* indeed, the entire action of the play turns on it. In a fury of wind, rain, and thunder, the old man vents his righteous anger, moving us to sympathy for a father being driven mad by the thought of his daughters' heartless rejection. How could a production duplicate the violence of a tempest without the benefit of modern lighting and sound effects?

Shakespeare achieves the impression through the force of his poetry. In the brief scene opening the act we gain some sense of the fury of the tempest as an unnamed Gentleman describes "the fretful elements" that Lear suffers himself to endure, striving "in his little world of man to out-storm / The to-and-fro-conflicting wind and rain." The lines prepare us for what is to follow, and advance the plot: Cordelia is bringing a French army to the aid of the misused old king, and she may already have landed at Dover.

3.2   In the storm scene itself, Shakespeare imparts the effect of the tempest in yet another way. Poetry, like music, achieves its effects by sound as well as meaning, and here the fury of the elements resonates in Lear's phrases. "Crack your cheeks" echoes a sudden onset of wind that shatters trees and splinters houses. "Rumble thy bellyful" recreates the unceasing surge of thunder through the clouds overhead. Those "fires" are "oak-cleaving thunderbolts" with the power to "strike flat the thick rotundity o'th'world." The sharp "strike flat" of the line startles as does a sudden flash of lightning, while the round vowels of "rotundity o'th'world" evoke the role of thunder as it diminishes in the distance.

Lear is at first submissive to the forces of nature, encouraging the elements to singe his "white head," and he acknowledges that they have a perfect right to do so since he never gave them land and they therefore owe him "no subscription [tribute]." But then he accuses the elements of collusion with his daughters in assaulting "a head / So old and white as this," and calls upon "the great gods," a higher force it seems, to right human wrongs by punishing those whose crimes are hidden, the "pent-up guilts" of those same daughters. He appeals to the "dreadful summoners" of divine justice to indict those who escape human laws, and ends with a desperate cry that he is "more sinned against than sinning."

It is almost too contradictory an episode for close analysis, but it is a powerful expression of a distraught man struggling to make sense of his distress. He first absolves and then indicts nature, and finally calls on "the great gods" for retribution before acknowledging that, though sinned against, he himself has sinned as well. His is the timeless cry of an uncomprehending humanity demanding to know why the universe seems empty of justice.

Lear wavers between rage and acceptance until he fears that his "wits begin to turn." At this moment, for the first time in the play, his distress awakens in him a compassion for another human being. He attempts to comfort his Fool—"Come on, my boy. How dost, my boy? Art cold?"— and acknowledges his humanity—"Poor fool and knave, I have one part in my heart / That's sorry for thee." Insanity and wisdom are never far apart in this play.

3.3   In the next few scenes the action alternates between the heath and the castle, as Shakespeare parallels Lear's descent into madness with the blinding of Gloucester, who is also to be thrust from the castle gates into the still-raging storm. Gloucester confides in Edmund that he has received a letter, the same one perhaps or a companion to Kent's from Cordelia. Edmund contemplates his luck. Revealing the letter to Cornwall will ensure his father's fall and his inheritance of the title, since Edgar is in disgrace. Evil leads on to evil. At first ambitious only for Edgar's status as heir, Edmund can now see no reason not to aim higher, observing philosophically that "the younger rises when the old doth fall." It is simply the way of the world!

3.4   Kent and the Fool finally lead Lear to a shelter, but he is scornful of comfort and has more to say, dwelling on the grievance that has prompted this rage and sorrow in him, "filial ingratitude!" whose sting has brought him to the edge of insanity: "O, that way madness lies; let me shun that! / No more of that." In his speech he mentions "this tempest in my mind," a phrase that puts the storm in a larger perspective. It is not just the chance occurrence of impersonal natural forces but a direct reflection of the turmoil within him. The phrase was more than an artful touch to Shakespeare's Elizabethan audience, who believed in a *universal order,* wherein all levels of existence, since they were created by God, were inextricably linked. The storm, then, complements Lear's state of mind and helps define it dramatically. It reflects, further, the state of the kingdom, foreshadowing the turmoil to come. In this sense, Lear and England and the heavens themselves are afflicted with the same distemper, as all existence participates in a single tempest.

As if to avoid the abyss of insanity, Lear's thoughts turn again to the suffering of the Fool, whom he urges to enter the hovel. Before seeking its comfort himself, he pauses to pray, his mind on those "poor naked wretches" who have no protection against the elements: "O, I have ta'en / Too little care of this!" This sudden compassion for the suffering of others, an outgrowth of his own distress, signals the beginning of what has been called Lear's "education" or "redemption." His trials have brought him to the verge of understanding who he is, but at this first sign of wisdom, he descends into madness. It is painful irony that at the very moment Lear seems to realize his own frail humanity, he slips over the edge of reason. Are we to conclude that such self-knowledge is gained only at the risk of sanity, that the truth of our nature is so terrible that we are safer with our illusions?

Lear's wits turn at the sight of madness itself, as in a stunning piece of dramatic timing, Shakespeare brings Tom o'Bedlam bursting on stage—Edgar, disguised as a wild-eyed lunatic, his filthy body twitching, with perhaps no more clothing than a ragged loincloth, babbling inanities about "the foul fiend" that torments him. Lear, now losing touch with reality, finds Tom ironically full of wisdom, a "noble philosopher," "good Athenian," and "learned Theban," one with whom he would hold conversation. As for his condition, well, he could have been brought so low only through the treachery of his daughters. Lear grows wise in his madness. He speaks the truth and we gain some understanding of its terrors when, gazing on Tom, he asks, "Is man no more than this?" and follows with the harsh insight, "unaccommodated man is no more but such a poor, bare, forked animal as thou art." Confirming his new wisdom, he seeks to join Tom in primal nakedness, tearing at his clothes, "Off, off, you lendings! Come, unbutton here!" to be deterred only by the restraint of his troubled companions.

3.5–6 The action returns briefly to the castle, where Edmund betrays his father. Cornwall orders the old man arrested for his treacherous collusion with the French and appoints Edmund Earl of Gloucester in his stead.

Back on the heath, Gloucester and Kent finally shepherd the others into the hovel, where Lear in his delusion stage-manages a scene that is true bedlam. He fantasizes a trial of his daughters before a tragicomic panel of three judges, one a madman, another feigning madness, and the third a Fool. It is a tragic parody of the justice Lear seeks, in its painful spectacle perhaps a revelation that no such justice exists. Lear is finally persuaded to lie down. He drops off to sleep murmuring, "we'll go to supper i'th'morning," to which the Fool replies, "and I'll go to bed at noon." The world, it seems, is topsy-turvy, a place where children seek their parents' death, where kings take refuge in a hovel, madmen utter wisdom, and fools speak the truth. Gloucester enters with news of a plot against Lear's life and urges Kent to carry him to Dover, where he will find "both welcome and protection."

This is the last we shall see or hear of the Fool, who at this point unceremoniously drops out of the play. There have been many suggestions why. Perhaps the most convincing is the thought that the Fool has been in a sense Lear's conscience, telling him over and over that he has done wrong, urging upon him that as a consequence he is himself at best a Fool, at worst "nothing." The Fool saw the truth, and aside from Kent, who paid dearly for his candor, he was the only one to voice it. But Lear now knows who he is and will henceforth speak the truth in a madman's ravings. And so the Fool's riddling is no more needed.

3.7 Shakespeare opens the next scene depicting Gloucester's apprehension and punishment with a brief glimpse of the sisters' malicious nature. When informed of Gloucester's treachery, they respond in chorus: "Hang him instantly." "Pluck out his eyes." On balance there is some justification for their harsh reaction. They are, after all, English and a French army is invading their country. So if one of their underlords is acting in concert with the enemy, they have every right to consider him a traitor. But their treatment of the old king overshadows all other sentiments, and now that they want him dead, our sympathies lie unfailingly with him and those intent upon his welfare. It is quite possible that an Elizabethan audience may have watched the ensuing scenes with some ambivalence. Although, as will be made clear, Cordelia has come in force solely to rescue her father—the French king is not with her—loyal English citizens may not have been entirely comfortable wishing their ancient enemies well. Shakespeare has worked the trick, however, by portraying the English as so irredeemably evil—and it gets worse—that no one could sympathize with them. Only Goneril's husband Albany escapes condemnation, for in what little we see of him he seems sensible and compassionate; and though he does nothing about it, he sternly disapproves of the treatment of the king.

Our sentiments are confirmed by Cornwall's cruel treatment of Gloucester, gouging his eyes out while Regan goads him on: "One side will mock another. Th'other too!" This is a difficult scene to stage, and an audience may be repulsed by it, even one more modern and accustomed to a steady diet of mayhem and mutilation on the screen. At any rate, we are witness to Cornwall's inhuman cruelty; he and Regan stand before us in all their stark wickedness, especially since the duke performs the deed with such obvious relish: "Out, vile jelly! Where is thy lustre now?" So unthinkingly cruel is such an act that one of Cornwall's servants rebels at the sight of it and dies in an attempt to stop his lord, but not before mortally wounding the duke.

Gloucester learns of Edmund's treachery and, with the added burden now of the knowledge of his error in abusing Edgar, is thrust blind and helpless onto the heath. As we learn later, Lear has slipped away from his benefactors and now roams free. So each stumbles alone into the wilderness, the one with his eyes destroyed, the other with his wits deranged, both afflicted with the knowledge that their own failings have brought them to this pass. Two old men wander a heartless heath, both blind in different ways, both victims of a failure to see where true love lies. Are we destined to a similar end by a failing so common to humankind?

4.1–5   The play picks up its pace. Edgar, still in the guise of mad Tom, undertakes to conduct his father to the cliffs of Dover, where Gloucester intends to unburden himself of his physical and mental torments by throwing himself from the heights.

At Goneril's castle, Edmund learns that Albany has been slow to rally his forces. Goneril declares her affection for Edmund, who marches off, and then exchanges harsh accusations with her husband, railing against him for his failure to join the army against the French. Albany retains his humanity in the face of her fierce insults—"Milk-livered man!" and "vain fool!"—displaying a compassion for the suffering of Gloucester and a prevailing loyalty to Lear.

Meanwhile Kent has conveyed Lear to Dover and learns of Cordelia's reaction to the news; she responds with mixed emotions, smiles and tears like "sunshine and rain at once." And the English forces are on the march.

Lear has escaped, and Cordelia sends soldiers in search of him. She sets the English audience at ease, declaring that the French have mounted the expedition solely to rescue the king, not for any "blown ambition" but for "love, dear love" alone.

It appears that Regan has also taken a fancy to Edmund, and a rivalry has risen between the two sisters, one which Regan, as a recent widow, is in a better position to do something about. She learns that Oswald is carrying a letter from her sister to Edmund and tries to persuade him to let her see it. He loyally refuses, so she gives him one to Edmund from herself.

4.6 In an episode that mixes the comic and tragic, Edgar, who has not yet revealed his identity, places his father in the middle of a field and persuades him that he stands on the edge of the Dover cliffs. After a prayer to "you mighty gods," Gloucester throws himself forward and falls on his face. Edgar, again disguising his voice and assuming the role of one who has watched the old man's fall from below the heights, convinces his distracted father that he has been under the influence of a demon and has miraculously survived. It seems a cruel joke to play on a blind old man, and it is not without its comic effect—a pratfall followed by pathetic bewilderment, as Edgar plays upon his father's Old World superstitions. The deception has its desired effect, however, as Gloucester resolves to live on and endure his fate: "Henceforth I'll bear / Affliction till it do cry out itself / 'Enough, enough' and die."

At this point Lear bursts upon the scene as plot and subplot converge in a painful reunion of the two men. The image is compelling because it is so familiar. We are accustomed to the sight of two age-encrusted survivors seated together on a park bench, passing the time of day with slow talk of the weather, local events, and old times, a scene repeated every day in every village. But Shakespeare raises the commonplace to agonizing art, shattering this innocent image with a dialogue ranging from insanity, blindness, suffering, injustice, and harsh children to a climax of climbing rage. These two, one blind, the other mad, sit down upon a barren heath to share a suffering far greater than human justice would impose upon them for their faults. From this point forward in the play, Lear's speech is filled with images of nature, here a mouse, birds, "the small gilded fly," the fitchew (polecat), and horse. Shakespeare conceives of Lear as gaining in wisdom in his madness, and such imagery builds on his recent recognition that man is "but a poor, bare, forked animal," drawing him ever closer to the natural world. He and the animals have a common bond now—they lack the gift of reason, and he has lost his.

On the other hand, Lear still conceives of himself as king, "Ay, every inch a king," but now a wiser one as he dispenses compassionate justice to imagined subjects. First he pardons one for adultery, citing the example of nature, where copulation thrives unburdened by "the plague of custom" that Edmund complained of. Indeed, in his ramblings this wise madman seems to have come around to Edmund's way of thinking, challenging the laws of society he had hitherto enforced. The difference, of course, is that Edmund's philosophy is handmaid to his ambition, while Lear's arises out of a newfound sympathy for the common man. Justice, he raves, breaks its lance against the wealthy but pierces the poor like "a pigmy's straw." In his madness he is untouched by Gloucester's affliction, addressing his loyal friend with what, had he his wits, would seem cruel jests. When the blind earl asks Lear if he recognizes him, the king replies, "I remember thine eyes well enough," and he later advises, "get thee glass eyes." In the end there is a glimmer of compassion as he seems to recognize Gloucester and offers his own eyes so that his friend may weep, advising that he be patient and endure the suffering the race is heir to: "When we are born, we cry that we are come / To this great stage of fools." His ramblings have no sustained thought, only themes: justice, nature, woman, the false pomp of office, the desire to undress, and finally the sudden thought of his oppressors. In an abrupt burst of anger he imagines stealing upon "these son-in-laws, / Then kill, kill, kill, kill, kill, kill!"

In the later stages of the play Shakespeare employs these verbal repetitions with increased frequency. It is not that Lear is at a loss for words— his lines are more than eloquent—but it seems that at times the language is inadequate to express his emotions of the moment, too frail an instrument for such intensity of feeling.

The scene ends in a burst of action. Cordelia's soldiers arrive to rescue Lear and he runs off, evading them; battle impends; Edgar, taking his father to safety, is confronted by Oswald, whom he kills; and we learn of Goneril's plot to have Edmund kill her husband, Albany, in the heat of combat. Gloucester sums up the spectacle of madness and inhumanity by wishing that he, like Lear, were mad as well, for then, he says, "should my thoughts be severed from my griefs, / And woes by wrong imagination lose / The knowledge of themselves."

4.7   The final scene of the act is the first of three in which Lear and Cordelia appear together, as we experience the tragic playing-out of their lives. Earlier, as we have seen, a French gentleman had given Kent an account of Cordelia's reaction to the news of her father's suffering and rescue: "You have seen / Sunshine and rain at once; her smiles and tears / Were like, a better way." Shakespeare wrote such lines with what seems a side glance at the audience, as if subtly to guide our response to unfolding events. Those lines prepared us for the reunion to come, and now we see that image performed. Our emotional response to Shakespeare's characters is seldom pure or unalloyed; and the success of his plays lies in just this evocation of the complex, often contradictory, movements of the human spirit. This is the way we are, here in the mixture of sorrow and joy that accompanies so many of the telling events of our lives, as when a mother weeps at her daughter's wedding. Thus Cordelia responds first to the news, and later to the sight, of her father with that conflicting combination of "sunshine and rain"—as do we.

The scene is painful. Lear has been rescued and lies helpless and sleeping in the safety of the French camp. He awakens unsure whether he is dead or alive, whether Cordelia is a spirit or a living being; but he seems to have emerged from his madness, as the doctor confirms: "the great rage, / You see, is killed in him." He finally recognizes the weeping Cordelia and begs her forgiveness: "Pray you now, forget and forgive; I am old and foolish."

This is a Lear we have not seen before. Were we able to pause here, we might ponder the spectrum of responses to the king that Shakespeare has aroused in us: disgust at Lear's folly in disinheriting Cordelia; embarrassment at his ignorance; pity mixed with admiration at the sight of him raging against his sufferings; fear, awe, and revulsion at his madness; sorrow and joy at his reunion with his daughter Cordelia. Shakespeare has put us through a virtual roller coaster of emotions, with more to come.

5.1–2   The armies clash. Under the command of Edmund, the English are victorious, and the newly reunited Lear and Cordelia are taken captive.

5.3   When they are brought before Edmund, Cordelia demands to see her sisters; but Lear, now more himself mentally and physically, responds with another of those intense repetitions: "No, no, no, no!" He is so overjoyed by his reconciliation with the daughter he loved most and feared lost forever that he has no fear of imprisonment, indeed welcomes it. The prospect of life with her, even behind prison walls, overshadows all other thought. Together, he imagines, they will "sing like birds i'th'cage," "laugh /At gilded butterflies," and "take upon 's the mystery of things." He seems completely unaware of the dangers of his position as he voices his joy, here again in the imagery of the natural world. But we see the sardonic Edmund standing over them, a presence that enhances the bitter irony of the idyllic picture the old man describes. Perhaps he does have some tragic sense of what awaits them—"Upon such sacrifices, my Cordelia, / The gods themselves throw incense"—but such is his joy at the moment that the perils of their captivity sink to insignificance.

Edmund orders the two to prison and arranges for their execution, but events turn against him. When Kent killed Oswald, he found on him a letter from Goneril to Edmund revealing the conspiracy to murder Albany in the midst of battle, one that Kent then turned over to the duke. Ironically, Edmund, who depended heavily on letters to advance his schemes, is defeated by yet another. Albany, after listening to the two sisters squabble over Edmund, arrests him for treason—and a curious scene ensues.

In the midst of all this high passion, Shakespeare inserts an episode in sharp contrast to the moving realism of events that come before and after it, an episode stiff with medieval ritual and chivalric ceremony. Edmund insists that if he is to be condemned, his guilt must be proven in a trial by combat. He asserts his right to challenge anyone who accuses him of treason, a right that no one questions. The trumpet sounds thrice and an armored figure appears, who, as custom requires, accuses him of all his crimes, concluding with the provocative remark that he is "a most toad-spotted traitor." Edmund accepts the challenge, and the two square off to decide by strength of arm who is the liar. This was the custom of a culture that believed in an immanent God who shaped human affairs during a time when, in the absence of a fixed body of laws, men sought justice on the battlefield, measuring right and wrong, truth and falsehood, in terms of an armed encounter, confident that a just deity would weigh in on the side of right and truth.

Edmund is mortally wounded; Goneril poisons Regan and, finding that her plot against her husband has been revealed, kills herself. Gloucester dies, a victim of the same mixed emotions that possess us. As Edgar reports, when the old man learned of his son's identity, his heart "'twixt two extremes of passion, joy and grief, / Burst smilingly." All that remains is the rescue of Lear and Cordelia. The dying Edmund has a redemptive moment, as other Shakespearean villains like Iago and Richard III do not. "Some good I mean to do, / Despite mine own nature," he exclaims, and rescinds his order for their execution. His penitence, however, comes too late for Cordelia.

Lear enters, bearing his daughter's body, calling upon all within hearing to "Howl, howl, howl!" the tortured cry of an animal in affliction. He indicts the entire race, "a plague upon you, murderers, traitors all!" raging ironically at a stage filled with those who have risked their lives to rescue him and avert the very tragedy that greets their eyes.

Shakespeare momentarily restores here the image of a robust Lear, his age no encumbrance. He is no longer the feeble invalid who acknowledges that he is old and foolish, nor the helpless prisoner who goes willingly to his cage. He enters as a figure of strength, bearing Cordelia in his arms, raging against the whole of humanity as he had against his daughters and the injustice of the heartless elements. And he reaffirms his vitality with the revelation that he has "killed the slave that was a-hanging" Cordelia. Shakespeare knew that our sense of tragedy would be dulled by the image of an old man, finally bowing under the weight of his years, slipping mildly into his grave; the sight would have left us saddened, perhaps, but largely untroubled. Rather he gives us a man with active years before him, one who succumbs not because nature in him "stands on the very verge / Of his confine," as Regan urged, but because his heart is broken by the loss of a love that only hours before had been miraculously restored to him. Age is not tragic; it comes to all. But the loss of love is a great misfortune, especially for those who turn it away in anger or ignorance.

Lear wavers between despair and hope. He mourns that "she's dead as earth." But then he is aroused by imagined evidence of life, placing a mirror at her lips to see if her breath will mist it, and then a feather to see if it stirs, a prospect that he says will "redeem all sorrows / That ever I have felt." Again despairing that "she's gone for ever," he hears her voice, "ever soft, / gentle and low."

The loyal Kent reveals himself to Lear and tries to tell him that he has been at his side all along, disguised as his servant, Caius; but the old king fails to connect the two, and our sympathies turn for a moment to Kent's distress. Lear receives the news of his elder daughters' deaths with a dismissive, "Ay, so I think," and Albany cautions that "he knows not what he says." But Shakespeare would not have us think that Lear is slipping out of reality again. It would not do for us to witness the death of a madman, which would be even less likely to arouse a tragic sense than that of an old man. No, he is sane; but the sight of the body before him, stark evidence of the enormity of his loss, so fills his mind that all other concerns sink to insignificance. He rails against the injustice of Cordelia's death in terms that might occur to anyone bereaved by the loss of a loved one: Why should life go on about her, in dogs, horses, and finally rats, and she have "no breath at all"? Then comes the despairing "never, never, never, never, never!"—the repetitions intoned in a kind of funereal chant. In a brief, final gesture, Lear asks to have a button undone, as Shakespeare reminds us of the wisdom that has come to him, the knowledge of his humanity and a sign of redemption. He dies in the belief that Cordelia lives. Edgar, shaken by the deaths, observes that this is a time to "speak what we feel, not what we ought to say," a sentiment that returns us to the opening scene of the play and the seed of folly that, nourished later by anger, ambition, cruelty, loyalty, and love, has finally led to this tragic end.

This final scene of *King Lear* proved so distressing for eighteenth-century audiences that producers altered it to provide a less traumatic staging, one in which Lear survives, retains his crown, and lives out his life in the tender care of a loving Cordelia. The play was performed this way for 125 years until a daring director determined that Victorian audiences were made of sterner stuff and could survive the full weight of Shakespeare's tragic vision. It has been staged faithful to that vision to our own day, but modern audiences are still stunned by the deep sense of loss at the spectacle of Lear and his innocent Cordelia, lying dead at the final curtain.

As mentioned at the outset, it is perhaps the great wealth of themes threading their way through the lines of *King Lear* that prompted A. C. Bradley to remark that the play "is too huge for the stage." Themes tumble so swiftly upon one another that we are barely conscious of being touched by them, of responding from some deep-bred memory of our days or intuitive sense of their truth. Shakespeare loads the final, harrowing scene with quick flashes of those many themes, calling them all to mind as if in summary of the play:

Lear's vitality and strength: "I killed the slave that was a-hanging thee."

His age: "I am old now."

His newfound wisdom: "pray you, undo this button." And his humility: "thank you, sir."

His ungrateful daughters, who now "desperately are dead."

The division of the kingdom, an exercise of "absolute power" that results in "the gor'd state."

The natural world: "a dog, a horse, a rat" and that despairing "Howl!"

And the supernatural: "if Fortune brag of two she loved and hated."

The fragile line between sanity and madness: "he knows not what he says."

Loyalty: "are you not Kent?" and forgiveness: "you are welcome hither."

Human justice: "all friends shall taste / The wages of their virtue, and all foes / The cup of their deservings."

And love: "Cordelia, Cordelia, stay a little."

All these themes are woven together by the swift shuttle of Shakespeare's art to create a final wrenching image of Lear wavering between hope and despair, between joy and grief.

But what is Shakespeare saying about these themes? The message is full of contradictions. Consider, for example the question of age. *King Lear* is surely a play about the conflict between the old and the young, about the inevitability of the time when those ripe in years must decide when and how to let go. Although all our sympathies are with Lear and Gloucester, we must admit to the stark wisdom of Edmund's heartless observation that "the younger rises when the old doth fall."

Again, nature is a central theme of the play, but its role in human affairs is far from clear. On the one hand, it seems a malignant force when Edmund, the "natural" son, proves treacherous and the storm assails the helpless old man. On the other hand, Lear's recognition that man is but "a poor, bare, forked animal" seems the height of wisdom, and his sensitivity to the natural world in his madness a mark of redemption.

Shakespeare's attitude toward social and political order is equally ambiguous. Edmund's challenge of society's "plague of custom" seems an almost demonic threat to stability. But that same "custom" empowers a willful father to disinherit a loving child on a whim, and Gloucester's "legitimate" son remains loyal while Lear's well-endowed heirs wish his death. Further, the traditional loyalty of servant to master, of nobleman to liege lord, and of subject to king, the personal bonds that kept the fragile medieval political world from chaos, seem altogether admirable in Kent but despicable in Oswald.

And what of justice, human or divine? Lear's world seems empty of it, except in the stiff, ritualistic staging of the trial by combat between Edgar and Edmund. All cry for justice, but the deaths of Lear and Cordelia seem a denial, indeed a mockery, of the belief that it exists in either the human or the spiritual domain. All appeal at one time or another to the gods, though each seems to have a different deity in mind. But whatever gods they call upon, whether primitive, Greek, or Christian, the final scene leaves us with the conviction that none of these deities is listening to human supplication. We are on our own, Shakespeare seems to say, and must suffer the consequences, however harsh, of our own failings. He shows us as well, however, that there is an inherent nobility in those who challenge such a judgment and rage against the want of justice.

In the end, the success of *King Lear* lies in Shakespeare's skill at evoking our pity for a man whose suffering far exceeds the all-too-human failing that gave rise to it, and our fear that his faults are so like our own that we may in time call down upon ourselves a similar fate.

HAMLET

⚜

HAMLET is Shakespeare's best-known and most enigmatic work. In the play the young prince of Denmark is called home from his studies because of the death of his father, only to witness his newly widowed mother hastily married to his uncle Claudius, who assumes the throne. Hamlet, while brooding over this course of events, is visited by his father's ghost, who reveals that Claudius is responsible for his death and swears his son to vengeance. For one reason or another, Hamlet delays fulfilling his vow, and Claudius becomes suspicious of his strange behavior. Eventually, each becomes intent upon the other's death, leading to a final encounter in which both die, as do all the remaining prominent figures of the court.

Halfway through the play, Hamlet accuses his two college mates, Rosencranz and Guildenstern, of scheming to "pluck out the heart of my mystery." This is another of Shakespeare's lines that cast a side glance at the audience, for we too are engaged in a bewildering effort to discover his "mystery"—whatever it is that prevents him from avenging the murder of his father. Because of Hamlet's inability, or reluctance, to do away with his uncle until the very end of the play, he kills three people instead of one, and is responsible for the death of at least four others, and himself as well. In following the frustrating progress of his procrastination, however, we are treated to a dramatic vision of the dilemmas facing any of us in this life, dilemmas about which Hamlet simply cannot make up his mind.

1.1 The opening scene of any play has the task of stirring the interest of the audience and providing enough information about past and impending events to enable the viewers to enter into the plot. *Hamlet* opens on two nervous sentinels walking their post at midnight on the dark battlements of the Danish royal castle at Elsinore. At the changing of the guard, they talk of a ghost that has appeared on previous nights and anxiously speculate as to whether it will walk again. Horatio, a minor but important figure as Hamlet's close friend and confidant, has come to confirm the report. The ghost suddenly appears, and as suddenly vanishes. It is a brilliant opening, immediately gripping the imagination of the audience, who share the curiosity and dread of the sentinels at the entrance of the apparition.

Horatio explains that Hamlet's father, also named Hamlet, has only recently died and that a war threatens, which clarifies the need for midnight sentinels on the ramparts of the castle. A Norwegian prince, Fortinbras, has asserted his right to lands lost to Denmark by his father in an earlier war, and is gathering an army to invade the kingdom and reclaim them. Horatio fears that the appearance of the ghost "bodes some strange eruption to our state," and he tells of similar strange manifestations preceding the death of Julius Caesar. There is no question that this *is* a ghost. Shakespeare's Elizabethan audience, and presumably he himself, believed that the world was full of spirits, supernatural beings whose visits promised no good for those so unfortunate as to see them.

The figure appears again and, as before, vanishes without a word. It bears such a striking resemblance to Hamlet's father, the recently deceased king, that Horatio determines to inform the prince of the apparition. And the night ends. Here Shakespeare's poetry evokes the hidden fears of deepest night and describes the dawn that dispels them. Again, some of his most memorable lines arise from the limitations of the Elizabethan *stage,* where daylight performances in an outdoor theater imposed a need to inform the audience of the passage of time and conditions of light: "But look, the morn in russet mantle clad / Walks o'er the dew of yon high eastward hill."

1.2 Having been introduced to the name of Hamlet in the opening scene, we now see him. It is immediately apparent that he has not succeeded his father on the throne. It is occupied by his uncle, Claudius, who has secured the crown by marrying the dead king's widow, Gertrude, with what seems uncommon haste so shortly after the death of her husband. Claudius justifies the haste as necessitated by an impending war with Norway and turns directly to that concern.

The setting is important here. Picture at stage right a colorful throne room where the king and queen hold court, surrounded by an active group of subjects, while to the left stands a brooding figure lost in thought, dressed in mourning black, and isolated from the bustle of courtiers to the crown. The king is engaged in the business of state, at which he proves himself adept. It would seem that the royal robes rest easily on his shoulders. He devises a scheme to prevent war, dispatching an envoy to the king of Norway with a request that he restrain his impetuous young nephew. He then turns to domestic matters—the request of Laertes, who had interrupted his studies to attend the funeral and stayed for the wedding, to return to Paris. The king, showing proper respect for family prerogatives, asks if he has permission from his father, and upon learning that Polonius has given his consent, readily agrees.

Next is the problem of Hamlet, which occupies the attention of both the king and queen. Addressing him, Claudius asks why he is so morose, why "the clouds still hang" on him. Hamlet replies, "Not so, my lord, I am too much in the sun," an answer that alerts us immediately to his penchant for wordplay, here punning on "sun-son" to reflect his sullen discontent. He will continue in this vein throughout the play with a wit and intelligence that outshines all others in the court. He can outtalk, outthink, and outwit them, sparing none the edge of his tongue. The line also hints at a possible cause for his melancholy—having failed to gain the crown, he is now "too much" the son of Claudius. The queen pleads with him to cast off his sorrow. The king echoes her, advising philosophically that we all must die sometime, and, while it is most proper to show respect for a dead father, it is a "fault" to heaven, fathers, and nature to persist in mourning. The king, to all appearances, is concerned about Hamlet's condition and the queen's distress; but with perhaps an underlying uneasiness about his behavior, Claudius detects that, unlike Laertes, the prince for the time being will not be permitted to return to his studies. Gertrude seconds the ruling and Hamlet, pointedly ignoring the king, agrees to obey his mother. The court disperses, and he is left on stage alone.

There follows the first of Hamlet's four great *soliloquies.* If we had wondered what he really thought of his situation and of the brief ex-

change with the king and queen, and been puzzled by his cryptic responses, we may now learn his true thoughts. Is he unnaturally distraught over the death of his father, or resentful at Claudius's assumption
of the throne and the prerogatives of a father, or is he just solemn and
melancholy by nature? The soliloquy is startling in its revelations. While
all these developments obviously disturb him, it appears that he is most
in anguish about something else entirely—his mother's hasty marriage to
Claudius, which he describes in heated and highly sensuous terms. Hamlet is so distraught as to be suicidal—and the reason? "Frailty thy name is
woman," he rages, and condemns her "most wicked speed . . . to post /
With such dexterity to incestuous sheets!"

These revelations introduce a source of Hamlet's "mystery" proposed by some, one much favored by psychological interpretations of the
play—an unnatural physical attraction between mother and son, described by Sigmund Freud as an Oedipus complex. Modern productions
of the scene either hint at this disturbance or display it openly by an untoward show of affection between Gertrude and her son, an immoderate
caressing, kissing, or embracing, and by casting her as a woman still
youthful in face and form. The implications of this reading are readily
seen: Hamlet, paralyzed by the guilt he feels over his barely repressed
sexual attraction to his mother, cannot bring himself to harm the father
figure, Claudius.

Horatio and Marcellus enter and inform a stunned Hamlet of the appearance of a ghost in the form of his late father, and he determines to
confront the apparition that night. The uncertain nature of the ghost, a
factor in later scenes, is reflected in Hamlet's agitated interrogation of
Horatio. Hamlet wavers between belief that the apparition is indeed the
ghost of his father and concern that it may be something else entirely.

1.3   Shakespeare now inserts a quiet, domestic scene into the action,
perhaps as a momentary relief from the sharp tensions of the episodes before and to follow, but perhaps also to delay the anticipated encounter
with the ghost and thus heighten our expectations of what is to come.
We meet Ophelia, who is bidding an affectionate farewell to her brother,
Laertes, upon his departure for Paris. He is concerned about her relationship with Hamlet, who, he advises, is a prince and not therefore free to
choose a wife for himself, since "on his choice depends / The sanity and
health of the whole state." He warns her not to "lose your heart, or your

chaste treasure" to him, for even though he may love her now, he may have to abandon her in the end and submit to the needs of the kingdom.

Polonius comes upon them, full of practical advice on how Laertes should conduct his life, sage insights which would carry more weight had Polonius himself more weight. We can imagine him as advanced in years, painfully long-winded and rambling in speech, somewhat pretentious and self-important, but nonetheless endearing—in brief, a comic figure, one of the few in the play, and all the more welcome for that. He had been the chief counselor to the old king and has been kept on in that capacity by Claudius, perhaps in the interest of continuity in the state, perhaps because of the queen's affection for him.

Laertes listens respectfully and, the lecture over, takes his leave. Polonius then turns his attention to Ophelia. He too has heard or observed that there is something going on between Hamlet and his daughter. Expressing the same concerns as his son, he forbids her to meet or talk with the prince. Ophelia dutifully agrees to obey; and while her meek submission may disturb a modern theatergoer, it is quite in keeping with the custom of the time, when the father had the final say in *arranging for the marriage* of his daughters.

The relationship between Hamlet and Ophelia will become a central concern in the play. It seems clear that she is smitten with him, but the strength of his affection is somewhat muddied, as we shall see, by the question of his uncertain mental balance. At the moment, however, the fears of her brother and father are not unfounded, and they seek to protect her from a liaison that could cause her disgrace should she continue to pursue the dictates of her heart with a prince not free to fulfill whatever promises he might make in moments of intimacy.

1.4　　That night Hamlet and Horatio, waiting on the ramparts of Elsinore to see if the ghost will walk again, occupy the late hours discussing the sorry state of Denmark. When they are startled by a sudden burst of noise from the courtyard below, Hamlet explains that the king keeps late hours, carousing with drunken companions—in sharp contrast, it is implied, to his father's more moderate behavior. It is a custom, Hamlet remarks archly, "more honored in the breach than the observance," and it gives Denmark a bad name. There is little else in the play to confirm this image of Claudius as a debauched monarch. Shakespeare does not demonize him. Claudius is not irredeemably evil, as are Iago and

Richard III; he seems, as we have seen, an able king and skillful diplo-
mat, and gives every evidence of genuine love for Gertrude. In subsequent scenes he voices a sincere regret for his crime and conceals a heavy
burden of guilt under a composed exterior. In his later plotting against
Hamlet, he protects himself from exposure, not out of any malicious animosity toward the prince but as a measure of self-preservation. Although
we have little sympathy for Claudius, Shakespeare avoids a stock confrontation between good and evil in order to focus attention on the "mystery" of Hamlet, who has faults of his own.

Shakespeare lifts the curtain a bit on Hamlet by placing in the
prince's own mouth an oblique allusion to such a fault, and in words that
interpret poetically Aristotle's definition of "the tragic flaw." * Speaking
of Claudius, Hamlet observes that no matter how virtuous or fortunate a
man may be, often "some vicious mole of nature" or "stamp of one defect"
may doom him to censure or scandal. Here, as elsewhere, a highly intelligent and philosophical Hamlet speaks pointedly of himself though unaware, it would appear, that he is doing so. A singularly introspective
Hamlet is at the same time blindly unself-conscious.

The ghost appears, beckoning Hamlet to follow him; and we are
given a the glimpse of the complex body of beliefs about the afterlife that
the Elizabethan age inherited from ancient and medieval lore. He addresses the apparition in terms reflecting doubt of its ambiguous origin:

> Be thou a spirit of health, or goblin damned,
> Bring with thee airs from heaven, or blasts from hell,
> Be thy intents wicked, or charitable,
> Thou com'st in such a questionable shape,
> That I will speak to thee.

As Hamlet moves to accompany the ghost, his companions attempt
to hold him back, voicing the same fear that the ghost may be a devil
who can appear in any guise to tempt a victim to sin or death, and, Horatio warns, "might deprive your sovereignty of reason, / And draw you to
madness." A frenzied Hamlet draws his sword upon his friends, so eager
is he to follow this spectral image of his late father.

1.5   The two now alone, the ghost calls upon Hamlet for vengeance.

*See "Tragedy," pp. 7–8.

But first he describes his suffering in the afterlife, a curious tale in its mixture of Christian and pagan beliefs. He died unshriven and as a consequence must endure unspeakable torments in a form of Christian purgatory to "burn and purge away" the sins of his life. But his fate reflects as well the ancient Greek belief that if the dead are not properly buried, their spirits are deprived of final rest and must wander the earth without solace. It is not an improper burial that condemns this ghost to reappear in the realm of the living, however, but a fierce desire that his death be avenged. Yet, curiously, there is no assurance that vengeance will end his suffering; and, further, it seems more Greek than Christian for a shade from the beyond to call upon one man to kill another, for the teaching of the church nowhere prescribes that avenging a treacherous murder will release the soul of the victim from purgatorial fires.

There is no time, however, for the audience to pause and contemplate the contradictions of the ghost's demands. Shakespeare is writing for effect, creating an atmosphere of awe, dread, and sympathy that leaves Hamlet in anguish. He is called to avenge his father's "foul and most unnatural murder," an act that assumes metaphysical dimensions in that it will seek retribution not only for his father's death but also for his spirit's suffering in the afterlife. The revelation that his uncle murdered his father stuns Hamlet, though his response, "O, my prophetic soul!" indicates that he had harbored such a suspicion. The manner of the murder was indeed "unnatural": Claudius stole upon the king, sleeping in his garden, and poured poison in his ear. The ghost departs with a final injunction that Hamlet is not to condemn his mother; it charges him to "leave her to heaven," and vanishes with a plaintive "remember me."

Hamlet reacts with a frenzy of impassioned oaths, pledging to wipe from his mind all thoughts but the death of his uncle. In a revealing gesture he declares, "my tables, meet it is I set it down / That one may smile, and smile, and be a villain." If the gesture is to be taken literally, at this moment of high passion he pauses to take out his "tables" (diary or notebook) to jot down his observations on the phenomenon, as would any detached scholar. If he does make an actual, rather than a mental, note, the action foreshadows yet another reading of his "mystery": Hamlet's mind is at odds with his emotions, and at times he thinks too much.

He rejoins his companions and insists that they swear an oath on his sword not to reveal anything of what they have seen. His behavior is indeed bizarre as he moves abruptly from one spot to another, chasing the voice of the ghost who is intoning "Swear." Should the staging make it apparent that Hamlet's companions do not hear the voice, we cannot escape the impression that the experience has unhinged him. He seems to recover quickly, however, and cautions them that if at any time he should seem to act in a similar fashion—that is, if he should "put an antic disposition on"—they are to give no hint that they know the cause of his conduct. It is not clear whether this is an embarrassed cover for his frenzied behavior toward his friends or the first step in a conscious design to avenge his father's death. If the latter, it is equally unclear what he means to achieve by feigning madness. At any rate, he requires them to take yet another oath to secrecy, and to the accompaniment of another subterranean "Swear" they do so.

Hamlet's final lines in this scene stand in sharp contrast to his earlier impassioned promise to the ghost: "The time is out of joint, O cursed spite, / That ever I was born to set it right." This note of reluctance leaves us to wonder about the strength of his resolve.

2.1 Act Two consists of one short and one very long scene filled with numerous entrances and exits, moving the action to its crisis. There are indications of a considerable passage of time between the two acts, perhaps a matter of some weeks. The first scene opens with Polonius dispatching Reynaldo to keep an eye on Laertes, who, he suspects, may not have fully appreciated the wisdom of his parting advice. Polonius rambles on characteristically, talking of this and that, at times losing track of his thoughts as he commissions his servant to report back on his son's behavior. However comic, the scene introduces an element that pervades the play. The several characters are continually spying on one another within the dark rooms and corridors of Elsinore. As we shall see, Rosencranz and Guildenstern are sent for to observe Hamlet; Polonius and Claudius lurk behind a curtain to overhear Hamlet's encounter with Ophelia, and Polonius does so again, to his distress, in Gertrude's bedchamber; Hamlet and Horatio eye the king during the play; and Hamlet steals upon him at prayer. The atmosphere is thick with plots and counterplots, suspicion, anxiety, and expectation as the several characters keep constant watch upon one another.

As Reynaldo departs, a distraught Ophelia enters. She has obeyed her father, and we hear from her lips an account of Hamlet's response to her rejection. Her description replicates the traditional image of the medieval *courtly lover* deprived of his lady's "pity," a young man careless of his appearance, speechless in despair, bizarre in his actions, and sunk in a melancholy so deep that, according to that tradition, it might prove life-threatening if not relieved. In his comedies Shakespeare has great fun with this figure. In *Hamlet,* however, the situation is more serious, as the prince, already distressed at the murder of his father and the marriage of his mother, finds himself inexplicably cut off by the woman he loves— emotional burdens enough to send any young man over the edge. Polonius concludes that "this is the very ecstasy of love" and determines to inform Claudius.

2.2   In another part of the castle, the king and queen greet Rosencranz and Guildenstern, Hamlet's fellow students at Wittenberg, asking their help in discovering what more than the death of his father is troubling Hamlet. They courteously agree. Polonius enters, prepared to confide in the king about Hamlet's "ecstasy of love," but first there is some state business to attend to. The ambassadors enter to report that the king of Norway has prevailed upon young Fortinbras to abandon his campaign against Denmark, thus averting war and confirming Claudius's diplomatic skills. The business completed, Polonius expounds on his theory about Hamlet's distraction and is again amusing in his long-winded way, prodded occasionally by the queen, who urges him to speak "more matter, with less art." Polonius proposes a scheme to test his theory; he will "loose" Ophelia on Hamlet, as he puts it, while they hide behind an "arras [tapestry]" to observe the result.

Hamlet enters at a distance, studiously reading a book, and the staging of his entrance has a critical effect on later events. He may be shown to overhear the plan to "loose" Ophelia on him, or to remain ignorant of it. The choice, as we shall see, offers radically different interpretations of his later behavior.

The king and queen depart and Polonius is left alone with the prince, who proceeds to toy with him, here clearly acting the madman, by answering his questions with seeming inanities, though even Polonius detects that "there is method" in them. On his departure, Hamlet reveals that he has been quite deliberate in his incoherent responses, declaring his contempt for "these tedious old fools!"

Rosencranz and Guildenstern enter and are greeted warmly by their fellow student. It would appear that they have already decided what it is that troubles Hamlet. They insist that he is disappointed in his thwarted ambition to gain the throne. Three times they attempt to bait him on the subject, in each instance receiving a witty denial. Hamlet, who sees through their designs, forces them to admit that they were sent for, and tells them why. He has not been himself of late, he confides, sunk so deep in melancholy that the earth seems "a sterile promontory," the air "a foul and pestilent congregation of vapors," and man but the "quintessence of dust."

The appearance of a troop of players provides an opportunity for Hamlet to toy further with Polonius, this time before an appreciative audience, and for Shakespeare to digress into some trenchant commentary on the contemporary stage. Hamlet asks the players to put on a work called *The Murder of Gonzago* and requests that they include some lines he will compose for the performance. It is so agreed and all depart, leaving him alone on stage.

The scene ends with another of Hamlet's soliloquies, in which we learn what he has in mind with these requests; but first we hear of his remorse that he has yet to act on his vow to the ghost. Taking his cue from the players' speeches, he contrasts the intensity of their acting a part in which they have no personal concern—"What's Hecuba to him"—with his own inaction in a cause so passionately close to him. He continues with an explosion of expletives, "Bloody, bawdy villain! / Remorseless, treacherous, lecherous, kindless villain! / O, vengeance!" as if attempting to spur himself into action. But he quickly expresses remorse for resorting to mere words.

"About my brains," he exclaims, and reveals that he has finally devised a plot against the king. He will put on a play reenacting his father's death and observe how Claudius responds. It is not a design to kill the king, however, but only to confirm his guilt. But how and when did Hamlet's new doubt arise? Moments before he was raging about vengeance, now he repeats Horatio's earlier fears that the ghost may indeed be a devil, who "hath power / T'assume a pleasing shape." Hamlet's "brains" have devised a plan to "catch the conscience of the king," but as yet he has no scheme to "catch" the king himself.

3.1 The first scene of Act Three has important implications for our understanding of Hamlet's state of mind. It opens innocently enough with Rosencranz and Guildenstern reporting to the king that they have been unable to gain insight into what Claudius now calls Hamlet's "turbulent and dangerous lunacy." They depart, and Ophelia is placed where Hamlet will come upon her while the king and Polonius conceal themselves to determine if the cause of his behavior "be the affliction of love or no." Before Hamlet enters, however, Claudius has a short speech delivered as an *aside,* a disclosure of the character's inner thoughts meant for the audience alone to hear. The passage confirms for the first time in the play that Claudius is indeed guilty of the murder and moreover suffers from the burden of his guilt.

The prince enters rapt in thought and in the most famous of his soliloquies makes no mention of Ophelia at all. He is brooding over the prospect of suicide, whether to "bear the whips and scorns of time" or end them with "a bare bodkin," thoughts that reveal him deep in a state of melancholy. It was a subject much studied in Shakespeare's time, though little understood. One theory held that the condition was a consequence of a natural predisposition (proposed today by genetic scientists), one of whose symptoms or, alternately, causes, was an excess of solitary contemplation. Hamlet concludes with a poetic expression of that theory, articulating an explanation of his "mystery" only hinted at earlier: he thinks too much! This extraordinarily intelligent young man, studious, contemplative, introspective, loses "the name of action" when a thought intrudes between his determination to act and the act itself, because, as we have seen, he must first pause to take out his "tables" and make a note. And, strangely, he knows this. "Conscience does make cowards of us all," he muses. But he is meditating on the fear of death and fails to apply the knowledge to his present circumstances, even as he had failed to consider his analysis of Claudius's "tragic flaw" applicable to himself as well.

But what have these reflections on suicide to do with Ophelia? Very little, really. They tell us that Hamlet is indeed severely depressed, but that his thoughts are not on Ophelia's rejection so much as on darker, more abstract matters. When he comes upon her, the encounter opens on a pleasant, though somewhat mocking, note as he asks her to remember him in her prayers. It is only when she attempts to return his gifts that he becomes incensed and answers her wildly, "Ha! Ha! Are you honest?" Dropping the pose of the melancholic rejected courtly lover, he first professes that he once loved her and then that he never did. Aroused now, he charges her to enter a nunnery so as to avoid breeding sinners like himself, but then abruptly asks, "Where's your father?" He bids her a curt farewell and perhaps dashes off stage, only to return in an even more agitated state and berate her further before taking his leave once more. But he is not finished. Returning again, now in a rage, he launches into a fierce tirade which, though directed at her, seems to be a general condemnation of women. He protests that they have made him mad, that marriage should be abolished, but that those already married shall live, "all but one," while "the rest shall keep as they are." Now Hamlet abruptly leaves, this time for good. To a distressed Ophelia he seems indeed mad, "a noble mind . . . o'erthrown"; and, mourning the change in him, she gives us a glimpse of the stature from which he has fallen:

The courtier's, soldier's, scholar's, eye, tongue, sword,
Th'expectancy and rose of the fair state,
The glass of fashion, and the mould of form,
Th'observed of all observers, quite quite down.

To her he seems now a "blown youth, / Blasted with ecstasy!"

The scene can be staged in a number of ways, depending on whether or not Hamlet is aware, or becomes aware, that he is being spied upon. If he is not, his outburst may be attributed the anger of a spurned lover venting his anger on the unhappy girl, or to a basically unstable state of mind. If, however, he had earlier overheard Polonius's plan to "loose" Ophelia on him, he knows he is being watched and may be deliberately putting "an antic disposition on" for the benefit of the king. The two interpretations are by no means incompatible, of course. He already feels himself betrayed by his mother, and the additional knowledge that his former love has not only spurned him but is in collusion with his enemies could certainly affect the balance of his mind.

Psychological critics see the scene differently. They note that Hamlet condemns not just Ophelia but all women, scorning them for their "calumny," their false "paintings [cosmetics]," and their "wantonness." "I say," he rages, "we will have no more marriages." Hamlet displays, they observe, symptoms of an Oedipal disorder, his spirit so twisted by a repressed sexual desire for his mother that he is unable to relate normally to

any woman. Thus, goes the analysis, his misogyny arises from an unconscious resolve that if he cannot have her, he will have none of them. However interpreted, it is a puzzling and disturbing scene.

If Polonius's scheme was intended to demonstrate that Hamlet is
"mad for love," it has quite the opposite effect upon Claudius, who
emerges from hiding to declare that "his affections do not that way tend"
and to conclude that Hamlet is troubled by "something in his soul, / O'er
which his melancholy sits brood." The king may not be certain what that
"something" is, but he is determined to take no chances, deciding immediately to rid himself of any possible threat by sending the prince off to
England. Polonius persists in his belief that the trouble arises from "neglected love" and suggests that the queen have a talk with her son—
while he once more conceals himself so as to overhear the exchange.

In the heat of his denunciation of marriage, Hamlet comes close to
giving himself away when he lets slip that impassioned "all but one." The
remark brings to the surface the underlying tension of the plot. He intends to kill Claudius, and as long as he keeps his intention hidden he has
the advantage over an unsuspecting victim. He was alert enough to swear
his companions to silence about the existence of the ghost, but the longer
he delays the greater the danger that the king will suspect his intent and
take measures to counter it. At this point in the play Hamlet is still free
to act, but his procrastination has served only to limit more and more the
opportunities open to him. It is not clear how much Claudius knows at
this point, but he is certainly perceptive and, unlike Hamlet, moves
quickly to dispose of possible danger. He announces for public consumption that a trip abroad will perhaps prove beneficial for the prince and,
more darkly, that "madness in great ones must not unwatched go." His
decision, further, raises the question as to what Hamlet means to accom-
plish by his "antic disposition," for if he is only feigning madness, the
total effect of the charade thus far has been to discredit him and arouse
the suspicion of the king.

3.2 In the shorthand of the theater, the next scene is called the
"mousetrap," the title Hamlet gives his play in an ironic reply to the
king. It opens with some of Shakespeare's advice to actors but quickly
gets down to business. The play is ready and the audience gathers, including Horatio, for whom Hamlet has some affectionate words. He
praises his friend for his constant, even-tempered, and moderate nature,

qualities that protect him from the uncertainties of fortune. Horatio, he says, is a man in whom "blood and judgment" are so well balanced that he is not "passion's slave." And so Horatio is a cherished friend whom he wears, as he puts it, at his "heart's core," his "heart of hearts." Hamlet values most in Horatio the qualities he finds lacking in his own mercurial nature—his mood swings, we would call them today—from a paralyzing despair that leaves him contemplating suicide to a wild exhilaration that incites rash action. Among the characters in the play, Horatio acts as the most prominent *foil* to Hamlet, a sturdy rock standing firm amidst the swirling waters of his friend's high emotions.

Hamlet informs Horatio of his purpose in arranging for the play, and the court enters to witness the performance. The prince indulges in obscure, witty replies to remarks by Polonius and Claudius, as well as an erotic exchange with Ophelia—"a fair thought to lie between maids' legs." Hamlet is clearly a master at such patter and continues to comment throughout the scene with quick remarks loaded with double meaning. All sit to watch the dumb-show, a theatrical practice of the time in which the characters mime the critical events of the play to come, presumably so that the audience may be sufficiently informed to appreciate the *dramatic ironies* of the plot. Hamlet and Horatio watch intently for the king's reaction as the players go through the motions of the murder in the garden. But they are frustrated because, as the scene is usually staged, Claudius and Gertrude are so intimately involved in a whispered exchange that they miss the pantomime. Hamlet must depend on the play itself for satisfaction, and it does not disappoint him. As the player nephew, Lucianus, steals upon the sleeping king and pours poison in his ear, Claudius rises abruptly from his seat, cries out for light, and rushes frantically from the hall, followed by all but Hamlet and Horatio. The prince is exultant; he leaps about, sings snatches of songs, and revels in his success—"I'll take the ghost's word for a thousand pound"—all again in contrast to Horatio, who is no less pleased but more measured in his response.

Rosencranz and Guildenstern return to inform Hamlet that the queen wishes to speak with him in her closet (bedchamber); and he toys with them once more, though this time with more bite. Apparently quite sincere, they ask why he does not share with his old friends the cause of his distemper; in response he taunts them with a reminder of their former baiting, "Sir, I lack advancement." Seizing a recorder (an early flute), he accuses them angrily of playing upon him as a musician would upon the instrument to "pluck out the heart of my mystery." Polonius enters, repeating the queen's summons. Hamlet, in his excited state, seeing nothing but enemies about him, toys with the old man again, until, puzzled and distressed by his antic behavior, they all depart.

Ironically, none of these figures is an enemy. Hamlet's dilemma is that he can take none of them into his confidence since he has only the ghost's word for the king's guilt—reinforced now, it is true, by Claudius's revealing response to the play, though even that serves only to strengthen suspicion. There is certainly no evidence to support a public accusation, which if he were to make it would only confirm fears about Hamlet's sanity. He must, therefore, consider everyone an enemy, hence the importance of Horatio, in whom alone he can confide.

In a brief soliloquy, Hamlet declares himself prepared, at this "very witching hour of night," to "drink hot blood, / And do such bitter things as the day / Would quake to look on." This renewed resolve, however, with all the force of its mounting emotion, is immediately diverted from its proper object, the king, by the thought of his mother.

3.3   Claudius, meanwhile, is determined to hasten Hamlet's departure and so informs Rosencranz and Guildenstern, who are to accompany the prince to England. Polonius departs for the queen's bedchamber, and Claudius is left alone on stage to ponder his guilt. He agonizes over it—"O, my offense is rank, it smells to heaven"—and then contemplates the possibility of repentance. "All may be well," he concludes, and kneels in prayer. Hamlet, on his way to see his mother, comes upon the king. Recognizing a rare opportunity, he steals up undetected, draws his sword, and prepares to "do't, and so a' goes to heaven." But a thought intrudes—"That would be scanned"—and he pauses. To kill the king while he is at prayer, in the very act of contrition, Hamlet reasons, would indeed send Claudius to heaven while the spirit of his father continues to burn in purgatorial fires. It would be better, he concludes, to kill him in the act of sin so that "his heels may kick at heaven" and his soul go straight to hell. Hamlet passes up the opportunity and leaves, whereupon we learn from Claudius that, ironically, his effort at repentance has been to no avail. He has mouthed his prayers but his thoughts were elsewhere, and as he knows, "words without thoughts never to heaven go."

The scene lies at the center of Shakespeare's play and at the heart of Hamlet's mystery. Why did he fail to "do't"? The intruding thought is not unreasonable for a believing Christian raised on the doctrine of the medieval church. But now Hamlet is toying with the fate of Claudius's soul, playing God, passing judgment on the immortal part of him, determining whether it will spend eternity in bliss or pain. In so doing, he has clearly stepped over the prescribed boundary of human concern into a forbidden realm. But is this the real reason he sheathes his sword? The two men's speeches share an underlying theme. Claudius laments that guilt "defeats my strong intent," robbing him of the will to act, and he attempts to shed that guilt by prayer and repentance. An oppressive sense of guilt can indeed paralyze the will, especially if the sin "hath the primal eldest curse upon't, / A brother's murder!" But Hamlet has no such sin on his conscience—something else entirely "defeats" his "strong intent." Claudius at least knows what his problem is, but Hamlet remains ignorant of his own. Of course, a Freudian critic could well argue that it is indeed guilt that gives him pause, preventing him from doing harm to a father figure.

3.4 Hamlet continues on his interrupted progress to his mother's bedchamber (in theater shorthand, this is the "closet scene"). The ghost had cautioned him not to trouble her, to "leave her to heaven," but it is beyond Hamlet to refrain. When summoned, he resolved "to be cruel, not unnatural. / I will speak daggers to her, but use none." As it turns out, he does use "daggers," but on Polonius, not her; and in "speaking " them he soon oversteps the bounds of the "natural" behavior of a son toward his mother. The dramatic effect is that of a Hamlet who, unable to purge himself of his boiling, pent-up emotions by killing the king, unleashes them on his mother!

Polonius conceals himself behind the arras and Hamlet enters, beginning immediately to "speak" daggers. Exasperated, the queen turns to leave; but he grabs her roughly, causing her to shout for help, a cry echoed by the hidden Polonius. Hamlet draws his sword and thrusts it through the arras, killing the old man. There is a moment of confusion as he asks, "is it the king?" He lifts the arras to disclose the corpse of Polonius; and in reply to Gertrude's exclamation at his "rash and bloody deed," he shoots back, "almost as bad, good mother, / As kill a king, and marry with his brother." Hamlet blurts out his deepest fear that she had been a party to the murder, but then strangely he says no more about it. Satisfied perhaps by her shocked reaction, he drops the accusation, which is never so much as implied elsewhere in the play.

Hamlet points to portraits of her two husbands on the wall, asking her to contrast them, and launches into a scathing denunciation of Claudius, with the desired effect. Stunned by a sense of shame, she asks her son to desist; but he cannot stop himself. The words flood out of him in a torrent of abuse while he is deaf to her anguished pleas, "no more," and again "no more." He is silenced only by the sudden reappearance of his father's ghost, come to chide him and "whet thy almost blunted purpose."

Part of the medieval lore about such spirits is their ability to be visible only to those whom they choose (as is Banquo's ghost at Macbeth's table). It is evident that Gertrude cannot see the figure, hence the spectacle of her son speaking to empty space unsettles her the more; she fears that he has indeed lost his wits. The ghost vanishes, and Hamlet turns to her with a warning that she should not dismiss her sense of shame because of his seeming madness. She submits once more, "O Hamlet, thou hast cleft my heart in twain." He tells her what she must do—and curious counsel it is!

It would seem that what troubles Hamlet most is that his mother sleeps with Claudius. "Go not to my uncle's bed," he urges, and then cruelly, "assume a virtue if you have it not." He repeats the admonition, "refrain tonight" so that later abstinence will be easier. Hamlet turns to go, but not yet satisfied he returns to embellish his advice in terms so explicitly erotic that he seems to relish them. Do not do this, he says, as if taking more pleasure in describing the intimate scene than he does forbidding it. Do not:

> Let the bloat king tempt you again to bed,
> Pinch wanton on your cheek, call you his mouse,
> And let him for a pair of reechy kisses,
> Or paddling in your neck with his damned fingers. . . .

In sum, he warns her not to be seduced into revealing to the king that her son is feigning insanity, that he acts "not in madness, / But mad in craft." She agrees, and he quickly turns to his upcoming trip to England, revealing that he has a plan to outwit Rosencranz and Guildenstern, one which he will enjoy as an opportunity "to have the engineer / Hoist with his own petar [blown up by his own explosives]." He finally leaves, dragging Polonius's body with him but showing no compassion or regret at the death of the innocent old man, who was guilty of little more than habitual meddling. To Hamlet he was but "a foolish prating knave."

The scene reveals two things at least about Hamlet's contradictory nature. First, he can act decisively, though perhaps only in moments of rashness before a thought intrudes. Second, he can devise a plot, as he does here against Rosencranz and Guildenstern. But when will he come up with one against Claudius?

At this stage in the play we have been exposed to all the forces bearing on Hamlet's puzzling behavior: grief over his father's death, the obligation to avenge the murder, his mother's marriage, his thwarted ambition, Ophelia's betrayal, his contemplative nature, and his melancholic state, complicated perhaps by Oedipal obsessions. How is an actor to convey the effects of these complex influences on the figure? In general terms there are two basic approaches to the character, which we may loosely label "the active Hamlet" and "the melancholy Dane." Productions that favor the former depict him as entirely sane, a forceful and energetic figure fiercely intent upon vengeance but restrained by physical circumstances—a king surrounded by a bustling court that leaves little opportunity for assassination. Those that favor the latter emphasize a figure whose genuine depression and near madness render him vulnerable to deeply psychological forces or philosophical doubts that inhibit him from carrying out his intent.

These alternatives are skillfully illustrated by the two most popular and effective film versions of the play. In Kenneth Branagh's 1997 production, the king is never alone except when he kneels in prayer. The film has a cast of thousands with a host of courtiers in constant attendance upon the monarch. Hamlet is brilliant, aggressive, and fully in control of his faculties throughout, engaging in carefully calculated descents into an "antic disposition." His "mystery" is still in evidence, of course, especially in the soliloquies, but it is overshadowed by the spectacle of the production and the boundless energy of the figure. In Laurence Olivier's earlier version (1948), on the other hand, Elsinore is a dark, brooding palace with long, empty, shadowed corridors and low-arched ceilings supported by large pillars, giving the impression more of a crypt than a castle, where death might lurk around any dimly lit corner. Olivier's Hamlet is very much the introspective "melancholy Dane," prevented by some unnamed inhibition from carrying out his vow of vengeance. Olivier is fond of the Freudian reading, particularly in the closet scene, where he attacks Gertrude as if in the act of rape, physically grappling with her, throwing her about on the bed as he assaults her with a torrent of words, to which she finally submits. It is here, Olivier seems to say, that Hamlet achieves a catharsis of his emotions, however misdirected his attack may be. The theater has the burden of presenting an audience with a coherent and emotionally plausible figure; but, that being said, too much of one or the other of these interpretations must necessarily fall short of Shakespeare's complex vision of this troubled spirit.

4.1–2 Act Four opens with Claudius learning of Polonius's death. He sends Rosencranz and Guildenstern to find Hamlet, which they do, only to be subjected once again to his obscure and biting wit. He runs off and they give chase.

4.3 In a meeting with his counselors, Claudius reveals why he must avoid direct action against the prince, whatever his behavior. There are many in the kingdom apparently unsympathetic to Claudius's assumption of the throne, hence he is reluctant to "put the strong law" on Hamlet. Even though he has killed a high government official, "he's loved by the distracted multitude," who presumably would rebel at his arrest no matter what he has done. Rosencranz and Guildenstern return to report that they cannot find the body of Polonius, and Hamlet follows under strong guard. He banters with Claudius, finally revealing, with heavy mockery, that "if indeed you find him not within this month, you shall nose him as you go up the stairs into the lobby." There follows a tense exchange in which Claudius informs Hamlet he is being sent to England. He replies, "good," to which the king responds darkly, "so is it if thou knew'st our purposes," and the prince comes back with "I see a cherub that sees them." Here, finally, are the two antagonists eye to eye, each acknowledging obliquely that he knows the other's designs. Claudius is now fully aware of the threat that Hamlet poses, and the prince in turn detects a danger in his trip to England. This is all very well, but it means that Hamlet in his procrastination has completely lost the advantage of his hitherto secret intent. Each now knows what the other knows; and Claudius, left alone again on stage, quickly confirms that the letters accompanying Rosencranz and Guildenstern require England to effect "the present death of Hamlet" upon his arrival there.

4.4   Hamlet, en route to his embarkation, encounters the army of young Fortinbras, which is marching through Danish land, as was agreed upon earlier by Claudius and the king of Norway, to conquer a relatively worthless piece of Poland. Hamlet, struck by the contrast between the Norwegian prince and himself, soliloquizes again on his own lack of resolve, wondering at his misuse of the gift of reason. It puzzles him that with every incentive to act, he fails to do so, musing that the cause is either some "beastial oblivion, or some craven scruple / Of thinking too precisely on th'event." "Examples gross as earth exhort me," he continues, and contemplates the contrast between Fortinbras's seemingly senseless cause and his own, "that have a father killed, a mother stained, / Excitements of my reason and my blood, / And let all sleep." He concludes with yet another effort to work himself up: "O, from this time forth, / My thoughts be bloody, or be nothing worth!"

4.5   A vulnerable Ophelia, despairing over the death of her father, which has come on top of Hamlet's harsh rejection, has lost her sanity. If we have puzzled over Hamlet's uncertain state of mind, his ravings at the sight of his father's tormented ghost, and his seemingly distracted exchanges with others, Shakespeare now places before us the pitiful spectacle of true lunacy, as if to leave to our judgment just how much "method" there is to Hamlet's "madness." In Ophelia we witness the behavior of one who has unquestionably sunk into insanity, as she dances among the shocked members of the court, singing snatches of songs that allude to her distress at both losses.

On her departure, Laertes enters. He has returned from Paris in response to the news of his father's death. Intent upon revenge against Claudius, whom he assumes is responsible, he has aroused the citizens against the king, confirming the unsettled state of Denmark. He bursts into Elsinore, backed by boisterous supporters who raise a cry of "Laertes shall be king!" and confronts Claudius. The outwardly composed king declares himself innocent, but before he can say more Ophelia reappears.

The sight of her further incites her brother. She passes out flowers to the sorrowing observers, with a wistful message for each. Laertes is overwrought by the sight—"Do you see this, O God?"—and Claudius calmly persuades him to a private conference, promising that if he does not satisfy the young man, he will surrender the crown to him.

4.6 Horatio receives a letter from Hamlet, giving an account of his adventures. His ship was overtaken by pirates and he, in the vanguard of the ensuing fight, boarded the pirate ship—he *can* act!—but was left their prisoner when his vessel was able to break contact and escape. The pirates, upon learning that he is a king's son, and sensing gain, are treating him well and conveying him back to Denmark.

4.7 The king and Laertes confer, and Claudius reveals that it was Hamlet who killed Polonius, and that he now seeks his own death. Laertes is incredulous, asking why the king had "proceeded not against these feats." Claudius justifies his inaction on two counts: first, "the queen his mother / Lives almost by his looks," and again because of "the great love the general gender bears him." The two men are informed of Hamlet's return, and Claudius reveals that he has a plan, apparently conceived on the spot, to dispose of the prince in such a way that "no wind of blame" will attach to them and "even his mother shall uncharge the practice, / And call it accident." The king asks Laertes what he would do to avenge his father's death, to which he responds viciously that he would "cut his throat i'th'church." Satisfied, Claudius outlines his plot. Relying on Hamlet's vanity, he will wager on a duel between the two, one in which, as is customary in such exercises, the foils will be "bated," that is, with their pointed ends protected by a round ball to prevent injury. Claudius proposes that they slip in among the foils offered for their choice one left purposely "unbated," which Laertes can then select so as to kill Hamlet and appear innocent of the oversight, claiming it was all a mistake. Laertes eagerly agrees and adds that, just to be sure, he will taint the point of the sword with a poison that nothing "can save the thing from death / That is but scratched withal." Claudius, not to be outdone, contributes a scheme to poison a chalice from which Hamlet will drink as he pauses between bouts. They leave nothing to chance.

The queen enters with the news that in her distraction Ophelia has drowned herself. Her lines are among Shakespeare's most poignant laments for the death of the innocent.

5.1 The last act opens on a graveyard—but it is a comic interval, intended to provide some relief from the intensity of the scene before and the episode to follow. Two grave-diggers, identified as "Clowns," are preparing a grave—as we learn, to receive the body of Ophelia. Death pervades this play, enveloping it like a thick fog from the first appearance of the ghost, to Hamlet's thoughts on suicide and murder, to the deaths of Polonius and Ophelia, and finally to the carnage of the ending, when the stage is strewn with bodies. Thus, even the comic relief is graveyard humor, as the two diggers joke together and with Hamlet and Horatio when they appear.

One of the diggers throws up a skull, which upon inquiry Hamlet learns is all that remains of Yorick, the court jester of his childhood. He responds with his famous lines beginning, "I knew him, Horatio," and contemplates the skull. It is a striking image, the two staring at one another across the chasm of death, mankind confronting his inevitable end. Hamlet alludes to the thought in his closing lines, bidding the skull to "get you to my lady's chamber, and tell her, let her paint an inch thick, to this favor she must come." The irony of the lines is heavy indeed, for he has yet to hear of Ophelia's death.

He is soon to learn of it, however. A funeral procession approaches, and Hamlet and Horatio conceal themselves to observe—more spying! Laertes is complaining bitterly that the deceased is denied the service of the dead; and he is informed that since "her death was doubtful"—that is, possibly a suicide—no such ceremony could be performed. Hamlet is startled by Laertes' revelation that the corpse is his sister's, and when her brother leaps into the grave for a final embrace, he rushes from hiding and jumps in after him. They wrestle until separated by others, and an incensed Hamlet swears fervently that he "loved Ophelia, forty thousand brothers / Could not with all their quantity of love / Make up my sum." Can this be true? If so, it may explain some of his earlier excesses, but it leaves unexplained his callous contempt for the corpse of Polonius when the thought never crossed his mind that he had killed his dear love's father. He showed scant regret for the deed at the time and has none now, unaccountably thoughtless of any grievance that Laertes might have against him. "What is the reason you use me thus?" he demands—a puzzling line. Is he so insensitive, so self-absorbed, wrapped up in his own concerns, that he has no idea why Laertes is angry with him?

As Hamlet leaves, the king takes charge, directing Horatio, Laertes, and Gertrude to different tasks.

5.2 In an abrupt change of tone, the final scene opens on Hamlet calmly describing to Horatio his deception of Rosencranz and Guildenstern, the success of which he attributes to his precipitate action. He pauses to philosophize on the thought:

> Our indiscretion sometimes serves us well,
> When our deep plots do pall, and that should learn us
> There's a divinity that shapes our ends,
> Rough-hew them how we will.

Shakespeare here gives us another key to Hamlet's character. He is capable of action, but only in a moment of rashness. Whatever our own "deep plots," he muses, fate ultimately will "shape our ends" no matter what we do. Hamlet is slipping back into melancholy, mulling over how powerless we are to determine our own destiny. It seems to him that acts of "rashness" or "indiscretion" offer the only way out of such fatalism; thus he determines to conduct himself impulsively and leave the outcome to "divinity."

He tells Horatio that he stole the king's letters from Rosencranz and Guildenstern and replaced them with forgeries calling for *their* execution, not his. He voices no regret over their impending deaths, observing coldly that it was their ill fortune to be caught up in a struggle between a king and a prince, to come, as he puts it, "between the pass and full incensed points / Of mighty opposites." Hamlet yet again recites his grievances against Claudius: "He hath killed my king, and whored my mother, / Popped in between th'election and my hopes, / [And] thrown out his angle for my proper life." But then he asks, "is't not perfect conscience / To quit him with this arm?" This is indeed puzzling; after all that has happened, Hamlet remains uncertain about the justice of his cause and turns to his friend for assurance that he may now kill Claudius with a clear conscience. Horatio does not answer him, as if to dismiss the question. He remarks only that the news of the executions of Rosencranz and Guildenstern will soon be known. Hamlet observes grimly that "the interim is mine," implying his resolve to act promptly to carry out his intent.

Having reaffirmed his resolve, however, his thoughts turn not to the means of accomplishing it but to something else entirely—his skirmish with Laertes. Again, whenever the thought or the opportunity arises to kill the king, something always intrudes to divert him from his purpose. Whether this is a quirk of an easily distracted melancholic temperament, or a subconscious resistance, even revulsion, at the thought, we cannot tell. It is apparent, however, that at no time during the weeks or months that pass in the course of the play does Hamlet devise a plan to kill the king, while Claudius hatches one plot after another to do away with the prince. Here again, when the brief "interim" is his, Hamlet fails once more to seize it. As for Laertes, he says, he will "court his favors"; he regrets "the towering passion" that caused his behavior and, calmer now, voices a compassion for the youth since "by the image of my cause I see / The portraiture of his." Both have had fathers murdered, but it never occurs to Hamlet that Laertes may want to kill him as passionately as he wants to kill the king.

Osric appears, inviting Hamlet to the duel. A brief interlude of levity follows. Osric is the stock character of a dandified court fop, who bows a lot and waves his hat about; and Hamlet mimics his extravagant speech, cleverly mocking him in such a way that he remains ignorant of the insults, much to Horatio's amusement. Hamlet agrees to the duel but confesses to his friend that he has undefined misgivings about the prospect: "thou wouldst not think how ill all's here about my heart." Horatio advises him to cancel the duel, but Hamlet scoffs at the thought, repeating his fatalistic philosophy about man's destiny: "If it be now, 'tis not to come—if it be not to come, it will be now—if it be not now, yet it will come—the readiness is all."

There is still no evidence of a plan to fulfill Hamlet's role as avenger, but we experience a mounting anxiety over what will happen to him as he falls into the trap laid by Claudius. All he seems capable of saying about his situation is, "the readiness is all." But "readiness" for what? Shakespeare loads his speech with a dramatic tension that has little to do with killing the king. The poet foreshadows a far more affecting event, the death of Hamlet himself—the "it" of "if it be now." We deplore his philosophizing, which has rendered him impotent from the outset; and we now watch apprehensively as, disarmed once again by his habit of thought, he prepares to walk, a "ready" victim, into that fatal trap. Hamlet's "readiness" strikes us as the sentiment of a man who has become a pawn in the game plan of Providence and who has a foreboding that death is near, that "it will be now."

The court enters, and Hamlet apologizes to Laertes for his behavior in the graveyard. In his apology we gain some notion of what he may have had in mind by putting "an antic disposition on." Hamlet's problem all along, not unlike the concern voiced by Claudius, has been how to kill his antagonist and achieve the throne. As we have seen, he has no evidence for the murder of his father except the word of a ghost and the king's sudden indisposition in the mousetrap scene. In feigning distraction, if he is feigning, he prepares an excuse for himself after the fact, one like that he now offers Laertes. Was it Hamlet who wronged him? No, it was his madness: "Then Hamlet does it not, Hamlet denies it. / Who does it then? his madness." Would it have worked? Well, it fails with Laertes, but the prince was "loved of the distracted multitude," as Claudius observed. If Hamlet had demonstrated the same magnanimity and composure as he does at this moment, the people may have considered the fit passed. They would not be the first, after all, to be ruled by a mad king.

The action that follows is swift and frenetic. Laertes secures the unbated foil, and the duel begins. Hamlet scores the first "hit," that is, he touches Laertes with the tip of his foil. They break to prepare for another round, whereupon the king raises a cup of wine into which he grandly drops a priceless pearl, or "union" (onion?), as he calls it, to be the reward for the winner. He offers the poisoned cup to Hamlet, who refuses. The prince scores another "hit" on Laertes, prompting the queen to take up the poisoned cup and drink to her son's success, to the impotent distress of Claudius. The third round of the duel ends in a draw—but during the break a frustrated Laertes treacherously thrusts at Hamlet, wounding him while his back is turned and enraging the prince. The two grapple, and in the confusion the foils are exchanged. Hamlet now wounds Laertes, who realizing his death is near, confesses to the whole scheme. The queen dies and Hamlet attacks the king, wounds him with the poisoned foil, and for good measure forces him to drink from the poisoned cup. Here again is "the enginer / Hoist upon his own petar." An overwrought Horatio reaches for the cup to end his own life, but Hamlet, gathering his last strength, dashes it from Horatio's hand, entreating his friend to "absent thee from felicity a while" and live to tell his story. Hamlet dies to Horatio's memorable lines: "Now cracks a noble heart. Good night, sweet prince; / And flights of angels sing thee to thy rest."

Fortinbras enters, returning from his Polish campaign, and is stunned that death "so many princes at a shot / So bloodily hath struck," a sight, the soldier observes, that "becomes the [battle]field, but here shows much amiss." The English ambassadors, who entered with him, report that "Rosencranz and Guildenstern are dead." Fortinbras, to whom the prince, for a brief moment the king of Denmark, had given his "dying voice," assumes the throne. He directs that Hamlet's body be borne "like a soldier to the stage, / For he was likely, had he been put on, / To have proved most royal," restoring the heroic image of this tragic figure.

What are we to make of this figure, and this play? Shakespeare only obscures the source of Hamlet's "mystery" by matching every facet of his character with another that contradicts it, in what seems at times an almost deliberate design to puzzle us. Consider:

Hamlet can act but he doesn't, except in rash moments.

He can plot but fails to do so against the king.

He loves Ophelia but abuses her and shows no remorse at killing her father.

He values composure in Horatio but is wildly erratic in his own behavior.

He is shrewdly attuned to human nature but blind to Leartes' hatred.

His temperament is subject to inexplicably abrupt shifts, moving from a deeply contemplative soliloquy to a sudden vicious attack on Ophelia, from a passionate outburst in the graveyard to a composed conversation with Horatio, from a grim resolve to act against the king to frivolous toying with the ridiculous Osric.

Further, his speech is full of contradictions:

He tells Rosencranz and Guildenstern that he has "foregone all custom of exercises," but to Horatio he says that he has "been in continual practice" with his sword.

He tells Ophelia that he did not love her, but to the queen he says that he did, more than "forty thousand brothers."

He tells his mother that he was not mad, but to Laertes he says he was.

In sum, Hamlet has a superior mind yet cannot focus it to his purpose; he is energetic yet immobilized by thought; intelligent yet ignorant of himself; compassionate yet cold to the suffering of others; philosophical yet unthinking; despairing yet sanguine; fearless yet hesitant; noble yet common.

In this forest of contradictions, then, Hamlet is the very image of the human condition, whose dilemmas ever puzzle us. He is, further, a consummate example of Aristotle's tragic hero brought down by his own "error or frailty." But the "mystery" remains: Which error? What frailty?

MACBETH

❧

SHAKESPEARE created several splendid villains—Iago, Richard III, Edmund in *King Lear*—but each is villainous from the outset, even announcing his treacherous intentions in opening lines; each undergoes little change in character during the course of the play. In *Macbeth* we watch the dark side of the human spirit emerge in slow degrees, transforming an initially upright and admirable figure into a monster. Here we see the forces that create a villain, tempting an essentially good man to embark on a course of action that sends him on the downward path to deception, cruelty, despair, and a final violent end. It is a chilling spectacle of evil leading on to further evil, all the more compelling in that it unveils the human potential to embrace ambition until it takes on a compulsion of its own, trampling underfoot the habits and beliefs of a hitherto unblemished life.

In the play two valiant and loyal Scottish thanes,* Macbeth and Banquo, encounter witches who predict that Macbeth will be king and Banquo beget kings. The prediction inflames Macbeth's ambition. Prodded by the urging of his wife, he murders the king and mounts the throne. Harrowed by insecurity and perhaps the burden of guilt, he has Banquo murdered and evolves into a ruthless tyrant, imposing a reign of terror on his subjects. The murdered king's son, Malcolm, finds refuge in England, where he raises an army and, accompanied by loyal Scots, returns to defeat Macbeth, upon whose death he assumes the throne. The play asks what forces might persuade a man or woman to take that first step on

---

*A heraldic title, like duke or count.

such an evil path, what crimes lie along its way, and how it may lead to a tragic end.

1.1   In *Macbeth* one of these forces is supernatural, and we are in its presence as the curtain rises. *Hamlet* opens on a ghost, *Macbeth* on witches—ugly, misshapen creatures that lived, it was believed, on the shadowed border between the spiritual and natural worlds. They are human but possess a power to see the future and shape events. Their appearance promises no good for those they choose to confront—and they have a rendezvous with Macbeth "upon the heath."

1.2   The scene shifts to the king's camp. Scotland is at war against rebels supported by the king of Norway, and it is in the reports of battle that we gain our first impression of Macbeth. He is a loyal thane of the Scottish king, Duncan, and has fought valiantly alongside Banquo, his comrade-in-arms, against the rebel forces. The two are equally courageous, the one an "eagle" among sparrows, the other a "lion" among hares; but it falls to Macbeth to kill the rebel Macdonwald and subdue the Norwegian invaders, hence it is he who is chiefly credited with the victory. The enemy had found an ally in that "disloyal traitor / The thane of Cawdor," and so the king announces that he will endow the "noble Macbeth" with the treasonous thane's title and lands as a reward for his service.

1.3   The witches reappear "upon the heath," and in their chanted exchange we hear of their powers. Although they cannot doom a ship, they can raise winds that render it "tempest-tost" and plague its captain with sleeplessness, causing him to "dwindle, peak, and pine." It is clear that they are not to be taken lightly and that they are working their charms to ensnare Macbeth. When, accompanied by Banquo, he comes upon them, they hail him as "thane of Glamis," which he is already, but further as "thane of Cawdor" and "king hereafter." Banquo asks them about himself, and they reply cryptically that he shall be less than Macbeth and not so happy, but at the same time greater and happier, and that though he shall not himself rule, he "shall [be]get kings." Macbeth is shaken. Apparently unaware of Cawdor's treachery, he questions the prophecies and demands to know why they have chosen him and Banquo for their revelations, whereupon the witches vanish.

Ross and Angus arrive to announce that Macbeth is indeed the thane of Cawdor, the second of the witches' announcements, which immediately lends substance to the third. Banquo is as surprised as he but urges caution:

> . . . oftentimes, to win us to our harm,
> The instruments of darkness tell us truths,
> Win us with honest trifles, to betray 's
> In deepest consequence.

Macbeth reacts to the news on two levels. Outwardly he thanks the messengers courteously while otherwise "rapt" in thought, as Banquo observes. Inwardly he is startled, and in a series of *asides* he reveals a troubled mind. He puzzles over the prophecies, which, he says, "cannot be ill; cannot be good," and wonders whether the one having proven true, the other may as well. The thought of the crown, he finds, "doth unfix my hair, / And make my seated heart knock at my ribs, / Against the use of nature"; it so "shakes [his] single state of man" as to unbalance his reason until it appears that "nothing is / But what is not." The intensity of his reaction suggests that he had already entertained thoughts of the crown, hence the prophecy merely brings that hidden ambition to the surface of his mind. He regains composure for a moment and concludes philosophically that "if chance will have me king, why, chance may crown me / Without my stir." He thanks the messengers again and leaves with them for the court.

What are we meant to make of these witches, and why have they chosen Macbeth as a victim of their charms? We do not know, but as they await Macbeth's arrival one of them provides a glimpse of their motive. She is angry because a sailor's wife refused to share some chestnuts with her, and in retaliation for the insult she schemes to inflict punishment upon the woman's innocent husband. In brief, the witches may act for any obscure reason, but it is clear that they do so out of malice, here tempting an essentially good man at his most vulnerable point—his secret ambition. In the play their motives are immaterial—the audience assumes that the witches are dark forces that mean Macbeth harm. They do so by unearthing a thought that had lain dormant in the hidden reaches of his mind and breathing life into it with their cryptic message. Supernatural forces, then, cannot dictate events, even as the first witch could not destroy the sailor's ship, but they can render their victim "tempest-tost," as they do Macbeth. Shakespeare would not have us think that we are the helpless toy of forces over which we have no control, for there would be little tragic in Macbeth's downfall were that the case. Rather, once set upon the path of ambition, as a result ironically of his own valorous deserving, Macbeth becomes the instrument of his own destruction. He does not become evil because of collusion with the forces of evil, as does Dr. Faustus, for example, but because he succumbs to the evil side of his own nature. *Macbeth* enacts the fatal course of anyone who thus submits, whether or not incited by the supernatural.

1.4 The following scene, though brief, is important on several counts. It reinforces the impression of Duncan as a benevolent king, generous to his loving subjects and perhaps a bit too trusting. Cawdor was, as he says, "a gentleman on whom I built / An absolute trust," as he does now on Macbeth and Banquo. The courtesies he exchanges with them may seem somewhat ornate, but they define the ideal relationship between king and subjects. In the imagery of husbandry, he is like the farmer who "plants" and nourishes them so that they grow, but their "harvest," as Banquo graciously replies, will be the king's. Shakespeare provides a brief glimpse of a virtuous ruler, against whom we can measure the tyrant that Macbeth becomes.

Duncan designates his son Malcolm as heir to the throne. In Macbeth's brief aside we learn that the witches' prophecy has already taken a firm hold on his imagination. Malcolm is an obstacle to his ambition, and in rhymed lines, as if to stress the emotional intensity of that ambition, he resolves to keep it hidden: "Stars, hide your fires! / Let not light see my black and deep desires." The irony of Duncan's nature is telling— his trust in the new Cawdor is apparently as misplaced as it was in the earlier one.

1.5 Aside from the witches, there is yet another force that sets the "noble Macbeth" on his course—his wife, his "dearest partner of greatness," as he calls her. Theirs is obviously a close relationship, and she knows him well. On hearing of the prophecy from his letter, she exults in the news but fears that he lacks the will to act on it. He is, she regrets, "too full o'th'milk of human kindness" to prey on others, too loyal to betray their trust, too honest to "play false." She will have to subvert his better nature if he is ever to be crowned.

Lady Macbeth sees in the king's impending visit an unanticipated opportunity to fulfill her ambition for her husband, and she invokes the forces of darkness, "spirits / That tend on mortal thoughts" and inhuman "murd'ring ministers" to prepare her for the task. "Unsex me here," she pleads, asking that she be drained of all human compassion, all the natural qualities of woman, wife, or mother. She entreats those "murd'ring ministers" to "make thick my blood," and turn the milk of her "woman's breasts" to gall, then calls upon "thick night" to conceal her intent so that her knife will "see not the wound it makes."

1.6 Duncan arrives at Macbeth's castle and observes that it has a "pleasant seat," a touch of *dramatic irony* in that we anticipate the terrors awaiting him within. Lady Macbeth emerges to begin another exchange of exaggerated courtesies. They enter the castle as Duncan reaffirms his great love for her husband.

1.7 Some hours pass, during which apparently Macbeth and his wife have spoken further of the plot, for he enters now and in an extended *soliloquy* contemplates the "assassination." He is uncertain of success and vacillates, remarking that "we still have judgment here" and marshaling all the arguments against it: Duncan is under his roof in "a double trust" as his kinsman, king, and guest. Further, he has proven such a good king that his virtues would cry out against his murder, and "pity, like a newborn babe" would cause all to weep because of it. Macbeth, with only "vaulting ambition" to prod him, is irresolute. When his wife joins him, he announces that "we will proceed no further in this business."

This soliloquy is important on several counts. First, it seems the final appearance of the "noble Macbeth," an honorable man wrestling with his conscience, knowing full well that those who engage in such plots have found that they can "return / To plague th'inventor" and that "vaulting ambition" often "o'erleaps itself / and falls on the other" side. On the other hand, he weighs the arguments for and against the plot not on moral grounds—the right and wrong of murder—but on its chance of success. Duncan's virtues do not trouble him; he fears only that the death of this highly revered king will excite his subjects to such an outpouring of grief that their "tears will drown the wind," that is, dampen and defeat the force of his claim to the throne. His later excitement over his wife's plan arises from its promise to absolve him of the murder and ease his way to the crown.

The soliloquy alerts us, further, to Macbeth's capacity for powerful poetry. It has been said that Shakespeare placed some of his most moving lines in the mouth of his most consummate villain, and that they reflect a mind possessed of a potent imagination. He has visions, he hears voices, he sees ghosts, he suffers nightmares, and he seeks the counsel of witches. To each experience he responds with soaring poetry, conveying the horror, the excitement, and finally the despair of one who delivers himself to the darker side of his nature. We find that we must be alert to the imagery of his lines in order fully to appreciate what is happening to him. The "naked new-born babe" is indeed a moving simile for pity, but this image of children acquires new meaning in scenes to come as their innocence contrasts starkly with Macbeth's darkening inhumanity.

Lady Macbeth is incensed at her husband's loss of resolve, and she demands to know what has changed his mind. She questions his love for her and finally attacks his manhood, asking if he is content to live with the knowledge that he is "a coward." Aroused by this charge, Macbeth defends himself, but she is not to be silenced. "What beast was't then / That made you break this enterprise to me?" she demands. Finally, now thoroughly "unsexed," she utters a terrible oath:

> I have given suck, and know
> How tender 'tis to love the babe that milks me—
> I would, while it was smiling in my face,
> Have plucked my nipple from its boneless gums,
> And dashed the brains out, had I so sworn as you
> Have done to this.

There is no other evidence of her children in the play; but nothing can diminish the horrifying image of the "new-born babe," only moments before imagined as a symbol of pity, now envisioned with its brains dashed out, and by its own mother.

Macbeth asks weakly, "if we should fail?" and she scoffs at his fears, disclosing a plan that apparently she alone has devised. She will ply the king's grooms with wine until they are insensible, providing an opportunity to kill Duncan and blame the murder on them. Macbeth is exultant in his admiration—"Bring forth men-children only!"—and then adds his own touch: they will use the grooms' daggers and then smear their bodies with the king's blood, confirming their guilt. Macbeth has needed little persuasion.

2.1   Some hours pass. The king has retired, and Banquo enters with his son, Fleance, remarking on the time of night. They encounter Macbeth, who at that very moment is on his way to the king's bedchamber. They exchange a few guarded words, then Macbeth dismisses his servant and prepares to move on to his task, only to be startled by the illusion of a dagger before him. The vision, he concludes, arises from his "heat-oppressed brain," but it is also a sign that "marshall'st me the way I was going." It is a chilling moment as he follows the bleeding dagger off stage, intoning some of Shakespeare's superb scene-setting poetry:

> Now o'er the one half-world
> Nature seems dead, and wicked dreams abuse
> The curtained sleep; Witchcraft celebrates
> Pale Hecate's off'rings; and withered Murder,
> . . . . towards his design
> Moves like a ghost.

2.2   Lady Macbeth enters moments later, apprehensive that something will go amiss. She has played her role by reducing Duncan's grooms to a drunken stupor. Macbeth reappears, having done his brutal part as well, and he is visibly shaken by the experience. After murdering Duncan he heard a voice cry, "Sleep no more! / Macbeth does murder sleep," and later, "Glamis hath murdered sleep, and therefore Cawdor / Shall sleep no more: Macbeth shall sleep no more!" The source of the voice may well have been his overheated imagination, aroused at the moment of murder, or perhaps his conscience condemning the act; but the lines echo the cadence and content of the witches' prophetic incantations.

In any event, sleep, mentioned briefly on earlier occasions, now becomes a central image of the play. In the contemplation of death—a recurring concern in Shakespeare's tragedies—the human imagination seizes on the figure of sleep as the closest parallel in mortal experience to that unknown and unknowable end. Christianity teaches that death is followed by an awakening, not in this life but in another, and indeed poets have at times pictured life itself as a sleep and death the waking from it. But no such promise brightens its dark dimensions in these plays, which work upon our conviction that the end of life is of all events the most tragic. The imagery is everywhere in Shakespeare, from Hamlet's "to sleep, perchance to dream" to Prospero's flowing lines in *The*

Tempest, "we are such stuff / As dreams are made on; and our little life / Is rounded with a sleep," providing in each instance a fleeting glimpse through the shadows surrounding that final mystery.

In *Macbeth,* however, though the implied parallel with death is never distant, sleep is benign, a solace to be sought and savored when it comes. The haunting voice foretells that Macbeth "shall sleep no more," and he wonders why he should be deprived of its healing powers:

> Sleep that knits up the raveled sleave of care,
> The death of each day's life, sore labor's bath,
> Balm of hurt minds, great Nature's second course,
> Chief nourisher in life's feast.

A troubled sleep, of course, is a traditional image of a guilty conscience, and so we shall find it in *Macbeth.* But it will not be forgotten that the "Weird Sisters"—the witches—can by their art deprive the innocent sailor of his rest, the lack of which will cause him to "dwindle, peak, and pine."

Macbeth, stunned by the enormity of his crime, has come downstairs unconsciously carrying the daggers of the sleeping grooms. He is so unnerved that he refuses to return to the scene of the murder, and his wife chides him for his fears, "the sleeping and the dead / Are but as pictures." It is she who must return the daggers to the grooms, and in her brief absence Macbeth stares at his bloody hands, asking, "will all great Neptune's ocean wash this blood / Clean." In his despair he concludes that they will be stained forever. Troubled by his fanciful ravings, his wife attempts to steady him, "a little water clears us of this deed." There is a knocking at the castle gate and they retire, as Macbeth, torn by remorse, exclaims, "wake Duncan with thy knocking! I would thou couldst!"

2.3 This tense scene is followed by a brief comic interlude, indeed the only one in this dark play, inserted here by Shakespeare between the murder and its discovery, as if to postpone that dramatic moment and heighten our anticipation of it. Even here, however, we are entertained with gallows humor, invocations to the underworld and allusions to hanging and treason. The drunken porter admits Macduff and Lennox, who banter with him until Macbeth comes upon them and we return abruptly to the grim tone of the play. He answers their inquiries tersely, and Macduff leaves to awaken the king, only to discover him beyond waking. The response to the news is frenetic: Macbeth and Lennox leave to view the scene, and the stage becomes quickly crowded as Lady Macbeth and Banquo appear, followed closely by Duncan's two sons, Malcolm and Donalbain. Macbeth returns to reveal that he has killed the two grooms in a fit of passion, for as he exclaims, "who could refrain, / That had a heart to love." It would appear that he has recovered quickly from his paralyzing remorse and has taken matters into his own hands to ensure that the grooms will never raise doubts about their guilt. Lady Macbeth faints. In a series of asides, Malcolm and Donalbain, fearing they will be the next victims, agree it is prudent to flee for their lives, the one to England, the other to Ireland.

2.4   The next scene opens with an account of nature's response to these unnatural events. Again, this is not mere scene-setting but one of several passages reflecting the belief of the time in a *universal order* in which dire events in human affairs are foreshadowed or echoed at all levels of existence. Here, "the heavens, as troubled with man's act, / Threatens his bloody stage"—owls kill falcons and horses eat one another as a king's death upsets the order of the universe, not only in the precarious balance of human society but in the heavens and the natural world as well. The flight of Duncan's sons casts strong suspicion on them; and Macbeth, his version of the murder unquestioned, is already en route to Scone for the ceremonial crowning. Significantly, Macduff will not attend the coronation, returning rather to his native Fife.

3.1   After the passage of several weeks, Macbeth is secure in the throne. Banquo enters alone, voicing a sullen acceptance of the fact, though he has suspicions that the king "play'dst most foully for't." He acknowledges that the prophecies of the "weird women" have all come true for Macbeth and wonders about the future they foretold for him. Macbeth enters, attended by his court, and in an outwardly courteous exchange between them—ostensibly to ensure Banquo's presence at a feast that night—the king inquires quite closely about his plans for the day. In Macbeth's soliloquy we learn what lies behind his questions: though he has achieved his ambition, the crown sits uneasily on his head—"to be thus is nothing, / But to be safely thus." The cause of his discontent is Banquo—"there is none but he / Whose being I do fear." His own prophecies having been fulfilled, his mind turns to the predictions for his friend; and the thought rankles that, should they prove as valid as his own, all his efforts will have only placed upon his head "a fruitless crown, / And put a barren sceptre" in his hand. Macbeth sees in those predictions a threat to his safety, and he is determined to remove it. "Come Fate into the list," he appeals, "and champion me to th'utterance." It is ominously ironic that he enlists fate in his cause, since his every act henceforth will only hasten his own end and ensure that Banquo's heirs will succeed to the crown. But Macbeth has long since abandoned the passive role he assumed when he first considered whether "chance may crown me, / Without my stir." He now seeks to frustrate the very forces that proved prophetic of his own success.

Macbeth secretly engages two men who hold grudges against Banquo in a plot to ambush and murder him and his son, Fleance, on their ride that day. In the confessions of these desperate men, Shakespeare subtly foreshadows Macbeth's own emotional aridity at the end of the play, when he finds life "but a walking shadow."

3.2   In the following scene we catch a glimpse of Lady Macbeth's inner thoughts, and it is immediately apparent that she is no longer the cold, hard, resolute woman who raged that she would dash her child's brains out rather than abandon a sworn resolve. She is now a much subdued figure who, over the intervening weeks, has fallen into a deep melancholy: "Nought's had, all's spent, / Where our desire is got without content." The cause of her distress, it would appear, is her husband's state of mind. Still able to rise above her own despair, she tries to prod him out of his brooding with practical advice: "Things without all remedy / Should be without regard: what's done, is done." But he will not be comforted, complaining that they now eat their meals "in fear, and sleep / In the affliction of these terrible dreams / That shake us nightly." And we recall that mysterious voice predicting that "Macbeth shall sleep no more." Such is his distress that he almost envies Duncan, for "after life's fitful fever he sleeps well." Macbeth is convinced that his mind, so "full of scorpions," can find relief only by the removal of Banquo and Fleance.

Macbeth confides in his wife vaguely that "there shall be done / A deed of dreadful note" that night. But when she questions him about it, he cautions her to "be innocent of the knowledge, dearest chuck, / Till thou applaud the deed." It is evident that the relationship between them, though still very close, has undergone a subtle change. While it is perhaps too much to say that their roles are reversed, she is no longer the moving force in their lives. It is now he who initiates plots, and he prefers that she remain "innocent" of them. He trusts her still but has become more secretive by nature. The scene closes with another instance of poetic splendor voiced by this villain, here on the contrast between the "good things of day" and "night's black agents." Macbeth concludes with a succinct summary of his newfound philosophy: "Things bad begun make strong themselves by ill."

3.3–4   The murderers successfully dispatch Banquo but blunder in allowing Fleance to escape.

At the palace, all is in readiness for the feast. The king and queen customarily take their meals on a raised dais while the assembled thanes dine at a long table at floor level, one which in this instance has a seat conspicuously empty. Macbeth, in a gesture of solidarity, proposes to join the thanes at their table. Before he can take his place, however, he confers aside with one of the murderers, from whom he learns of Banquo's death and the escape of Fleance. "Then comes my fit again," he murmurs, "I had else been perfect."

Returning to the banquet, he exchanges courtesies with his wife and expresses disappointment at the absence of Banquo, whose bloodied ghost has meanwhile appeared and, undetected by Macbeth, taken its seat at the table. The king glances about and recoils at the terrifying sight, inadvertently blurting out his guilt in a protest of innocence: "Thou canst not say I did it." It is clear that no one else sees the ghost, since Lady Macbeth, in a series of asides, reproaches her husband for his strange behavior in terms reminiscent of the night of Duncan's murder. "Are you a man?" she demands. As before, he defends himself. The ghost vanishes, and Macbeth returns to the company, apologizes, and raises a cup in a toast to the absent Banquo—when suddenly the ghost reappears, setting him off again, to everyone's consternation. Lady Macbeth attempts to calm the guests, who look on amazed; but the king raves on, again defending his courage—"What man dare, I dare." He commands the specter to quit his sight, and when it does, he collects himself once more—"I am a man again." Lady Macbeth, sensing that the evening is in ruins and perhaps dreading another outburst, dismisses the guests.

Macbeth interprets the meaning of the apparition—"It will have blood; they say, blood will have blood"—and his thoughts turn to one whom he suspects might indeed want his blood. Macduff was absent at his coronation and rejected an invitation to the banquet, reason enough for one consumed by mistrust to doubt his loyalty. Macbeth assures his wife that he will soon have sure knowledge of Macduff's intentions, however, since he keeps a paid informer in all the houses of his thanes. He is clearly shaken. The ghostly visitation suggests to him that the supernatural may hold the answer to his uncertainties—he will seek out the witches. Macbeth feels the need for swift action, whatever the cost: "I am in blood / Stepped in so far that, should I wade no more, / Returning were as tedious as go o'er." His wife counsels the need for rest and he agrees—"come, we'll to sleep." The two, joined now in distress as they were once in ambition, leave together, seeking a bed we suspect will offer little comfort.

In some modern productions this scene is played without the ghost, implying that the visitation is but a figment of Macbeth's imagination, as were the dagger and the voice at Duncan's bedside, hence a manifestation of his heavily burdened conscience rather than the metaphysical meddling of greater forces. Shakespeare's audience, however, who believed in ghosts, were more likely to take the apparition as real, a vengeful spirit, like Hamlet's father, so incensed by betrayal that it returns to "plague th'inventor." We may take it either way, or both, for the two interpretations are not incompatible. Whether we think of Macbeth as a man suffering under the weight of guilt or urged along the path of self-destruction by malevolent, otherworldly forces, the effect of the ghost's appearance is the same. It persuades him of the need to shed further blood in deeds "which must be acted ere they may be scanned," since, he fears, even to think on them might give him pause. He is now committed to a course of action that will brand him as an unrelenting tyrant.

3.5–6 The appearance in the next scene of Hecate, goddess of the earth and the underworld, is thought to be an addition by Thomas Middleton, a contemporary of Shakespeare's. He is said to have edited the play, adding the figure presumably because audiences delighted in such supernatural manifestations and no play could have too many of them.

Macduff has been "disgraced" because of his failure to attend "the tyrant's feast" and has defected to England, joining Malcolm, Duncan's eldest son and heir, who has found asylum there under the protection of "the pious" Edward the Confessor. This detail provides a time frame for the play. Edward reigned from 1042 to 1066 and was regarded as an ideal Christian prince, thus a useful *foil* to Macbeth, though we learn of him only by report.* A conversation between two Scottish thanes reflects mounting discontent and opposition to Macbeth in Scotland. With guarded irony, one voices his doubts about the death of Duncan, and the other commends the mission of Macduff, hoping it "may again / Give to our tables meats, sleep to our nights."

4.1 Act Four opens on the witches. In an eerie dance about a boiling cauldron, they weave a demonic charm to the recurring incantation of "Double, double toil and trouble; / Fire burn and cauldron bubble." They are brewing an infernal concoction, composed of such grizzly ingredients as the "finger of birth-strangled babe," and it is apparent that the "toil and trouble" of their chant is intended for Macbeth. He bursts upon them and, in a chilling invocation of all things unnatural, demands to know his destiny. In answer, apparitions arise from the enchanted cauldron and address him, not this time in prophecies so much as in cryptic warnings and assurances. The first, an armed head, warns him to beware of Macduff; the second, a bloody child, informs him that he need fear none "of woman born"; the third, a child again, bearing a tree, assures him that he will not be vanquished until "great Birnum wood to high Dunsinane hill / Shall come against him." These visions resurrect the image of the child, earlier portrayed as a "naked new-born babe" evoking pity, later as a victim of violence, its brains dashed out, and the "birth-strangled babe" of the witch's brew, and yet to come, Macduff's murdered son. They lure Macbeth into a false sense of invulnerability.

He is reassured by the witches' revelations but demands a less cryptic answer to the question that most troubles him: Will Banquo's heirs succeed him? In response, he is treated to a ghostly procession of eight

---

*At times Shakespeare plays fast and loose with history in order to create compelling drama. In the play, Macbeth's reign appears to have been short and filled with turmoil, but he actually ruled for seventeen years and was considered an able and virtuous king. The image of perfidy was apparently concocted by advocates of the House of Stuart (James I, Shakespeare's king, and his successors), who laid claim to the Scottish throne through the mythical Banquo and his son, Fleance, and through it to the English crown.

kings, followed by the figure of Banquo, who, eyeing Macbeth, points
mockingly to them. It is a mixed message indeed; and when Lennox enters with the news that Macduff has fled to England, Macbeth's thoughts
turn to the armed head's warning and he decides to "give to th'edge
o'th'sword / His wife, his babes, and all unfortunate souls / That trace
him in his line." Macbeth is not one to philosophize, Hamlet-like, on the
state of man and submit to fate with a resigned "readiness is all." A man
of action, he is true to his doctrine that "things bad begun make strong
themselves by ill," and he responds to events, natural and supernatural,
with abrupt resolve. But his responses are increasingly irrational. He is
incensed as he watches helplessly the vexing spectacle of Banquo's successors. Impotent to oppose them, he now vents his anger on the first of his
enemies to come to mind, lashing out at Macduff's successors, those that
"trace him in his line." It is "Banquo's issue" that infuriates him, but in
his crazed frustration he turns his wrath on any "issue" at hand, whether
they pose a threat or not.

4.2 In order to bring home to the audience the depths to which
Macbeth has sunk, Shakespeare includes a scene of senseless slaughter.
Lady Macduff resents her husband's flight to England, and Ross, a Scottish thane, attempts to justify his absence. She will not be pacified, however, and it is soon apparent that her fears are well founded. Two
murderers enter, kill her son before her eyes, and, pursuing her off stage,
slay her as well. The implication of the scene is that this is not an isolated
incident, affirming that all Scotland now lives in fear of a ruthless tyrant.

Thus far in the play, Shakespeare has traced the career of a man who
has achieved his ambition by devious means and suffers from the effects
of his own deception. When he takes the crown, Macbeth is a murderer
but not necessarily a tyrant. In the passage of time, however, the seeds of
his crime take root. Having proven untrustworthy himself, he now trusts
no one about him. Having committed murder to achieve his ends, he assumes that others plot his death as well. At first Banquo is the only man
"whose being I fear"; but once that threat is removed, it is replaced by another, Fleance, and then by yet another, Macduff. The tyrant will always
fear someone and in acting on his fears commit himself to more and more
inhuman measures, even to the slaughter of innocent women and children. Macbeth is, to be sure, plagued by nightmares; but, as will appear,
his recurrent crimes dull his conscience and leave him in the end devoid

of all feeling, in a condition of callous disregard for any blows that fate may inflict upon him, even death itself.

4.3 The scene shifts to England, where Macduff is attempting to persuade Malcolm to return to Scotland, rally support against Macbeth, and claim the crown. This is a long and rather dry scene, empty of action, but it serves several purposes, the first of which is to confirm the state of Scotland under the tyrant. Macduff reports that at home "each new morn / New widows howl, new orphans cry, new sorrows / Strike heaven in the face." Malcolm is cautious, however, and voices his concern that Macduff may have been sent to lure him back to Scotland and his death. It is suspicious, he notes, that Macduff came without taking leave of his family and seems to have no concern for their safety. Malcolm declares himself unfit to be a king, insisting that he is so steeped in voluptuousness and avarice that he would be worse than Macbeth. Macduff is shocked, and in despair he turns to leave. Malcolm, apparently no longer doubtful of Macduff's intentions, confesses that this description of his own sinful nature was but a test of the thane's loyalty, and that he is guilty of none of the "taints and blames" he has laid on himself. He readily agrees to the campaign, plans for which are apparently already well advanced with the support of King Edward, who has committed "old Siward" and ten thousand English soldiers to the cause.

Although the saintly Edward does not appear in the play, Shakespeare continues to set up the qualities of this good king as a foil to those of the tyrant Macbeth. Malcolm reports that Edward is preparing to administer "the king's evil," the power to cure illness by touch, a gift that monarchs of the time were said to possess. Certain days were set aside for suffering subjects to approach the king and receive the therapeutic laying on of hands.* The contrast between the two monarchs is striking: Macbeth spreads sickness among his subjects while Edward cures the ills of his people.

Ross arrives to inform Macduff of the murder of his wife and children, prompting more references to the virtues of manhood. Malcolm's remark to Macduff that he should "dispute it like a man" may seem unsympathetic, even callous, but his cause has need of such men, and he

---

*The custom prevailed until as late as the eighteenth century, when Samuel Johnson's mother carried her sickly child to London to be touched by Queen Anne.

tries to dissuade his grief-stricken friend from acting rashly on his own. Macduff responds with a prayer, appealing to the "gentle heavens" to bring him "front to front" with Macbeth in single combat, setting the stage for their final, cruel encounter.

5.1   The last act opens upon Lady Macbeth's famous sleepwalking scene. She appears in her nightdress, carrying the candle that she has always by her bed to hold the terrors of darkness at bay. Her unconscious monologue is a chronicle of the crimes that trouble her rest. She rubs her hands to cleanse them of stain—"Out, damned spot! out, I say!"—bringing to mind her confident "a little water clears us of this deed" on the night of Duncan's murder. Imagining that night, she chides her irresolute husband—"Fie my lord, fie! a soldier, and afeard?"—and afterward she is surprised at all the blood. Her still-sleeping mind jumps about, collapsing different events into a single thought. In the cadence of a nursery-rhyme jingle, "the Thane of Fife had a wife," she dismisses the slaughter of Macduff's family. In the same breath she anguishes over her bloody hands and reproaches her husband for his reaction to Banquo's ghost—"You mar all with this starting"—all the while rubbing, rubbing, rubbing to remove the spots she imagines there. Finally, in her fancy she takes his hand, counseling, "what's done, cannot be undone," an echo of her earlier "what's done, is done," and leads him off to bed and sleep.

This scene is the culmination of the recurring image of sleep, with its implied allusion to death, that has run through the lines of the play. This Lady Macbeth is a far cry from the resolute wife who first feared that "the milk of human kindness" would keep her husband from the throne, or even the queen who voiced her discontent on the evening of the banquet; but her lines revive that image in our minds and remind us of her former strength. What has reduced her to this pathetic sleepwalker, rambling on distractedly about their crimes? The answer may lie in her earlier prayer, asking dark powers to "unsex me here," that is, to make her something she was not. In her terrible prayers and curses, she abandoned the protection that society and nature were said at the time to provide a woman, wife, and mother, leaving her adrift in a world where "blood will have blood." She had asked that nothing in her woman's nature be allowed to "shake [her] fell purpose," and the dark spirits she prayed to granted her wish. Now nature takes its toll.

Here, finally, we are witness to the nightmares, only alluded to earlier, that have plagued the rest of husband and wife. Lady Macbeth remains loyal to her husband until the end. What disturbs her most is the corrosive effect of his crimes upon him. The burden of guilt distracts a spirit severed from its natural strengths, contaminating her sleep and reducing her to despair. As in her dream she leads her husband off to bed, the imagery of sleep and death merge into a single meaning. For this is the last we see of her.

5.2   In the scenes to come we observe the effect of all these crimes on Macbeth himself. There is no more talk of nightmares for him, for all his worst fears will be played out in broad daylight. As the English forces advance, his thanes desert him, and one of them conjectures that he is either mad or possessed of a "valiant fury." Shakespeare has the task now of resurrecting the earlier image of the "noble Macbeth" so that his fall will strike us as tragic, and he does so in subtle changes in the language describing him. In the phrase "valiant fury" he reminds us of Macbeth's bravery in battle, as reported in the opening scene.

5.3   Macbeth has been absent from the stage for some time, and we now see him responding defiantly to the news of the defection of his thanes: "The mind I sway by and the heart I bear / Shall never sag with doubt nor shake with fear." The image of heroic defiance is immediately undercut, however, by his abusive treatment of his lowly servant—"The devil damn thee black, thou cream-faced loon!"—and we observe the further deterioration of the tyrannical mind. Before this scene his demeanor toward his subjects had always been outwardly courteous, whatever he thought of them, but now all pretense of courtly decorum has been discarded and, plagued by distrust of all about him, he is harsh to those who remain in his service. Learning of the approach of the English forces, he lapses into a reverie, a sour lament that at his stage of life he is denied the comforts of age, "honor, love, obedience, troops of friends," and is afflicted rather with "curses, not loud but deep, mouth-honor, breath / Which the poor heart would fain deny and dare not." "The poor heart" indeed! Could we possibly pity such a figure? He utters not a single note of regret about the actions that have brought him to this pass, and nothing he says could possibly be interpreted as penitence. And yet . . .

He recovers quickly from this self-pity and calls for his armor: "I'll fight, till from my bones my flesh be hacked." Lady Macbeth's doctor en-

ters with more ill tidings—"She is troubled with thick-coming fancies"—and the king demands sharply, "canst thou not minister to a mind
diseased?" He immediately relates her mental state to the ills of his kingdom, challenging the doctor to examine "the water of my land, find her
disease, / And purge it to a sound and pristine health." The irony here is
stunning. Confronted by the plague of an invading army, he is blind to
the fact that he is himself the source of Scotland's illness, that it is he who
has infected his "land." Again arousing himself, he resolves to oppose the
English, but his show of courage is undercut by the witches' warning allusion to Birnum forest and his confidence in their assurances.

5.4–5 The English advance, and it is ordered that each soldier cut a
bough from Birnum Wood to conceal their approach to Dunsinane. At
the castle Macbeth is encouraging his soldiers, but his speech is interrupted by a cry of women off stage. He reflects that at one time such a
sound would have terrified him; but now, having "supped full with horrors," he finds himself drained of feeling. Seton enters with word of the
death of the king's wife, once his "dearest partner of greatness" and "dearest chuck," his closest, indeed his only confidante, loyal to him through
all his troubled reign. But her loss does not reduce him to grief. As he has
only just confessed, he is no longer capable of responding to events on a
human level. News of Lady Macbeth's death prompts some of Shakespeare's most memorable lines, though they are spoken in sour contemplation of the meaninglessness of life, which as Macbeth says, "creeps in
this petty pace from day to day, / To the last syllable of recorded time,"
leading only to a "dusty death." Shakespeare employs one of his favorite
analogies—life has no more meaning than does the play before us. It is
but a shadow of reality, and we are "poor players" with but an hour of
eternal time to "strut and fret" our brief part and then disappear from the
stage of life, to be "heard no more." Life, like the play we are watching,
"is a tale / Told by an idiot, full of sound and fury, / Signifying nothing."
Whether these are words spoken in stark despair or stolid resignation,
they reflect a spirit void of emotion. The accumulated horror of Macbeth's crimes has left him unable to feel terror, love, or sorrow.

Any pity we might have for one so reduced is quickly dispelled by yet
another angry outburst of contempt for his subjects. A fearful messenger
enters with the news that Birnum Wood has indeed come to Dunsinane.
Macbeth recoils at the report and begins to sense that he has been tricked:

"I pall in resolution, and begin / To doubt th'equivocation of the fiend / That lies like truth." He recovers quickly, however, and, shouting his defiance at those forces, natural or supernatural, that seek his ruin, prepares for battle: "Blow wind! come, wrack! / At least we'll die with harness on our back."

5.6–7 The English forces advance, discard their camouflage, and assault the castle. Macbeth enters the battle, still confident that he need fear "none of woman born," and is challenged by Siward's son, whom he, the more seasoned warrior, slays. He moves off stage and Macduff enters, seeking him out to avenge the murder of his family. The scene ends with Scotland's thanes fighting "on both sides," an ironic renewal of the conflict with which the play opens.

5.8–9 Macbeth reappears, his castle by now occupied and his forces scattered; but he rejects suicide, the resort of "the Roman fool." Confronted finally by Macduff, he attempts to avoid battle. As he confesses, his "soul is too much charged" already with the blood of the thane's family. Here we detect a touch of remorse in Macbeth, which humanizes him briefly in our eyes. Pressed by Macduff, however, they engage and fight to a draw. As they catch their breath, Macbeth explains his reluctance, whereupon Macduff reveals that he is indeed not "of woman born" but was "from his mother's womb / Untimely ripped." Momentarily fearful, cursing the "juggling fiends" that "palter with us in a double sense," Macbeth refuses to fight further. Confronted with the spectacle of his fate should he surrender, however, he resolves not to yield and issues his final challenge: "Lay on, Macduff, / And damned be him that first cries 'Hold, enough.'" The tyrant is slain and his head brandished by Macduff on the end of a pole, as Malcolm begins the task of healing the wounds of his ravished kingdom.

In contemplating our response to the play, we must wonder whether Shakespeare has restored the heroic image of Macbeth sufficiently to move us to sense that his death is somehow "tragic." The message is mixed. In one sense, Macbeth may be seen as a victim incited by powerful forces that propel him to his fate—the pull of his own "vaulting ambition," the thrust of his relentless wife, and the trickery of the witches, who "lie like truth." As he faces his fated end, he seems to hurl that final challenge at them all, rather than at Macduff alone. For reasons unknown, the powers of darkness single him out for destruction. Playing upon his weakness, they deceive him with prophecies that promise him glory and apparitions that persuade him he is invulnerable to the fate of other mortals. So in the end he defies them all, throwing his warrior heart against those who have plagued his sleep and reduced him to a human shell devoid of feeling, a man who has supped so "full with horrors" that he cannot even mourn the death of his wife. The frequent references to manhood throughout the play perhaps foreshadow this moment when Macbeth once more assumes the stature of the noble thane, a mere man again, stripped of what he thought was supernatural protection, and defies the human weaknesses and otherworldly powers that brought him to this end.

On the other hand, his death seems righteous retribution for his crimes; and the spectacle of his bleeding head, held high so that all Scotland can see, confirms that he richly deserves such an end. Those crimes are justly on that severed head. No "supernatural soliciting" compelled him to kill his king and his comrade-in-arms, slaughter the family of Macduff, and drench his land in blood. Having once embarked upon the path to his own destruction, he is soon "in blood / Stepped in so far" that he cannot turn back. Having murdered to secure the crown, he must embark on a murderous career to retain it. The fault is his own, born of a flawed nature. But Shakespeare is careful not to place before us a figure sunk in decadence, a self-indulgent voluptuary, drunken and carousing, intent only upon sensual gratification. In all qualities other than his ambition, he is a sober and outwardly upright man, entirely devoted to his wife, and until the end courteous to his subjects. In brief, he might be any of us, flawed only in that one respect.

But this is not a morality play with the line between good and evil so clearly drawn that we are edified by the defeat of the wicked. The downfall of Macbeth, though richly deserved and brought on by a fault in his own nature, can be felt as tragic in that he is incited by forces beyond his control, reminding us of Gloucester's words from *King Lear:* "As flies to wanton boys are we to th'gods; / They kill us for their sport." We abhor the tyrant and welcome his death; but we know full well that the seeds of such ambition, when nourished by insidious agents, be they natural or supernatural, can blossom in any human spirit to match the scale of Macbeth's monster inhumanity.

OTHELLO

MOST OF Shakespeare's tragedies chronicle the lives and deaths of royalty, the kings, queens, and princes who, for good or ill, preside over the affairs of their kingdoms. *Othello,* on the other hand, is a domestic tragedy, the tale of a husband's jealous rage at the suspected infidelity of his wife. It is a common enough experience, to be sure, but Shakespeare explores it in uncommon depth, touching on *themes* often associated with it: the tension between passion and reason, the deceptive difference between appearance and reality, the nature of evil, and the several shadings of truth.

Othello himself is certainly a distinguished figure, in keeping with Aristotle's definition of a tragic hero.* He is the highly respected commander of the armed forces of Venice, a city then at the height of its power, with possessions reaching into the eastern Mediterranean as far as the island of Cyprus, where it comes into conflict with the Turkish Empire. Othello is a Moor with origins presumably in North Africa, a soldier who has gained his martial reputation in a lifetime of fighting, and he is highly valued by the Venetian senate.

The play opens on Iago, who is Othello's trusted subordinate but in fact hates the Moor. Othello has secretly married Desdemona against the wishes of her father, a senator of the city, and Iago attempts to ignite animosity between the two men. His plot fails as Othello is directed to lead an expedition against the Turks, who threaten the Venetian colony in Cyprus. As the Turkish fleet founders in a storm, Othello lands on the island, to be greeted by Desdemona, Cassio, his faithful lieutenant, and

*See "Tragedy," pp. 7–8.

Iago. Moved by his hatred, Iago plagues Othello with subtle insinuations and finally an open accusation that Desdemona is having an affair with Cassio. Othello, finally convinced of his wife's infidelity, murders her in a jealous rage. Confronted with evidence of her innocence and Iago's duplicity, he kills himself—and we are left with the final mystery: What could have possessed Iago to pursue the death of this virtuous couple?

1.1   We are offered one explanation for Iago's animosity in the early moments of the play. As the first scene opens, he is in conversation with a character named Roderigo, to whom he complains that he has been passed over for promotion to the rank of Othello's lieutenant. The position has been awarded instead to Michael Cassio, a mere "arithmetician [administrator, staff officer]," he claims, with no experience in battle. Iago in consequence has been left in a lesser post as "his Moorship's ancient." * Roderigo asks why then he remains in Othello's service, and Iago, in a long, candid speech, reveals the duplicity of his nature. "I follow him to serve my turn upon him," he explains, remaining the Moor's faithful ancient and acting as do those who feign "shows of service" but serve only themselves. From the very outset of the play, then, we know Iago as a man who hates Othello but will hide his antipathy behind a mask of loyalty and duty. As he openly admits, "I am not what I am."

Iago suddenly proposes that they "call up her father," leaving the audience perhaps puzzled about which daughter he means. Shakespeare frequently opens a scene in the midst of a conversation between two characters, as he does here; and it is evident that the two were discussing the elopement of Othello and Desdemona as they entered, the "this" of Roderigo's opening speech. Iago refers back to the matter with an abruptness that reflects his skill at improvising schemes on the spur of the moment. It is late at night as they stand under Brabantio's balcony and awaken him with the alarming news that his daughter (Desdemona) has been seduced. Iago has a richly erotic vocabulary, here inciting Brabantio with word that "an old black ram / Is tupping your white ewe" and "your daughter and the Moor are making the beast with two backs." Roderigo

---

*"Ancient," or "ensign-bearer," was a military rank in medieval armies, comparable in modern times to a position somewhere between commissioned and noncommissioned officers. Pistol, in *Henry V,* is an "ancient."

identifies himself, and we learn that he has been an unwelcome suitor for the daughter's hand. Iago conceals his identity, however, by remaining in the shadows. He leaves it to his companion to convince Brabantio that she is in "the gross clasps of a lascivious Moor." Iago, his purpose served, leaves to join Othello, toward whom, he says, he "must show out a flag and sign of love." Brabantio, by now alarmed at his daughter's absence, emerges from his house, and learning that she has married the Moor, calls up armed guards to search for the couple.

This opening scene introduces two critical elements of the play. The first is Iago's hatred of Othello, which would seem to exceed the resentment of a soldier passed over for promotion. Although he later reveals additional reasons for his anger, not even the sum of his grievances could be said to explain the depth of his loathing. Shakespeare does not explore the motivation for such hatred here. Some people hate others, he seems content to say, and often for incomprehensible reasons, so he simply sets before us such an instance. The other element is Othello's race, often referred to in the scene. Roderigo slurs him as "the thick-lips," and to Iago, as mentioned, he is "an old black ram." Later, Brabantio, confronting Othello, will show his contempt for "the sooty bosom / Of such a thing as thou art," so there is no doubt that race is a factor in his alarm over the marriage.

1.2   The next scene finds Iago with Othello, whom he attempts to anger with an account of the "scurvy and provoking terms" Brabantio used in referring to his commander—a total fabrication, for the only one who said anything "provoking" was Iago himself. His purpose is clear, however: having stirred up one side, he now seeks to incite the other. Iago's slander fails to move Othello, who is calmly confident that his services to Venice "shall out-tongue" Brabantio's complaints. Cassio enters with a summons from the duke to consult with him about "something from Cyprus," and the three men set out for the palace, only to be intercepted by the angry father and his guards. In an effort to precipitate a fight, Iago draws his sword and challenges Roderigo, but he is thwarted by Othello himself. The general commands, "keep up your bright swords, for the dew will rust them"—that is, if left out of their scabbards—and he addresses Brabantio with measured courtesy: "Good signior, you shall command more with years / Than with your weapons."

This is our first impression of Othello. He has a commanding presence, that of a man who by his bearing and voice demands obedience, so that when he orders the opposing sides to "keep up" their swords, they instinctively comply. Bloodshed is prevented, but Brabantio attacks verbally, accusing Othello of seducing his daughter "with foul charms . . . drugs and minerals." He cannot conceive of any other explanation for her submission. There is a subtle implication of racism here in Brabantio's assumption that someone of Othello's background would be skilled in the black arts. But the Moor either misses or ignores the slight and reveals that he has been summoned by the duke and his council. Brabantio agrees to accompany him, eager to lay his case before that body, the highest court in Venice.

1.3   In the council chamber the duke receives reports that a powerful Turkish fleet is bearing down on Cyprus, and he is relieved to see the "valiant Othello" appear in answer to his summons. Before they can address the crisis, however, Brabantio charges Othello with corrupting his daughter with "spells and medicines bought of mountebanks." He claims that only through "witchcraft" could a properly modest young woman, "in spite of nature / Of years, of country, credit [reputation], everything," have fallen "in love with what she feared to look on!" Othello requests that Desdemona herself be questioned and that he be given an opportunity to defend himself against the charge with an account of their courtship.

The duke agrees, and Othello begins by describing how Brabantio had often invited him to his home, encouraging him to recount his life, his battles, his suffering, and the strange sights he had seen in his wanderings. Desdemona, he says, listened when her household duties permitted and later asked him to repeat his tale for her alone. On hearing of his trials, she wept, he goes on, and asked that if he knew of someone who loved her, he should "teach him how to tell my story, / And that would woo her." This, he claims, is how she was won, not with witchcraft: "She loved me for the dangers I had passed, / And I loved her that she did pity them."

Desdemona enters, and Brabantio attempts to assert his authority. He reminds her obliquely that in marrying Othello she has violated the prevailing social code that bestows upon the father the right to *arrange for the marriage* of his daughter, and that she is obliged to defer to him in the matter, wherever her heart may lie. She courteously but firmly defies the custom, replying that although she owes her father respect, being now married she must show "so much duty" to "the Moor my lord." Confronted by her resolution, Brabantio submits ungraciously, addressing Othello: "I here do give thee that with all my heart, / Which but thou hast already, with all my heart / I would keep from you." The duke attempts to heal the breach between father and daughter, but to no avail; and the council now turns to the Turkish threat.

Othello agrees to lead an expedition against the Turks and requests that his wife be properly accommodated during his absence. The duke suggests that she stay with her father, but all three refuse the proposal; and Desdemona rather boldly asks that she be permitted to accompany her husband. Othello seconds her, and the duke agrees. But the general must leave immediately, and it is decided that Iago will remain behind. He will follow later with the duke's official orders and so be available to escort Desdemona to Cyprus. Othello has complete confidence in a man of such "honesty and trust," only the first of many references to Iago as "honest." As Othello leaves, a disillusioned Brabantio condemns his daughter, "look to her, Moor, if thou hast eyes to see: / She has deceived her father, and may thee," to which Othello loyally responds, "my life upon her faith." All depart, leaving Iago and Roderigo on stage alone.

What do we make of this union of two such different people? Brabantio cannot comprehend why his daughter married "in spite of nature / Of years, of country, credit, everything." He is bewildered that one of her "nature," a carefully brought up Venetian maid, modest in demeanor and respectful of her elders, protected and schooled in social graces and the traditional duties of a wife, could have run off with someone so unsuitable—a soldier, moreover, whose rough life in the field has left him awkward in the sophisticated society of an urban court. There is also the question of "years," for it is apparent that Othello is much older than Desdemona. Iago is to make much of this disparity.

The difference in race is mentioned only obliquely—Brabantio remarks that Othello is from another "country"—but the contrast is visible to all and lies just below the surface of the exchange. The Venetians are cosmopolitan merchants, accustomed to commerce with a great diversity of people, and may indeed be more tolerant than most, but they are not free of prejudice. In an effort to soften Brabantio's intransigence, the duke remarks that he may in time come to value Othello's virtues and find that his "son-in-law is far more fair than black." It is a gracious gesture, but his meaning is clear—"fair" is preferable to "black."

Desdemona, Brabantio further complains, will lose her "credit," or reputation; and one can well imagine the salons of Venice buzzing with gossip about the unconventional marriage and behind-the-hand speculation about how long it will last. And the audience may wonder as well. We admire the "noble Moor" for his dignified, straightforward manner and his calm in the face of provocation, and we feel the profound respect in which he is held by the Venetian duke and senators. In Desdemona's brief appearance, we admire as well her directness and commonsense sincerity, her loyalty to her husband, and her willingness to put behind her a familiar, comfortable existence to share the inconveniences and dangers of his life. We have heard much of their love but have been able to witness none of it in the stiff formality of the duke's court. Perhaps it will see them through.

Iago thinks not. He is left alone on stage with Roderigo, and their relationship becomes clearer in the exchange that closes the act. The young man has fancied himself a suitor for Desdemona's hand, and in the face of her father's intransigence has employed Iago to deliver costly gifts to her on his behalf—or so he supposes. The marriage is a setback to his suit, of course; but Iago, who has been benefiting from the income gained by selling Roderigo's gifts, and is anxious to keep the poor fish on the hook, contends that the union of "an erring barbarian and a supersubtle Venetian" cannot last. For Iago, human behavior is a simple matter of a contest between passion and reason, and love is no more than "a lust of the blood and a permission of the will." He insists that Desdemona cannot "long continue her love for the Moor," who is so much older. She will eventually "change for youth." As for Othello, "these Moors are changeable in their wills," and he will soon find the marriage "bitter" to him. Iago's advice to Roderigo, as he never tires of saying, is to "put money in thy purse" and follow them to Cyprus, where he will surely "enjoy her." Since they both now hate the Moor, he concludes, they can conspire to avenge themselves upon him. Roderigo, excited at the prospect, dashes off, shouting inanely, "I'll sell all my land."

The scene closes on Iago's soliloquy, which begins with his contemptuous dismissal of Roderigo—"thus do I ever make my fool my purse." He reaffirms his hatred of the Moor, giving yet another motive for revenge—he imagines that Othello has been sleeping with his wife! He plots to secure Cassio's place and to discomfort the Moor by insinuating that the lieutenant is "too familiar with" Desdemona. Othello, he says, "is of a free and open nature / That thinks men honest that but seem so," and he means to exploit that quality, which he considers a weakness. It is a plan devised, it would appear, on the spur of the moment. He has no idea what this "monstrous birth" will develop into as it matures, nor does he much care as long as it serves his purpose.

2.1 The setting for Act Two, and for the balance of the play, is the island of Cyprus. We encounter first the Venetian governor, Montano, whom Othello will replace as military governor when he arrives, as appropriate for a frontier colony in a war zone. The talk is all of the storm, which has scattered the Turkish fleet but raised anxiety about the fate of Othello's vessels, still at sea. The first ship to reach port safely bears Cassio, who responds to Montano's query about the marriage with high praise for "the divine Desdemona." She arrives in the second ship, accompanied by Iago, his wife Emilia, who is her maid, and the hapless Roderigo. Cassio comes forward to greet the party. He is young and handsome, with all the graces and courtesies of an accomplished courtier, which may explain why he was chosen as lieutenant over the more experienced but more common ancient—perhaps another source of Iago's grievance. He welcomes Desdemona with gallant praise and greets Emilia with a courteous kiss, which leads to an extended exchange that shows Iago in a new light. The ancient entertains Desdemona with witty jests, songs, and riddles, much as would a court jester, beguiling the time as they await news of Othello's ship. The entertainment over, Cassio, indulging in a courtly ritual of the time, takes her by the hand and kisses his fingers. The gesture incites a vicious *aside* from Iago, who promises that "with as little a web as this I will ensnare as great a fly as Cassio."

Othello arrives safely and greets Desdemona, "O my fair warrior!"—a high compliment from the soldier he is. Shakespeare's poetry soars in this brief scene as he captures Othello's passion for his wife: "O my soul's joy! / If ever after tempest came such calms, / May the winds blow till they have wakened death!" It is the consummate moment of his life—"If it were now to die, / 'Twere now to be most happy"—and he is so moved that words fail him—"I cannot speak enough of this content"—and so they kiss. This brief exchange is critical to our response to the play, for it is the only scene in which the two visibly demonstrate their love for each other. Modern cinematography is able to present them in a passionate clinch to the accompaniment of soaring strings, or intrude with quick flashes of them in the act of love; but Shakespeare had no such license and was further constrained by the requirement to cast boys in female roles. It is the poetry alone that conveys the intensity of their love.

This short interval is enough, it would appear, to incite Iago, who responds to the joyous reunion with another malevolent aside: "O you are well tuned now! But I'll set down the pegs that make this music, as honest as I am." Iago has a satanic air about him from the outset, and we may detect in his speech the smoldering anger of one infuriated by the display of love and beauty. In the Christian tradition the devil was said to detest such a sight; by his very nature he was a tortured being compelled to seek the destruction of anything that reminded him of the bliss he had lost in rebelling against God.

All depart, leaving the stage again to Roderigo and Iago, who is especially loquacious here, perhaps agitated by the display of mutual affection. He argues at length that Desdemona is in love with Cassio, and that he desires her in return. Improvising still, he notes that Cassio will command the guard that night, and he instructs Roderigo to pick a quarrel with him. The poor dupe is a willing tool, and on his departure Iago, in another soliloquy, refines his scheme. He will incite Othello into a jealous rage against Cassio, quite justifiably, he adds, since he suspects the lieutenant of sleeping with his wife as well—Iago thinks that Emilia has bedded the entire army! He is not yet sure how to work his revenge— " 'tis here, but yet confused"—but he is confident that the opportunity will present itself.

2.2–3 Othello declares a festival to mark the destruction of the Turkish fleet, as well as "the celebration of his nuptial." We are suddenly aware that he and Desdemona have yet to consummate their marriage, an obligation he means no longer to neglect: "Come, my dear love, / The purchase made, the fruits are to ensue; / The profit's yet to come 'tween me and you." His long service to Venice has him speaking like a merchant.

As the couple leave, Iago, pursuing his scheme, attempts to inflame Cassio with erotic allusions to Desdemona. She is "sport for Jove" and "full of game," her eye "a parley to provocation," her speech "an alarurn to love." The proper Cassio responds only with chivalric platitudes, however—she is "an exquisite lady," "a most fresh and delicate creature," and "indeed perfection." Failing in this device, Iago succeeds in getting Cassio drunk and prods Roderigo to provoke him. The resulting melee ends with Cassio battering Roderigo and wounding the old governor, Montano. Othello enters and Iago suddenly turns peacemaker—"The general speaks to you; hold, hold, for shame!"

Othello is enraged and calls a halt to "this barbarous brawl," threatening that anyone who "stirs next to carve for his own rage / Holds his soul light; he dies upon his motion." All stand back, awed by Othello's commanding presence, as he demands to know the cause of the disturbance. But those involved are all reluctant to speak, only angering him more:

> My blood begins my safer guides to rule,
> And passion, having my best judgment collied,
> Assays to lead the way. If I once stir,
> Or do but lift this arm, the best of you
> Shall sink in my rebuke.

He commands Iago to explain the brawl, and the ancient, first proclaiming his devotion to Cassio, gives a vivid eyewitness account of the altercation—omitting, of course, his own role. It is an accurate description as far as it goes; and since Roderigo has limped away, no one present can find fault with it. Othello, accepting the account, dismisses Cassio—"never more be officer of mine"—and appoints Iago commander of the watch.

This is our first exposure to Othello in anger, and it is a sobering sight. There are fires beneath that calm, commanding exterior. He warns here that his "blood begins his safer guides to rule" and passion "assays to lead the way," a spectacle that no one present could wish to see. The scene also highlights Shakespeare's skillful use of *place*. In Venice, Iago's attempt to provoke an armed confrontation failed because of Othello's composed command to "keep up your bright swords." In Cyprus, however, he succeeds not only in causing a brawl but in arousing the Moor's passionate nature. The contrast is striking. Venice is a civil city under the rule of law, a place where passions are held in check and grievances are resolved in a court whose decisions are respected. Cyprus, on the other hand, is a

frontier where emotions run close to the surface and Iago's insidious influence can prevail unrestrained. American viewers may well compare the
atmosphere on the island to the myth of their own early West, where
Judge Roy Bean was "the only law west of the Pecos" and the hangman's
noose and six-gun were the instruments of raw justice.

Iago is in his element. Left alone with Cassio, he feigns sympathy for
the disgraced lieutenant. Cassio laments the loss of his reputation, "the
immortal part" of him, but Iago scoffs at his distress, declaring that "reputation is an idle and most false imposition; oft got without merit and
lost without deserving." He advises his friend to ask Desdemona to plead
with Othello on his behalf: "Confess yourself freely to her; importune her
help to put you in your place again." Cassio gratefully accepts the counsel
of "honest Iago" and leaves.

Left alone on stage, Iago soliloquizes ironically—"What's he then
that says I play the villain" in giving such useful advice. Does not Othello
so love Desdemona, he asks archly, that "she may make, unmake, do what
she list"; and what better way for Cassio to restore himself to favor? "How
am I then a villain?" he protests mockingly, and proceeds to answer his
own question. While Cassio presents his case to Desdemona, Iago will
persuade Othello that his lieutenant does so out of lust for her, so that "by
how much she strives to do him good, / She shall undo her credit with
the Moor." His motives have taken a subtle turn—they now include a design to "undo" Desdemona.

Roderigo reenters, his head perhaps swathed in bandages, complaining that he has run out of money and all he has to show for the expense is
a beating. He intends to return to Venice, he says, but Iago, glib as ever,
persuades him to remain, and then dismisses him. Warming to his
scheme now, he refines it—he will maneuver Othello so that he comes
upon Cassio soliciting Desdemona, a sight ripe with possibilities for mis-
interpretation.

3.1 The third act opens with a brief comic interlude, a device
Shakespeare often uses to relieve momentarily the tension building in the
audience; but the play quickly returns to its grim business. Iago advises
Cassio once again to seek out Desdemona and promises to occupy Othello
elsewhere while they talk. As we know, he plans to do quite the opposite,
and the *dramatic irony* cuts deep here as a grateful Cassio declares that he

"never knew / A Florentine more kind and honest." He asks Emilia to arrange an interview, and she agrees to help.

3.2–3 We catch a glimpse of Othello and Iago engaged in military duties and quickly move on to Cassio in conversation with Desdemona. The success of any performance of the play depends upon the effectiveness of this extended central scene, almost five hundred lines long. At its opening, Othello is a loving husband, doting on his new wife. At its close, convinced of an adulterous affair between Cassio and Desdemona, he condemns them both to death. Can a man's affections take such an abrupt turn in such a short space of time? Or, we may ask, does Shakespeare persuade us that Othello is capable of such an emotional upheaval? A great deal depends upon our perception of the marriage. How much have we been swayed by Iago's words, or by Brabantio's? As we have seen, the couple are from sharply contrasting backgrounds—he a soldier whose character has been shaped by the rough usages of war, she a modest maiden raised in the protective cocoon of Venetian society. He is advanced in years and experienced in the world; she is young and vulnerable in her innocence.

And then there is the question of racial difference. Shakespeare, significantly, does not pander to the perception. "The Moor," for example, is not a racial epithet. Only Iago and Roderigo abuse Othello with the term, but Desdemona, Cassio, Emilia, and the Venetian senators employ it with various degrees of respect, admiration, and affection. Yet an audience watching the play is ever conscious of Othello's color. Desdemona is often played by a slim, blond actress who contrasts sharply with his bulk and complexion. But the point is not so much that he is black and she is white, as that he is darker-skinned. Shakespeare plays upon the stereotypical perception that swarthy-complexioned people are more passionate than those lighter in color, more likely to let their emotions rule. Even today we find the "Latin lover" an attractive figure, to be preferred over those perceived as the thin-lipped, pale-skinned, repressed suitors of more northern climes. The stereotype survives in the summertime obsession for sunning at the shore, acquiring a "savage" tan intended to render the sunbather somehow more attractive to the opposite sex. Stereotypes are offensive, of course, but a playwright makes use of everything at his disposal, and Shakespeare's audience would have expected the passions of a Moor to be closer to the surface than those of his northern neighbors.

It has been suggested that Othello's trust in Iago displays the innocent gullibility of a "free and open nature," a man out of his depth in a society whose sophisticated members conceal their intent behind masks of custom and propriety. In fact, however, Iago deceives everyone, including the foppish Roderigo, to whom he candidly admits his duplicitous nature—"I am not what I am." He is an unknown quantity even to his wife Emilia, who, as the scene opens, voices her confidence that Cassio's disgrace "grieves my husband / As if the case were his."

Cassio pleads his cause to Desdemona, who promises to intercede with her husband on his behalf. Othello and Iago enter at a door some distance from the couple; Cassio, who sees them but is too embarrassed to remain, quickly leaves. Iago begins his campaign of innuendo. "Ha!" he remarks, as if to himself, "I like not that." They speak here out of earshot of the others, and Othello asks if it was Cassio he has just seen talking to his wife. Assuming a troubled air, Iago replies that he thinks it unlikely, since he can't imagine why the lieutenant "would steal away so guilty-like, / Seeing you coming." The insinuation is checked by the simple honesty of Desdemona, who readily acknowledges that it was indeed Cassio she was talking to. She goes on to praise him, even reminding her husband that he had been his frequent companion during their courtship. Othello is initially evasive but finally agrees to see Cassio. "I will deny thee nothing," he promises fondly, and she, content with his decision, takes her leave. As he watches her go, Othello murmurs to himself, "excellent wretch! Perdition catch my soul / But I do love thee; and when I love thee not / Chaos is come again."

Chaos, in Renaissance belief, was the source of all matter, the substance out of which God created the universe. It was a realm where the elements were said to exist in a state of constant conflict with one another, a condition of "Eternal Anarchy" in John Milton's phrase from *Paradise Lost,* until God shaped them into the sun, the stars, Earth, and humankind itself. Othello means, then, that should there come a time when his love fades, the consequence would be not just emotional turmoil or social disorder, but for him the equivalent of cosmic dissolution. His short speech is a striking evocation of the strength of his passion for Desdemona, and a foreshadowing of the depth of his despair upon losing her. But, more to the point, why should he even contemplate a time when he would not love his wife? Are we to assume that he is insecure in the marriage from the outset, thus offering fertile ground for Iago's seeds of doubt? The challenge for any actor in this scene is to portray Othello's subtle transition from love to jealousy. We await anxiously the moment when he submits to the suspicions that Iago weaves, the point at which his growing anguish turns to rage. When does it occur?

Not yet, of course, but Iago, seizing on Desdemona's chance remark, asks Othello a seemingly innocuous question: "Did Michael Cassio, / When you wooed my lady, know of your love?" Othello replies that he did, and asks what Iago means by the question. Iago is evasive, playing with simple words like "indeed" and "think," spoken with knowing inflections, as if hiding a thought he is reluctant to voice. In this way he makes Othello pry the accusation from him. Iago raises the question of Cassio's integrity by saying he thinks him "honest"—and then casts the thought in doubt with the remark that "men should be what they seem," an ironic inversion of his earlier admission that "I am not what I am." Othello, by now troubled, continues to press Iago to voice his suspicions; but he resists, confessing that he may be making too much out of "his scattering and unsure observance," hence is reluctant to upset the husband by revealing his thoughts. An increasingly agitated Othello insists, but Iago refuses to make a clear accusation. Instead, assuming the stance of friend and counselor, he cautions Othello against excesses, and in doing so he indirectly raises two issues designed to disturb Othello even more.

The first of these is reputation, Othello's "good name," which Iago declares to be a man's most precious possession. His advice here contrasts sharply with what he had earlier voiced to Cassio on the subject, when he asserted quite the opposite, calling reputation "an idle and most false imposition." His duplicity is blatant here as he adapts his philosophy to fit the occasion. His words strike home with Othello, however, as he plays on the perception of a cuckolded husband as a figure of ridicule whose wife wanders, it was said, because of his own lack of "manhood." The second subject Iago raises is jealousy itself, which he introduces again by indirection, warning against it, describing the pain experienced by a cuckold "who dotes, yet doubts, suspects, yet fondly loves." Othello's response, "O misery," can be uttered in different ways, either as an indication that his affections are beginning to sour, or simply as a dispassionate expression of pity for any man so abused.

It may be that his response owes something to both sentiments, as Iago's slow poison begins to work. Othello now contemplates how he would react to evidence of an unfaithful wife, and it is obvious that he has been affected by the ancient's warnings about reputation and jealousy. The Moor is a soldier, accustomed to the clear distinction between friend and foe on the field of battle; and he is not one to harbor uncertainties for long. For him, "to be once in doubt / Is once resolved." He would demand proof, he says, and on seeing it, "away at once with love or jealousy." The soldier in Othello declares that there is no room in his heart for two such contrary emotions. Iago feels a tug on the line and, sensing that he may have hooked the catch, cautions that he speaks "not yet of proof," advising only that Othello keep an eye on his wife—"Observe her well with Cassio." He knows these Venetian women well, he confides: those who "let heaven see the pranks / They dare not show their husbands." And he reminds Othello of Brabantio's parting remark about his daughter: "She did deceive her father, marrying you; / And when she seemed to shake and fear your looks, / She loved them most."

Iago must take great care with what he says here. One of the dramatic tensions of the scene is the possibility that he may discredit himself too soon with a direct accusation. Should he do so prematurely, he will only incur Othello's wrath. So he backs off momentarily and cautions the now troubled husband that he should not interpret his meaning "to larger reach / Than to suspicion." Iago must maintain a certain level of deniability so that should the truth come out, he can argue that he never accused anyone of anything. If he has misjudged Othello's state of mind at this stage, he can still retreat and retain his general's trust. Or has he gone too far already? If he has not, just where does he cross the line beyond which there is no turning back?

A downcast Othello reasserts his confidence in his wife's fidelity. Iago, in mock agreement, declares, "long live she so!"—and then doubtfully, "long live you to think so!" "And yet," the Moor begins; but Iago jumps in to complete the thought for him. "And yet," he continues, it is strange that in choosing Othello she should reject suitors of her own "clime, complexion, and degree." It would not be surprising if in time she were to "repent" of her choice. Othello, now thoroughly distressed, dismisses Iago and, suspecting that his loyal ancient knows more than he is telling, agonizes, "why did I marry?" Iago, anxious perhaps that he may have gone too far too soon, returns to urge Othello "to scan this thing no further," but at the same time he sets the stage for the next step in his intrigue. He advises Othello to delay restoring Cassio to his post and observe if Desdemona continues to plead his case. "Much will be seen in that," he suggests slyly.

Left alone again, Othello nurtures his suspicions. Iago, he is confident, is "of exceeding honesty" and, moreover, experienced in "human dealings," while he himself is "black," unskilled in society, and "declined / Into the vale of years." "She's gone," he decides suddenly, "I am abused and my relief is but to loathe her." But then Desdemona appears, and the sight of her restores his love—"If she be false, O, then heaven mocks itself! / I'll not believe't." But this is the very state of mind he had earlier vowed he could not abide, one in which he is torn between the conflicting emotions of "love or jealousy." He pleads a headache, and she produces a "napkin [handkerchief]" to soothe his brow. But he dashes out, and she drops it in her urgency to follow him. Emilia picks it up, remarking curiously that her "wayward husband hath a hundred times / Wooed me to steal it." Iago comes upon her and secures the handkerchief, which with sudden inspiration he decides to leave in Cassio's chambers to confirm suspicion against him. "Trifles light as air," he observes, "are to the jealous confirmations strong / As proofs of Holy Writ."

Othello reenters, and Iago notes with satisfaction that the Moor is now thoroughly distracted, so much so, he gloats, that no medicine can restore him "to the sweet sleep / Which thou ow'dst yesterday." Shakespeare employs a clever piece of stagecraft here. Aware of the difficulty an actor might experience in portraying the transition from a man who disclaimed, "I'll not believe't" to the infuriated husband who raves, "Ha! Ha! false to me," the playwright has taken the unresolved Othello off stage and returned him after an interval, a man now thoroughly convinced of his wife's betrayal. Iago seems somewhat taken aback by his success, as the Moor rages, "O, now for ever / Farewell the tranquil mind! farewell content!" and laments the loss of his life's work, "the big wars / that make ambition virtue." Now, he cries out, "Othello's occupation's gone!" a burst of emotion that reveals the depth of his passion for Desdemona and his utter despair at the loss of her love.

He turns fiercely on Iago and, grasping him by the throat, adamantly demands "ocular proof" of his wife's infidelity, threatening, "if thou dost

slander her and torture me, / Never pray more; abandon all remorse."
Iago has clearly crossed the line now, but he meets the challenge of this
new development, replying in mock outrage that "honesty is not safe"
and loving friends no longer valued. His protests seems to appease
Othello, who voices his dilemma: "I think my wife be honest, and think
she is not; / I think thou art just, and think thou art not." Desperate now,
he all but pleads for "proof,"and Iago asks indignantly what sort would
satisfy him. Would he "behold her topped," the mere mention of which
maddens the Moor further: "Death and damnation! O!"

Iago, more daring now, fabricates an account of Cassio uttering endearments to Desdemona in his sleep, and testifies that he has seen him
wipe his beard with her handkerchief. The audience will appreciate the
delicious *dramatic irony* of the scene, since Iago has the "napkin" in his
pocket the entire time. (As a reminder, more audacious actors in the part
have been known to leave a corner of it showing.) Othello, now completely persuaded, utters a terrible oath: "Arise, black vengeance, from
thy hollow shell! / Yield up, O love, thy crown and heated throne / To
tyrannous hate!" Iago, perhaps startled by the intensity of the emotions
he has aroused, counsels patience, but Othello responds with a yet more
awesome outburst: "O blood, blood, blood!" Iago recovers quickly and in
a ludicrous scene kneels with Othello to vow his loyalty, promising to do
away with Cassio. Perhaps intoxicated by his power over the Moor, he
again directs by indirection, advising him to spare Desdemona, the mere
mention of which is enough to incite Othello to seek "some swift means
of death / For the fair devil." The general concludes by appointing Iago
his lieutenant. This was the ancient's only concern at the outset, but
events have carried him well beyond his original intent, an instance of
Shakespeare's persistent theme that evil leads on to greater evil. Iago
must now do away with both Cassio and Desdemona in order to protect
himself from discovery of his deceit.

It may seem that we have been examining this episode in excessive
detail, and I admit to a fascination with its psychological insight and theatrical achievement. Such detail is necessary, I think, because *Othello,*
more than any other of Shakespeare's plays, depends for its success on the
convincing performance of a single scene. It is the ultimate challenge for
an actor, for if he does not persuade us that jealousy can be aroused in
such a man within such a short space of time, all that follows is mere
melodrama—there is nothing tragic about it.

So, does the scene work? Is this the way jealousy arises, in a sudden passion erupting in explosive intensity? And is it irreversible thereafter? The success of the scene also depends on the impressions left by the first two acts. Critical, of course, is our perception of Othello. He is a noble figure, we have seen, a relatively uncomplicated man and a soldier impatient of ambiguities that leave one irresolute. Above all, he has a passionate nature, responding with sudden anger to Cassio's dereliction, where he warns that his "blood begins [his] safer guides to rule." And he loves his wife with a burning intensity.

Othello's confidence in Iago is certainly misplaced, but it is not necessarily naive. As mentioned, the ancient fools everyone! He is, to all appearances, an entirely admirable figure, known to be honest, trustworthy, valiant, kind, bold, and wise, to cite only the terms used to describe him by the various characters at one time or another. Othello has trusted him on the battlefield and so trusts him in personal matters as well, especially since he is native to Venice and professes familiarity with "the country disposition" of the city's women. Shakespeare, it may be said, has meticulously prepared the ground for Othello's swift transformation. But it is not an easy part for an actor to play.

3.4 After the emotional turmoil of this long scene, Shakespeare relieves the tension with another brief comic interlude between Desdemona and the clown; but Othello's entrance soon restores the dark tone of the play. The scene is full of frightening dramatic ironies. The Moor, in an aside, agonizes, "O, hardness to dissemble!" a difficult task for one of his honest, direct nature. He takes his wife's hand, but she dismisses his cryptic remarks and begins to plead for Cassio. Othello distracts her by asking for her handkerchief and, on learning that she does not have it with her, reveals that it has special powers to "subdue" the owner to love. "There's magic in the web of it," he warns, and presses her to produce it. His revelation raises a question about his earlier insistence that he had used no "witchcraft" in wooing Desdemona, and conjures up again the troubling image of an alien Moor skilled in the black arts.

Taken aback by his intensity, Desdemona insists that the handkerchief is not lost. Recovering her composure, she claims playfully that he mentions it only to put her "from her suit" for his lieutenant. Othello with mounting fury demands to see the handkerchief while she persists in her praise of Cassio, unaware that in her husband's mind the two matters are one. The altercation reaches a crescendo as he dashes off stage, shouting "Away!" This prompts Emilia, who has witnessed the scene, to ask, "is not this man jealous?" Emilia is a familiar character, the devoted handmaiden, older, more experienced, and worldly-wise in her ways. She knows jealousy when she sees it, in contrast to her innocent lady.

Iago and Cassio appear, learning of Desdemona's lack of success and Othello's unexplained anger. She attempts to excuse her husband, but Emilia persists in her belief that he is jealous. Desdemona is still doubt-ful, since she knows she has given him no cause, but Emilia replies that guilt or innocence is beside the point to those in that state of mind— "They are not jealous for the cause, / But jealous for they're jealous: 'tis a monster / Begot upon itself, born on itself." Desdemona promises to renew her efforts on Cassio's behalf, and the women depart as Bianca, Cassio's paramour, enters. He produces the handkerchief, which Iago has left in his chambers, and asks her to copy it for him. She sullenly agrees after exacting a promise that he will come to her that night.

In a way Bianca acts as a *foil* to Othello. She is yet another figure eaten by jealousy, though in her case it is with cause. She complains that she has not seen Cassio for "a week," and we are presented with a puz-zling instance of the play's "double-time." Our sense of the action is that we are still in the day following the arrival in Cyprus, with only the night when Othello "makes wanton" with Desdemona intervening. But there are several references to a longer time frame, in the present instance Bianca's complaint about Cassio's absence for so many days. These anom-alies need not distract us. In the swift pace of a performance, they go un-noticed.

Indeed, the pace is essential to Iago's success, for his web of lies would surely come unraveled had anyone the opportunity to pause and examine Othello's sudden change. The scene just past between the husband and wife is characteristic of several to follow. Dramatic tension rises in Oth-ello's encounters with various characters, any one of whom could discover the cause of his distemper with the right question or a chance word that would give him pause. We watch with mounting anxiety as he speaks with Desdemona, Emilia, and the Venetian envoys, waiting for someone to discover what is bothering him. Iago's purpose is to bring matters to a swift conclusion before this can happen.

4.1 Iago relishes his newfound power over Othello. He torments him with explicit erotic allusions to the adulterous lovers "naked in bed" and reminds him that Cassio has the handkerchief. Othello asks if Cassio has said anything, and Iago taunts him with a play on the word, "lie," concluding casually with the provocative "with her, on her, what you will." This is too much for Othello, who is reduced to babbling incoherence and falls senseless to the floor. If this seems excessive, remember that he is afflicted with sexual jealousy, which may be the most powerful and destructive of emotions, as the pages of any daily newspaper will attest, and it is a torment especially devastating to a man of Othello's passionate nature.

This is Iago's supreme moment as he stands over the prostrate Othello and exults in the success of his schemes, gloating maliciously, "work on, / My medicine, work!" Imaginative actors in the part have been known to deliver a contemptuous kick to the fallen body. Cassio comes upon the scene, but Iago sends him away and turns his attention to the reviving Othello. Seizing the opportunity, Iago reveals that Cassio will soon return and advises Othello to conceal himself nearby where he can overhear them. The "valiant Moor" is reduced to a base eavesdropper.

When Cassio returns, Iago steers the conversation around to Bianca, avoiding the use of her name, and the lieutenant boasts, as soldiers will do, about his sexual exploits. Othello misconstrues his words as callous pride in the seduction of Desdemona. When an angry Bianca returns, we anxiously wait for someone to let something slip at last to plant a seed of doubt about Iago in the mind of the lurking Moor. But she only confirms his conviction! Indignantly throwing the handkerchief at Cassio, she rejects his story that he found it in his chamber. She accuses him of accepting it as a gift, "some minx's token," from another woman. Othello is stunned at the sight of the handkerchief. As Bianca stalks off with Cassio in pursuit, he emerges from concealment, muttering, "how shall I murder him?" Iago continues to incite him as Othello reaffirms his intention to kill Desdemona without delay—he will do it "that night." Such is his control over the Moor now that Iago need no longer lead by indirection. He proposes openly that she be murdered in "the bed she hath contaminated," and Othello finds that "the justice of it pleases."

Lodovico, an official, arrives from Venice with instructions from the senate. Perhaps now, we dare hope, an outsider will be able to see what those too close to the turbulent events have been blind to. Alas, no. He is as distraught and mystified at his general's behavior as any on Cyprus, especially when Othello strikes his wife and, raging incoherently, storms off. Lodovico's speech reminds us of how far Othello has fallen. "Is this," he asks, "the noble Moor whom our full senate / Call all in all sufficient," a man "whom passion could not shake," whose virtue was unassailable? Iago replies that "he is much changed" and guilefully suggests that Lodovico watch and see for himself.

4.2 The next scene opens on a conversation between Othello and Emilia, another occasion when the misunderstandings might be cleared up, since she at least suspects the source of his anger. She assures him of Desdemona's fidelity, and he orders that she be brought to him. Now at last, if he will only accuse her directly, or even mention the handkerchief, she can defend herself. But Othello is too incensed, more intent upon abusing her and venting his own anguish than getting to the bottom of the affair. He will not say with whom he suspects she has been "false," and, ultimately reduced to tears, he can only lament his loss. He could endure anything, he says—sickness, poverty, captivity, scorn—but not betrayal "where I have garnered up my heart" in love for her. She pleads with him to reveal what "ignorant sin" she has committed, but he only raves on, calling her "that cunning whore of Venice." He calls in Emilia and stalks out.

She attempts to comfort her distraught mistress, who asks to see Iago, and he enters full of compassion at her distress. Emilia is enraged, convinced that "some eternal villain, / Some busy and insinuating rogue" has slandered her "to get some office." She comes too close to the bone for Iago, who insists there is "no such man." But she raves on: "The Moor's abused by some villainous knave, / Some base notorious knave, some scurvy fellow." She does not suspect her husband, but the dramatic irony is especially thick here as, inwardly irritated by her outburst, Iago attempts to silence her. Finally the trusting Desdemona asks his help, kneeling before him to protest her innocence in yet another triumphant moment for Iago. Othello has fallen at his feet and now his wife is on her knees before him. Such is the power of the lie.

The women depart, Roderigo enters, and Iago's plots begin to come unraveled. To this point he has been in control of events, but now he must respond to them, putting out fires. Roderigo declares that he has abandoned his suit of Desdemona and will return to Venice. He has given Iago countless jewels to deliver to her—none of which, as we know, has she received—and now he has decided to make himself known to her, ask for their return, and leave. It is all Iago can do to reassure him. Othello has been ordered to Mauritania, he discloses, and will take Desdemona with him, leaving Cassio in command on Cyprus. The only way to keep Desdemona accessible, Iago counsels, is to delay the couple's departure, which may be accomplished by eliminating Cassio, the general's replacement as governor. He proposes they do so that very night. Roderigo has his doubts but agrees to the scheme.

4.3 As the next scene opens, Othello instructs Desdemona sternly to get to bed and dismiss Emilia for the night, adding ominously that he will join his wife "forthwith." There follows a long, intimate exchange between the two women as Desdemona prepares to retire. The interval serves several purposes. First, it inserts a quiet interlude between two scenes packed with passion and violence. Further, it reaffirms Desdemona's innocence and arouses our pity for her. In her sorrow she foreshadows her own death, calling to mind the tale of a young woman whose lover "proved mad / And did forsake her." It was said that she sang an old song "of 'willow'" and died doing so. Desdemona sings the plaintive song herself and then asks Emilia if there are indeed women who "do abuse their husbands / In such gross kind." The earthy Emilia assures her wittily that there are, and explains that it is really all the husbands' fault. Desdemona bids her good night and prays that she will learn something good from the "bad" that afflicts her. The quiet intimacy of the scene further heightens the dramatic tension of the moment, for we know Othello is approaching.

5.1 The first scene of the final act is fairly frenetic. It is nighttime now. Iago places Roderigo where he can intercept Cassio and, in a duplication of the scene under Brabantio's balcony, withdraws into the shadows. When the lieutenant appears, Roderigo lunges at him but misses, and Cassio, defending himself, wounds his assailant. Iago emerges and, striking from behind, wounds Cassio, whereupon both injured men cry out for help. Othello comes upon them unseen but makes no effort to stop the brawl—no "keep up your bright swords" in Cyprus! Confident that Cassio has been dispatched, he moves on to his purpose, vowing ominously that Desdemona's "bed lust-stained shall with lust's blood be spotted." Lodovico and Gratiano approach but are fearful of venturing further in the dark. Iago, pretending to defend Cassio, comes upon the injured Roderigo and kills him. Bianca suddenly appears, responding to her lover's cries; and the quick-witted Iago casts suspicion on her for Cassio's injury. He takes charge now that the altercation has drawn a crowd, tends to the wounded Cassio, his "dear friend," and sends Emilia to the citadel to inform Othello of events.

5.2   The long final scene takes place in Desdemona's bedchamber, where Othello enters and pauses over her sleeping form, lit by the candle he carries. How does he perceive himself at this moment? As an abused husband intent upon revenge? Well, yes, but to perform this unnatural act he must convince himself that he is playing a larger, more significant role. He is a priest performing a perfect sacrifice as he enters intoning a solemn chant, "it is the cause, it is the cause, my soul." He promises that he will not "shed her blood, / Nor scar that whiter skin of hers than snow." He sees himself as an instrument of higher justice, serving a "cause," so "she must die, else she'll betray more men." He has reduced himself to a near trancelike state as he contemplates the consequences of what he intends. Staring at the candle's flame, he compares it to the life he is about to extinguish—"put out the light, and then put out the light." He can restore the flame of the candle but, should he repent, never again Desdemona's "vital growth." His words reflect a spirit torn between love and hatred, but words fail here, as Shakespeare's moving lines reveal his inner torment in phrases opaque in their contradictions. Kissing her once, and then again, Othello murmurs, "be thus when thou art dead, and I will kill thee, / And love thee after. One more, and that's the last. / So sweet was ne'er so fatal." Shakespeare reduces the poetry to the spare eloquence of simple one-syllable words as Othello expresses the inexpressible.

Desdemona awakens and her husband urges her to repent of her sins before he kills her. Frightened by the threat and by his appearance, as he rolls his eyes and gnaws at his lip in anguish, she professes herself innocent of any sin except loving him. Fearful perhaps that the sight of her will dissuade him, he finally blurts out a direct accusation—she gave her handkerchief to Cassio. She denies having done so and only enrages him further as he feels the justification for his role slipping away—"Thou dost stone my heart, / And mak'st me call what I intend to do / A murder, which I thought a sacrifice." The tension mounts here. Surely he will come to his senses! And where in the world is Emilia?

Desdemona pleads with him to ask Cassio, but on hearing that he is dead, as Othello thinks, she abandons all thought of reasoning with him and begs for more time, a day, an hour, a moment for prayer. Refusing, he smothers her, even as Emilia beats on the door. He is uncertain what to do, since he knows she will want to speak to his wife, a thought that brings home the full horror of his act: "My wife! my wife! what wife? I have no wife." Dazed and ineffectual, all he can do is draw the curtains about the bed and unlock the door, admitting Emilia.

As Othello learns that Cassio is not dead, Desdemona momentarily revives and declares herself "falsely murdered," but in reply to Emilia's frenzied question, she reverses herself. No one killed her, she says, it was "I myself"; and she dies, loyal to Othello at the end—"Commend me to my kind lord: O, farewell." The physiology of her brief revival may trouble us momentarily, but there is no denying its dramatic impact. Othello at first tries to hide behind her dying words, but he lacks Iago's duplicitous ingenuity and in the end he admits openly, " 'twas I that killed her." On hearing from Othello that Iago is the source of his jealousy, Emilia is speechless, uttering only an uncomprehending "my husband" over and over again, until an exasperated Othello exclaims, "I say thy husband; dost understand the word? / My friend, thy husband, honest, honest Iago."

Emilia is unrestrained in her response as she defends Desdemona's innocence and discloses her true feelings about the marriage, a "filthy bargain" with a man not worthy of her. Montano and Gratiano enter, accompanied by Iago; and Emilia continues her tirade, accusing her husband of "a lie, an odious, damned lie; / Upon my soul, a lie, a wicked lie!" Iago attempts to silence her but she is relentless, crying out "villainy, villainy, villainy!" at which Othello exclaims, "O! O! O!" and falls across the bed upon Desdemona's body. The dramatic tension of the scene arises from the audience's anticipation of the moment when Othello fully comprehends the enormity of what he has done, and from our fearful expectation of his reaction to the knowledge.

But there are some realities the mind simply refuses to accept, and

Othello is not yet ready to bear the burden of his error. He rises from the bed to condemn his wife. "O, she was foul!" he exclaims, and charges that "she with Cassio hath the act of shame / A thousand times committed." He cites the handkerchief, and now that the fatal evidence is in the open Emilia can refute it, revealing that she had found the "napkin" and given it to her husband. Othello, suddenly aroused, lunges at Iago but is disarmed, whereupon the ancient eludes him, stabs his wife to silence her, and makes his escape. The others chase after him, leaving Othello and the dying Emilia alone. She sings her lady's plaintive song, "willow, willow, willow," and in her last breath assures him "she was chaste; she loved thee, cruel Moor."

Shakespeare must now revive the image of the "noble Moor" of earlier scenes, before he was reduced by Iago's devices to irrational rage and babbling incoherence. The ending would be less than tragic were Othello simply to bow under the weight of his sorrow and meekly submit to his destiny. The poet has the task of restoring him to his former stature in our eyes and persuading us that the passion of such a man is paradoxically both an affliction and a virtue. He does so by reducing the Moor to an ominous calm and reminding us of the imposing figure he was. Othello finds another sword and defies the returning company, grimly confronting his fate. His eyes turn to the bed, however, and he crumbles as the full impact of his loss suddenly hits him, "O Desdemon! dead Desdemon! dead! O! O!" the abrupt cadences of his lament proclaiming the core of his despair.

Iago is brought forth and Othello looks at his feet, declaring "if that thou be'st a devil, I cannot kill thee," suggesting the image of cloven-hoofed demon, motivated solely by malice. Othello lunges at Iago, wounding him before surrendering his sword. He then asks why the seemingly loyal ancient sought to "ensnare" him. Iago replies defiantly, "demand me nothing: what you know, you know; / From this time forth I never will speak word"—and he never does.

Iago's treachery is now finally disclosed and Othello, realizing the full folly of his deed, submits and requests a final word. He asks those present to speak in their reports "of one that loved not wisely but too well; / Of one not easily jealous but, being wrought, / Perplexed in the extreme." Regaining some of his former dignity, he reminds them of his long and honorable service to the state, of how "in Aleppo once" he killed a "turbaned Turk" who was beating a Venetian. Taking the account as a cue, he draws a hidden dagger and stabs himself, falling upon the body of Desdemona, "to die upon a kiss." Cassio acknowledges that he feared such an end, "for he was great of heart"; and Lodovico turns on Iago, accusing him of "the tragic loading of this bed." At the curtain all eyes are upon the enigmatic ancient, wondering, as do we, what possessed him to desire the destruction of innocent love.

Jealousy permeates the play. Aside from Othello's passion, we see the fury of Bianca and Roderigo's impotent resentment. Iago is jealous of everyone—of Cassio for his promotion, and of both the Moor and his lieutenant, whom he suspects have been sleeping with his wife. But there is more to Iago's malice than simple jealousy. With an almost satanic intensity he is pained by the sight of anything good. Othello's virtues offend him. Cassio is a "proper man" with "a person and a smooth dispose"—in brief, handsome, with, as Iago fumes, "a daily beauty in his life / That makes me ugly." If virtue and beauty disturb him, Desdemona must torment his spirit even more. When he sees her with Cassio, as they await Othello's arrival, he is incensed; and the sight of the husband and wife in a loving embrace provokes him to fury. He is compelled by forces that Shakespeare only hints at.

While Iago may remain an enigma, Othello is all too familiar a figure, a jealous husband enraged at the infidelities, real or imagined, of his wife. But is it possible that the "valiant Othello," whom the Venetians see as "all in all sufficient," a man whom "passion could not shake," whom even his enemy acknowledges has "a free and open nature"—is it possible that such a man could fall victim to a tissue of lies? We accept such a possibility if the play effectively portrays the essential elements of the tale: Iago's ability to deceive everyone, the unconventional marriage, the passion between Desdemona and Othello, and the Moor's tragic flaw of innocently loving "too well." Convinced of all these, we must agree that such a man might well fall into a murderous rage on the basis of "trifles light as air," which Iago tells us "are to the jealous confirmations strong / As proofs of Holy Writ."

ROMEO AND JULIET

❧

THIS IS a tragic love story, but not as Aristotle defined tragedy, unless, of course, to be young and to fall in love are considered fatal flaws of character.* The tragic hero in the play is romantic, passionate, and rash; the heroine romantic, innocent, and impressionable. Both, in brief, are young and subject to the excesses common to those of their years in any era. Their love is doomed not by some error or frailty in their nature but by the fateful circumstances in which it flowers—an ancestral hatred between two feuding families in a time when fiery youths strode about the streets of a Renaissance city openly armed with sword and dagger, ready, indeed eager, to meet with their despised adversaries. Shakespeare does not describe the source of this ancient animosity. These things happen, he is content to say, offering a spectacle of fathers, mothers, children, and servants who never question why they hate, knowing only that they do.

The tale was a familiar one in Shakespeare's time, that of "star-cross'd lovers," one from each of two feuding families, whose devotion falls victim to some forgotten cause, their deaths the occasion for a reconciliation between penitent elders who had nurtured the mindless strife. The lovers die, it is true, as a result of the compassionate intercession of a kindly friar who meddles in medieval medicine, and because of a fatally undelivered letter. But it is not such tricks of plot that doom them. The cause is the spilling of "civil blood," which as the prologue tells us "makes civil hands unclean." This condition, Shakespeare seems to say, would have claimed them in any event.

*See "Tragedy," pp. 7–8.

1.Pro.   The first two acts of *Romeo and Juliet* open with a *Chorus* who delivers lines, all in rhyme, introducing us to the action. The play is a love story, and rhyme, even to this day, is considered an appropriate means of conveying the emotions aroused by love. Indeed, most of the lines in the early acts, which explore the *theme,* are rhymed, giving way later, when the tragic note intrudes, to blank verse. The speech of the Chorus is also a sonnet, which in Shakespeare's day was a verse form reserved almost exclusively for love poems. Indeed, among his works are 154 sonnets on the theme, many of whose opening lines will be familiar to the reader, those such as "Shall I compare thee to a summer's day," and "That time of year thou mayst in me behold."

The Chorus gives a brief synopsis of the plot, preparing us for its tragic outcome. An "ancient grudge" between "two households" in the city of Verona causes "a pair of star-cross'd lovers [to] take their life." This will be a tale of "their death-mark'd love," we are told, brought about by "their parents' rage." Thus the tragic theme is announced at the outset, perhaps to remind us that although there are many moments of playful levity to come, they will lead ultimately to that "death-mark'd" ending.

1.1   The levity is apparent at once as two minor figures of the house of Capulet engage in a witty exchange of the sort that will enliven the dialogue throughout, a play on similar sounding words: "coals," "collier," "choler," and "collar." These servants of the house boast that they will conduct themselves honorably should they encounter any Montagues, answering insults with their swords. As the servant Gregory says, "the quarrel is between our masters and us their men."

Two Montague servants approach, and it is the Capulet servant Sampson, who "bites his thumb" at them to provoke a fight, a particularly insulting gesture of the time (one still in use today). Benvolio, a Montague, enters and attempts to separate the combatants, only to be confronted by the fiery Tybalt, a Capulet, who leaps into the fray and challenges him in a way that honor compels him to answer. Soon advocates of both houses join the general melee, and finally the elders themselves come upon the scene, calling for their swords. In a comic touch the women restrain their men, Lady Capulet scornfully urging her husband to call for a "crutch" rather than a weapon, and Lady Montague demanding that hers "not stir one foot to seek a foe." This chance encounter between swaggering servants, then, degenerates into a street brawl between the two houses, confirmation of the "civil blood" foretold by the Chorus. The prince enters and separates the feuding families, complaining angrily that this is the third time they have "disturb'd the quiet of our streets." He threatens the elders that should there be another disturbance, "your lives shall pay the forfeit of the peace." The Capulets depart, leaving Benvolio to give an account of the fray to the Montagues.

The subject and tone of the scene shifts abruptly with Lady Montague's query about Romeo. Her son has been behaving strangely, Benvolio acknowledges, rising before dawn and secluding himself in darkness during the day, a solitary, melancholy figure whose conduct puzzles his parents. Romeo approaches, and Benvolio urges the elders to leave him alone with their son, promising to probe the source of "his grievance."

Benvolio knows what is wrong—Romeo is in love—and, the more to be pitied, he has been rejected. The disheartened youth describes himself in the tradition of the *courtly lover* whose lady has spurned him, speaking of his "sighs" and "groans," of eyes that wound and of himself as "dead." He elaborates on the paradoxes of love. Its painful contradictions, he declares, are like a "feather of lead, bright smoke, cold fire, sick health," everything "that is not what it is," and he mourns the loss of a woman who "hath forsworn to love." Benvolio, in a telling touch of *dramatic irony,* counsels him to forget her and "examine other beauties," but Romeo is inconsolable.

Thus in this opening scene we are immediately aware of the two themes that will thread through the play, love and hatred, and of their tragic intertwining as reflected in Romeo's plaintive exclamation: "O brawling love, O loving hate." There has been no mention of Juliet, who is not as yet the object of Romeo's love.

1.2 She is introduced indirectly in the following scene. The noble Paris, a kinsman of the prince, meeting Capulet on the street, asks his permission to woo his daughter. Capulet gives every appearance here of a reasonable and compassionate man. He first acknowledges the justice of the prince's edict—"'tis not hard I think / For men so old as we to keep the peace"—and then cautions Paris that his daughter is not quite fourteen, perhaps too young to marry. In contemporary versions of the tale, from which Shakespeare drew inspiration for the play, Juliet is more advanced in years, and we may wonder why he insisted on her extreme youth. It was not unusual, however, in medieval and Renaissance times for women to marry as soon as they reached childbearing age. Paris remarks that "younger than she are happy mothers made," but Capulet still has his doubts. Nonetheless he agrees, but with the understanding—in sharp contrast to his later angry insistence on the marriage—that the decision will be entirely hers: "Within her scope of choice / Lies my consent and fair according voice." The young man will have an opportunity that very evening, he suggests, when the Capulets will host a feast for their friends and relatives. The matter settled, he hands a list of guests to a clownish servant and orders him to seek them out and deliver invitations—unaware, it seems, that the man cannot read.

The two walk off together as Romeo reenters, accompanied by Benvolio, who continues to press his friend to find another love. They come upon the servant and read the list of guests for him. Benvolio seizes upon the feast as an opportunity for Romeo to survey "all the admired beauties of Verona," one of whom is sure to compare favorably to the unresponsive Rosaline, whose name is on the list. Romeo agrees but replies with passionate hyperbole that it will be a waste of time, since "the all-seeing sun / Ne'er saw her match since first the world began."

1.3 In the following scene we finally encounter Juliet—and her nurse. Lady Capulet has important news for her daughter but is delayed by the nurse's rambling reminiscences about her charge's childhood. She is a familiar figure in Shakespeare, seen also in the person of Emilia, Desdemona's maidservant in *Othello*. Well-meaning and loyal, indeed devoted, to her mistress, she is very much a woman of the world, given to bawdy quips about Juliet's future as a wife. She is a cherished figure, largely comic in effect, garrulous and earthy in her view of life, serving as somewhat of a *foil* to Juliet's innocence, romantic exuberance, and untried idealism. The nurse's favorite memory is an occasion when her husband picked up the three-year-old Juliet, who had fallen on her face, and remarked in a broad humor matching her own, "thou wilt fall backward when thou hast more wit, / Wilt thou not, Jule?" at which the infant ceased her crying and answered, "Ay." So pleased is the nurse with the jest that she repeats it over and again in her rambling account, to the exasperation of both Juliet and her mother.

Finally able to quiet the irrepressible nurse, Lady Capulet broaches the subject of marriage to Juliet, confiding that "the valiant Paris seeks you for his love." The nurse is ecstatic at the news—as a kinsman of the prince, Paris is a highly desirable "catch"—but Juliet seems less than enthusiastic. Her mother suggests that she take special notice of Paris at the feast that night, and Juliet agrees to observe him discreetly. Our first impression of Juliet, then, is that of a properly obedient daughter of a prosperous family, no doubt carefully raised and protected—though a childhood under the care of the earthy nurse, we would expect, has left her not entirely innocent of the world and the flesh. Although only a few days shy of fourteen, a subject much discussed in this scene, the actress in the part can project the impression of a young woman a bit more advanced in years and fully capable of the mature passion she later displays.

1.4 That evening finds Romeo and Benvolio outside the Capulet house, accompanied by Mercutio, like Paris a kinsman of the prince, and a close companion of the young Montagues. He is a boisterous, engaging man-about-town, whose outgoing nature serves as a foil to the brooding Romeo. He mocks both the devotion of lovers and the senseless feuding of the families, declaring love and hate frivolous emotions, though he remains bound by the code of honor so important to his culture. Both he and Benvolio are greatly amused by Romeo's romantic obsession and pass up no opportunity to jest at his expense. They prepare to join in the Capulet festival.

The fact that Montagues are able to intrude on a Capulet affair, uninvited and for a time undetected, is justified in some productions by staging it as a masked ball or by masking the intruders only, portrayals supported by brief allusions in the lines. But other versions simply ignore the complication. The Montagues are aware of the danger, as Benvolio acknowledges by his remark that they should be prepared to take to their "legs," but the daring of it excites the blood of the young men. Before entering, however, Romeo confides in his friends that he has had a dream, a remark that launches Mercutio into a satiric account of the myth of Queen Mab, a small fairy creature who incites dreams appropriate to the sleepers, lovers of love, courtiers of curtsies, lawyers of fees, ladies of kisses, soldiers of war, and so forth. The lengthy speech has little to do with the plot but is much admired as a flight of poetic fancy. The practical-minded Mercutio puts no store in the substance of dreams, but when his companions finally quiet him, Romeo reveals that his have left him with a sense of foreboding that something fearful will begin with "this night's revels," something that will result in a "vile forfeit of untimely death." Shakespeare offers Mercutio's skeptical view of the influence of the supernatural in our lives and contrasts it immediately with Romeo's confirmation of its power to foretell "untimely death."

Thus far in the play Shakespeare has offered a representative cross section of Verona's young gallants while portraying each as a distinct personality. Mercutio is a highly entertaining free spirit, engaging in his wit and vitality, one who loudly proclaims a cynicism that often passes for wisdom and worldliness with the young. Benvolio, as his name implies, is by nature "benevolent," a mild-mannered youth careful to avoid hostile encounters and anxious to resolve them when they occur. Romeo is in the grip of passion throughout the play, hence alternately languid and abrupt in his actions. At the outset he is the grieving courtly lover, the butt of his friends' jests; but once he sets eyes on Juliet he becomes an ardent and eloquent suitor who thoroughly engages our sympathies. Tybalt is a hot-blooded bully, quick to take offense, rising to any perceived slight to his personal honor, a man who seems to live on the edge of anger. Paris is considerably less interesting than the others: a perfect gentleman, properly respectful of his elders and careful to follow the prescribed protocol of courtship. It is tempting to think of him as a simpering fop or a haughty snob, but there is no need to do so. He is an entirely presentable, if somewhat wooden, young man, whose only defect is that he is not Romeo. Shakespeare gives us a rich variety of individuals, a group like any to be found in a local street or tavern today.

1.5   The friends enter upon a busy scene in the Capulet house—servants bustling about and the genial host calling for music and light before settling down with an elderly relative to recall the masques of their youth. Romeo spies Juliet and is immediately stricken, all thought of Rosaline dismissed: "Did my heart love till now? Forswear it, sight, / For I ne'er saw beauty till this night." He is recognized by Tybalt, however, who calls for his sword and threatens violence until restrained by Capulet who, conscious of the ancient privilege of a guest, is anxious that nothing "here in my house do him disparagement." A seething Tybalt is an ominous presence in the background of this first meeting of the "star-cross'd lovers."

Shakespeare fashioned the first exchange between Romeo and Juliet in the form of a sonnet, fourteen lines long with a set rhyme scheme and a closing couplet, the traditional verse form, as mentioned earlier, for a love poem. A theater audience will not be aware of the poetic artifice upon hearing it, though they may be conscious that the dialogue has turned to rhyme in recording this delicate moment. The subject is surely appropriate—he is asking for a kiss, and does so with the image of religious devotion, a pilgrim approaching a holy shrine. She replies prettily, pursuing the same image, and shyly submits. Then, with further play on the thought, he kisses her once more. The brief moment of their meeting is interrupted by the nurse, but the bond between them has been irreversibly sealed. Each inquires eagerly about the other's identity, and both are dismayed to learn that they are the children of hostile families. Romeo exclaims, "my life is my foe's debt"; and Juliet is stunned to find "my only love sprung from my only hate" and mourns that she is fated to "love a loathed enemy."

Thus Shakespeare brings together two young people whom he describes as quite different in their response to love. Juliet is innocent of its power and skeptical of its prospects, and this is for her a first love with its bewildering swirl of unfamiliar emotions. She has been taken by surprise and finds it all the more bittersweet for its strangeness. Romeo, on the other hand, has felt its force before, but until now he has seemed more in love with the idea of love than with the object of his desire, appearing even to relish the misery it causes him. He is in love for the entire play, the image of Rosaline simply erased by the sight of Juliet; and if this sudden transference of affection leaves us with the impression of a somewhat shallow youth, later events will reveal new depths to him. The different backgrounds prove inconsequential in the end, swept aside by a mutual affection so intense that it elevates both to a new, shared level of experience.

Romeo and Juliet become enamored of each other at first sight, as do almost all of Shakespeare's comic and tragic couples. If this sudden blossoming, brought on by no more than coincidental glances across a busy room, seems too facile or theatrically contrived to some audiences, it may be because they have forgotten or have yet to learn that this is indeed how it happens. The poet has no interest in explaining why they fall in love. His concern is only to explore the consequences.

2.Pro.   The second act opens with yet another sonnet by the Chorus, this one, however, without the grim foreshadowing of a tragic end. It simply dwells on the obstacles facing the lovers, he "being held a foe," unable to woo her traditionally, and she cut off from "a way to meet her new beloved anywhere." But, we are assured, love will find a way.

2.1   After leaving the Capulets, Romeo slips into the darkness while his friends search unsuccessfully for him. Mercutio calls out mockingly, "Romeo! Humors! Madman! Passion! Lover!" He playfully attempts to revive the "dead" Romeo with a litany of Rosaline's charms—her eyes, forehead, lips, foot, leg, and, more provocatively, her thigh. Mercutio's speech is full of erotic allusions—"in his mistress' name / I conjure only best to raise him up"—and bawdy puns based on beliefs of the time that a good set of textual footnotes will illuminate. He is having fun at his lovesick friend's expense. Predictably, he draws no response from Romeo. Those who find Mercutio's jests less than friendly may not be familiar with a curiosity of male bonding, to use a modern term for the process. In the company of young men, insults often carry the same affectionate weight as endearments, especially in matters of the heart, as anyone who has attended a prenuptial bachelor party will attest. Shakespeare understood well this idiosyncrasy of male friendship (see the treatment Benedick receives at the hands of his companions in *Much Ado About Nothing* and the banter between Prince Hal and Falstaff in the *Henry IV* plays).

2.2   As his friends leave, Romeo emerges, muttering his well-known response to Mercutio's gibes: "He jests at scars that never felt a wound." He stands beneath a balcony where Juliet suddenly appears, inspiring him to rhapsodize on the sight of her. She is the sun, her eyes two stars that outshine any in the night sky. She is his love, but, he regrets, she is unmindful of it—"O that she knew she were!" Not yet aware of his presence, she unburdens her heart into the night, and her thoughts are of his name, which must keep them apart. They can abandon their names, she imagines, and he in compensation for the loss can "take all myself."

This is the tenderest moment of any love's history, when both discover what they hardly dared hope—their affection is returned. This sudden revelation creates the world anew, daylight sparkles, stars shine with added intensity, and all things are possible. Romeo reveals himself and, echoing Juliet's thought, declares that "henceforth I never will be Romeo." He continues in this vein, pouring out his love and defying the danger of his presence there. Juliet's first surprise is replaced by a fear of his discovery by her kinsmen, but she soon submits to the joy of the moment and responds in kind. "Dost thou love me," she asks innocently. Setting aside all customs of courtship, she acknowledges her "true-love passion," begging him not to "impute this yielding to light love." He prepares to swear to his devotion but she prevents him, voicing a maidenly fear that the emotion is "too rash, too unadvis'd, too sudden," and bids him good night. Romeo, reluctant to leave, asks for an "exchange of thy love's faithful vow for mine." But, as she says, she has already given hers and only wishes she could recapture the moment when she did, so as to give it again.

The nurse calls Juliet away while a dazed Romeo questions whether the encounter has been "but a dream, / Too flattering sweet to be substantial." For both, then, the emotions accompanying an avowal of mutual love are so unearthly as to cause them to wonder at it. Juliet returns and, all modesty aside, asks him to name the time and place to "perform the rite" of marriage. He promises to inform her by nine the following morning. After further endearments she finally withdraws, to the famous lines, "parting is such sweet sorrow / That I shall say good night till it be morrow." Romeo rushes off to find a priest.

It may escape the notice of a viewing audience that this moving scene, save for an occasional couplet, is entirely unrhymed. Romeo's rhapsodizing over Rosaline, as we have seen, is heavily so, the convention for love poetry at the time. Shakespeare, perhaps to distinguish between the merely fanciful and the true emotion, discards the convention and adopts blank verse as a freer form, better able to convey the quality of the moment.

2.3 Romeo's final words and the opening lines of Friar Laurence's speech in the following scene signal the arrival of dawn. The good priest, puttering about in his herb garden, philosophizes about the mixture of good and evil in nature, marveling at the paradox of a single plant containing both "poison" and "medicine powers." Romeo enters, and the friar chides him for his infatuation with Rosaline. When the young man informs him of his new love, however, one who miraculously returns his affections, the friar readily agrees to assist, seeing an opportunity to change the two "households' rancor to pure love."

2.4 Meanwhile, Mercutio and Benvolio puzzle over Romeo's disappearance, the former ridiculing his friend's lovesick state with more ribald humor. We learn that Tybalt has issued a challenge to Romeo, and

Mercutio worries that someone in his moonish condition will not be able to muster the resolve to face an accomplished swordsman like the fiery Capulet. When Romeo comes upon them, they engage in a witty exchange, punning at length on the erotic implications of words like "sole" and "goose." The nurse enters and they banter with her too, finally leaving Romeo alone to hear her message. After submitting to her stern warning that he not lead Juliet into "a fool's paradise," he is able to arrange for the wedding that very afternoon, and for the delivery of a rope ladder so that he can reach her bedchamber that night.

2.5–6   Juliet waits impatiently for the nurse's return, but when she finally appears she insists on delaying the news while she settles her "bones" and catches her "breath." The old woman seems to enjoy her importance in the affair, delaying even further, to Juliet's exasperation, with complaints about aches in her head and back. She finally reveals the marriage plan, urging Juliet, "hie you to church," while she goes off to arrange for a ladder. Later that day, Romeo and Friar Laurence await Juliet in the church. When she arrives, after an exchange of affection they leave to be wed.

3.1   Act Three opens on a Verona street somewhat later in the day. Benvolio urges Mercutio to retire so as to avoid a confrontation with the Capulets, but Mercutio launches into a lengthy speech chiding his friend for being quarrelsome—remarks that seem to apply more to himself than to the good-natured Benvolio. Tybalt enters and Mercutio taunts him, but he is more intent on finding Romeo, who comes upon them, we may assume, fresh from his wedding. Tybalt challenges him—"thou art a villain"—but Romeo brushes aside the insult and answers cryptically that Capulet is a name "I tender / As dearly as my own." Mercutio is incensed at what he sees as Romeo's "calm, dishonorable, vile submission" to Tybalt's taunts, and he draws his sword. Romeo desperately attempts to separate them, but in doing so he interferes with Mercutio's sword arm, allowing Tybalt to stab him. Tybalt retreats, and the injured Mercutio, asked if his wound is serious, replies with characteristic irony that "'tis not so deep as a well, nor so wide as a church door, but 'tis enough, 'twill serve." He is not a Montague, it will be recalled, but a kinsman of the prince, hence his heartfelt, "a plague o' both your houses," which he repeats over and again as he is carried off.

Romeo contemplates his dilemma, but on hearing of Mercutio's death he becomes enraged. Seeing Tybalt return, he challenges him. They clash and Tybalt falls, leaving Romeo momentarily stunned by what he has done. "O, I am fortune's fool," he cries in despair and dashes out. The prince, accompanied by both families, comes upon the scene and demands an explanation. It is Lady Capulet who responds most angrily to Benvolio's account. She demands justice: "Romeo slew Tybalt. Romeo must not live." But the prince, knowing full well where the fault lies, sentences him only to exile and imposes heavy fines on both families. At the same time he is prophetically troubled by his own leniency: "Mercy but murders, pardoning those that kill."

3.2 Juliet, meanwhile, awaits Romeo with growing impatience. In an ardent *soliloquy* she wishes the day gone. "Come night, come Romeo, come thou day in night," she pleads, caught up in a rush of desire for him: "O, I have but bought the mansion of love / But not possess'd it." The nurse enters, wailing about the murder, and it is some time before a distraught Juliet can make out that it is not Romeo who has been killed but her cousin Tybalt, at his hand. She is subjected rapidly to a range of conflicting emotions—joy that Romeo is alive, sorrow that Tybalt is dead, despair that her husband is banished, and anguish that she, but a "three-hours wife," must suffer separation from him. She reflects her inner turmoil in a series of paradoxes—Romeo is a "beautiful tyrant, fiend angelical . . . a damned saint, an honorable villain!" The good-hearted nurse, upset at the distress of her young mistress, offers to find Romeo and bring him to "comfort" her that night.

3.3 Romeo has sought refuge in Friar Laurence's cell, where he learns of "the Prince's doom." His response is as anguished as Juliet's, and nothing the priest can say is of comfort. Friar Laurence scolds him, insisting that he should be glad to be alive and grateful that "the kind Prince, / Taking thy part, hath rush'd aside the law." Romeo raves on, complaining that "every cat and dog" can look on Juliet, but not he, and asking for poison or a knife as a "sudden means of death."

The word *banished* echoes throughout these two scenes.* Lest we respond to the lovers' ravings as so much adolescent hysteria, we should re-

*It is pronounced with three syllables, *ban-ish-ed* to preserve the rhythm of the lines.

member that theirs are not uncommon sentiments. Lovers simply *want to be* with each other. To them, hours spent apart are so much of life suspended, to be renewed only when they are once more together. A forced separation, for weeks perhaps or months, is a kind of death, or so it seems to Romeo and Juliet. On learning that he is "banished," she laments that "there is no end, no limit, measure, bound, / In that word's death"; and he grieves that "exile hath more terror in his look, / Much more than death." For him the word itself "is death, misterm'd," and for them both separation is unendurable, its only analogy that final dissolution.

The nurse gains entrance and gives Romeo an account of Juliet's state—she "but weeps and weeps." He raves on until reprimanded by the priest, who shames him for his talk of suicide: "Wilt thou slay thyself? / And slay thy lady that in thy life lives?" With the stern voice of reason, he admonishes the young man that he should be happy that Juliet lives, that Tybalt did not kill him, and that his punishment is only exile. "Go, get thee to thy love as was decreed, / Ascend her chamber," he concludes, but warns him that he must leave her before "the Watch be set." Then find refuge in Mantua, he counsels, and he will find a means to communicate. A chastened Romeo departs to join his love.

3.4   In a brief scene, Paris expresses his regret to the Capulets that "these times of woe afford no times to woo." They are under the impression that Juliet is mourning the death of Tybalt, and her father is annoyed at her refusal to join them. In contrast to his earlier compassion for her, his concern for her youth and his willingness to leave the decision of marriage to her, he resorts to the parent's prerogative to *arrange for the daughter's marriage* and peremptorily announces that the wedding will take place the following Thursday, regardless of her desires in the matter.

3.5   Much later, after their wedding night together, the lovers watch the first signs of dawn. Shakespeare once again pens memorable lines for an audience surrounding a *stage* bathed in midday light within the Globe Theater's "wooden O": "Look, love, what envious streaks / Do lace the severing clouds in yonder east." Juliet, reluctant to let Romeo leave, insists it isn't so and that the birdsong they hear is not the lark but the nightingale. He submits, sighing that he has "more care to stay than will to go"; but when he adds, "come death, and welcome," she urges him to be gone—it is the lark after all. Lady Capulet's approach interrupts the moment, and with Juliet wondering sadly if "we shall ever meet again," Romeo leaves.

Juliet maintains the posture of mourning Tybalt's death with her mother, prompting the lady to promise that "we will have vengeance for it, fear thou not." Told of her impending marriage to Paris, Juliet rejects the proposal with purposefully deceptive irony, claiming she would rather marry Romeo, "whom you know I hate." Capulet enters and on hearing of her refusal flies into a rage, threatening to drag her to church if she fails to appear. He is incensed—"Hang thee young baggage, disobedient wretch!"—and sweeps aside the women's efforts to calm him. He has bent every effort to arrange a suitable marriage for his daughter, he rages, and if she insists on defying him, then she will "hang! Beg! Starve! Die in the streets!" He storms out, followed shortly by his wife, who washes her hands of the whole affair. Juliet has only the nurse to turn to, but she proves scant comfort, advising her to go ahead with the marriage to Paris, who she claims is "a lovely gentleman. Romeo is a dishclout to him." Juliet pretends to agree and leaves to seek the aid of Friar Laurence, vowing to trust the nurse no further.

4.1   The opening scene of Act Four finds Paris in Friar Laurence's cell, where he has come in search of Juliet. He informs the priest of the impending marriage, justifying it as her father's effort to lift her sorrow over Tybalt's death. The friar is momentarily distraught but is saved further comment by the appearance of Juliet herself. Paris, addressing her, undertakes some heavy-handed wooing and receives in return a cold reply, full of double meanings. In balance, however, while he seems somewhat overbearing in this, his only scene with her, his expectations are no more or less than any other suitor of the time.

When he leaves, Juliet bursts out in a frantic plea for help from the friar, drawing a knife with the threat to kill herself rather than marry Paris. She declares that she will endure unimaginable horrors, walk "where serpents are," chain herself to "roaring bears," or hide at night in a charnel house so as to "live an untainted wife to my sweet love." While her words may border on melodramatic excess, they, and the dagger in her hand, convince the friar that she is in a desperate state of mind and might harm herself. He calms her with an alternate plan. He has among his stores, he says, a potion, perhaps one of those he had earlier described as at once poisonous and medicinal. When taken, it induces all the symptoms of death, but the effect wears off in forty-two hours and the person is restored without harm. Juliet is to agree to the marriage with Paris and drink the "mixture," appearing to die. Meanwhile the priest will write to Romeo to inform him of the scheme and urge him to rescue her when she recovers her senses, carrying her off then to Mantua. A custom of the time was to leave the bodies of the dead uncoffined, so Juliet will lie atop her bier in the Capulet crypt until Romeo comes. She eagerly agrees—"Give me, give me!"—and praying "love give me strength," she dashes out.

4.2–3 The Capulet household is again bustling with activity, this time in preparation for the sudden wedding. Juliet appears before her father, begs his pardon for her "disobedient opposition," and agrees to the marriage. Capulet, both relieved and pleased at her submission, unexpectedly moves the wedding up to the following day. It is clear that he is simply impatient to have the whole worrisome matter over with.

Shortly thereafter, in Juliet's bedchamber, she asks her mother and the nurse to leave her to herself for a time. When they are gone, she addresses them plaintively with her same words at Romeo's departure— "God knows when we shall ever meet again." It is a touching time of farewells for Juliet. She addresses the vial of Friar Laurence's "mixture" in a soliloquy full of anxious doubts. What if it doesn't work and she has to go through with the wedding? Or what if it is poison? Most frightening of all, what if she awakens in the crypt before Romeo arrives and, surrounded by the bones of Capulet corpses, is driven mad by the "terror of the place"? Finally, shaken by the thought of Tybalt's armed ghost stalking Romeo, she drinks the potion and falls upon her bed.

4.4–5 The activity in the Capulet household continues into the morning until it is time to summon the bride. The nurse finds her, apparently dead, and her cries alert the others. The scene of general lamentation is joined by Paris and Friar Laurence, and the priest chides the family for their outburst of grief, reminding them, rather disingenuously, that she has gone to a better place. This distressing scene is framed by two comic interludes, the confusion of the wedding preparations and the dismissed musicians, whose chief lament is that they will not be paid.

Shakespeare again balances the tragic with the comic vision of our life. Are we meant to laugh at this spectacle of grief? Well, perhaps so, since we know Juliet still lives.

5.1–2   Exiled in Mantua, Romeo is unexpectedly buoyant, ironically because his "dreams presage some joyful news at hand." His mood is abruptly shattered, however, by Balthasar, who arrives with word of Juliet's death. Romeo greets the news with an ominous calm, simply directing his man to hire horses for a voyage. We soon discover his mind, an impulsive resolve to die: "Well, Juliet, I will lie with thee tonight." He seeks out an apothecary to secure a deadly poison to take with him "to Juliet's grave, for there I must use thee." Meanwhile, Friar Laurence's letter to him, explaining the scheme, has gone undelivered. Friar John, who was to place it in his hands, was delayed by a mishap. He was boarded up for a time in a house infested with the plague and, not realizing the letter's import, upon his escape has returned with it. Friar Laurence rushes out to be with Juliet when she awakens.

5.3   The long final scene of the play is set in the Capulet crypt, and Shakespeare heightens the tension by filling the stage with people. First Paris and his page appear, then Romeo and Balthasar, finally Friar Laurence. All the while the alerted watch officers are approaching. We wait apprehensively in expectation that someone, anyone, will deter the mad young man from his fatal intent.

Paris enters and approaches Juliet's bier to strew flowers over her "bridal bed," but he is interrupted by a signal from his page that someone approaches. Romeo arrives, directing Balthasar to leave him, but the faithful servant, uneasy about his master's state of mind, conceals himself nearby. Romeo enters the tomb, only to be confronted by the grieving Paris. Convinced that Juliet died of sorrow at Tybalt's death, Paris draws his sword to challenge his murderer. Romeo attempts to dissuade him— "good gentle youth, tempt not a desperate man"—but Paris persists and is killed in the ensuing fight. Romeo recognizes his assailant and regrets the loss—but not for long, as his attention is drawn to the still body of Juliet. His emotions at the sight of her are familiar to any newlywed. He is moved by a sudden, unendurable void in his life, by the loss of her love and beauty, and by the unimaginable prospect of living on without her. Convinced that she died of sorrow at their separation, he is determined to be with her in whatever reunion death may hold. After a long, despairing speech in which he marvels that she is "yet so fair," he drinks the poison and dies.

Friar Laurence finally arrives, encounters Balthasar, enters the crypt, and surveys the scene. But as Juliet awakens, he hears others approaching and, fearing disclosure, he leaves her alone. Seeing the corpse of Romeo and moved by the same sentiments as was he, Juliet draws his dagger and stabs herself, even as the page comes upon the scene with the watch. They usher in Balthasar and Friar Laurence as the prince arrives with the Capulets, followed closely by Montague, whose wife has died of sorrow at her son's exile. Friar Laurence is brought forward to give a long account of the events that have led to the bloody scene before them. His speech rehearses much of what the audience already knows. But it is all new to the stunned listeners, and the dramatic impact of the scene arises from their anguished response to his revelations and the belated recognition of their role in the deaths.

The prince is moved to pity for the devastated families. While he is not harsh with them, he places the blame where it belongs. "Where be these enemies?" he demands accusingly, eyeing the elders who have harbored the generations of hatred that led to the senseless deaths of five vital young members of the city, three of whom lie lifeless within their sight. Indeed, he does not exonerate himself from blame. He was troubled by his earlier leniency with Romeo, observing at the time that "mercy but murders, pardoning those that kill"; now he acknowledges his fault in "winking at your discords," which have cost him "a brace of kinsmen" as well. If he had been more severe with the feuding families, the carnage in that dismal crypt might have been prevented. This realization, and the sorrowful reconciliation between Montagues and Capulets, come all too late, however, for "Juliet and her Romeo."

The lovers' fault, if it can be called that, is not that they learned to love "too well" like Othello, or too late like Lear, but that they did so too soon, before time could temper their youthful passion and smooth its edges with the abrasive stuff of life. But that passion is the very source of their appeal for us; it evokes our ambivalence toward a half-remembered time when we too might have been captive to such a love and reminds us perhaps that we no longer are. Romeo and Juliet are dear to us in their devotion, which causes them to take their own lives. It is a measure contemplated by many who suffer such a loss, oblivious to the sorrow wrought on others by such an act and tragically unmindful of future happiness forfeited thereby. They are lost, these two, but cherished in their loss because it carries us back to a time when we too were convinced that love conquers all, unaware as yet that the world will marshal forces to cloud that dream. Oddly, we leave the theater with a sense that it may be true after all, persuaded not so much by the ritualistic reconciliation between Montagues and Capulets but by the ability of Shakespeare's poetry to evoke the pure force of youthful love.

JULIUS CAESAR

❧

ANYONE ATTENDING one of Shakespeare's Roman plays might suspect that his audiences were more familiar with ancient history than are theatergoers today. Such seems to be the case. These plays are based largely on Plutarch's *Parallel Lives of Greeks and Romans,* composed about 100 A.D., a book apparently more widely read then than it is today. Allusions in Shakespeare to past events and characters such as Pompey and Cato, who are dead as the play opens, would have had more meaning for a Renaissance audience than they do for us. Shakespeare, as was his custom, adapted history to his dramatic purposes, but such references are nonetheless likely to leave us puzzled. The plays are highly effective tragedies despite these allusions, but a brief summary of the history they record will make them more accessible to a modern audience.

In the four hundred years before the time of Caesar—that is, to the middle of the first century B.C.—Rome had flourished under a republican form of government that was dominated by a powerful Senate. Each year the Senate elected two "consuls" to act in the capacity of an executive body. To balance their authority, two "tribunes" were designated to protect the rights of the common citizens or "plebeians." Rome was a republic, however, only in so far as it was not ruled by a single head of state, a king or dictator. The Senate was an oligarchy, composed of men from the aristocratic families of Rome, ever vigilant to protect their traditional prerogatives.

Julius Caesar spent years in the service of the Senate conquering provinces for Rome. When that body, fearing his fame, acted to discredit him, he marched on the capital with his loyal legions and forced them to appoint him to the high office of consul. He joined in a political union with Pompey, another highly respected general, and Crassus, a man of great wealth, to form "The First Triumvirate," an alliance powerful enough to overawe the Senate. When Crassus was killed while campaigning in Syria, the two men, Pompey and Caesar, fell into contention for control of Rome. Caesar prevailed, largely because of his generous contributions to the welfare of his soldiers and the common people.

It is at this point in Roman history that *Julius Caesar* opens. The Senate perceives Caesar as a threat to their ancient liberties and traditional authority, and they plot to remove him. In a conspiracy led by Brutus and Cassius, they assassinate Caesar in the capitol, precipitating a series of civil wars fought to decide the fate of the Senate. As Caesar's devoted follower, Mark Antony expects to be designated his heir; but instead Caesar's young nephew, Octavius, is named to inherit his considerable wealth and authority. The two settle their differences, however, and joining with Lepidus to form "The Second Triumvirate," set about to destroy the Senate. They initiate a bloody purge of that body, ruthlessly executing its chief members and their families, and finally eliminate the last hope of the republic by defeating Brutus and Cassius at the battle of Philippi.

Thus the history according to Plutarch. Shakespeare animates the dry narrative with richly drawn characters—an imperious Caesar, a noble Brutus, a "lean and hungry" Cassius, and a vengeful Mark Antony, all competing for the ultimate prize, sovereignty over the known world.

1.1 The play opens on a group of "commoners"—carpenters and cobblers—who have swarmed to catch sight of Caesar in a rare public appearance. The tribunes, Flavius and Murellus, who were elected to protect the liberties of Roman citizens, are angry with their constituents, chiding them for their fickle allegiance. They cheered Pompey when he was Caesar's enemy, Murellus complains, and now they idolize the man who "comes in triumph over Pompey's blood." This *theme,* the uncertain loyalty of the common people, their frivolous submission to the sway of oratory, pervades the early acts of the play, emphasizing the danger of placing faith in the shifting sentiments of the mob, who may flock to a charismatic leader one day and repudiate him the next. The tribunes recognize Caesar's threat to Roman liberties and are angry because the commoners' attraction to spectacle leaves them blind to the danger.

1.2 Caesar appears, surrounded by family and supporters, to participate in the festivities of Lupercalia. A soothsayer emerges from the crowd to warn him, "Beware the ides of March," but Caesar ignores him and the party passes on.* Our first impression of Caesar depends upon the gestures and demeanor of the actor in the part, since there is little in the lines to define him. He is surrounded by his court who insulate him from the admiring crowd of commoners. He has cultivated their support and depends upon them for his authority, but he appears aloof from them. Caesar allows the ragged, wild-eyed soothsayer to approach his person but then dismisses his warning with a contemptuous wave of his hand. Shakespeare's audience, well aware that Caesar will be assassinated, could well perceive his haughty dismissal as a sign of the overweening pride of a man who thinks himself above the will of fate.

But, again, there is little to go on. Brutus and Cassius, left alone on stage, engage in a kind of verbal ballet, each reluctant to voice his inner thoughts to the other. A shout from the nearby marketplace finally shakes out of Brutus the admission that he fears "the people / Choose Caesar for their king." Cassius, responding to his candor, insists that Caesar is as mortal as any man. He had to be rescued from drowning and suffered a fever while campaigning in Spain, during which " 'tis true, this god did shake," grow pale, and cry for drink. But now, he goes on, this vulnerable man "doth bestride the narrow world / Like a Colossus," reducing the rest of humanity to "underlings." In an appeal to his friend's vanity he calls Brutus as worthy as Caesar, and to his patriotism by reminding him that his ancestor had expelled the kings from Rome centuries before. Both men are on dangerous ground here, Cassius proposing treason and Brutus contemplating it, so they speak in veiled terms, referring only obliquely to their hidden meaning. Brutus says only that he will think about it.

Caesar reenters with all his followers, and he confides in Antony that he has concerns about Cassius, who, he says, "has a lean and hungry look; / He thinks too much: such men are dangerous." The party passes on as Brutus intercepts another senator, Casca, asking him the cause of the cheers they heard. Antony, he reports, offered Caesar a crown on three occasions, and each time he rejected it the people applauded wildly. Casca

---

*The "ides," or middle day of the month, fell on the 15th of March under the old Roman calendar.

makes no effort to conceal his contempt for the Roman commoners: "The rabble hooted and clapped their chapped hands and threw up their sweaty night-caps and uttered such a deal of stinking breath" that Caesar swooned. He is subject to "the failing sickness," as Brutus observes, a form of epilepsy, further evidence that he is but a mortal man. Cicero is mentioned, a famous Roman orator and senator revered for his learning, integrity, and dedication to the republic. He spoke, says the mundane Casca, but in Greek, and he could not understand a word—"it was Greek to me." As the men prepare to go their several ways, Brutus promises to confer further with Cassius on the unspoken matter alluded to in their conversation.

1.3   As the next scene opens, it is the midnight before the "ides." Thunder and lightning rage as Casca informs Cicero of the strange events he has witnessed: a slave with a burning hand, a lion in the capitol, a screech owl at noon, and a group of women who swore they had seen "men all in fire walk up and down the streets." Nature is in disarray, a sign according to the belief in *universal order* that human affairs are in a similar state.* Cicero acknowledges that "it is a strange-disposed time," but he questions the superstitions about such events, which, he says, "men may construe" any way they please. As he leaves, Cassius enters, and as if to confirm Cicero's doubts, he remarks vaguely that they bring to mind "a man / Most like this dreadful night." Casca asks if he means Caesar; but Cassius remains cautious, unwilling as yet to speak his mind openly: "Let it be who it is."

Casca has heard reports that the Senate intends to appoint Caesar king. Cassius, sounding him out evasively, declares himself well armed against tyranny. When Cassius finally admits his hatred of "so vile a thing as Caesar," Casca eagerly commits himself to the conspiracy, prompting Cassius to confide in him that he has arranged a meeting "of the noblest-minded Romans" that very night to confer on a plot, "most bloody-firing and most terrible." Cinna, one of the conspirators, comes upon them and stresses the critical need to include Brutus in their plans. That very night, Cassius responds, they will visit Brutus to "be sure of him."

---

*In *Hamlet,* Horatio compares these same manifestations in Rome to the appearance of the ghost, concluding that such phenomena foreshadow "fierce events."

Cassius is justly cautious, for as the conspiracy expands it runs the danger of including in its ranks one who will betray them. Brutus, though essential to their success, is also their greatest threat, since they know that if he refuses to join them, he will feel honor-bound to expose the plot.

2.1   Act Two acquaints us more intimately with both Brutus and Caesar, who in successive scenes are found at home in the company of their wives. We see Brutus first, a man whom Shakespeare portrays as a patriot of spotless honor and unshakable integrity. He is a model of the virtues that were said to have made Rome great, chief among them a stoic disregard for self and a total dedication to the welfare of the empire. Widely admired by both the common people and the aristocracy, he is essential to the conspiracy as a symbol of the justice of the cause. If he can be persuaded to join in the assassination, it will be seen not as an act of ambitious men jealous of Caesar's power, for Brutus is neither ambitious nor jealous, but as the painfully necessary removal of a threat to Roman liberties.

The opening lines of the scene inform us that it is still nighttime. Brutus has already resolved the issue in his conscience, musing "it must be by his death," and justifying the decision to himself in a lengthy *soliloquy*. He has nothing against Caesar, he admits, but fears that he might become tyrannical if entrusted with the absolute authority of a monarch. Caesar, Brutus acknowledges, shows none of the marks of a tyrant at present, but many so empowered soon do, "so Caesar may; / Then lest he may, prevent." Although, he admits, Cassius "first did whet me against Caesar," the decision is entirely his own, arising from a carefully considered concern for the welfare of Rome.

Cassius enters, accompanied by his fellow conspirators, and after some initial guarded pleasantries, Brutus comes directly to the point. He openly acknowledges himself one of them and immediately assumes the leadership of the group. As they plan the assassination, Cassius makes a series of proposals, all of which Brutus rejects for one reason or another. It is suggested that they all swear their allegiance to one another, but Brutus argues that there is no need for such a gesture among honorable men joined in a righteous cause. Cassius proposes that Cicero be included in the conspiracy because, as Metellus urges, "his silver hairs" will add authority to the act. Brutus opposes his inclusion, arguing that Cicero is too self-important to join them. Cassius then argues for the death of Antony, but Brutus vetoes this proposal as well. "Let us be sacrificers, but not butchers," he urges, and "carve him as a dish fit for the gods." Brutus can only condone the assassination if it is seen as a religious rite, a sacrifice on the altar of Roman liberty, with "a purpose necessary and not envious" so that the conspirators will "be called purgers, not murderers." Cassius persists, but Brutus will have none of it, so determined is he that their purpose remain unsullied by ambition or malice. The men then discuss the details of the plot, most critically a means of ensuring that Caesar attends the Senate meeting. Brutus assures all that he will enlist another senator, Caius Ligarius, in the cause. Morning breaks and they disband.

As the conspirators leave, Brutus is confronted by his wife, Portia. Deeply concerned about his state of mind, she asks what is distracting him. Shakespeare portrays her, as he does many of the women in his history plays, as living on the periphery of great events, anxious about the fate of the family when her husband engages in a dangerous struggle for political power. Portia kneels before her husband, pleading that he share with her, "your self, your half," what is troubling him; but he remains evasive until she reveals a wound she has given herself in the thigh as a pledge of her constancy. The sight of her blood so moves Brutus that he promises to confide in her, but they are interrupted by a knocking at the door, and she withdraws. It is Ligarius, who has been excluded from the conspiracy thus far, and Brutus enlists him in the cause. This minor figure is introduced to confirm the profound respect the Romans have for Brutus. Ligarius is not privy to the plans but pledges himself "to do I know not what; but it sufficeth / That Brutus leads me on."

Although *Julius Caesar* has been enormously popular over the years, some viewers have found it difficult to identify with the characters. They are too inclined, it is said, to give speeches rather than converse with one another. Even in the most intimate scenes between husband and wife, they seem to speak as if they were in a public forum. In this scene Portia pleads with Brutus as if she were before a court of law. He is outwardly unmoved by her words, submitting only when in a dramatically visual gesture she shows her wound. Shakespeare, perhaps conscious that he is representing the Romans as so many orators delivering so many sententious speeches, mocks his own invention in the scene that follows. It is a companion to the one just ended, presenting Caesar, like Brutus, in the company of his wife and later among the conspirators.

2.2   Calphurnia, Caesar's wife, has slept unquietly, crying out that her husband will be murdered. Uneasy, Caesar orders priests to perform sacrifices that, it was believed, could foretell the future. Calphurnia enters, pleading with him to stay at home, and in his reply he sounds as if he is addressing the Senate. He refers to himself rather grandly in the third person, "Caesar shall forth" and "Caesar shall not," supremely confident, it would appear, that he is insulated by his greatness from the fears and dangers of common men. Shakespeare portrays him as an almost comically pompous figure, puffed up with his own importance; and the scene is heavily layered with *dramatic irony,* since no audience, in his time or our own, could be unaware of what happened on "the ides of March." Shakespeare has taken pains to undercut this image of the great man by including details that emphasize his mortality: he can suffer from fevers, is deaf in one ear, and is subject to "the falling sickness," all these in ironic contrast to his perception of himself as an almost godlike being. His exalted opinion of his powers lends substance to the fears Brutus has expressed about the dangers of his rule once he is entrusted with the absolute authority of a king. Shakespeare's Caesar is not a sympathetic figure, and this scene does little to endear him to us.

Calphurnia voices her fears, citing the strange events of the night, but he is unmoved, proclaiming grandly, "cowards die many times before their deaths; / The valiant never taste of death but once." These are memorable words no doubt, but their heroic effect is somewhat compromised by the fact that Caesar is speaking privately to his wife and both of them are standing about in their nightgowns. At this point he receives a report that the priests have found a sacrificial victim without a heart—an ominous sign. Calphurnia kneels before him, as Portia had before Brutus, with further entreaties. He changes his mind, shaken perhaps by the priests' findings, perhaps moved by his kneeling wife—he "will stay at home."

Decius enters, come to escort Caesar to the Senate, only to be informed of his decision. Asked his reason, Caesar replies haughtily, "the cause is my will," but he continues with an account of Calphurnia's dreams. Decius first attempts to sway Caesar with an appeal to his ambition, informing him that the Senate intends to declare him king and may change their minds should he not appear. He then engages the great man's vanity, asking what would be said of him if it became known that he feared to come because of a woman's dreams. Impressed by these appeals, Caesar changes his mind yet again and agrees to go, at which point the entire party of conspirators enters, to be greeted with his customary courtesy and affability. It is a stunning scene, the great man surrounded by those who will shortly encircle him again with drawn daggers. To add to the dramatic irony, he insists that they all leave together "like friends," and Shakespeare accents the irony by repeating the word *friends* three times in as many lines.

2.3-4   In the next two short scenes, Shakespeare builds the tension. Artemidorus has somehow learned of the conspiracy and has written a warning letter he intends to pass to Caesar on his way to the Senate. His discovery justifies the caution that Cassius exercised earlier in disclosing the plot to Brutus and Casca—his fear that widening knowledge of it runs the danger of compromise. Portia, meanwhile, is in a frenzy as she awaits news of the fate of her husband, and the soothsayer who had earlier warned Caesar to "beware the ides of March" will try again.

3.1   Act Three opens on Caesar in procession approaching the Forum, and Shakespeare raises the tension a notch. The soothsayer presses forward and warns Caesar that although the ides have come, they have not yet passed. Artemidorus thrusts his letter at him, urging that it contains matter important to him personally, but the great man ignores it, seizing the moment to proclaim to all that his personal concerns "shall be last served." Another senator, Popilius, draws him aside in private conversation, raising fears among the conspirators that they have been betrayed. Their anxiety proves groundless, however, and they proceed as planned. Trebonius draws Antony off and, as agreed, Metullus appeals to Caesar for the pardon of his banished brother. He kneels to present his petition and Caesar scoffs at the gesture—"these couchings and lowly courtesies," he declares, "might fire the blood of ordinary men" but leave him unmoved. The conspirators gather about him, as if to add their pleas for clemency, and Caesar in answering them is insufferably pompous. "I could well be moved," he proclaims, "if I were as you"; but, he goes on, "I am as constant as the northern star," the one fixed "spark" in the sky, "unshaken by motion." He conjures up the image of universal order, comparing his constancy in human society to the one unchanging star in the heavens. The irony of this comparison is inescapable, since we have just seen Caesar change his mind twice, "moved" by the appeal of his wife and "shaken" by the taunts of Decius.

Casca, as planned, strikes him from behind and the noble Brutus from in front, the latter blow provoking the famous "Et tu, Brute? Then fall, Caesar!" The deed done and tension broken, the conspirators exult with shouts of triumph—"Liberty! Freedom! Tyranny is dead!"—and the more measured voice of Brutus—"Ambition's debt is paid." They urge Brutus and Cassius to speak to the people in justification of the cause, and senators not involved in the assassination are ushered out. Fear of reaction sets in, for all are aware that Caesar was greatly loved by the people. The first thought is of Antony, who, they are told, "has fled to his house amazed," and Brutus philosophizes about death. They all stoop and in solemn ritual bathe their hands in Caesar's blood as a pledge of their solidarity. A servant enters with a message from Antony asking that he be allowed to join them safely to hear "how Caesar hath deserved to lie in death." The message is full of praise for Brutus, promising that, once satisfied, Antony "shall not love Caesar dead / So well as Brutus living." Brutus agrees, confident that Antony will be reconciled to the justice of the deed. But Cassius has serious doubts.

Antony enters, kneels by the corpse, and takes his farewell. Rising, he confronts the murderers, professing himself ready to die. This is not mere rhetoric, for he knows well that political prudence would call for his death now. Indeed, all that stands between him and the assassins' knives is Brutus, whose conviction that they must be seen as "sacrificers, but not butchers" and "purgers, not murderers" restrains them. Brutus, confident that Antony will accept the purity of his motives, assures him that he is received "with all kind love, good thoughts and reverence." Cassius, less assured that these lofty sentiments will satisfy Antony, offers more practical inducements, promising that he will have an equal voice "in the disposing of new dignities." As a gesture of amity, Antony shakes hands with all, staining his own with Caesar's blood, but he glances once more at the body and is momentarily carried away by grief. An anxious Cassius interrupts, and Antony recovers to reaffirm his friendship with the party, asking only that he be permitted to display the corpse in the marketplace and deliver a eulogy. Brutus consents, though Cassius, again the realist,

argues against it. In the end it is agreed that Brutus will speak first and
that Antony will say nothing against the assassins. They depart, leaving
Antony alone with Caesar's body, and in his soliloquy we learn the
thoughts he has kept hidden under the mask of conciliation with "these
butchers," as he calls them. He is furious and promises vengeance for the
murder, prophesying that all of Italy will suffer "domestic fury and fierce
civil strife" when Caesar's spirit will "cry 'Havoc,' and let slip the dogs of
war" as a consequence of "this foul deed." Antony, burdened with grief
and inflamed by anger, is determined that not only the murderers but
Rome itself will answer for Caesar's death.

A servant enters to report that Octavius is en route to Rome, having
been summoned by Caesar, and Antony sends him back with the message
that the city is not yet safe for him.

3.2   The vast events to come, both in this play and next (*Antony and
Cleopatra*), Shakespeare implies, are precipitated by this next central
scene, where the fate of Rome seems to turn on the aroused instincts of its
volatile citizens. He has portrayed a vivid cast of factions competing for
power: Caesar is closely attuned to the concerns of the people and uses his
popularity to satisfy his boundless ambition. Brutus, high-minded, honest, and virtuous, represents the very best tradition of the old rule; others,
like Cassius and Casca, appear to be motivated chiefly by envy. The Senate itself seems an ineffectual body, the seat only of intrigue, and all are
subject to the whim of a dangerous and unruly Roman mob, who in
Shakespeare's portrayal can be swayed this way and that, pledging themselves to whomever speaks last.

In the Forum the plebeians demand satisfaction, and Cassius moves
off, followed by a body of citizens, leaving Brutus to justify the deed to
those who stay. We do not hear Cassius speak, but we may assume that
his words echo those of Brutus, who argues that Caesar's ambition was a
threat to Roman freedom. He was slain to save them from the fate of
"slaves" and "bondsmen." It is not an inspiring speech—Brutus is not a
charismatic orator—but it serves the purpose. As Antony appears, bearing Caesar's body, the crowd responds with favor to Brutus, some crying,
"let him be Caesar," others, "this Caesar was a tyrant." Satisfied, Brutus
leaves, asking them to attend to Antony.

Having agreed not to condemn the assassins, Antony begins cautiously, "I come to bury Caesar, not to praise him," and acknowledges

that "Brutus is an honorable man; / So are they all; all honorable men." He repeats this praise of the "honorable" Brutus time and again as he continues, slyly calling his sterling reputation into doubt, as Antony recites the phrase at first with subtle irony and eventually with biting sarcasm. He has no intention of abiding by his agreement to avoid criticism of the assassins, but given the sentiments of the crowd, who warn him initially to "speak no harm of Brutus here," he must tread carefully. To answer the claim that Caesar was ambitious—the only reason given for his murder—Antony reminds the people that he had refused the crown, a point that impresses the plebeians, who conclude that "'tis certain he was not ambitious." Antony then shifts his ground. Disclaiming any desire to "stir / Your hearts to mutiny and rage"—which he does indirectly by the very mention of them—he brings up the matter of Caesar's will, but begs that he not be called to read it for fear "it will inflame you, it will make you mad." The will, he says, appoints the people Caesar's heirs, a testament of his love for them. Urged on by the crowd, who now cry out that these "honorable men" are traitors, villains, and murderers, Antony overcomes his show of reluctance and agrees to read it. But first he will inflame them the more. He draws attention to Caesar's corpse, pointing out the holes in his mantle made by the knives of Cassius, Casca, and especially Brutus, "the most unkindest cut of all." Dropping all pretense now, he rages about "bloody Treason." In a dramatic gesture, he rips aside the mantle, uncovering the body itself, mutilated, he storms, by these same "traitors."

Antony has whipped the Roman crowd into an angry mob, who respond with cries of "Revenge! About! Seek! Burn! Fire! Kill! Slay! / Let not a traitor live!" He quiets them for a moment, but only to incite them further, again by indirection. He is no orator like Brutus, he says, but if he were, he would "move the stones of Rome to rise and mutiny." It takes no more than the mention of Brutus to focus the mob's wrath on him and raise the cry to burn his house. Having inflamed the Roman plebeians, Antony now throws tinder on the fire with an account of Caesar's will, which, he says, leaves a bequest to every citizen and donates his lands for use as public parks. The enraged mob rushes out to put all the conspirators' houses to the torch, missing an opportunity to slaughter them only because they have been forewarned and fled the city. Antony is well pleased: "Now let it work. Mischief, thou art afoot, / Take thou what course thou wilt." It is a masterful performance, opening with subtle innuendo and indirect accusations, ending with outright condemnation and a call to mutiny.

3.3   In the short scene that follows, Shakespeare offers insight into what is called today "crowd psychology." The plebeians confront Cinna the poet and attack him simply because he has the same name as one of the conspirators. The innocent suffer as well as the guilty, Shakespeare tells us, when they fall victim to the indiscriminate frenzy of an aroused and remorseless mob.

4.1   The opening scene of Act Four would seem to follow closely on these events. In order to achieve dramatic continuity, though, Shakespeare actually vaults over several months of civil conflict between Octavius and Antony, who became bitter antagonists, the former supporting the Senate, the latter seeking to destroy it. Octavius prevailed, but eventually the two became uneasy allies, forming with Lepidus "The Second Triumvirate." In the time sequence of the play, they are now the absolute rulers of the empire. Their purpose in meeting is to plan the utter destruction of the Senate as an effective force in the political life of Rome by eradicating the old aristocracy. They are drawing up a list of those to be executed, and each must agree to the deaths of friends and family in order to preserve the unity of their rule. Antony sends Lepidus off to secure Caesar's will, and when he leaves dismisses him as "a slight unmerited man." Octavius reproves him cautiously; and Antony replies that he has "seen more years than you" and is more experienced in public affairs, raising the issue of the disparity between their ages, alluded to frequently throughout these plays. At Caesar's death (45 B.C.) Octavius was a mere eighteen years old and Antony twice his age. The young man had only just been thrust into the public arena, while his companion was a seasoned soldier who had endured hard campaigns and had a reputation for both a dedication to his legions and a notoriously dissolute private life. As mentioned, Antony was devoted to Caesar and had expected to be designated his heir, only to find that Octavius was named instead. Shakespeare implies a strained relationship, one sustained only by the two men's shared love for Caesar and a common cause of perpetuating his legacy.

Antony has received information that "Brutus and Cassius / Are levying powers," and he announces that they must do likewise to meet the threat. The mobilization of armies sets the stage for the final confrontation between the new dictatorial rule of Rome and the old aristocracy, who are devoted to the sadly corrupted Senate and the faded ideal of the republic.

4.2–3   The balance of the play dramatizes events leading up to and including the battle of Philippi. Brutus and Cassius did indeed "levy powers," the former from the Roman provinces of Greece, the latter from Syria and the Middle East, while the triumvirate drew its forces from Italy and the West. Given the limitations of Shakespeare's *stage,* he could not depict the clash of great armies, hence his history plays dwell at some length on conferences and confrontations before the actual battle. We are presently in the camp of Brutus and Cassius, where it appears that a serious breach has developed between them. They retire to the privacy of a tent to air their grievances out of sight and hearing of their soldiers, who would be demoralized by the spectacle of their commanders in angry dispute.

Cassius complains first that Brutus has condemned one of his followers, Lucius Pella, for bribery, and Brutus responds that he cannot condone such measures to raise funds. They killed Caesar in the cause of justice, he proclaims, and none of their party should dishonor that cause by contaminating "our fingers with base bribes." Cassius is incensed, responding throughout the confrontation as if his anger might escape his control: "O ye gods, ye gods! must I endure all this?" and "Do not presume too much upon my love. / I may do that I shall be sorry for." Brutus, haughtily secure in his virtue, dismisses such threats, declaring himself "armed so strong in honesty" that he can chide those who are less so. Governing himself by a higher standard, he insists that he "can raise no money by vile means"—though in the same breath he complains that Cassius failed to send him gold to pay his legions, gold, it may be assumed, gained by these same "vile means." Cassius denies the accusation, and the argument grows more heated until, in a despairing gesture, he offers his dagger and bares his breast, urging Brutus to "strike, as thou didst at Caesar." This physical act, like Portia's display of her self-inflicted wound, reduces Brutus to submission, and the two are reconciled.

They call for wine to seal their reconciliation, and Brutus suddenly reveals the source of his ill humor: Portia has killed herself, and in an unimaginably horrible manner. Cassius is aghast: "How scaped I killing when I crossed you so?" but the stoic Brutus turns aside his sympathy— "Speak no more of her." Messala enters to confer, and Shakespeare brings us quickly up to date: "young Octavius" and Antony are on the move toward Philippi with a large army, having carried out their ruthless plan by executing a "hundred senators," the highly respected Cicero among them.* Messala asks cautiously if Brutus has had letters from his wife, and finally, after some prompting, reports on the death of Portia. This a strange moment in the play, as Brutus unaccountably acts as if he is hearing the news for the first time, seemingly staging the exchange for effect. His only response is a stoic, almost offhand "why, farewell, Portia. We must die, Messala"; and it seems to have the desired effect, for Messala is awed by his fortitude—"Even so great men great losses should endure." We can admire the self-control of Brutus and accept his desire to avoid a show of emotion to his friends or receive their sympathy, but it is troubling to watch him orchestrate a public display of his stoic composure in the face of a devastating private loss. Shakespeare leaves open the question of his state of mind, of just how much this "great loss" clouds his judgment during the hours ahead, but it has clearly shaken his spirit.

This entire scene has found disfavor with some observers, who remark that it does nothing to advance the plot or create dramatic tension. But it is clear what Shakespeare is about. These two men are to die, and Brutus, at least, has many of the marks of a tragic hero.† They have been absent from the stage for some time, however, and we need to know them better if their deaths are to have an impact on us. The bond between them is indeed a close one, and the fact that we sense they are doomed makes the scene all the more poignant.

Without further comment, the generals turn to a debate over military strategy. Cassius is opposed to confronting the enemy at Philippi, counseling a "nimble" defense to wear them down; but Brutus insists upon an open battle. "There is a tide in the affairs of men," he argues, "which taken at the flood leads on to fortune," and this is such a moment, an opportunity to be seized before it is lost. One must wonder how much his

---

*According to Plutarch, the death toll in their purge of the aristocracy was actually far larger, including wives and children of the leading Roman families.
†See "Tragedy," pp. 7–8.

impatience to join in battle is influenced by Portia's death. It is as if her loss renders questions of empire less important to him now, and he simply wants the matter settled without further delay. It is unclear whether the decision is a wise one—other factors entirely decide the outcome of the battle—but the strategy proposed by Cassius would have stretched the campaign out indefinitely, something Brutus is obviously unwilling to do. So he has his way and the others depart, leaving him alone.

The brief exchange that follows between Brutus, his servant Lucius, and the guards highlights his humanity and his concern for the well-being of those who serve him. Brutus is no martinet, nor is he distant and aloof from his subordinates. He is a deeply compassionate man whose stoic philosophy leaves room for a genuine love for his fellow humans, and Shakespeare stirs our sympathy for him. All settle down to sleep save for Brutus, whose studies are suddenly interrupted by the appearance of Caesar's ghost. It speaks ominously of meeting him again at Philippi, to which he responds with the same equanimity that marked his reaction to his wife's death: "Why, I will see thee at Philippi then." He is clearly unnerved by the apparition, however, for he shouts his sleeping guards awake and asks if they have seen anything. None have, so he is abruptly all business, sending an order to Cassius directing him to "set on his powers."

5.1   The final act opens on Antony and Octavius, where the younger man is obviously chafing at his elder's assumption of command. Octavius, perversely disregarding Antony's direction, demands that he lead the right wing of the army, and he will not be denied. The four opponents meet in parley, during which they do nothing but abuse one another, Cassius concluding with a contemptuous characterization of his enemies as "a peevish schoolboy . . . joined with a masker and a reveller!" They part to prepare for battle, and as Brutus speaks with Lucillius, Cassius confides in Messala that he has misgivings about the battle, citing the appearance of ignoble birds, "ravens, crows, and kites," which have replaced the eagles that accompanied them on their march.* Brutus returns, and the talk between the two is all of what they will do in the

---

*In ancient times the flight of birds was said to foretell the fate of humans.

event of defeat. Cassius begins with the thought that should they lose the battle, "then is this / The very last time we shall speak together"; and Brutus echoes him: "whether we shall meet again I know not. / Therefore our everlasting farewell take." These are stirring words, and we can be sure that Shakespeare is playing on the sentiments of the audience, who know the outcome of the battle. On the other hand, their state of mind almost sets them up for defeat. It is axiomatic in any contest, whether in sports, debate, or war, that those who compete convinced that they will lose, almost invariably do.

5.2–3 Shakespeare necessarily simplifies the battle for stage presentation, but he follows Plutarch in its general outline. Each side has two commanders and so each army has two wings, Brutus facing Octavius and Cassius facing Antony. When the forces clash, Brutus prevails over Octavius, but Antony overpowers Cassius. We join the action at the moment when Antony is pressing Cassius, who sends Titinius to determine whether some troops within sight are friend or foe. He asks his bondsman, Pindarus, to report on how his messenger is received, since, as he says, "my sight was ever thick." Pindarus sees Titinius "enclosed round about / With horsemen" and concludes that he has been taken prisoner. Cassius, convinced now of defeat, orders Pindarus to kill him, and he dies with the name of Caesar on his lips. Titinius, who has in fact been greeted with joy by Messala and his troops, returns to discover Cassius dead, and he finds the consequences catastrophic: "The sun of Rome is set! Our day is gone." He regrets that "mistrust of my success hath done this deed"; but Messala interprets his death in a wider context: "O hateful error, melancholy's child. / Why dost thou show to the apt thoughts of men / The things that are not?" We are reminded of the pessimistic parting of the two generals. Cassius, who was distressed at the decision to meet the enemy at Philippi and profoundly affected by his "melancholy" farewell from Brutus, seems to have been resigned to defeat, and so saw it where it was not. His death is, in modern terms, a self-fulfilled prophecy.

Messala leaves to inform Brutus, and the loyal Titinius, distraught by the death of Cassius, kills himself. Brutus comes upon the scene and is struck by its significance: "O Julius Caesar, thou art mighty yet!" There is no time for sorrow or funerals, however; he returns to the battle, where he has had success against the wing led by Octavius.

5.4–5 Antony, having disposed of Cassius's wing, now comes to the aid of Octavius and encounters Lucilius, who, in an effort to distract the advancing forces from his leader, claims to be Brutus. But Antony knows him and, admiring his courage, spares him, declaring that he would "rather have / Such men my friends than enemies."

As Antony's forces sweep all before them, Brutus, surrounded by his comrades, asks each in turn to slay him; but none will agree, replying as does Volumnius, "that's not an office for a friend, my lord." Shakespeare subtly elevates the stature of Brutus above that of Cassius, who had no difficulty finding someone to do the deed. His army scattered and his companions fled, Brutus is left alone with the loyal Strato, whom he persuades to hold a sword while he runs himself on it. His dying words, like those of Cassius, return us to the central event of the play: "Caesar, now be still: / I killed not thee with half so good a will." Antony and Octavius come upon the scene and it is Antony who speaks Brutus's epitaph: "This was the noblest Roman of them all." "His life was gentle," he concludes, "and the elements / So mixed in him that Nature might stand up / And say to all the world 'This was a man!'"

Unlike Shakespeare's other tragedies, *Julius Caesar* has no central figure, no Hamlet or Othello, about whom the play revolves. Caesar is the dominant character in the early scenes, though he has far fewer lines than the others; but he is killed at the beginning of Act Three to appear thereafter only as a corpse and briefly at the end as a ghost. Is he the tragic hero here? Certainly his spirit pervades the play, as Antony and Octavius complete his work by bending the Senate to their will. Antony emerges prominently in the central scene, though he must share the stage with Caesar's corpse, but it is the enigmatic Brutus who engages our sympathies in the final acts. So whom is the play about? If Brutus, then he is brought down not by a fatal flaw in his character but paradoxically by the nobility of his nature and his refusal to abandon principle—unless, of course, we perceive these qualities as flaws. But perhaps it might more properly be said that the central figure of the play is Rome itself, or the idea of Rome, whose ancient liberties under the republic were crushed beneath the weight of its greatness. The enormous wealth and scope of its empire, the absolute sway of its power over the known world, proved too much of a temptation to human ambition, and the republic fell, Shakespeare seems to say, a victim of its own success.

ANTONY AND CLEOPATRA

❧

THE EVENTS of *Antony and Cleopatra* follow closely upon those of *Julius Caesar*, but it is a very different play. Prominently, there can be little doubt as to whom the chief character is. Although the plot carries us from Rome to Alexandria, from Athens to Syria, the audience is never allowed to forget Cleopatra. Even when the action centers on Rome, Shakespeare constantly returns us to Egypt, as if to say that world-shaping events take on importance only in terms of her response to them, and the entire fifth act dramatizes her final hours. Shakespeare gives us a captivating woman who ensnares two emperors in the web of her allure and attempts to work her charms on a third. She plays throughout for high stakes, control of an empire, while remaining subject to the doubts and vacillations of a queen in love, torn between duty to her ancient kingdom and passion for Antony.

Because *Antony and Cleopatra* takes up where *Julius Caesar* leaves off, readers will find it useful to refer to the introductory remarks of the latter play for the earlier historical background. Having extinguished the last hope of the Senate and the republic at the battle of Philippi, and established themselves as the undisputed dictators of Rome, "The Second Triumvirate" divided up the empire, Caesar* to rule Rome and the western provinces, Mark Antony to preside over Greece, Egypt, and the East, and Lepidus over the lesser important kingdoms of Africa. Shakespeare's principal source, again, is Plutarch's *Parallel Lives of Greeks and Romans.* There this arrangement is recorded, Lepidus becoming in time inconsequential, until dissension arose between Caesar and Antony over the latter's seem-

---

*The "Octavius" of *Julius Caesar* is called "Caesar" in this play.

ing indifference to a threat posed to Rome by the powerful forces of the son of Pompey the Great, who bore his father's name.

It is at this point that *Antony and Cleopatra* opens. Captivated by the Egyptian queen, Antony immerses himself with her in a life of idle luxury and dissolute self-indulgence and neglects his responsibilities to the empire. Breaking away from Cleopatra, Antony returns to Rome, where he temporarily patches up his differences with Caesar. They neutralize Pompey, and as a sign of his good intentions Antony marries Caesar's sister, Octavia, and for a time settles down in Athens to a responsible life. But the draw of Egypt is too powerful. He deserts Octavia, returns to Cleopatra, and marries her. The two emperors raise forces in preparation for the inevitable clash, which comes at Actium, where Caesar prevails. Antony flees to Egypt with Caesar in pursuit. There, hearing erroneously that Cleopatra has committed suicide, he wounds himself fatally; rather than submit to Caesar, she ends her life with the bite of a poisonous asp. Caesar emerges as the sole dictator of Rome, establishing a line of emperors that rule for the next four hundred years. Shakespeare, making allowances for dramatic effect, is faithful to this history, animating the bare chronicle with compelling characters and memorable poetry.

In this play, more perhaps than any other, Shakespeare employs the image of *place* to dramatic effect. Egypt is a world devoted to the senses, to frivolous diversion and the pursuit of pleasure. In Cleopatra's extravagant court, the nights are filled with sumptuous feasts, drunken revelry, and sensual excess. An infatuated Antony, who is known already for his earthy instincts and loose behavior, gives himself over entirely to these decadent delights. Enslaved by his own nature and Cleopatra's seductive appeal, he neglects his duties as one of the "triple pillars of the world" and is transformed, in the judgment of one of his captains, "into a strumpet's fool."

In contrast, Rome is the image of civic responsibility, filled with grave men who talk of governance and power, peace and war, of order, conquest, and dominion. A statesmanlike Caesar strives to hold the empire together against the threat of Pompey and complains bitterly that Antony has lost himself in lascivious pursuits, neglecting his imperial duties. Egypt, then, is an image of a human desire to throw off the irksome restraints of an ordered life, and Rome of the need for dedicated labor and sacrifice in the cause of stable society—the one a surrender to fantasy, the other a stern call to reality. Antony is torn between the two, and as the play opens Cleopatra feels her hold on him weakening. *Antony and Cleopatra* is not a morality play, however, and Shakespeare does not judge between Rome and Egypt, each of which has its own dark dimension. He is content simply to place them before us as twin impulses of the same human spirit, reflecting our ambivalence toward the inner conflict between the attraction to sensual pleasure and our anxious desire for order and continuity in life.

1.1   The play opens in Egypt, where two minor figures set the scene for us. Philo, one of Antony's officers, describes to Demetrius, who has just arrived from Rome, the degree to which their master has fallen under the sway of Cleopatra. This mighty captain, whom they had often admired as he surveyed "the files and musters of war," now has eyes only for "a tawny front." Cleopatra is imagined as darker-skinned than the Romans; and in Philo's mind Antony's warlike nature has been subdued to serve "a gipsy's lust."

Antony and Cleopatra enter, speaking of love, and are approached by an attendant with a report from Rome. Antony addresses him impatiently—"grates me! the sum"—but Cleopatra insists that he hear the news. She taunts him with the mocking implication that he is at the beck and call of others. Perhaps Fulvia, his Roman wife, is angry with him, she scoffs, or "the scarce-bearded Caesar" has tasks for him. Octavius Caesar, his co-emperor, is some twenty years Antony's junior, a matter of frequent comment both here and in *Julius Caesar.*

Antony's response to her mockery is to dismiss the call to duty that Rome represents and instead to embrace Cleopatra: "Let Rome in Tiber melt, and the wide arch / Of the ranged empire fall! Here is my space." "What sport tonight?" he asks. When she taunts him again to hear the news, he utters the first of many passages in which Shakespeare captures the paradoxical appeal of the woman: "Fie, wrangling queen! / Whom every thing becomes, to chide, to laugh, / To weep." She can do anything, even as here "to chide" Antony about his wife and his duty, and it only adds to her allure. He is indeed enthralled. Demetrius is shocked that he should dismiss a message from Caesar in so cavalier a fashion. Philo explains that he has not been himself of late.

1.2   In the following scene we enter the court of Cleopatra, which modern productions can furnish lavishly with all the trappings of a sumptuous and decadent Eastern palace. On Shakespeare's bare *stage,* however, the poet had to reflect the flavor of the court in the words of its attendants—here Charmian and Iras, Cleopatra's handmaidens; Mardian, a eunuch; and Alexas, frequently portrayed as homosexual. We also see Enobarbus, of whom more later. They wile away the hours with erotic wit and as a diversion consult a soothsayer, a palm reader who tells their fortune in brief, obscure predictions packed with *dramatic irony* for an audience well aware of Cleopatra's fate. They banter back and forth about marriage, children, sex, cuckolds, and whores, until Cleopatra approaches. She is concerned because Antony was at one moment "disposed to mirth" but grew abruptly solemn, she complains, when struck with "a Roman thought."

Antony enters, more attentive now to the news from Rome, and Cleopatra leaves with her court. The news is not good. His wife, Fulvia, has been making trouble in Rome, finally joining with her brother to challenge Caesar. In the east the forces of Parthia have overrun "Syria / To Lidia and Ionia," threatening control of Antony's third of the empire, all this while he has been dallying with Cleopatra in Alexandria. He is all too aware of his bondage: "These strong Egyptian fetters I must break, / Or lose myself in dotage." Next comes news of Fulvia's death, which strengthens his resolve: "I must from this enchanting queen break off."

Antony announces his decision to Enobarbus, who responds with a series of witty comments on Cleopatra's anticipated reaction. When informed of Fulvia's death, he replies that "when old robes are worn out there are members to make new,"—that is, Antony is now free to marry Cleopatra. Enobarbus's chatter annoys Antony, who silences him with an abrupt "no more light answers" and then informs him of the threat to Rome. Sextus Pompeus, the son of Pompey the Great, has gained control of the seas, and they must return to confront him.

Enobarbus is a complex figure. At times, as here, he acts the clown, entertaining with his sometimes biting wit; but he is also a knowing man, entirely loyal to Antony. He is somewhat dissolute himself, an apt companion to his master, one who seems to fit comfortably into the life of the Egyptian court. He is, however, the essential cynic, the arch observer of others' follies, a jaded realist whose evaluation of events we come to rely on. He realizes that Antony can never break Cleopatra's hold on him and seems inordinately fond of her himself. When a frustrated Antony remarks that he wishes he had never seen her, Enobarbus replies, "O, sir, you had then left unseen a wonderful piece of work." He acts at times in the role of a *chorus,* interpreting events from the point of view of one close to the action but at the same time standing outside it, the observer who sees developments clearly.

These scenes give us a sense of the vast setting of the play. The dialogue skips across three continents in a moment, from Egypt to Italy, from Syria to Sicyon (Greece), where Fulvia lies dead. Shakespeare's stage in *Antony and Cleopatra* is the known world, but the dramatic center of that world is Cleopatra's chamber. The great events chronicled in the play—the wars, deaths, battles, and shifting alliances of the empire— seem to matter only in so far as they affect the passions of that "enchanting queen."

1.3 Cleopatra tries to prevent Antony's return to Rome, and we have a glimpse of the ways in which she retains her hold over him. She attracts him through perversity, by keeping him emotionally off balance; and since everything becomes her, "to chide, to laugh, to weep," she has had some success. She sends Alexas in search of him with instructions that "if you find him sad, / Say I am dancing; if in mirth, report / That I am sudden sick." Charmian disapproves of her design to counter his every mood, advising that she should "in each thing give him way, cross him in nothing." But Cleopatra scoffs at the thought: "Thou teachest like a fool: the way to lose him."

Antony enters, and she decides to be sick. He cannot get a word in edgewise in the exchange that follows, as she accuses him of deceiving her. "Bid farewell, and go," she says plaintively. But her suffering has a sting—if he does "go" to Fulvia, she declares, he will be branded the world's "greatest liar." Finally in exasperation he commands, "hear me, queen," and explains that Pompey's rebellion demands his presence in Rome. He concludes with the news of Fulvia's death, but Cleopatra turns even that to her advantage, claiming that, since he mourns Fulvia's loss so little, she can see how her own death will be received. She continues to accuse him of "excellent dissembling" until, now thoroughly vexed, he announces abruptly, "I'll leave you, lady," and turns to go. Sensing his resolve, she drops all pretense. "Courteous lord, one word," she pleads, and attempts to convey her sense of desolation at his departure. They have loved and must part, she says, "but that's not it," the cause of her despair. Emotion rises to a level where language falters, and Shakespeare's poetry soars beyond meaning as she cries out, "O, my oblivion is a very Antony, / And I am all forgotten." The phrase is almost incomprehensible but it captures perfectly the essence of her sorrow. Resigned now, she recovers, bids him farewell, wishes him success—"upon your sword / Sit laurel victory!"—and they leave together.

The question of the play—and of history—is the depth of Cleopatra's love for Antony. Certainly the autonomy of Egypt as a nation depends upon the good will of the emperor Antony; at this point her devotion to her ancient kingdom is not in conflict with her love for him—but this will not always be the case. She expresses no interest in the threat of Pompey; her talk is all of Fulvia. She shows no concern here for the empire or for Egypt, though political concerns are never far from the surface of their talk. Clearly in this scene Shakespeare's Cleopatra is a woman in love, suffering from the pain of Antony's departure, in comparison to which questions of dominion, so prominent in Rome, sink to insignificance.

1.4 The next scene carries us to Rome, where the other two members of the Second Triumvirate are in conference. Caesar complains about Antony's dalliance in Alexandria, and Lepidus attempts to excuse him. Lepidus is the least of the three men and is disposed of later in the play, but here he has the essential role of mediator between the other two. Caesar is unmoved—"you are too indulgent"—and while admitting that there is nothing wrong with a "tumble in the bed of Ptolemy," he argues that a grown man should be able to recognize his public obligations. A messenger reports that Pompey is "strong at sea" and pirates prey on shipping at will, a perilous threat to a Rome almost entirely dependent on imports to feed the city's volatile population. A frustrated Caesar pleads, "Antony, / Leave thy lascivious wassails," and recalls his courage and tenacity on an earlier occasion when had been defeated and was on the run. They depart to muster their forces against Pompey.

1.5 In Alexandria, a short time after Antony's departure, Cleopatra is beside herself. "O Charmian," she asks, "where think'st thou he is now? Stands he, or sits he? / Or does he walk? or is he on his horse?" Alexas enters, having seen Antony off earlier, and Cleopatra questions him eagerly: "What was he, sad or merry?" The diplomatic Alexas, who knows his

place and means to keep it, reports that he was neither. Cleopatra interprets his words to please herself, reasoning that for Antony to appear sad
would discourage his followers, and to be merry would reveal that his
thoughts were with her. Her mind jumps about restlessly as she first asks
Alexas if her letters are being delivered, then reminisces with Charmian
about her former conquests. "Did I," she asks, "ever love Caesar so?" This
is the dead Julius, whom she had charmed during his Egyptian campaign, and, it was said, by whom she had a son, the boy Caesarion. She recalls with delight her power over Pompey the Great as well, who, she
says, "would stand and make his eyes grow in my brow."

Cleopatra recalls her time with Caesar as "my salad days. / When I
was green in judgment, cold in blood," one of two references in the scene
to her perception of herself as "an older woman," the first being her remark that she is "with Phoebus' amorous pinches black / And wrinkled
deep in time." In fact, at the time she was twenty-nine years old, at the
height of her beauty and appeal (Antony was forty-three), and indeed
lived another ten years. Shakespeare seems to conceive of her as older, perhaps to heighten our sympathy for a woman who is conscious of her fading beauty and regrets the passing of her youth. The poet collapses time
in many ways, speeding us across the years as readily as he carries us back
and forth from one corner of the empire to another, and he does so to create a sense of continuity in the action of the play. He chooses what to include and what to omit of that eventful decade between the meeting and
the death of the two lovers, so as to maintain a dramatic focus on their
tragic passion.

2.1   Save for one scene, Act Two is set in Italy, but the continual talk
of Egypt keeps Cleopatra ever before us. She is on the thoughts of every
man, a silent presence at the council tables of the great. Pompey is convinced that Antony is still with her, and he utters the hope that she will
keep him ensnared in "the charms of love" so that "sleep and feeding may
prorogue [suspend] his honor." News arrives that Antony is in Rome,
however, and though Menas alludes hopefully to the enmity between him
and Caesar, Pompey thinks it prudent that they prepare, since "fear of
us / May cement their divisions."

2.2   In Rome, Lepidus has arranged a meeting of the feuding rulers.
He urges Enobarbus "to entreat your captain / To soft and gentle speech,"

though Enobarbus, if anything, seems more incensed than Antony. The two emperors enter, pointedly ignoring one another until Lepidus addresses them. After a brief moment of strained uncertainty as to who will sit first, they begin their parlay. Caesar has grievances: Antony's wife, Fulvia, had made war on him; his messengers have been rudely dismissed; and he was refused the promised "arms and aid" from Antony against her. Antony excuses his neglect at a time "when poisoned hours had bound me up" so that he hardly knew himself. He asks pardon for Fulvia, who, he says, made war only "to have me out of Egypt."

The two are reconciled, but Caesar expresses doubt that the alliance will last. Agrippa proposes that to seal the bond between them Antony marry Caesar's sister, Octavia. It is so agreed, and the triumvirs depart to confer on the matter at hand, Pompey's growing strength. The stage is left to Enobarbus and Caesar's captains, Agrippa and Maecenas, who have heard tales of Egypt, of "eight wild-boars roasted whole at a breakfast" for one thing, and are eager to question Enobarbus about life in the East. He embellishes somewhat on the tales and offers to tell them of the meeting of the two lovers.

Shakespeare is faithful here to Plutarch's account, which describes Antony seated in state at the marketplace in Tarsus, prepared to receive the tribute of the empire's kings and magistrates, among them Cleopatra. She chose not to attend him there but arrived instead on the banks of the river Cydnus in an elaborately decorated and perfumed barge, where she lay in her golden pavilion, "o'er-picturing that Venus where we see / The fancy outwork nature," as Enobarbus puts it. Agrippa listens, slack-jawed in fascination: "O, rare for Antony!" The citizens of Tarsus, hearing of her approach, rushed to the riverside, leaving Antony seated alone in the marketplace. Agrippa is speechless: "Rare Egyptian!" Antony took no offense, however, and invited her to supper, but she replied with an invitation of her own—and the rest, as they say, is history. Shakespeare reduces Plutarch's prose to some thirty lines of incomparable descriptive poetry, which engage all our senses in the telling.

These are memorable lines, as are those that follow, in which Enobarbus describes Cleopatra herself in terms that recall Antony's praise of her as a woman "whom every thing becomes." He recalls seeing her out of breath after running, when even as she "panted" she made "defect perfection." Enobarbus is convinced that Antony will never desert her, for "age cannot wither her, nor custom stale / Her infinite variety," a woman who "makes hungry / Where most she satisfies." Again, her every act "becomes" her, so that even "the holy priests / Bless her when she is riggish [wanton]." Enobarbus acts somewhat in the role of a *chorus* here, bringing us up to date and interpreting the unfolding events. But he is entirely in character, enjoying the attention of a rapt audience as he spins his tale of strange sights in distant lands.

2.3–4 In the brief scene that follows, the marriage between Antony and Octavia is arranged. When Antony is alone, a soothsayer enters, urging him to avoid competing with Caesar, for "if thou play with him at any game," he warns, "thou art sure to lose." Antony dismisses him but acknowledges that truth of what he says. "I will to Egypt," he resolves, "and though I make this marriage for my peace, / I'th'East my pleasure lies." Meanwhile, matters of state occupy his attention: Ventidius is to lead an army against the Parthians, and Lepidus arranges for a rendezvous at Misenum, where they will parlay with Pompey.

2.5 We return to Alexandria to learn how Cleopatra responds to these developments. She is restless, calling for music and then silencing it, suggesting a game of billiards, and then conjuring up an elaborate fantasy about fishing for Antony. She reminisces in striking lines that capture their passionate relationship:

> I laughed him out of patience; and that night
> I laughed him into patience; and next morn,
> Ere the ninth hour, I drunk him to his bed,
>
> . . . .
> [And] wore his sword Philippan.*

It is the image, again, of attraction through adversity, keeping Antony off balance and ending with reconciliation in the pleasures of the bed. She revels in her former power over him—but now he is beyond her reach.

The play abounds in Shakespeare's erotic imagery. His Egypt is a land famed for the pursuit of sensual pleasure, and his lovers are a mature man and woman, not teenage novices. On the Elizabethan stage, Cleopatra was played by a boy buckled into stiff brocade to hide his masculinity, and the play's Romans strutted about swathed in bedsheets, leaving little

---

*The sword he wielded at the battle of Philippi.

opportunity for the intimate embraces that pass for love on the modern stage and screen. Shakespeare's moralistic monarch, James I, proscribed indecency on the stage; but the poet found many ways to enhance Cleopatra's sensuality, among them a liberal sprinkling of phallic symbols in her lines: "I would I had thy inches"; "I wore his sword Philippan," and all references to "sword"; and "The soldier's pole is fallen."

A messenger arrives with news from Rome, but before he can begin, an excited and apprehensive Cleopatra warns him that if he values his life, the news had better be good. She finally calms down long enough to be told that Antony has married Octavia, at which she becomes so incensed that she beats the messenger, finally drawing a dagger to slay him. She is unmoved by his reasonable plea that though he brought the news, he "made not the match." He wisely runs off, only to be summoned back. Now more in control, she asks him to confirm the report, and when he does, she angrily dismisses him once more, only to order him to return and give an account of Octavia's appearance. She is desolate: "Pity me Charmian, / But do not speak to me. Lead me to my chamber."

2.6 The next two scenes are really one, dramatizing the accord reached with Pompey and the celebration thereafter. Such scenes must have appealed enormously to Shakespeare's audiences, as he imagines conversations between the great and near-great deciding the shape of their world. His characters are not wooden statesmen, however, and his scenes are animated by undercurrents that make them compelling figures, in this case the barely healed animosity between Antony and Caesar, the obvious mistrust between Pompey and the triumvirs, Antony's oversensitivity to any mention of Egypt, and the apparent danger of accepting Pompey's invitation to feast aboard his ship.

The emperors enter and are greeted by a bit of bluster from Pompey—"we shall talk before we fight"—bluster because, while he is "absolute master" at sea, he knows he cannot match their strength on land. The return of Antony, the most seasoned soldier of the three, weighs heavily in their favor. Pompey has taken up arms, he declares, in order to restore his father's good name. The emperors listen patiently but quickly come to the point when he is finished—will he accept their offer? He is to have Sicily and Sardinia and must agree to rid the sea of pirates, this last uttered with perhaps a glance at Menas, who is one of them. Pompey accepts the offer, they shake hands, and he begins to ask Antony about

Cleopatra and Egypt. Enobarbus, sensing a rising anger in the volatile Antony, anxiously deflects the questions. The four principals depart to attend a celebratory feast, leaving Enobarbus alone on stage with Menas, who is also curious about the relationship between Antony and Cleopatra. He is surprised, he says, to hear of the marriage to Octavia, and Enobarbus offers the opinion that it will not last. Octavia, he observes, "is of a holy, cold, and still conversation," and Antony in time "will to his Egyptian dish again," so that the source of present amity will be the cause of future enmity between the two emperors.

2.7   In the following scene the feast aboard Pompey's galley is well advanced and all have drunk too much, especially Lepidus, who is much the worse for it. Antony is explaining to Caesar about the ebb and flow of the Nile when Lepidus intrudes to ask about the crocodile. Antony's answer reveals his contempt for the man: it is as broad as it is broad, as high as it is high; it is of its own color and moves and eats. Lepidus, very much in his cups, is fascinated by this mockery of an answer and can only repeat, " 'tis a strange serpent." Egypt is a constant source of conversation in these scenes and Cleopatra never far from the thoughts of the men.

During this exchange, Menas draws Pompey aside to propose that they cut the ship's cable, set it adrift, and murder the three emperors. Pompey's sense of honor will not permit him to violate the strong tradition of a host's sacred obligation to his guests, however, and he refuses, regretting that Menas had even mentioned it to him: "This thou shouldst have done, / And not have spoke on't." If Menas had acted on his own, Pompey says, he would have praised him for it, but under the circumstances he "must condemn it now"—reasoning that prompts Menas to abandon him. Pompey's honor, like that of Brutus, proves his downfall.

They return to the feast, where Lepidus is now falling-down drunk and has to be carried off. Enobarbus suggests an Egyptian dance and song—"cup us, till the world go round"—but a more sober Caesar finally calls a halt to the celebration. They leave and, as Enobarbus watches Pompey start down the gangplank, he mutters sardonically, "take heed you fall not." He and Menas remain aboard to continue the festivities. For them the night is still young!

3.1   Act Three opens on the plains of Asia, where Antony's captain, Ventidius, has defeated the Parthian army. Silius, one of his officers, urges him to pursue the enemy into Mesopotamia and thoroughly crush them, but Ventidius replies with the acquired wisdom of a survivor in this world divided between proud and contentious emperors. It would be unwise, he cautions, to be too successful, else he will arouse Antony's envy: "Better to leave undone than by our deed / Acquire too high a fame when him we serve's away." Rather, he says, they will report the victory in Athens and take care to attribute their success to Antony's "name, / That magical word of war."

3.2 In Rome, Agrippa, Caesar's captain, and Enobarbus, Antony's, try to outdo each other in heaping praise on the other's master, and by implication to diminish Lepidus. They stand aside as the triumvirs enter with Octavia to bid farewell to the couple as they leave for Athens, designated Antony's capital of the Eastern Empire. The scene lends emphasis to Caesar's strong affection for his sister and his fear, echoing Enobarbus, that while she is meant to be "the cement" of amity between the two emperors, she might become "the ram to batter / The fortress of it." Antony, as we know, has long since decided that he will return to Cleopatra, so his pledges of devotion ring hollow, rendering Caesar's fears an ominous foreshadowing of the break between them.

3.3 In Alexandria we take up the action where the previous scene there left off, as if to imply that the serious events we have witnessed carry little weight in Egypt, where time ticks to a different measure. Cleopatra calls the messenger back to question him about Octavia, but having once been subject to her anger, he is reluctant to repeat the experience. He is persuaded to return, and in the interval, it would appear, has received some advice about how to address Cleopatra. Octavia, he observes cautiously, is shorter than the queen and low-voiced. Cleopatra hears what she wants to hear—"dull of tongue and dwarfish"—and asks if there is majesty in her gait, reminding the messenger that he is in the presence of majesty. Warming to his task, he reports that "she creeps," that her demeanor is more like that of a statue than a woman. Cleopatra is pleased. "He's very knowing," she concludes, a man of "good judgment." She rewards him and promises to employ him, now a man "most fit for business," to carry letters back to Antony.

3.4–5 The next three scenes record the falling out between Antony and Caesar, and Shakespeare must pass over or condense a great deal of history. After an interval of some months during which Antony has been behaving himself in Athens, he learns that Caesar has taken steps to discredit him. He complains to Octavia that Caesar has insulted him in public and waged war on Pompey in violation of their agreement. She pleads with him for patience, grieving that when a brother and a husband are in conflict, whoever wins, it is the wife who loses. He claims his honor is at stake but agrees to employ her as a go-between to Caesar. It is clear what he intends: as soon as she leaves for Rome, he sets sail for Alexandria, and Cleopatra.

The conversation between Enobarbus and Eros, both in Antony's camp, fills in some of the intervening events. In the war with Pompey, Caesar finds occasion to discredit and imprison Lepidus until, as Eros says, "death enlarge his confine." * Pompey has been killed, as it happens by one of Antony's own officers, which infuriates him, since it deprives him of a potential ally against Caesar. The two emperors are gathering forces in anticipation of a war.

3.6 Some time still later, it is Caesar's turn to complain about Antony's actions. He has returned to Alexandria and divided up the Eastern Empire, declaring Cleopatra and her children, by Julius Caesar and himself, to be rulers of its several kingdoms. Octavia enters, and Caesar is angry that she has been received with so little ceremony. She learns from him that Antony has returned to Cleopatra and is marshaling his forces.

3.7 As the opposing armies converge on Actium, Cleopatra insists that she accompany Antony. Enobarbus argues that her presence will distract him, but she is determined to stay. Antony enters, puzzled by the swiftness with which Caesar has crossed the sea to confront him. He announces that he will fight him by sea, a resolve that Cleopatra seconds. When asked why, Antony replies curtly, "for that he dares us to't." Enobarbus argues against such a strategy, contending that their navy is ill-manned by inexperienced conscripts while Caesar's ships, fresh from the war with Pompey, are served by seasoned sailors. He urges that they fight on land, where Antony has the advantage of his "absolute soldiership." Antony remains adamant, however, and is supported again by Cleopatra, who is proud of her Egyptian fleet of "sixty sails." Antony's captain,

---

*Shakespeare is unhistorical here, leaving the impression that Lepidus has been disposed of. In fact Caesar simply stripped him of his powers as emperor and appropriated his land. He was relegated to a lesser position and indeed outlived Antony by many years, dying in 13 B.C.

Canidius, observes that nothing can be done now that "our leader's led, / And we are women's men."

It is not clear why Antony makes the controversial decision to fight at sea, where he will be at a disadvantage, rather than on land where he is in his natural element. Shakespeare strongly implies that Cleopatra persuades him to adopt the strategy but gives no reason other than Antony's remark that Caesar "dares us to't." The play, following Plutarch, leaves the impression that had Cleopatra not been present, Antony would have chosen otherwise. Caesar, we learn, is in the vicinity of Actium at the mouth of Greece's Sea of Corinth.

3.8–10 Three short scenes dramatize the battle itself.* Briefly, the armies remain in place while the navies fight it out, and Caesar's proves the superior of the two. At a critical point in the battle, Cleopatra inexplicably hoists the sails of her fleet and flees, and Antony, disheartened by her desertion, abandons his forces to pursue her. His navy is soundly defeated; his army either disperses or, as in the case of Canidius, joins forces with Caesar.

3.11 We return to Alexandria some time later, where Antony is distraught over his desertion at Actium. He urges his soldiers to flee, offering them his treasure to divide among them, but they refuse. Cleopatra enters in what is dramatized as their first encounter since the defeat, and Eros urges her to comfort Antony, who is reminiscing about his courage at Philippi. He finally acknowledges her presence: "O whither hast thou led me, Egypt?" She pleads that she did not anticipate his response to her flight—"forgive my fearful sails! I little thought / You would have followed"—but he replies that she knew full well he would, that "my sword, made weak by my affection, would / Obey it on all cause." Her tears subdue his anger—"give me a kiss; / Even this repays me." Actium is forgiven.

3.12 Caesar has followed up his victory by pursuing Antony into Egypt. At his camp outside Alexandria he receives Antony's envoy, who presents his offer: he asks that he be permitted to retire to private life in Athens and that Cleopatra, after she has submitted to Caesar, be allowed

---

*Actium was a massive military effort for ancient times. Contemporary accounts, perhaps exaggerated, estimate the strength of the opposing forces as: Antony—500 warships, 100,000 foot soldiers, and 12,000 cavalry; Caesar—400 warships, 80,000 foot soldiers, and 12,000 cavalry.

to see her heirs continue the line of Ptolemies as monarchs of Egypt. Caesar dismisses Antony's request, but will consider Cleopatra's if she will drive her husband from Egypt or have him killed. He then employs Thidias as an envoy to Cleopatra, with instructions to separate her from Antony by promising her whatever she asks.

3.13 In Alexandria, Enobarbus places blame for the defeat at Actium entirely on Antony, who, he says, erred in making "his will [lust] / Lord of his reason." Antony enters, attending to his envoy's reply from "the boy Caesar," and in a gesture of defiance sends him back with the challenge of individual combat between the two, "sword against sword," to decide the issues between them. After Antony departs, Enobarbus scoffs at the proposal, convinced now that his master has completely lost "his judgment."

Thidias enters and attempts to win Cleopatra to Caesar's side, He cleverly reports to her that his master is aware that "you embraced not Antony / As you did love, but as you feared him," to which she replies with an enigmatic "O!" The actress in the part will guide our response to Cleopatra by the manner in which she delivers that single "O!" Does she do so with a dismissive shrug, or as if she welcomes the suggestion and is encouraging Thidias to continue? She loved Antony as long as he was emperor and rewarded her with the crown of Egypt, but now that he has been brought low and her only hope of remaining in power is to embrace Caesar, does she betray him? Enobarbus, at any rate, has heard enough. He addresses the absent Antony: "Sir, sir, thou art so leaky / That we must leave thee to thy sinking, for / Thy dearest quit thee." But is he a reliable judge? Thidias, too, finds her reply receptive and warms to his task, promising her anything she desires if she will desert Antony and place herself under Caesar's protection. Cleopatra replies in carefully veiled terms that she will "kiss his conqu'ring hand" and lay her crown at his feet. Thidias, satisfied that his mission has been accomplished, asks if he may kiss her hand as a courtly gesture upon his departure. She extends her hand and he bends over it—as Antony bursts upon the scene.

However we may interpret the episode, Antony sees only betrayal in it. "Ah, you kite [whore]!" he rages at her, and then orders Thidias whipped. This is an egregious insult, since an envoy traditionally traveled under his monarch's protection, and any injury to the servant was considered a hostile act against the master. Antony then turns on Cleopatra, accusing her of harlotry, of seducing Julius Caesar, Pompey the Great, and many others "unregistered in vulgar fame." He rages against her for letting anyone "be familiar with / My playfellow, your hand." She can only respond with exclamations of distress: "O, is't come to this?" and "Wherefore is this?" Thidias, having been whipped, is brought back, and Antony turns his wrath on him for playing with "the white hand of a lady." Caesar "has made me angry with him," he storms, and sends the suffering Thidias back with the message that in retaliation he should feel free to "whip, or hang, or torture" any of Antony's hostages he holds.

When Thidias leaves, Antony seems to sink into deep despair, plaintively asking Cleopatra if she is "cold-hearted toward me." She replies with an impassioned speech, declaring that if it be so, then she, her children, and all her "brave Egyptians" should be destroyed and "lie graveless, till the flies and gnats of Nile / Have buried them for prey!" Her ardent words are enough for Antony. "I am satisfied," he replies simply, and, buoyed apparently by her profession of love, is himself again. Alive now with his old confidence, he will fight on, challenge Caesar, and restore his honor, even if he must die in doing so. "Call to me / All my sad captains," he orders, and together they will "have one other gaudy [festive] night" in which he will speak to them and raise their spirits. They hurry off on this hopeful note, leaving behind Enobarbus, who finds the scene ludicrous. "A diminution of our captain's brain / Restores his heart," he observes, and decides to "seek / Some way to leave him."

4.1–3 Predictably Caesar is incensed by Antony's reply. He refuses the challenge to individual combat, since as he says caustically, he has "many other ways to die," and gives orders for an attack the following day. In Cleopatra's palace, Antony is disappointed at his refusal but prepares himself for battle.* He calls for his servants and, in a scene almost maudlin in its sentiment, asks them to serve him well tonight, for "haply you shall not see me more." Cleopatra is dismayed at his behavior, and Enobarbus, in an *aside* to her, sees it as yet another mark of Antony's instability: " 'Tis one of those odd tricks which sorrow shoots / Out of the mind." He weeps at the sight and reproaches Antony, who laughs off the

---

*Antony calls Enobarbus "Domitius" here, the historical figure in Plutarch upon whom the character is based.

display and assures him that he is confident of victory the next day—but tonight they will feast.

In a brief scene, some common soldiers hear strange music and interpret it as the departure of Hercules, Antony's godlike patron. This is the only intrusion of the supernatural in the play. Like the soothsayer's predictions, it foreshadows Antony's fate.

4.4   Some hours later, Antony dons his armor in preparation for battle. In a brief, brilliant episode, Shakespeare adds a lighthearted touch to the play as Cleopatra insists on helping him and with playful impatience he attempts to dissuade her. Several soldiers enter, whom Antony encourages; he then takes his farewell of Cleopatra with "a soldier's kiss." "I'll leave thee / Now like a man of steel," rendered impregnable, he implies, by her love.

4.5–9   The next few scenes depict the battle itself, with human interest provided by the tragic fate of Enobarbus. In brief, Antony's forces prevail on land, but he loses the battle at sea, ushering in what Caesar rather grandly calls "the time of universal peace" when the world "shall bear the olive freely."

Enobarbus deserts and joins Caesar's camp. Antony, in a sadly magnanimous gesture, directs that all his belongings be sent to him. This act of generosity weighs heavily on the load of guilt that Enobarbus bears— "I am alone the villain of the earth"—so much so that he refuses to fight against his former master, preferring rather to "seek / Some ditch wherein to die." He does indeed die, with Antony's name on his lips, apparently of a broken heart.

4.10–12   Caesar prepares to challenge Antony by sea, and defeats him when the Egyptian fleet deserts and joins the imperial navy. Antony places the blame for their treachery on Cleopatra, raging, "this foul Egyptian hath betrayed me." She comes upon him and he turns on her, threatening to kill her and deprive Caesar of his triumph, when, he predicts, she will be forced to "follow his chariot, like the greatest spot [disgrace] / Of all thy sex." Frightened by his threat, she leaves, and he resolves that "the witch shall die" for her treachery in selling him "to the young Roman boy."

The tantalizing question, of course, is the degree to which Antony's suspicions are justified. Does Cleopatra intend to abandon him now that he has lost everything? She has a history of allying herself with the victor in the power struggles that afflicted Rome during her lifetime, and Antony is convinced that she has done so again. The scenes to follow leave no doubt that she loves him, but they leave open the question whether she loves Egypt more. As Shakespeare portrays her, she represents the classic conflict between love and duty. He leaves it to us to decide which rules her.

The prospect of Caesar's "triumph," first mentioned here, becomes increasingly important in the plot. When a Roman general, or as here an emperor, won an important victory, he was honored with a parade through the capital, one in which his captive enemies, often in chains, walked submissively behind his chariot, subject to the jeers of the spectators. The "triumph" was all the more effective if an enemy king or general was among the prisoners, on display as a symbol of the victor's prowess. Anticipating such an event, Caesar orders that Antony be captured alive and later directs that every effort be made to prevent Cleopatra from killing herself.

4.13–14 Cleopatra, fearing for her life, seeks refuge in her "monument," a secure structure in her palace built for easy defense. She orders Mardian to tell Antony that she has killed herself, a device that recalls her earlier masquerade to maintain her hold over him. Once again she will cross his mood in the hope that sorrow will subdue his anger, but the stakes are much higher now.

A despondent Antony laments his loss, more of Cleopatra, it seems, than his empire, but his anger rises again as Mardian approaches him: "She hath betrayed me, and shall die the death." When Mardian relates her supposed dying words, grief so overwhelms Antony that he utterly surrenders: "Unarm, Eros, the long day's task is done, / And we must sleep." In a long lament as he discards his armor, he can think only of joining her in death: "I will o'ertake thee, Cleopatra," and "I come, my queen." He orders Eros to kill him, but the loyal servant stabs himself instead. In desperation Antony falls on his own sword but succeeds only in wounding himself, though, as it turns out, fatally. He pleads with his soldiers to dispatch him, but they refuse. Diomedes enters to reveal that Cleopatra yet lives, and Antony asks to be taken to her.

4.15 Moments later, Diomedes, bearing Antony, arrives at Cleopatra's monument, where she looks down on them from an upper window. Antony asks to be admitted for one last kiss, but she dares not open the gates for fear of capture, vowing that she will take her own life rather than become a trophy for Caesar. Instead, in an involved bit of stage business, she lowers ropes to lift him up to her, where he has his last kiss. In his final words, he cautions her to trust only Proculeius (which turns out to be bad advice) and then dies, as he says, with honor, "a Roman by a Roman valiantly vanquished." Cleopatra pleads with him not to leave her. "Shall I abide / In this dull world," she asks, "which in thy absence is / No better than a sty?" and grieves at her loss as if it were indeed the passing of a world: "The crown o'th'earth doth melt . . . and there is nothing left remarkable / Beneath the visiting moon." She repeats her resolve to end her life, for when "all's but naught," she mourns, it is no sin "to rush into the secret house of death, / Ere death comes to us." They will bury Antony, she concludes, "and then, what's brave, what's noble, / Let's do it after the high Roman fashion, / And make death proud to take us."

5.1   In the last act of the play, Caesar and Cleopatra engage in an elaborate verbal ballet, a contest of words for the ultimate prize—her life. In this first scene Caesar receives word of Antony's death and wonders, with mixed emotions, why "the breaking of so great a thing should [not] make / A greater crack," since in Antony's name "lay / A moiety [portion] of the world." As Agrippa observes, "Caesar is touched." Indeed, he seems to mourn the loss, as he puts it, of his "brother" and "competitor," his "mate in empire, / Friend and companion in the front of war." This mood is interrupted by an envoy from Cleopatra, and Caesar quickly returns to the business at hand. She asks his intentions toward her, to which he sends the reply that he means to deal honorably with her, since, he adds somewhat disingenuously, he "cannot live / To be ungentle." As the Egyptian envoy leaves, Caesar turns immediately to Proculeius, ordering him to speak to her and promise that "we purpose no shame" so as to deter any thought she may have of killing herself, for, as he says, "her life in Rome / Would be eternal in our triumph." We know his intentions at the outset, then, and can watch him play out his game with her. In a sense he is like a false lover, courting Cleopatra for his own gain, and the dramatic tension arises from the ambiguity of her response. She has, after all, seduced two emperors; why should she fail with a third?

5.2   In the monument, Cleopatra still contemplates her death: "It is great / To do that thing that ends all other deeds." Proculeius appears before the gates, and while he speaks to her, Gallus and his soldiers gain access to the monument. Shakespeare left no stage directions for the complicated movements of this scene, but it would appear that Cleopatra is now on the ground floor, replying to Proculeius through barred gates. She bargains with him, announcing her terms. She will submit to Caesar, she says, if he will acknowledge her as queen of Egypt, or, if that does not please him, appoint her son king.* Proculeius, biding his time, smoothly assures her of Caesar's clemency, until Gallus appears behind her and throws open the gates. Cleopatra draws a dagger to kill herself but is disarmed by Proculeius, who attempts to calm her. She is adamant, however, vowing not to be put on display "to the shouting varletry / Of censuring Rome." "Rather a ditch in Egypt," she declares, "be gentle grave unto me!"

Dolabella enters to inform Proculeius that Caesar has sent for him and to assume responsibility for guarding Cleopatra. As he attempts to make himself known to her, she launches into an impassioned tribute to Antony and he cannot get a word in. He finally is able to express his profound sympathy for her, "a grief that smites / My very heart at root," and confirms her fears that Caesar intends to lead her in triumph. The play casts no light on Antony's misplaced trust of Proculeius or Dolabella's compassion for Cleopatra. In these matters Shakespeare is simply following Plutarch, who is equally unhelpful, saying only that Dolabella bore her no ill will.

Caesar enters, and Cleopatra kneels to him. They exchange assurances: he will treat her gently; she submits to him, the "sole sir o'th'world." But then he abruptly discards the mask of the benign conqueror, threatening that should she take her own life, he will put her children to death. As an apparent gesture of compliance, she submits a list of her possessions and calls for her treasurer, Seleucus, to confirm it. That worthy reveals that she has concealed half her wealth, gaining himself a beating for his disloyalty. She pleads that she is saving only some "innocent toys" as gifts for Octavia and Caesar's wife, Livia, "to induce their mediation" when she is taken to Rome. Cleopatra's scheme to hide her wealth is indeed puzzling. Is it an attempt to lull Caesar into the be-

---

*Probably Caesarion, her son by Julius Caesar. He was later put to death because he represented a threat to Caesar's inheritance.

lief that she has no intention to take her own life, or is she confident she can charm Caesar, as she has others, and so prudently puts away provision for the future? Caesar, addressing her as "dear queen," assures her that he intends to take nothing from her and will treat her only as "yourself shall give us counsel." On that note he leaves. The scene resonates with dramatic ironies as each plays false with the other—we know what he intends and that she knows as well.

Cleopatra leaves no doubt of her mistrust: "He words me, girls, he words me, that I should not / Be worthy to myself." She whispers instructions to Charmian as Dolabella enters to confirm Caesar's intent. When he leaves, she paints a verbal picture of their fate should they be forced to participate in Caesar's triumph. "Mechanic slaves / With greasy aprons" will put them on display; comedians will mock them in extemporaneous street theater; Antony will be shown drunk; and some "squeeking" boy will portray her "i'th'posture of a whore." To avoid this humiliation she intends "to conquer / Their most absurd intents," and so calls to be dressed in her royal raiments, crown and all, as if she were "again for Cydnus, / To meet Mark Antony."

At this, one of the most intense moments of the play, Shakespeare introduces a comic figure, a "rural fellow" bearing a basket of figs that hide a serpent beneath. His is gallows humor, to be sure, but his appearance releases the tension momentarily and probably draws more nervous laughter from the audience than his antics would normally warrant. Cleopatra listens to his ramblings patiently and finds that he is difficult to be rid of. She dismisses him three times but he persists, delighting in his macabre wit, until he is finally ushered out, wishing her the "joy o'th'worm." The tragic mood returns. Cleopatra calls for her robe and crown, declaring, "I have / immortal longings in me." "Husband I come," she exclaims, echoing Antony's, "I come, my queen," and then kisses her loyal servants farewell, the intensity of the moment breaking the heart of Iras, who falls dead. She applies the asp to her breast and dies with the name of Antony on her lips. As she does, her crown slips askew, and in a moving gesture Charmian pauses to straighten it before applying the asp to herself.

Caesar enters onto a stage draped with the dead, and though he regrets the loss, he praises Cleopatra's end. "Being royal," he observes in a brief eulogy, she "took her own way," and in such a manner as to leave no blemish on her features: she looks still as if "she would catch another Antony / In her strong toil of grace." The two will be buried together, he announces, and "no grave upon the earth shall clip in it / A pair so famous."

So ends what is possibly the most "famous" love affair in history or literature, to borrow Caesar's word. But Shakespeare's message in the play, if indeed there is one, is obscure. It abounds with *themes:* love versus duty, loyalty versus self-interest, passion versus reason, self-destructive ambition, the lure of power, and more—but Shakespeare leaves it uncertain what the choices should be. Why did Cleopatra flee at Actium? When Antony's star was fading, did she sincerely consider siding with Caesar? The play offers examples of those who desert their masters—Canidius, Alexas, Enobarbus, Dercetus—as well as those who remain loyal—Eros, Iras, Charmian. What prompted Cleopatra to kill herself? Certainly the loss of Antony left her deeply grieved, and some do die of grief—Enobarbus, Iras—but if Caesar had left her Egypt, would she have chosen to live? The chief reason she gives for taking her life is to avoid the humiliation of Caesar's triumph, and it was that threat, added to her sorrow, that decided her. But which proved the most compelling?

Their deaths are tragic, to be sure, and perhaps brought on by loving, like Othello, "too well." Antony dies at the lowest ebb of his fortunes, however, when every other option is closed to him. Cleopatra dies knowing that her "fearful sails" at Actium and the false message of her death were responsible for his destruction. In any event, it is her figure that stays with us in later hours as we think back over the play, and this not only because she dominates the final scene. She is the most puzzling of the characters in the play, the one who leaves us with that wealth of unsolved mysteries that surround Shakespeare's most tragic figures.

TITUS ANDRONICUS

❧

THERE SEEMS little doubt that *Titus* is Shakespeare's earliest tragedy, hence its defects are excused as the work of an apprentice playwright. The critics have not been kind to the play, from an early writer who dubbed it "a heap of rubbish" to later opinion that it is the "stupidest," "most ridiculous," and "uninspired" play ever written. Modern scholars have come to its rescue, proposing that it is actually a parody of the tragic form, the playwright having a bit of fun composing a sixteenth-century version of *The Rocky Horror Picture Show*. This, it appears, is the only way they can accept the evidence that Shakespeare actually wrote it, which they would prefer to deny.

The play is criticized as a spectacle of brutal excess, with by rough estimate fourteen deaths by seven different murderers, including episodes of mutilation and self-mutilation, ritual human sacrifice, rape, and the final barbarism, an unknowing mother served the heads of her sons baked in a pie. But it would be unwise to underestimate the audience appeal of brutal excess, on stage or screen, in Shakespeare's time or our own. *Titus* seems to have been quite popular with Elizabethan playgoers, published in three quarto editions during the poet's life; and the blood and gore of its severed heads and chopped-off hands have been splashed across the screen in a modern film version, a critical though not a box office success. The action is admittedly quick and dirty, allowing little pause to explore motive or revenge, or to develop character, but the play deserves attention.

Act One The Roman general Titus Andronicus returns home in triumph after years of successful campaigns against the Goths, bringing with him their queen, Tamora, and her three sons. His first act is to sacrifice Tamora's eldest in the belief that his death will permit his own sons, lost in the wars, to rest in peace. She pleads for his life to no avail, and vows revenge when Titus kills him. The general's brother, Marcus, greets him as the new emperor, but he declines. He defers to the dead emperor's heir, Saturninus, who then announces that he will marry Lavinia, the daughter of Titus. The marriage is clouded by contention, however, since Saturninus is attracted to Tamora, and his brother, Bassianus, is betrothed to Lavinia. Bassianus and Lavinia defy Saturninus and hurry off, pursued by Titus, who is angered by their defiance. He finds his way barred by his son, Mutius, and he kills him.

Saturninus announces that he will not marry Lavinia after all, but will take Tamora as his empress. She cools tempers, pleading publicly for Titus and assuring Saturninus privately that she will be avenged on the entire Andronicus family. All are outwardly reconciled for the moment.

Act Two   Aaron the Moor, Tamora's lover, meets her two sons, Demetrius and Chiron, both of whom desire Lavinia and are arguing over who will have her. Aaron advises that during a court hunt to be held that day, they abduct and share her—"take your turns [and] serve your lust." Aaron meets Tamora in the forest and temporarily resists her amorous advances while he plots the death of Bassianus. Lavinia and Bassianus come upon them, followed shortly by Demetrius and Chiron. Demetrius kills Bassianus, tossing his body into a pit, and the brothers force Lavinia off with them. Titus's sons Quintus and Martius enter and fall into the pit, as Aaron brings the emperor on the scene and accuses the brothers of Bassianus's murder. Titus pleads for them, but Saturninus condemns them to be executed for the crime.

When all have left, Demetrius and Chiron enter, dragging the mutilated Lavinia. They have ravished her, cut off her hands, and torn out her tongue so that she cannot incriminate them. They abandon her and Marcus rescues his suffering niece, carrying her off to her father's house.

Act Three   In Rome, Titus pleads for the lives of his sons, but no one will listen. Marcus enters, bearing Lavinia, a sight that devastates Titus and his son Lucius. Aaron enters with a message from Saturninus, offering to pardon Titus's sons if one of the Andronicus family will sacrifice a hand. The three argue over who will suffer the loss until Titus tricks the others into leaving and asks Aaron to sever his own hand. The Moor readily agrees and delivers it to Saturninus, who returns it treacherously with the heads of Quintus and Martius. Titus sends Lucius off to raise an army of Goths and return to punish Rome for its iniquity.

Act Four   Later in the house of Titus, he seems to have lost his wits. Lavinia, desperate to explain her injuries to him, fumbles her way through a book, pausing pointedly at the legend of Philomela, who like her was ravished and had her tongue torn out. Coached by her uncle Marcus, she succeeds in naming her abductors.

Aaron finds that Tamora has been delivered of a child, by its dark complexion obviously his. His sons urge him to do away with the baby, but he is determined to keep it and substitute a white infant in its place. He kills the nurse and midwife, the only witnesses to the birth, and decides to entrust the baby to the Goths, who he assumes will care for it as their queen's child.

Saturninus learns of the approach of Lucius and an army of Goths and he despairs, knowing that the Roman people prefer Titus's son to him. The devious Tamora has a plan, however. She will persuade Titus, who she is convinced is mad with grief, to invite Lucius to a meeting with the emperor at his father's house. There, she says, she will entice Titus to persuade his son to abandon the Goths.

Act Five   A Goth discovers Aaron and his child and brings them before Lucius, who condemns them both to death. To save his son, Aaron reveals the entire history of his duplicity, reciting the list of his evil deeds with such relish that Lucius decides to postpone his execution, convinced that "he must not die / So sweet a death as hanging."

Tamora and her sons, taking advantage of Titus's supposed madness, present themselves to him disguised as the mythical figures of Revenge, Rape, and Murder, offering to torment his enemies. Playing along, he agrees to arrange a parlay between Lucius and the emperor, but he privately plans to be avenged. Assisted by Lavinia, he cuts the throats of Tamora's sons and bakes their heads in a pie. Lucius arrives and sits down to dinner with Saturninus and Tamora. Titus slays Lavinia in their presence to save her from shame, and reveals that Tamora has been enjoying a meal of her sons. He stabs her, is himself stabbed by Saturninus, who in turn is killed by Lucius. With all of them dead, Lucius is declared emperor. He disposes of Aaron, who is unrepentantly evil to the end, and abandons Tamora's body to the mercy of "beasts and birds of prey."

Titus Andronicus is not a play to everyone's taste, but it contains characters that are said to foreshadow later, more familiar figures in Shakespeare's greater tragedies. The unrelentingly wicked Aaron is more fully developed in Iago. Titus himself in some ways prefigures the tortured Coriolanus, torn between conflicting loyalties to family and empire. And the malicious Tamora emerges later as Lady Macbeth or the heartless sisters Goneril and Regan in *King Lear*. It would not do to carry such analogies too far, but it is clear that all these figures owe something to this, Shakespeare's apprentice tragedy.

CORIOLANUS

❧

IN ITS EARLY HISTORY Rome was a city surrounded by enemies, including the Volsci to the south. *Coriolanus* is the tale of a renowned warrior, possessed of martial qualities much prized at the time, who leads the Roman armies to victory over the Volsci. Raised to achieve nobility in battle by his ambitious mother Volumnia, to whom he is devoted, he is a virtuous man, but one so conscious of his virtues that he has nothing but contempt for those with aspirations less noble. He is not, in brief, a complex tragic figure but one who is defeated by the contradiction between his devotion to an abstraction called Rome and his haughty scorn for the Romans who comprise it.

Act One The Roman people are rioting against the wealthy patricians, who, they protest, retain storehouses of grain during a time of famine. They single out Caius Marcius (later Coriolanus) as their chief enemy. The elderly Menenius attempts to calm them, but they are not subdued until Marcius confronts them. Outbreaks elsewhere in the city have been pacified with the promise that the common people may appoint tribunes to represent them in the Senate. News arrives that the Volsci under Tullus Aufidius are in arms against Rome, and the Senate summons Marcius to repel the invasion. In the Volsci city of Corioli, Aufidius relishes an opportunity to confront Rome's famed warrior.

In Marcius's house his mother, Volumnia, is pleased with the news. She has raised her son to seek honor in battle; the war promises another opportunity for him to distinguish himself. But his wife, Virgilia, is upset and vows not to leave the house until his safe return.

Before Corioli the Roman army is forced to retreat, and Marcius rages at them for their cowardice. They refuse to follow his attack on the city gates, leaving him to fight the Volsci single-handed. His fellow general, Titus Lartius, arrives to support him, and the Romans take the city. Marcius, though wounded, rushes off to the aid of another part of the army, led by Cominius, which has been forced to retreat. He rallies the Romans and, having run Aufidius off in single combat, achieves the victory.

Cominius announces that Marcius will be rewarded with a tenth of the booty taken, but he refuses, protesting that he cannot "take / A bribe to pay my sword." Since he will not accept gain, Cominius declares that he will be honored with the name "Caius Marcius Coriolanus," in recognition of his role in capturing the city. Meanwhile, Aufidius nurses his hatred of Marcius.

Act Two   In Rome, awaiting the return of Coriolanus, his mother is pleased that he has received wounds, which, she says, are additional marks of his greatness—this much to the distress of his wife. He arrives in triumph and kneels to his mother. He and Menenius retire to the Senate, where he is to receive more honors. As they leave, the tribunes of the people, Sicinius and Brutus, voice their resentment of the great man, whom they understand will be appointed consul, the highest office in Rome. They comfort themselves, however, with the thought that Coriolanus is so contemptuous of the commoners that he will alienate them.

In the Senate, Coriolanus, with seeming modesty, refuses to stay and hear, as he puts it, "my nothings monstered." In a long speech Cominius recites his many services to Rome, and Coriolanus returns to hear that the Senate has indeed appointed him consul. He first must seek the approval of the people, however, and he asks to be excused from the customary ceremony, resentful that he must brag of his achievements and display his battle scars to gain their favor. The tribunes insist, however, and leave, confident that he will defeat himself.

In the Forum the citizens are divided in their judgment of Coriolanus, and when he appears they ask him the customary question: What have you done to deserve the office? Assuming a haughty air, he insists that his deeds speak for themselves and asks brusquely for their approval, deploring the fact that he must request an honor he so obviously deserves. Although doubtful, the citizens agree to his appointment. The patricians depart for the Senate, leaving behind the tribunes, who are seething with indignation. Addressing the citizens, they warn that once in power Coriolanus will strip them of their liberties. They urge the aroused crowd to revoke their "ignorant election," and lead them off to the Capitol.

Act Three   Coriolanus and several senators make for the marketplace, but their way is barred by the tribunes, who report that the citizens are incensed against him. They incite him into a fury until he flares against the "mutable, rank-scented" rabble, raging that they demand free food from the state but, cowards all, refuse to bear arms in defense of Rome. The tribunes, having provoked him to a public revelation of his disdain for the people, accuse him of treason and call their police, the Aediles, to arrest him. They enter, backed by a crowd of commoners, but the patricians draw their swords and beat them back. Coriolanus is persuaded to retire while Menenius attempts to quiet the mob, promising to bring the candidate to the marketplace, where, he assures them, he will be more conciliatory in his manner.

The Roman nobles urge Coriolanus to return and answer the people more "mildly." Troubled, he refuses at first, asking "must I / With my base tongue give to my noble heart / A lie that it must bear?" But, taunted by his mother, he finally agrees. The tribunes plot to enrage him again, and when he appears they accuse him of seeking "power tyrannical." He replies in a fury, and they demand that he be banished from Rome. He agrees, since now he despises the city so much that he will turn his back on it and seek a "world elsewhere."

Act Four   At the city gate, Coriolanus bids farewell to his family and supporters, still declaring his scorn for the people, "the beast with many heads." He enters the Volscian city of Antium and makes himself known to Aufidius, offering to join them in their war against Rome. Aufidius greets him joyfully and gives him command of half the army.

In Rome the tribunes pride themselves in the peace that prevails, but soon they learn that Coriolanus is marching against them at the head of a Volscian army. In the enemy camp, Aufidius chafes at his ally's haughty demeanor and wonders about his downfall in Rome—a consequence, he suggests, of "pride" or "defect of judgment" or his very "nature" as a soldier who is accustomed to command rather than persuade. Ominously, he predicts that in the end Coriolanus will be "mine."

Act Five   The fearful Romans send emissaries to Coriolanus, pleading with him to withdraw. Cominius fails to move him, as does Menenius, and he is finally confronted by his mother, wife, and son. Volumnia pleads with him in long speeches, accusing him of treading on his "mother's womb" and endangering his wife and son. "There's no man in the world / More bound to's mother," she claims. Because of that bond, it seems, her son finally relents, calling off the siege and returning to Corioli with the Volscian army.

The Romans rejoice, but in Corioli Aufidius plots his revenge. The great man returns, extolling the peace, only to be confronted by Aufidius, who challenges him with the unforgivable epithet: "Boy!" Coriolanus flies into a rage at the insult, a prearranged signal for the Volscians to fall upon and kill him.

With his exalted sense of his own worth, Coriolanus falls victim to those who exploit it as a weakness. His pride is a hot button that anyone can push. The tribunes twice incite him to wrath, his mother reduces him to submission, and finally Aufidius challenges his manhood. His single-minded pursuit of honor leaves him vulnerable to more complex human motives, of which he seems innocent and hence has no defense against.

TIMON OF ATHENS

❧

ALTHOUGH SET in ancient Greece, *Timon* is a very modern story, the tale of a man who runs through a fortune, is beset by creditors, goes bankrupt, and ends up dying in poverty. It is a tale with a twist, however. The tragic hero is generous to a fault, giving away his wealth in lavish hospitality, unsecured loans, and gifts to anyone who appears at his door. He is, however, a poor accountant, and when his money runs out, his appeal for help falls on deaf ears among his erstwhile friends and admirers. He ends a bitter misanthrope, cursing all mankind, even those who offer him aid.

Act One Timon of Athens is generous to a fault. He pays the debt of Ventidius to free him from prison and refuses repayment, insisting that the money was given in friendship. He bestows a dowry on the daughter of an elderly Athenian so that she may marry her lover. He invites any and all to feast at his table and repays every gift received seven times over. The senators and nobles who benefit from his generosity praise him unreservedly, and return for more. Only two men question his great heart, the surly philosopher Apemantus, who will accept nothing from him because he will not flatter him in return, and his faithful steward Flavius, who knows that his largesse comes "all out of an empty coffer." He does it all, Timon says, in the name of friendship and prides himself in the wide circle of those who call him "friend."

Act Two A senator to whom Timon is in debt learns that he owes large sums to others as well, and he sends a servant to collect. At Timon's door the servant finds others on a similar mission, and they press their demands on the uncomprehending man. On learning of his debts, Timon scolds Flavius for failing to keep him informed, but the steward insists that he has tried to do so frequently to no avail, and that now he owes twice the amount he owns. Timon is confident that his host of friends will come to his aid, however, and sends his servants out to borrow the needed money.

Act Three   Each of his "friends" finds a reason to refuse him, however—Lucullus because "this is no time to lend money," Lucius because he is temporarily short of funds, and Sempronius because he feels slighted that Timon did not come to him first. His creditors' clerks press their bills upon him once again. Now enraged, he sends his servants out to invite his friends to another feast.

Meanwhile, Alcibiades, an honorable Athenian captain, pleads with the senators to remit the death sentence passed on a fellow soldier who has killed a man in an affair of honor. They refuse, citing reports of the man's history of such "outrages." Alcibiades presses his case until the exasperated senators declare him banished from Athens. He leaves, determined to retaliate by leading his "discontented troops" against the city.

Timon welcomes his guests to the feast where he serves them dishes that, when uncovered, are seen to hold nothing but warm water. He denounces them angrily and throws both water and dishes at them, chasing them from the house. Thoroughly disillusioned now, he rages that "henceforth hated be / Of Timon, man, and all humanity."

Act Four   Timon has been transformed from the generous, outgoing benefactor to a bitter misanthrope, raging against Athens: "Degrees, observances, customs, and laws, / Decline to your confounding contraries; / And yet confusion live!" The faithful Flavius shares his last funds with Timon's dismissed servants and sets out in search of his master. Timon, now a hermit living in the forest, digs for roots to eat and uncovers a hoard of gold. He receives a sequence of visitors, to each of whom he gives gold as profligately as he had spent his wealth earlier, though this time he does so out of spite rather than generosity. Alcibiades, leading a vagabond army against Athens, comes upon him, and Timon gives him gold to pay his troops, urging him to slaughter the Athenians. He also gives money to the whores accompanying the army, telling them to spread venereal disease. The dour Apemantus seeks him out and the two, a pair of cynics now, rail at one another and at mankind. Bandits discover him and he gives them gold, raging that all "the earth's a thief" and sending them off to rob in Athens. Flavius finds him finally and tries to comfort him, but Timon mistrusts his kindness, suspicious that, like his earlier "friends," he wants something in return. He offers the steward gold, sending him off to "hate all, curse all, show charity to none." Flavius begs to stay, but Timon casts him out.

Act Five   Next appear a poet and a painter who have heard that Timon has new wealth and have come to seek his patronage. Separating them, he gives each money, warning them not to trust the other, and drives them out. He is approached by Flavius and two senators, who plead with him to return and assume power to repel Alcibiades. He replies that he "cares not" about the fate of the city and is concerning himself now only with composing his epitaph, which, he says, they will find inscribed on his gravestone.

The senators return to Athens and negotiate with Alcibiades, agreeing to open the gates to him on the condition that he execute only his and Timon's enemies, and no more than a tenth of the population. Word arrives of the death of Timon.

The closing scenes of *Timon* do not convey a sense of tragedy. During the play the hero, in true Aristotelian fashion, undergoes a change from good fortune to bad, and his fall is a consequence of an "error or frailty" in his character. But his flaw is an innocent generosity arising from an altruistic view of humankind, not from ambition, or passion, or greed, or melancholy. He is not led astray by evil, for indeed no one in the play is evil; his "friends" are no more than shallow, self-serving sycophants who fade when he is in need. And there is no final wrenching scene—a Lear mourning the loss of Cordelia, a Macbeth challenging his furies, or an Othello reminding us that he has "done the state some service" before plunging a dagger into his breast. Indeed, we don't even see Timon die. We hear only the brief account of a man who simply rolls into his grave without further ado.

And yet a tragic sense pervades the play. A curtain drops on one man's vision of benevolent mankind, leaving only the dark image of a race without compassion or kindness. The wicked have at least one re-deeming feature: they believe in something and act on their belief. Ed-mund's creed in *Lear* is "now, gods, stand up for bastards"; Iago plots because he "hates the Moor"; and Richard III declares, "I am determined to prove a villain." Timon's "friends," however, are empty of meaning. They worship nothing and value only themselves. And that, indeed, is tragic.

The Comedies

What is love? 'tis not hereafter;
Present mirth hath present laughter.
—*Twelfth Night*

Love is merely a madness, and I tell you, deserves as well
a dark house and a whip as madmen do.
—*As You Like It*

Dost thou think, because thou art virtuous, there shall be
no more cakes and ale?
—*Twelfth Night*

COMEDY

ARISTOTLE'S DEFINITION of comedy was very broad indeed: If tragedy records a character's change from good fortune to bad, comedy is rather the account of a change from bad fortune to good.* A comic work then, according to him, was not necessarily funny; and it was in this sense that Dante called his long poem *La Commedia,* for though there is precious little in the *Inferno* to laugh at, the pilgrim starts out in hell and ends up in heaven. By Shakespeare's time the term had come to mean more or less what it does today—a work intended chiefly to amuse.

And Shakespeare's surely do. But a reader will miss the "sight gags" in which audiences delight—the pratfalls and doubletakes, the bungling keystone cops and reeling drunks and lemon meringue pies in the face that enliven Charlie Chaplin films, reruns of "I Love Lucy," and modern sitcoms. On the other hand, the reader is more likely to appreciate Shakespeare's principal comic device—wordplay—his inexhaustible store of puns, insults, and erotic allusions, as well as his subtle and not-so-subtle put-downs. Both reader and viewer may find it difficult to catch on to his humor the first time through, since his quips on the customs and events of his time in particular may leave us at a loss without a footnote.

The playgoer is not at a complete loss, however, because a character's tone of voice can key us to the joke. A line may be delivered "dripping with irony" in a way that gets the point across. In the opening scene of *Much Ado About Nothing,* for example, Beatrice refers to Benedick as "Signor Mountanto." It is unlikely that a modern audience would know that a "montant" is a thrust of the sword, and that she is ridiculing him

*See "Tragedy," p. 6.

as a mere fencer rather than a valorous soldier. But if she delivers the line with a derisive inflection, her meaning will be clear. Again, in *Twelfth Night,* when Sir Toby Belch introduces Maria to the dim-witted Aguecheek, he urges his friend, "Accost, Sir Andrew, accost," and we may be momentarily puzzled by the unfamiliar use of the word. But the joke is that Sir Andrew doesn't know what it means either and, thinking it is her name, addresses her as "Good Mistress Accost"—and we *know* that's not what Sir Toby meant. So good acting conveys the humor, though of course a familiarity with the play, either through reading or seeing it, can only add to our delight in Shakespeare's word play.

The comedies are rich in *malaprops,* the unconscious distortion of language. Some characters, in an effort to impress their social superiors, attempt a vocabulary of sophisticated words and misuse them, as in *Much Ado About Nothing* when Dogberry remarks to Leonato that "comparisons are odorous." In other instances they just simplemindedly turn the meaning on its head. In *The Merry Wives of Windsor,* for example, young Slender, when asked if he can love Anne Page, replies that he doesn't know her very well as yet but that "if there is no great love in the beginning, yet heaven may decrease it upon greater acquaintance."

A reader's search through the critical literature on Shakespeare's comedies may prove disappointing. Scholars and teachers are understandably reluctant to dwell on the humor of the plays, since any effort to explain a joke is more likely to be rewarded with a groan than a laugh. In brief, a joke explained is not very funny. Serious discussion of the comedies is more likely to be, well, serious, rather than amusing, which they were meant to be. Commentary more often dwells on the "dark" side of the plays. In the words of one distinguished scholar, "all Shakespeare's 'comedies' lie close to sorrow; close at least to heart-ache, sometimes close to heart-break." *

These plays do have their dark side, of course, often developed as one of dual plots, the one light, the other heavy. *The Merchant of Venice,* for example, traces the fall of Shylock from good fortune to bad in proper Aristotelian fashion, and the rise of Bassanio from bad to good—he is penniless in Act One, but he gets the girl and she is rich. As it happens,

---

*Sir Arthur Quiller-Couch, in his introduction to *Much Ado About Nothing* (Cambridge, England: Cambridge University Press, 1923), p. xv.

the tale of Shylock is the far more interesting of the two and scholars tend to dwell on it, slighting all the fun of the comic plot, which arises from disguises, misunderstandings, tricks, and, again, word play and the mangling of language. While we cannot neglect the dark side, certainly not in the instance of so compelling a figure as Shylock, it will be more to our purpose to dwell on the comic elements of the play, even at the risk of explaining the jokes, so that readers will be more apt to enjoy them in performance.

The antics of these plays arise from a single subject, really—love—and Shakespeare explores all the comic possibilities of the *theme*. He had a ready-made tradition to play upon—the medieval *courtly lover*. In that tradition the figure was an object of pity. Having fallen in love and been either rejected or otherwise deprived of the object of his affections (it is almost always the male who suffers the affliction), he declines into a painful melancholy. Shakespeare's gently satiric pen explores other dimensions of the theme. Among his many love-struck figures are confirmed bachelors who scorn marriage just moments before they are stunned by the sight of their destined bride; pretentious nincompoops who preen themselves, fancying they are admired by a lady who has not the slightest regard for them; lustful predators with but one thing in mind; and dried-up ancients, invariably rich, in absurd pursuit of blooming maidens.

Several features of Shakespeare's comic treatment of love are worth mentioning. First, his lovers almost always fall in love at first sight. He does not attempt to explain why people fall in love—for in truth, who knows?—but he delights in exploring the comic possibilities once they do. This romantic phenomenon should not violate our willing *suspension of disbelief*, since that's how it happens most of the time anyway (doesn't it?). Another feature arises from the social custom of the time, the father's prerogative to *arrange for the marriage* of an eligible daughter. The tradition lent itself to comic plots in which young lovers devise means to outwit the paternal designs. Finally, love almost always ended in marriage—no cohabiting with a significant other to explore the relationship. Although we may at times have our doubts about the compatibility of the pair and wonder just how long they will last, Shakespeare is not inclined to speculate on their future. In the comedies the lovers realize their most passionate desire, a lawful union with a cherished partner—and that's where most of the plays end, drawing the curtain on whatever tribulations may follow.

Shakespeare's comedies have qualities in common with his darker plays. Their characters display the same human flaws—pride, passion, and ambition—that are fatal to figures in the tragedies, but here they do not lead to sorrow and death. His comic characters may possess these same faults, but they survive their follies under the redeeming influence of love and compassion. The evil forces that propel the tragedies, Shakespeare seems to tell us, need not prevail if one can retain a faith in human nature and look upon it with a lively sense of its absurdities. The most potent weapon against evil, it is said, is laughter.

THE MERCHANT OF VENICE
(A Tragic Comedy)

⚜

THIS PLAY is customarily listed as a comedy, but anyone seeing it in performance must question whether its most memorable and controversial character, Shylock the Jew, is a comic figure. There are two distinct plot lines in *The Merchant of Venice*; according to Aristotle's guidelines, one is a comedy, the other a tragedy. Bassanio's fortunes change from bad to good, for he starts out penniless and ends up winning the wealthy Portia. Inversely, Shylock is a successful moneylender at the outset, but when last seen he is a defeated man, stripped of his wealth and dignity.* This is a comic work, surely, in the traditional sense of the word, but its antic elements seem muted against a backdrop of the Shylock's malignance and misfortune.

In the play Bassanio, a handsome young man-about-Venice, borrows money from his friend, Antonio, in order to equip himself to woo the wealthy Portia. Antonio, since his funds are all invested, must arrange for a loan from Shylock, and the two agree that should he default on the payment, the forfeit will be a pound of his flesh. Bassanio travels to Belmont, Portia's country estate, where he meets the challenge of choosing the correct casket from among three, one each of gold, silver, and lead, thereby winning her hand. When Antonio's cargoes are all reported lost in shipwrecks, Shylock demands his pound of flesh. Bassanio races from Belmont to offer him payment, but when the matter is brought before the Venetian court, Shylock refuses the offer and demands the forfeit agreed

*See "Tragedy," p. 6.

upon. According to the laws of the city, as the Duke acknowledges, it must be paid. Portia arrives in disguise as a judge and resolves the case in Antonio's favor, penalizing Shylock heavily. Defeated, he withdraws to the scornful jeers of the court. The principals return to the serene and secure Belmont, where, after some of Portia's trickery, the play concludes on a note of love and harmony.

1.1 The action opens with the confession by Antonio, the "merchant" of the title, that he is sad and doesn't know why, a sentiment appropriate to a comedy which will see him, it can be expected, in better spirits at the end. His young friends, Salerio and Solanio, commiserate with him, suggesting that he is worried about the fate of his ships, now all at sea. But this is not the cause, he assures them, since like any good businessman he has diversified his investments. They then suggest he is in love, which he cursorily dismisses, leaving them at a loss for an explanation. They conclude only that "you are sad / Because you are not merry."

Three other friends appear, all equally concerned about Antonio's depression. One of them, Gratiano, attempts to cheer him, but with little effect, and so he departs with Lorenzo, leaving the stage to Antonio and Bassanio. Antonio, who is the older of the two, asks his young friend to elaborate on a plan he had mentioned earlier to embark on a "secret pilgrimage" to woo a lady. Bassanio freely admits that he has been profligate in his expenses, having "disabled my estate," as he puts it, and incurred considerable debt, most of it owed to an overly generous Antonio, a condition he intends to remedy by winning "a lady richly left." He explains that he met the lady, Portia, at Belmont, her father's estate, before his death. Moreover, he adds, aside from her wealth she is both fair and virtuous, and, he is confident, has looked upon him with favor. He now needs funds to equip himself as a worthy suitor. Antonio readily agrees to the loan but explains that since all his assets are presently invested "at sea," on ships bound for foreign ports, he will have to secure the money on his "credit."

The relationship between Antonio and Bassanio moves both the tragic and later the comic action of the play. It is clear that theirs is a close and long-standing friendship, and it would appear that the source of Antonio's melancholy is his young friend's announcement earlier in the day that he is planning to seek a wife. The older man is saddened by the thought that the bond between them will be severed, a prospect that has reduced him to a state of despondency. But he is either unaware of or unwilling to admit the cause. Another concern introduced by the scene is the character of Bassanio, who at first sight seems a mercenary youth, a spendthrift who has gone through his own fortune and has borrowed heavily to support a scale of living he can no longer afford. He is a gentleman, that is, of "gentle" birth, and is obviously a popular figure, but his chief interest, it would appear, is to marry this "lady richly left" so as to repair his fortunes—not, on the whole, an entirely sympathetic figure.

1.2   The following scene takes us to Belmont, where Portia confesses that she "is aweary of this great world." The comedy opens, then, with its chief characters at low ebb—Antonio melancholy, Portia "aweary," and Bassanio bankrupt. Her story is an old one, told in various versions throughout the ages. Her father on his death left three caskets, one each of gold, silver, and lead, with instructions that Portia is obliged to marry only the man who opens the one with her portrait in it. It was customary among the monied classes of the time for the father to *arrange for the marriage* of an eligible daughter, but Portia's father is surely carrying the custom to extremes by insisting on his prerogative from beyond the grave. In complying with his wishes, his daughter has been plagued with suitors from all over Europe, each of whom, it appears, has failed the test.

Nerissa, Portia's maidservant and close companion, asks her opinion of the suitors thus far, and she answers with a litany of the stereotypically unfavorable characteristics of the men of various nations, a sequence that today might be called "racial slurs." To her mind they are all ludicrous: the Neopolitan talks only of his horse; the Count Palatine is dour and humorless; the French lord is an effete braggart; the Englishman is insular, having learned no language but his own, and, the more to his discredit, wears bizarre clothes; the Scot is quarrelsome; and the German is a drunkard. Nerissa reminds her of Bassanio, upon whom both look with favor, and they prepare to meet a new suitor, the Prince of Morocco.

1.3   Back in Venice we find Bassanio attempting to secure a loan from Shylock, using Antonio's credit. Shylock ponders the arrangement, observing that the merchant is indeed "sufficient"—that is, financially sound—but voicing a concern that at the moment the report "upon the

Rialto" is that his assets are all "squand'red abroad."* Nonetheless Shylock agrees to "take his bond." He will loan the money with security so that if it is not repaid in three months, whatever is bonded—usually goods, chattels, or a house—will be forfeit. Shylock asks to speak with Antonio, but when Bassanio invites him to dine with them, he declines with sudden sharpness. He will trade and talk, Shylock says, with followers of "your prophet the Nazarite," but he will not eat, drink, or pray with them.

Antonio approaches, and in an *aside* Shylock reveals his hidden thoughts about him, a man whom he despises "for he is a Christian" who "hates our sacred nation." His chief grievance, however, seems to be the merchant's monetary dealings. Shylock depends for his livelihood on loaning money at interest, which is the very reason Bassanio has consulted him, and he asks whatever the market will bear. Antonio "lends out money gratis," thereby lowering the rate in the marketplace, a practice that Shylock takes personally since the merchant also abuses him in the process. "Cursed be my tribe," he mutters fiercely, "if I forgive him!"

In medieval times loaning money at interest was considered sinful, since it was deemed unnatural to profit from the exchange of a commodity that was not the product of human labor. Although "usury" in our day has come to mean exorbitant interest, in earlier times it meant any interest at all. Christians, in brief, were forbidden to make money out of money; indeed, one of the lower levels of Dante's hell is reserved for the eternal punishment of such "usurers." No such prohibition applied to Jews, however, nor was it considered improper for Christians to borrow from them at interest when the need arose. In loaning money "gratis," therefore, Antonio shows himself a proper Christian gentleman, though it may seem somewhat hypocritical of him to borrow at interest and at the same time to rail against Shylock for asking it.

Shylock seems intent upon seizing the occasion to justify his practice, and does so in a rather involved passage citing biblical precedent. Antonio responds scornfully that "the devil can cite Scripture for his purposes," the first of a number of references in the play to the Jew as a devil.

---

*The Rialto was the Venetian exchange where merchants met to trade and share news, so called because of its proximity to the famous bridge of the same name, which today spans the Grand Canal.

The merchant is impatient to conclude the agreement, but Shylock is determined to exploit this rare opportunity to voice his grievances. He has borne Antonio's abuse patiently, he complains, while the merchant has continually called him a "misbeliever, cut-throat dog, / And spet upon my Jewish gaberdine [coat]." In return "for these courtesies," Shylock asks with heavy irony, should he lend him money? Antonio replies with open candor—"I am as like to call thee so again, / To spet on thee again, to spurn thee too"—behavior, it would seem, not considered inappropriate for a Christian gentleman.

Shylock protests that he has been misunderstood. "I would be friends with you, and have your love," he insists, and to show his sincerity he offers to forgo interest on the loan. Interest is one thing, security quite another, however. Shylock proposes to Antonio "in a merry sport" that if the sum is not repaid in the required time, the forfeit will be a "pound of your fair flesh." The merchant, confident that his ships will make harbor safely, finds the offer a gesture of friendship, surprised that "the Hebrew will turn Christian, he grows kind." But Bassanio is not so sure.

Nor are we, having just heard Shylock admit to a fierce desire "to catch [Antonio] once upon the hip [and] feed fat the ancient grudge I bear him." Shylock calls it a "merry bond," protesting that it is unthinkable he should collect on it. But it is an open question whether he actually contemplates doing physical harm to Antonio at this stage of the play or is simply suggesting an absurd contract, really no bond at all, as a gesture of amity. Audiences in Shakespeare's time would have had little doubt of his malicious intent. The Jews were an alien presence in the cities of medieval and Renaissance Europe, vilified for their religion and mistrusted for their sharp commercial practices. They were largely unassimilated in early Western culture, which was both a cause and a consequence of the intolerance toward them in communities whose members seldom strayed far from their birthplace in a lifetime and were suspicious of strangers of any sort. Forbidden to own land or engage in trade, Jews gravitated toward medicine, banking, and the marketing of precious gems, trades at which they were highly successful, some amassing fortunes that only added to the resentment against them. A Christian monarch would endure their presence because they were a ready source of loans to finance his wars and courts, and when the debt became too onerous, he could simply cancel it by banishing all Jews from the kingdom, a move generally popular with his subjects who found the race a ready scapegoat for the many misfortunes of their lives. Jews were banned from England, for example, at the end of the thirteenth century and allowed to remain in the country only if they conformed outwardly to Christianity. Even those who were tolerated were required to live in a segregated section of a city, preserved on present-day maps as the Ghetto Nuovo in Venice and Old Jewry in London.

Given this background, how is Shakespeare's Shylock to be presented on stage? Is he the caricature of the miserly Jew, the acquisitive, hawk-nosed villain, the hunched-shouldered wily schemer, wringing his hands in sly obsequiousness to strike a bargain and reveling with ruthless satisfaction when he has the upper hand, indulging in unscrupulous practices and gloating over his mounting hoard of gold? Or is he an admirable figure, striking back at his oppressors, showing them up for the hypocrites they are in his struggle for revenge, not only to repay them for the injuries he himself has suffered but for the ancient injustices endured by his people at the hand of Christians? Is he a figure of ridicule or a hero? Do we condemn or admire him?

One cannot avoid the conclusion that, given the sentiments of Shakespeare's audience, he meant Shylock, in part at least, to be a comic villain. *The Merchant of Venice* is a comedy, and the joke is on ethnic groups, few of which escape mockery. Portia impresses us at the outset with her wit and intelligence as she ticks off the absurdities of national types, a list soon lengthened by the arrival of the pompous Prince of Morocco and the overbearing Prince of Arragon, whose puffed-up egos beg to be punctured. Given this pervasive tone of ethnic ridicule, it can hardly be expected that the Jew would escape unscathed. Shakespeare composed a comedy for the amusement of his Elizabethan audience, and if a Jew appeared in a comedy they would certainly have expected to enjoy the mockery of his idiosyncrasies in speech and gesture, and to applaud when he was outwitted. For the first two hundred years of the play's stage history, Shylock was portrayed either as a figure of ridicule by actors known for comic parts, or as maliciously evil.

But Shakespeare gave the Jew speeches that seem to undercut any scornful satisfaction his audience may have felt at his humiliation. In the early nineteenth century serious actors, inspired by the performances of Edmund Kean, began to portray a very different Shylock, one whose grievances were all too real, whose defiance of his oppressors evoked sympathy. He became "the noble Jew," seeking justice for his people, a valiant figure facing down centuries of mindless prejudice that had driven him to desperate measures to right old wrongs, and he has been so portrayed ever since.*

The remarkable quality of the play is that it allows for both interpretations. Shakespeare does not judge Shylock. The Jew is presented as a complex human being with the flaws of any man or woman long oppressed, a nature twisted into malignancy by injustice, but retaining a dignity that draws substance from the long history of a proud people. In a post-Holocaust world an audience may smile indulgently at Shylock's human frailties; but we are no longer amused by the trials of those who, whatever their ethnic idiosyncrasies, are victims of intolerance. Shakespeare lays bare the stark reality of that intolerance, neither condemning nor justifying a man so incensed by the indignities that have been heaped upon him that he is prepared to carve flesh from the breast of a fellow human being.

2.1–2   We return to Belmont, where the Prince of Morocco, very full of himself, has come to try his fortune with Portia's caskets. She reminds him of the penalty for choosing wrong—he is never to marry— and he agrees.

Much of the act is concerned with the elopement of Shylock's daughter, Jessica, with the Christian Lorenzo; but there are one or two glimpses of the Jew, as well as comic interludes provided by the clown, Launcelot Gobbo. Launcelot is babbling to himself about his desire to leave the service of Shylock, whom he calls "the very devil incarnation." He plays a rather cruel trick on his old, blind father, and then urges him to plead with Bassanio to take his son into service. Bassanio, flush now with Shylock's loan, is gathering a retinue of servants to accompany him in proper style to Belmont. He supplies them with "liveries," matching uniforms appropriate to the household of a prosperous gentleman of the time.

Part of the comic element of the scene is the tendency of the Gobbos to mangle the language. When addressing their social betters, they pre-

---

*I am indebted to the distinguished scholar William Kerrigan for setting me straight on the stage history.

tend to a sophisticated vocabulary in remarks rich in *malaprops*, as in the elder Gobbo's "he hath a great infection sir, (as one would say) to serve" and Launcelot's "in very brief, the suit is impertinent to myself." At any rate, Bassanio takes the young man on, apparently on Shylock's recommendation. Gratiano enters and asks to accompany his friend to Belmont. Bassanio consents but, remarking that Gratiano is at times "too wild, too rude, and bold of voice," insists that he behave himself, to which his friend wittily agrees.

2.3–6 At Shylock's house, Jessica bids farewell to Launcelot and complains of her life there. "Our house is hell," she declares, and gives him a letter to be delivered to Lorenzo in which she professes her hope to "become a Christian and [his] loving wife!" Launcelot conveys the letter, which proposes a plan, Lorenzo confides to Gratiano, to "take her from her father's house" with "what gold and jewels she is furnish'd."

Meanwhile, back at Shylock's house, he reveals that, despite his earlier refusal, he intends to dine with Christians, though he finds the prospect distasteful. Since there is to be a festival that night with the streets full of celebrating masquers, he insists that Jessica lock up the house and admonishes her to avoid watching "Christian fools with varnish'd faces." Launcelot leaves, but not before delivering a cryptic rhymed message informing Jessica that her plan will go forward. Later that night Lorenzo arrives with a troop of friends. Jessica, dressed as a boy, escapes the house to join them, carrying with her a considerable portion of her father's hoard of gold and jewels.

2.7, 9 At Belmont the pompous Morocco and overbearing Arragon choose respectively the gold and silver caskets, neither of which contain the hoped-for portrait of Portia. As they leave she exclaims in relief, "O these deliberate fools!" A messenger brings news that Bassanio has arrived to try his hand at the caskets, a prospect that excites Portia.

2.8 In Venice, meanwhile, Salerio and Solanio bring us up to date on the departure of Bassanio and Gratiano for Belmont and Jessica's escape with Lorenzo. They report gleefully Shylock's impassioned response, with Solanio quoting him at length, doubtless with a mocking Jewish accent: "My daughter! O my ducats! O my daughter! / Fled with a Christian! O my Christian ducats!"—in effect ridiculing him for caring more about his ducats than his daughter. They then turn their thoughts to

Antonio, who Solanio observes ominously, "shall pay for this," and his companion reports on the grave news that one of the merchant's ships may have been lost.

Salerio gives a moving account of Bassanio's parting from Antonio, a description that has further implications for our understanding of the relationship between the two men. He first confirms our impression that Antonio is an altogether admirable man, "a kinder gentleman treads not the earth." We retain this impression despite the report of his reprehensible behavior toward Shylock, perhaps because we never actually hear him abuse the man, nor do we ever see him "spet upon [his] Jewish gaberdine." Any ambivalence we may have about Antonio's character certainly is not shared by the two Venetians, nor was it, we may assume, by Shakespeare's audience, who would have found nothing untoward in such a gesture. Salerio goes on to describe Antonio's response to his friend's departure: With tears in his eyes, "turning his face, he put his hand behind him, / And with affection wondrous sensible / He wrung Bassanio's hand, and so they parted." Solario's comment is certainly suggestive: "I think he only loves the world for him." They determine to seek out the merchant and attempt to relieve "his embraced heaviness."

3.1 Act Three finds us still in Venice, once more with Solanio and Salerio. The two figures, virtually indistinguishable from one another, reflect the general attitude of the ordinary citizen of the time, in both their respect and affection for Antonio and their scorn for Shylock. A modern audience will find them objectionable, a pair of Jew-baiting bigots mindlessly parroting the animosity of the age. But did Shakespeare intend them as a criticism of intolerance? Perhaps, though as has been often observed, the poet does not preach, nor does he judge his characters. He presents humanity as he sees it—indeed, it may be said, as it is—and he leaves it to us to reflect on its follies and virtues.

The two lament the "news on the Rialto" about their friend's losses and restate their apprehension about the consequences for "the good Antonio, the honest Antonio" as they note the approach of Shylock, again characterized as a "devil." They bait him about the defection of his daughter and ask if he has heard of Antonio's losses. He replies darkly that the merchant would do well to "look to his bond." Salerio asks, quite reasonably, what use he would have for Antonio's flesh. Shylock spits back, "to bait fish withal"—it will feed his revenge, he says, if nothing else.

Shylock continues with one of the most powerful passages in literature condemning racial intolerance. No one, in Shakespeare's time or our own, could possibly escape the force of its appeal to a higher standard for the human spirit. We Jews are no different from Christians, he protests, with the same eyes, "hands, organs, dimensions, senses, affections, passions," a people "fed with the same food, hurt with the same weapons, subject to the same diseases, healed by the same means, warmed and cooled by the same winter and summer as a Christian is." He goes on to ask "if you prick us do we not bleed? if you tickle us do we not laugh? if you poison us do we not die?" But then he casts a shadow over this eloquent plea for compassion and understanding: "If you wrong us shall we not revenge?" Yes, he concludes, all humans are indeed alike; and if a Christian seeks vengeance on a Jew, may he not reply in kind? This impassioned speech ends, then, not as an appeal for tolerance but as a justification for revenge. It is difficult to cite another passage in which Shakespeare presents his audience, then and now, with a more stark dilemma, a conflict of sentiments between a conviction that all are equal in the eyes of God and the instinctive mistrust of others who do not think, act, look, or pray as they do. Shakespeare sets the choice before us in all its troubling dimensions.

The two young Venetians have no reply, but they are, it seems, unmoved. They note the approach of Shylock's friend Tubal and again link the Jew with the devil. Tubal comes with some bad news and some good news, and he seems almost to relish his role as he badgers Shylock with alternating accounts of Jessica's extravagance and Antonio's misfortune. The exchange serves to fuse the two developments together in Shylock's mind. It matters not to him that Antonio was in no way responsible for Jessica's flight; it matters only that she eloped with a Christian, so some Christian must suffer for the Jew's indignities and losses. For him the issue has become much larger: "The curse never fell upon our nation till now," he agonizes, "I never felt it till now." If Shylock's original suggestion of a pound of Antonio's flesh as a bond for the loan was indeed only a gesture of friendship offered "in merry sport," it has now become an opportunity for retribution.

3.2   In vivid contrast to the angry passions heating up in Venice, at Belmont love finds a way. Bassanio approaches the caskets as Portia orders music to be played and a song sung, one that may offer some broad hints—for one thing, the first three lines all rhyme with *lead*. At any rate, after much consideration Bassanio chooses the right one and wins the lady. Portia is ecstatic, presenting herself modestly to Bassanio as "an unlesson'd girl, unschool'd, unpractised, / Happy in this, she is not yet so old / But she may learn." In view of later events, it may be said that she protests too much. As we will see, there is considerably more to her than this somewhat disingenuous self-description. She commits herself to Bassanio "to be directed, / As from her lord, her governor, her king," and declares that she and everything she owns "is now converted" to him. These lines may be distressful to modern ears, but such was the custom of the time. As a token of her love, she gives him a ring which she says he must never "part from, lose, or give away." He gallantly pledges that if it ever "parts from this finger, then parts life from hence." Gratiano and Nerissa enter with the news that they have fallen in love as well, and the two couples happily plan a double wedding.

Lorenzo and Jessica approach along with Salerio, who bears a letter from Antonio to his young friend. Bassanio reads it and turns pale, prompting Portia to ask that he share its message with her. First, however, he clears up any doubts we may have had about his motives, revealing that before he undertook the challenge of the caskets he had told her of his penniless state. But at the time, he confesses, he failed to mention that he was deeply indebted to Antonio. Now all the merchant's ships are reported lost, and he cannot repay his debts. Shylock is pressuring the Duke of Venice for the rightful payment of his "bond," which, Jessica confirms, her father said he would rather have than "twenty times the value of the sum" owed. Portia insists that Bassanio go to his friend's aid with enough of her wealth to repay the debt many times over. It would appear that though she has committed all she owns to him, she still has a say in its distribution—but then they are not yet married, a want she means to remedy without further delay. At her request Bassanio reads her the letter, in which Antonio absolves him of the debt, asking only that he be present during his final moments. Portia urges him to "dispatch all business and be gone!"

3.3   In Venice, Antonio, on his way to prison, encounters Shylock in the streets and attempts to speak with him, but the Jew will not hear him. He insist only on the forfeiture of his "bond," confident that the duke will award it rather than "impeach the justice of the state." In the background of this entire inhuman episode is the integrity of Venetian law. The prosperity of the city depends on trade, the success of which in turn depends on its reputation for paying its debts. Antonio is a wealthy man, but with all his assets committed to cargoes at sea, he has no ready funds. Like his fellow merchants, he is able to accumulate capital through credit in contracts backed by Venetian law, which demands that the contracts be honored so that all who trade with the city may do so with confidence that their investments are secure. Shylock knows this, and he is confident the duke will not arbitrarily cancel a contract for fear it would put the city's reputation in jeopardy. In a sense, by insisting on his bond Shylock will have his revenge on all Christians, exposing the hypocrisy of a mercenary oligarchy that is quite prepared to see one of their number slaughtered rather than endanger their credit rating.

3.4–5   At Belmont, Lorenzo praises Portia for "bearing the absence of [her] lord." She replies that if Bassanio loves Antonio, the man must be worthy of her sacrifice. She then entrusts her estate to Lorenzo, explaining that she and Nerissa will retire to a nearby monastery "to live in prayer and contemplation" until their husbands return. Left alone with Nerissa, she confides that she has in mind a scheme involving her cousin, one "Doctor Bellario." She intends to dress the two of them as men, adding playfully that she will "prove the prettier fellow." After their departure, Launcelot the clown engages in some witty banter with Lorenzo and Jessica, and she confirms our impression of Portia: "The poor rude world / Hath not her fellow." She is confident that Bassanio, now married to such a remarkable woman, will henceforth "live an upright life," leaving unsaid what "life" he has been leading.

4.1–2   Act Four records the defeat and humiliation of Shylock. In Shakespeare's time this story about the thwarting of a Jew was an old one, told and retold in prose, verse, and song; but in the play's many sources he is a remorseless villain, void of any touch of humanity. Shakespeare, it may be said, gives the Jew his day in court, and with such persuasion that modern audiences are sorely torn between sympathy and revulsion as he pursues his revenge. The duke voices the old tradition in warning Antonio that he faces "a stony adversary, an inhuman wretch, / Uncapable of pity, void, and empty / From any dram of mercy." When Shylock enters, however, the duke appeals to his "human gentleness and love," asking him to abandon a suit against a man who has already suffered crushing losses, ending with the austere admonition that "we all expect a gentle answer, Jew!" Shylock replies sharply with a reminder of the commercial interests of Venice, demands his bond, and warns that should it be denied, "let the danger light / Upon your charter and your city's freedom." Although he is a Venetian like all the others in the room, it is clear that he considers himself an alien presence in their midst, since it is "your," not "our" charter and freedom that are at stake. As to why he prefers a pound of flesh to the money owed, he replies casually, "say it is my humor," a natural inclination that defies reason, born of "a lodg'd hate, and a certain loathing" he has for the merchant. Further appeals fail to move Shylock. Finally Antonio, who is strangely passive during the entire episode, urges his friends to abandon their efforts "to soften that— than which what's harder? / His Jewish heart." He simply wants the ordeal over with.

Bassanio offers Shylock double the money owed, but again he demands the bond guaranteed by Venetian law. The duke asks why he will show no mercy and receives in reply another indictment of Christian commerce. The Venetian merchants all own slaves, he notes, whom they consider mere property. "Shall I say to you," he taunts them, "let them be free, marry them to your heirs?" The bond is his property as much as the slaves are theirs, he contends, and if they deny it to him then "fie upon your law! / There is no force in the decrees of Venice."

The duke has summoned a learned doctor of laws—the same Bellario to whom Portia has written—asking for an opinion on the case, and Bassanio sees a ray of hope: "Good cheer Antonio! what man, courage yet!" But the merchant seems indifferent to his fate. He is quite prepared to die, an outwardly calm center in the storm of pleas and accusations swirling about him. Nerissa enters, disguised as a law clerk, and presents the duke with a letter from Bellario. Shylock, meanwhile, prepares for the verdict by openly sharpening his knife, an act whose cruel defiance unleashes a tirade of invective from the impulsive Gratiano: "O be thou damn'd, inexorable dog." In this scene Gratiano confirms Bassanio's earlier concern that his friend is at times "too wild, too rude, and bold of voice." He reacts to Shylock's provocative gesture with unrestrained anger, hurling abuse with a vehemence that has caused at least one irate scholar to brand him "that Nazi."

Bellario's letter pleads illness and asks the duke to accept in his stead one Balthazar, a young doctor of laws, to adjudicate the case. Portia enters, dressed in a lawyer's garb, and identifies the disputants. We are asked to *suspend our disbelief* that neither Bassanio nor Gratiano have an inkling that these two "men" are their wives, and we willingly do so in anticipation of the use the women will make of their disguise. This is a common device in Shakespeare's comedies—Rosalind in *As You Like It,* for example, and Viola in *Twelfth Night*—and we readily accept the deception as a prelude to comic developments. These will come in time, but for the moment the disguises have a darker purpose.

Portia advises Shylock to show mercy, and when he asks why he should, she responds with what are surely the best-known lines in the play, perhaps in all of Shakespeare: "The quality of mercy is not strain'd, / It droppeth as the gentle rain from heaven / Upon the place beneath." Shylock, despite this eloquent plea, remains adamant. Bassanio, revealing that his offer to pay the debt "ten times o'er" has been rejected, pleads with Portia to set aside the law and deny the Jew's suit. She replies that the law must stand, drawing praise from Shylock, who compares her to Daniel, a biblical hero famous for his justice. She once more advises him to "be merciful" and accept the money, but he again refuses and urges her impatiently to "proceed to judgment." She does so, directing Antonio to "prepare your bosom for his knife," which elicits further praise from Shylock. She asks if he has brought scales to weigh the flesh, which he has, and if he has provided for a surgeon to attend to Antonio's wounds, to which he replies callously that nothing in the bond requires him to do so.

Antonio, given the opportunity for some last words, addresses them to Bassanio, whom he entreats not to feel guilt at his death but to mourn only that he had "once a love" whom he has lost. Bassanio and Gratiano, both distraught at the prospect of their friend's fate, declare to him impulsively that they would gladly sacrifice their lives, and their wives, to save him. The two women respond to these declarations in ironic asides. Portia that Bassanio's "wife would give you little thanks for that" and Nerissa that Gratanio's offer could well make for an "unquiet house."

Portia is particularly struck by the close affection between her husband and Antonio, and productions on stage and screen often position the three figures to emphasize the suggestion that this is in some ways a lovers' triangle. The relationship between the two men is obviously close and long-standing, whereas she has known her husband for only a few days and not yet in the biblical sense. Although she stands by her conviction that Antonio must be a worthy man since Bassanio values him so highly, she may be a bit uneasy at her husband's impassioned offer. What she will do about this situation remains to be seen, but for the moment the compelling issue of Shylock's bond must be dealt with.

Portia announces the verdict: "A pound of this same merchant's flesh is thine," she tells Shylock, "the court awards it, and the law doth give it." He approaches Antonio, brandishing the knife he has so provocatively sharpened, a moment critical to our response to the figure. Does he actually mean to carve on the merchant? Has he become so incensed by the betrayal of his daughter that he can take the life of Antonio—for he cannot survive such a trauma—a man guilty only of spitting on him in public and lowering interest rates? Does he so relish the opportunity to avenge the ancient wrongs visited upon his oppressed people that he will take the life of an innocent man while his fellow Christians stand helplessly by? Shakespeare's audience would not have doubted his determination to carve, and modern viewers agree. But do we today think he is justified in doing so? If we do not, how does his obvious intent affect our sympathy for Shylock?

Mercifully, Portia intervenes and spares our spirits the burden of this agonizing dilemma, the conflicting emotions of at once sympathizing with Shylock and condemning him for his cruelty. He is to be prevented from committing this inhuman act, and further, to be reduced and humiliated, ironically by the letter of the very law he has appealed to. Portia stops him in the act by cautioning him that he may have his pound of flesh, but that the strict wording of the bond, which he had cited with such heartless satisfaction in the matter of a surgeon's presence, allows him "no jot of blood." Moreover, according to Venetian law, should he "shed / One drop of Christian blood," all his wealth is forfeit to the state. Accepting defeat, Shylock agrees to take the money in repayment of the loan. But Portia is adamant that, since he has refused it twice over, he must have his bond or nothing. He scornfully opts for nothing and turns to leave, only to be called back by Portia. It seems there are other laws: if "an alien" seeks the life of a Venetian citizen, which he clearly has, his intended victim may seize "half his goods" while "the other half comes to the privy coffer of the state," and his life "lies in the mercy / Of the Duke." Portia advises him to kneel and plead for his life, and in this posture he remains until dismissed.

During this entire exchange, Antonio and Bassanio are speechless bystanders, leaving the stage to Portia—and to Gratiano, who spits hatred. He is exultant, goading Shylock with praise of Portia—"O Jew! an upright judge, a learned judge"—throwing his former admiration for her back in his teeth—"a Daniel shall I say, a second Daniel"—and finally declaring that he "must be hang'd." But the Christian court rejects his heated intolerance, demonstrating to all appearances the "quality of mercy" Shylock failed to show. The terms of the settlement are a bit tangled. Briefly: The duke pardons Shylock's life and offers to fine him rather than seize half his wealth, provided he shows sufficient "humbleness." Antonio approves and asks that the other half be given to him only "in trust," to be left to Lorenzo on Shylock's death. He imposes two conditions, however, one that the Jew convert to Christianity and the other that he sign a will leaving his entire worth to Lorenzo and Jessica upon his death. The duke forces the issue, threatening to revoke his pardon should Shylock refuse—and so the broken Jew submits. Gratiano is dissatisfied with the outcome, but in some productions he achieves a kind of vindictive triumph by forcing the prostrate Shylock to kiss a cross.

Thus Christian mercy! Shylock leaves deeply humiliated, but he walks out a free man, sentenced for his attempted murder only to a fine and loss of the use of half his wealth. Modern audiences may feel that the sternest punishment he receives is the demand that he abandon his religion. Gratiano gloats over the sentence, but Antonio may have meant it charitably. Jews, according to Christian belief at the time, were damned from birth, and an Elizabethan audience may well have seen the good merchant's requirement as an offer of salvation. So the Christians are merciful according to their own lights and laws, but such a conclusion begs the question of the justice of those laws themselves, which brand as "alien" a man who may have lived and worked in this Christian community for all his days.

Antonio and Bassanio attempt to reward this young doctor of laws for his services, but Portia graciously declines, observing that "he is well paid that is well satisfied." They press her further, however, until she finally agrees, asking only for Bassanio's ring as a token of their gratitude. He protests that he cannot part with it, and Portia stalks off in mock indignation. Antonio persuades his friend to surrender the ring—little enough payment, he says, for the great service done. Bassanio reluctantly agrees, sending Gratiano to catch up with the departing lawyers and deliver it. When he does so and takes his leave of the women, Nerissa confides that she will separate him from a like ring she has given him.

5.1 The last act finds us once more at Belmont, where Lorenzo and Jessica are exchanging witty endearments while enjoying a stroll in a wooded grove on a moonlit night. A messenger arrives with news that Portia is returning, and Launcelot enters to tell them that Bassanio is on his way as well. The couple sit to admire the peaceful scene as musicians arrive to play for them.

This opening episode, in which nothing really happens, stands in sharp contrast to the preceding scene in Venice, emphasizing the importance of *place* in Shakespeare's works. The city is a center of commerce, symbolized by the marketplace at the Rialto, where merchants scheme and barter, and fortunes are made or lost. Belmont, on the other hand, is a country refuge to which all happily return to find a haven from the tension and distress of the contentious metropolis.

Consider the contrasts Shakespeare sketches for us. At Belmont a dutiful daughter obeys the wishes of her father, even those voiced from beyond the grave; in Venice a rebellious daughter flees her father's house, robbing him of money and jewels. At Belmont foreign guests are greeted with courtesy and decorum, even when unattractive and unwelcome; in Venice one citizen abuses another, spitting on him as something "alien." Money is plentiful at Belmont, enough to pay off any debt ten times over; in the city merchants haggle over interest rates, spendthrift youths go through fortunes and sink under crushing debt, and merchants suffer losses that leave them bankrupt. In Belmont love flourishes; in Venice hatred seethes beneath the surface of every encounter. In one place humankind is in concert with nature and music soothes the soul; in the other men shout in anger and plot unnatural deeds. In one there is wedded harmony; in the other attempted murder. Each location has a role in the play as important as that of any single character.

The women arrive at Belmont first, and Portia cautions all there to remain silent about their absence. The men appear, and Portia is welcoming Antonio when a squabble breaks out between Gratiano and Nerissa, who has taken notice that he no longer wears her ring. He claims he gave it in gratitude to a doctor's clerk, "a kind of boy, a little scrubbed boy," but she insists that if it was a gift to a clerk, it was to one who "will ne'er wear hair on's face." Portia, with a mock superior air, chides Gratiano, expressing confidence that her husband would not part with her ring "for all the wealth / That the world masters." Bassanio is at a loss for words, but Gratiano, determined not to take all the heat alone, impulsively blurts out that his friend has given his ring away as well. Portia is indignant, accusing her husband of giving it, like Gratanio, to a woman. Bassanio tries to explain that it was a gift to "a civil doctor" who had saved his dear friend's life, a claim Antonio confirms, but she will have none of it. The knife is in now, and Portia gives it a twist. She reveals that unknown to their husbands, she and Nerissa have taken that same doctor and his clerk as bedfellows. The men don't believe them until they produce the rings, claiming they were gifts from their supposed paramours. Bassanio is again speechless, but Gratiano is seldom without words. "What," he exclaims, "are we cuckolds ere we deserv'd it!"

There is a subtle undercurrent of purpose to Portia's trickery. She has witnessed the close bond between Bassanio and Antonio, and though perhaps not exactly threatened by it, she senses that a point must be made about her husband's priorities. Hers is an innocent jest, after all, and once it is explained the men good-naturedly accept the fact that they have been the victims of a clever joke. Nonetheless they have also been put on notice that they are now married and will have to reexamine the order of their obligations. To love Antonio is all very well, but wives will henceforth take precedence in the allotment of affections. Portia takes nothing away from Antonio here, she simply sets the record straight. Indeed, she gives him something—a letter with news that, contrary to former reports, three of his ships have come safely to harbor. So harmony is restored, and all retire to the house with the earthy Gratiano considering his options—whether to bed Nerissa now or later.

Portia is a superb figure. The only question we may have about Shakespeare's construction of her character is whether our early view of her prepares us adequately for the transformation to the learned judge and subtle schemer of the final acts. There seems at first glance a troubling disparity between the obedient daughter—raised, we may assume, in a traditionally protective environment to perform household duties—and the daring young woman who convincingly carries off her disguise as a learned doctor of law in the court of the Duke of Venice, outwits Shylock, and saves the life of her husband's friend.

We can perhaps dismiss her earlier protest that she is "an unlesson'd girl, unschool'd, unpracticed," the conventional image of a Renaissance maiden, as a touch of virgin modesty as she offers herself to the delighted Bassanio. There's obviously more to her than that. It seems she has become maturely cosmopolitan during her ordeal of the caskets, greeting prospective suitors from all corners of Europe with poise and confidence, and dismissing them courteously despite her secret contempt for them. She easily adopts the mask of decorum and has grown wise in the ways of the world. Like most of Shakespeare's comic heroines, she is much more interesting than her male counterpart, who on our first encounter seems an appealing but somewhat feckless youth. He reveals a streak of common sense in choosing the lead casket, but he cannot compare to the fascinating creature who defeats the vengeful Jew and cleverly tutors her husband about his obligations.

Once Shylock retires in disgrace, he is never heard from again—indeed, save for two brief remarks, is never heard *of* again, leaving us only to imagine how he will spend the balance of his days. Shakespeare purges him from the play toward the end of Act Four so that his troubling presence is not allowed to intrude on the serenity of Belmont. It is indeed a relief for us to put him from our minds and sit back to enjoy the clever word play, delightful ironies, and comic possibilities of Portia's deception. It is as if his dejected figure has been erased from the thoughts of the young Venetians. But it doesn't quite work for us. Shylock will not go away, and we are left with that unresolved dilemma, torn between sympathy for his suffering and disgust at his inhumanity. The playful banter between the lovers cannot lift the heavy weight of the trial scene. We cannot forget the humiliated Shylock, bereft now of family, wealth, and even his precious religion, sitting among possessions no longer his, nursing his hereditary anguish. Certainly Portia has a somewhat serious purpose in mind at the end—to show Bassanio where his true affections should lie—but in comparison with Shylock's stark tragedy, the play of sentiments in Belmont seems somehow trivial. We cannot relish his defeat with the satisfaction of an Elizabethan audience. We cannot turn so lightly to lovers' comic tricks with that dark figure brooding over our spirits.

AS YOU LIKE IT

❧

THIS PLAY is a vacation in the country, a romp in the woods. In the *pastoral* tradition, it demonstrates the healing powers of nature upon spirits oppressed by the artificial values of the court, where life is marred by jealousy, hatred, and violence. The forest is a *place* of kindness, generosity, and good humor, where love can flourish. The most prominent *theme* of *As You Like It*, however, as in all of Shakespeare's comedies, is love. The poet surveys the subject with more scope than in any other play, placing before us the whole spectrum of its effects, exploring it with broad humanity, as he does warfare in *Henry V.* He displays its delights and absurdities, its joy and pain, in characters that experience emotions ranging from the lust of a predatory suitor, to the agonizing despair of a *courtly lover*, to the pure affection of a romantic couple. Love, nurtured by the forest, flowers in a rich array of colors.

The play opens in the court, a place where brother hates brother. Frederick has usurped the dukedom and banished his elder brother. Meanwhile, Orlando attacks his brother Oliver, demanding to know why he has been treated unjustly. When Oliver seeks his death, Orlando must flee. When the duke banishes his niece Rosalind, his daughter Celia, out of affection for her friend, vows to accompany her into exile. The seeds of love are sown: Orlando and Rosalind meet and are immediately smitten with each other.

But love is doomed in the court, and all seek refuge in the Forest of Arden, where Rosalind's father, the banished Duke Senior, lives a life of pastoral simplicity in the company of his loyal followers. Rosalind and Celia disguise themselves for protection, one as a young man, the other as a maid in peasant dress. The lovesick Orlando composes verses to Rosalind and tacks them on the trees of the forest. The lovers meet, but she retains her male disguise and, though in love herself, playfully offers to cure him of his sickness. And then the fun begins.

1.1   As the play opens, Orlando is complaining to the faithful old family servant, Adam, that his older brother Oliver has deprived him of his rightful inheritance and kept him in a state of penniless servitude. Oliver enters, and after heated words Orlando locks him in a wrestler's grip, demanding the thousand crowns left him in his father's will. Oliver agrees but secretly plots to take other measures.

Oliver sends for Charles, a professional wrestler. As will become evident, wrestling was a serious sport at the time, often ending in broken bones from which contestants did not always recover. Oliver asks him the news in court, and Charles replies that there is only "old news": Duke Frederick has usurped the title and banished his older brother. The old duke's daughter, Rosalind, has been permitted to remain in court because she and the new duke's daughter, Celia, are very close, "never two ladies loved as they do." Rosalind's father, known only as Duke Senior, has taken refuge in the Forest of Arden with a group of retainers loyal to him.

Charles reveals that Orlando has challenged him to a bout and suggests that Oliver attempt to deter his brother. Oliver replies that he has already tried to do so and goes on to advise Charles maliciously that "I had as lief thou didst break his neck as his finger." It is an open question why he hates Orlando so fiercely—indeed, he doesn't even know why—but Shakespeare does not explore the matter. Brothers are often jealous of one another, and such seems to be the case here. Orlando is simply more attractive, and as a result Oliver feels "misprised [diminished]," so he plots to dispose of his younger brother. These things happen.

1.2   In contrast to this episode of violence and hatred, the next scene introduces the theme of love—the close affection between Rosalind and Celia. As it opens, Rosalind is sad, as befits a comedy which will trace the change in her fortunes from bad to good, and Celia is attempting to cheer her. After lively banter between them about falling in love and the relationship of nature to fortune, Touchstone enters. He is the court jester, or fool, full of songs, riddles, and witty cynicism about life, all relatively harmless, meant only to entertain. This first encounter is characteristic of his style. Celia challenges his use of the phrase "by mine honor," implying that he has none, and through a circuitous and highly questionable chain of logic he ends up doubting the "honor" of one of her father's courtiers. Touchstone's wit is often directed at court manners, and Celia warns him that he could be whipped for such "taxation [fault-finding]." He replies with mocking self-pity that it is a shame "fools may not speak wisely when wisemen do foolishly."

Le Beau enters. He is a stock character in Shakespeare, the court fop who in his elegant attire and exaggerated gesture is a parody of formal manners. He is customarily dim-witted as well, a figure of fun as here, where the three mock him by twisting his words into insulting quips that go right over his head. He is finally able to get his message out, an invitation to the wrestling match, to which Touchstone replies archly, "it is the first time that ever I heard breaking of bones was sport for ladies."

The court enters with Orlando and Charles stripped for the bout. The duke asks Celia and Rosalind to persuade Orlando to withdraw, but he refuses with a speech full of courtesy toward the "fair and excellent ladies" and an account of himself that could only raise their pity. If he is killed, he says, he will not wrong his friends, "for I have none to lament me," nor do injury to the world, for "in it I have nothing." This combination of courtesy and pity is apparently enough to win the heart of Rosalind—"O excellent young man!" Orlando wins the wrestling match and the duke approaches to congratulate him, only to hear that he is the son of Sir Rowland de Boys, who before his death had been a loyal courtier to the old duke. Frederick remarks sternly, "I would thou hadst been son to some man else," and departs. The two women approach Orlando, who as Rosalind places a congratulatory chain about his neck, is struck speechless. They turn to go; but Rosalind, hearing him mutter to himself, turns back to ask, "did you call sir?" Still stunned at the sight of her, however, he remains dumb, and she must turn again, leaving him with the assurance that he has "overthrown / More than [his] enemies."

So the two have fallen in love at first sight, as Shakespeare's lovers invariably do. But the road to romance will be rocky indeed. Le Beau approaches Orlando and warns him that he had best "leave this place," for the duke has taken a dislike to him and "the Duke is humorous [temperamental, unpredictable]." Orlando asks the identity of the young women. Le Beau tells him but goes on to reveal that the "humorous" duke has taken a dislike to Rosalind as well, because "the people praise her for her virtues, / And pity her for her good father's sake." Orlando takes the advice and determines to leave, with a parting thought of "heavenly Rosalind."

1.3   For her part, Rosalind is seriously smitten, and in the next scene Celia attempts to cheer her with an exchange of puns about her condition. Rosalind complains that the world is full of "briers," which then become "burs" that get caught on petticoats. But the burs are in her heart, she says, and Celia, returning to petticoats, advises her to "hem them away," whereupon the "hem" becomes "him"—and so it goes. The play abounds in this kind of mock-serious play on words.

Duke Frederick interrupts them with an order for Rosalind's banishment. She defends herself stoutly, asking why this sudden change of heart. But he is adamant—"thou art thy father's daughter, there's enough"—and he warns her to leave under pain of death. He stalks off, but such is the love between the two young women that Celia determines to accompany Rosalind in exile. They decide to join her father in the Forest of Arden and to assume disguises for protection. Rosalind, being the taller, will dress as a young man, taking the name of Ganymede, and Celia will wear the guise of a country maid, "in poor and mean attire," called Aliena. They decide to take along the court fool for company and, to sustain themselves, what jewels and wealth they can collect.

2.1   The first act serves to move the principals to the forest. The second act finds us there, and Shakespeare's concept of place assumes importance. The court bristles with hatred and violence, and Duke Senior, a victim of its intrigues, asks in his opening speech, "are not these woods / More free from peril than the envious court?" In famous lines he declares, "sweet are the uses of adversity," and takes pleasure in a life that can find "tongues in trees, books in running brooks, / Sermons in stones, and good in everything." Although the forest is depicted as a place where good prevails, Shakespeare does not describe life there as entirely ideal, as it is pictured in the fanciful pastoral tradition. As the duke says, "the winter's wind . . . bites and blows upon my body" at times, but even this discomfort can be redeeming, since the wind and cold are unflattering "counsellors / That feelingly persuade me what I am."

There is hunger and death in the forest as well. After a somewhat idealistic appreciation of the state of nature, the duke finds himself with an appetite and suggests, with a touch of regret to be sure, that they kill a deer for supper. The thought leads to the introduction of the melancholy Jaques (pronounced *Jak*-weeze), not in person as yet, but through a description by the unnamed first lord. Jaques was discovered lying by a stream contemplating the plight of a wounded deer, weeping at the sight, and comparing the suffering of the animal to the human condition. In his ruminations Jaques is said to pierce "through / The body of country, city, court, / Yea, and this our life," in a way an apt description of the play itself.

2.2   The next scene returns us briefly to the court, where Duke Frederick has discovered the flight of his daughter and niece. He is told that they might be with Orlando, for whom they had expressed admiration, so the duke angrily orders his arrest, or if that fails, the apprehension of his brother Oliver. This short interlude sets up a pattern for future scenes, where we watch love flower in a pastoral setting but are transported from time to time back to the contentious court, lending emphasis to the contrast between the two settings.

2.3   As he prepares to flee the city, Orlando once again encounters Adam, who urges him to avoid Oliver, who still seeks his death. The loyal old servant offers his life's savings to Orlando, vowing to join in his flight and continue to serve him. Orlando praises the old man for his devotion, "the constant service of the antique world, / When service sweat for duty, not for meed." It is a sentiment to be heard in any age, though generally from an older generation that laments the passing of the virtues of an earlier time.

2.4   Rosalind, Celia, and Touchstone, the fool, arrive in Arden. Touchstone is a creature of the court and feels entirely out of place in a pastoral setting, where his wit is lost in the unsophisticated society of forest and meadow. As he puts it, "now I am in Arden, the more fool I." They conceal themselves upon the approach of two shepherds, the one, Corin, much older than his companion, Silvius, who seems to be in some distress. He is in love, and is convinced that his passion is unique in the history of the world, more intense, he is certain, than any Corin could have possibly experienced in his youth. He rushes off, exclaiming, "O Phebe, Phebe, Phebe." Thus, no sooner do these transplanted creatures of the court find themselves in the forest than they encounter a young man in love, one whose "wound," Rosalind confesses, reminds her of her own. The passion of Silvius and the mention of "wound" alert us to the introduction of the theme of courtly love: the young man is in pain, wounded by the lady's eyes, and can only be saved by her "pity." Touchstone immediately parodies this fanciful image with a comic description of his own rough wooing of "Jane Smile," apparently a servant girl. "True lovers," he concludes, "run into strange capers." They approach Corin and through him purchase a cottage and flock of sheep.

2.5   We return to the banished court, where Amiens is singing "Under the Greenwood Tree," a ballad that extols the pastoral life, where the only enemy is "winter and rough weather." And here we meet Jaques, who asks Amiens to continue and identifies himself for us in a phrase: "I can suck melancholy out of a song, as a weasel sucks eggs." After some banter, Amiens ends his song and Jaques adds a chorus ridiculing the pastoral theme—only an ass would leave "wealth and ease" for a country life. He substitutes "Ducdame" for Amiens's "Come hither," and when asked what it means replies, "'tis a Greek invocation, to call fools into a circle." This is a visual joke, a piece of stage business, in which as Jaques sings the group gather about him and so become the "fools [in] a circle." He is not without wit, we discover, but it targets the whole human race, even here the amiable Amiens, who has sung at his request but is included in the circle of "fools."

2.6   In another part of the forest, Adam and Orlando are in flight from the court, but the old man is failing for lack of food and Orlando vows to find him some. A minor theme of the play is the relationship between youth and age, as enacted in this brief scene and the earlier encounter between Corin and Silvius.

2.7   We move to the banished court, gathered for supper. Their conversation is of Jaques, as it was when last we met them. It seems he provides entertainment for the exiles, in much the same role as Touchstone at court—playing tricks on them, singing satiric songs, mocking their customs, and at times singling out individuals as targets for his wit. But, again, the object of that wit is the world itself, not just the immediate company. He avoids society, except necessarily at meals, preferring either solitude or individual company. Further, unlike the fool, he does not seem to be playing a role—he means it all. Nonetheless, the duke and his followers are amused by him and seek him out for distraction—there's not much to do in the forest.

Again they wonder where he is. This time he appears in person, raving about a meeting with "a motley fool," motley being the multicolored costume traditionally worn by jesters. He has encountered Touchstone, who seized upon his simple greeting, "good morrow, fool," to weave an elaborate jest on time, ending with the pessimistic observation that "from hour to hour, we ripe, and ripe, / And from hour to hour, we rot, and rot." Jaques confesses that he laughed for an hour at the jest, though, we can be assured, not at the humor of it. He delights rather in a gloomy description of life that fits well with his philosophy, and he is pleased to have found someone who seems sympathetic with his own disposition. He admires the fool's license to speak freely and claims that, had he the same license, he would "cleanse the foul body of th'infected world." The duke challenges him and receives a reply—this is why they enjoy his company—only to have the exchange interrupted by Orlando, who bursts upon them, sword in hand.

Orlando demands food. When told he is free to eat all he wants, he is surprised at their generosity, explaining that he had expected a hostile reception in such a "savage" place. He leaves to fetch Adam, pledging not to eat until his friend "be first suffic'd." While Orlando is gone, Jaques delivers his famous speech, beginning "all the world's a stage, / And all the men and women merely players." This is a favorite theme of Shakespeare's, which we find time and again in the plays, most notably in Macbeth's "poor player / That struts and frets his hour upon the stage," and in Prospero's prediction that the world shall dissolve, and like the *masque* he has just dismissed, "leave not a rack behind." The stage, the poet observes, is unreal, a mere fiction; and life as well may be but a dream, as Prospero would have it, or simply a place where one "plays many parts" in Jaques's phrase. In his melancholy view of life, he finds humankind moving pointlessly through seven ridiculous ages, from "the infant / Mewling and puking in the nurse's arms" to the second childhood of old age, "sans [without] teeth, sans eyes, sans taste, sans everything."

Orlando returns with Adam, who offers thanks. Amiens sings again, a not entirely happy ballad that reminds us again that the pastoral life is less than ideal. "Blow, blow, thou winter wind," he begins, and compares it to life, finding its unseen bite "not so sharp / As friend remembered not." Save for the last line—"this life is most jolly"—it is a sentiment worthy of Jaques. The duke identifies himself and welcomes Orlando as the son of a father he had loved.

3.1   Meanwhile, hatred and jealousy prevail at court. Duke Frederick demands that Oliver find his brother and bring him back "dead or living." Until he does, the angry duke rages, all of Oliver's wealth and lands are forfeit.

3.2   In a sharp shift in tone, the next scene finds the lovelorn Orlando writing poems to the absent Rosalind, as many a lover has been known to do, and hanging them on the trees of the forest, which is a new twist to the old story. He dashes off to "carve on every tree / The fair, the chaste, and inexpressive she." He is far gone.

Touchstone and Corin enter and enact a classic encounter between court and country. The old man asks the sophisticated fool if he is enjoying the shepherd's life, and Touchstone responds with a series of witty contradictions that reflect the ambiguity of human desire—"in respect it is in the fields, it pleaseth me well; but in respect it is not in court, it is tedious." And so it is with us—paradoxically we want both Eden and the World, enjoy the pastoral for its peace and solitude but need the court with its bustling society. Touchstone engages in questionable chains of logic to demonstrate that Corin is damned because he has never been to court. The simple shepherd attempts to stay with him in the exchange but finally admits good-naturedly, "you have too courtly a wit for me, I'll rest." Pushed further, he affirms his uncomplicated creed, defining the pastoral ideal:

> Sir, I am a true laborer: I earn that I eat, get that I wear; owe no man
> hate, envy no man's happiness; glad of other men's good, content with
> my harm; and the greatest of my pride is to see my ewes graze and my
> lambs suck.

Touchstone insists on having the last word, accusing Corin of making a living by the copulation of sheep, because of which he is indeed damned. In the end our sympathies lie with the natural man whose ambition goes no further than the enjoyment of what he has. The courtly fool wins his clever argument but loses the case.

The play returns abruptly to the theme of love, where it is most to be enjoyed. Rosalind enters, reading one of Orlando's poems, which she has found on a tree. It rhymes, though imperfectly (the last syllable of her name is sounded "lined"), demonstrating that Shakespeare could write bad verse when he put his mind to it. Touchstone responds with verses of his own, mocking Orlando's romantic excesses by couching his in the more earthy terms of animals pursuing mates, and ending with the bawdy, "he that sweetest rose will find / Must find love's prick, and Rosalind." In modern terms, it may be said that Touchstone's mind is in the gutter.

Rosalind matches his wit until Celia comes upon them with more verses that further extol the virtues of her friend. Celia, who anticipates confidences with Rosalind, asks the others to leave. She then toys with her friend about the identity of the versifier, and Rosalind, who at first affects indifference, finally presses her impatiently to tell who he is. Celia, delighting in Rosalind's ignorance—"O wonderful, wonderful! And most wonderful wonderful!"—finally reveals that it is Orlando who is acting so absurdly. Rosalind's immediate response is distress over her "doublet and hose," that is, her male attire, and she bursts into an impatient series of questions about him, which Celia, still amused, attempts to answer. But they are interrupted by the appearance of Orlando himself, accompanied by Jaques. The women conceal themselves.

Jaques has a moment with each of the main characters, here with Orlando, later with Touchstone and Rosalind, in each case, it would appear, seeking them out. The encounter with Orlando does not go well, however, as they dismiss one another with mock courtesy: "God buy you: let's meet as little as we can," and "I do desire we may be better strangers." Jaques stays to ridicule Orlando's lovesick state, but he gets as good as he gives from the young man until they finally part: "Farewell, good Signior Love," and "Adieu, good Monsieur Melancholy."

Rosalind steps boldly out of hiding, and we are asked to exercise a *suspension of disbelief* in accepting the proposition that Orlando does not recognize her. She embarks on an extended display of wit on the subject of time, designed to attract his attention. It succeeds admirably, for he is clearly intrigued by the clever Ganymede. He continues to question her until finally she mentions the poems, and he admits that he is the one "so love-shaken," asking if she has a remedy for his condition.

Rosalind is clearly setting the pace of the entire exchange, with Orlando tamely following her lead. She invents an uncle who told her how to recognize a true lover, and taunts Orlando by telling him he has none of the telltale marks. Those she mentions are drawn directly from the tradition of the courtly lover suffering from the pangs of unrequited affection—"a lean cheek," a sunken eye, an irritable spirit, "a beard neglected," a lack of concern for his appearance, and "everything about [him] demonstrating a careless desolation." Orlando is no such lover, since, as she puts it, "you are rather point-device in your accoutrements," his tidy appearance more characteristic of one who loves himself rather than another. Orlando insists that he is the author of the verses, that "unfortunate he" who worships Rosalind.

She assumes the stance of a rather cynical, worldly-wise young man who declares that love is "merely a madness," and offers to cure Orlando of his affliction. She claims to have succeeded on a former occasion when she persuaded a lovesick youth to imagine that she was his mistress and in response to his wooing acted out all the most objectionable qualities of a flighty young woman who may or may not have loved him. She "would now like him, now loath him; then entertain him, then forswear [reject] him, now weep for him, then spit on him" until he finally rejected the world and retired "to live in a nook merely monastic." She proposes to repeat the remedy if Orlando wishes to be cured. He is to woo her as he would Rosalind, had he the opportunity, and, still intrigued, he agrees. The proposal sets up a dizzying complexity of gender identities. Since female characters on the Elizabethan stage were played by boys, we have a male actor in a female role, who in turn adopts the disguise of a male and then proposes to act the part of a female. The comic possibilities are legion.

3.3   But before we can learn how this curious charade will work itself out, we are introduced to two additional couples, each markedly different from the other and from the central affair between Rosalind and Orlando, completing Shakespeare's survey of love. The first is Touchstone in pursuit of Audrey, a young, wholesome, unlettered country girl, the female counterpart to Corin, though without the experience and wisdom of his years. Touchstone literally lusts after her. She is not unaware of his desire, but, though receptive, she virtuously succeeds in fending him off as he presses his attention upon her. Jaques is concealed nearby, watching this curious courtship.

All of his wit, Touchstone has discovered, is lost on the simple Audrey, so he is reduced to pursuing her with speeches full of double meanings, some addressed to her, some to an invisible, more appreciative audience. She claims to be "honest," which he takes to mean "chaste," which he wishes she were not. He claims that honesty is wasted on a "foul slut," which seems a gross insult, but she takes "foul" to mean simply plain looking and "slut" merely untidy, and takes no serious offense. Touchstone seems to be talking to himself half the time, rambling on about "horns," which were said to grow on the brow of a cuckolded husband, for all but him to see. He resigns himself to the fact that he can have his way with the "honest" Audrey only by marrying her. Since she seems quite willing, he has arranged for Sir Oliver Martext to perform the rites. Sir Oliver is a comic figure, an unlettered country vicar whose only requirement for this most uncanonical wedding is the presence of someone to give the bride away.

Jaques steps out and volunteers for the role but frowns on the proceedings. Touchstone explains his motives in the most elemental terms, comparing his desire to that of animals, and Jaques reproves him for marrying improperly. The fool shamelessly admits that he has purposely chosen Sir Oliver, since if they are not "well married, it will be a good excuse for me hereafter to leave my wife," but he accepts Jaques's counsel. Touchstone here is a prototype of the slick city sophisticate preying on the affections of a simple country girl. He is endlessly amusing though not an entirely attractive figure, but we must admit that love sometime follows this pattern, so it deserves consideration in Shakespeare's survey of the subject.

3.4   The next two scenes present other patterns entirely. Rosalind is in distress because Orlando has promised to meet her that morning and has not appeared. The levelheaded Celia has some sharp words about men in general and Orlando in particular, who, she says, certainly "writes brave verses" and "speaks brave words" but will prove false in the end. Corin enters, asking if they would like to see Silvius woo "the proud disdainful shepherdess / That was his mistress." Rosalind agrees, since "the sight of love feedeth those in love."

3.5   Concealing themselves, they observe yet another pattern of love, this time between a shepherd and a shepherdess. All is not well with them, however, for Silvius is pleading with Phebe not to scorn him. His language is drawn from the tradition of courtly love, where the rejected suitor was said to be dying from the disdain of his mistress, having been wounded by her eyes. The literal-minded Phebe denies that she has injured Silvius since he bears no outward evidence of harm; but he insists that his are "wounds invisible." The tradition, again, prescribes that his wounds can be cured only by the lady's "pity," but Phebe declares haughtily that she wants no part of him.

At this point Rosalind emerges from hiding and demands of her, "and why I pray you?" She proceeds to chide Phebe for her pride, but notices that the shepherdess is paying particularly close attention—"I think she means to tangle my eyes too!" She turns to Silvius, calling him "a thousand times a properer man / Than she a woman," and then back to Phebe with what is one of the most devastating put-downs in literature. Fall on your knees, she admonishes the haughty maiden, "thank heaven, fasting, for a good man's love" and "sell when you can, you are not for all markets." Phebe, however, is captivated by the youth, and an exasperated Rosalind exclaims impatiently, "he's fallen in love with your foulness, and she's fallen in love with my anger." Rosalind leaves after more sharp words for her, but Phebe has indeed fallen for the abrasive Ganymede, and Shakespeare gives her a line from Christopher Marlowe: "Dead shepherd, now I find thy saw of might, 'Who ever lov'd that lov'd not at first sight.'"*

But Silvius, ever faithful, stands by, uttering the plaintive plea of the courtly lover, "sweet Phebe pity me," and she agrees in so far as to say, "I will endure; and I'll employ thee too." The pathetic Silvius, who has observed her attraction to Ganymede, is content. He will gladly accept any affection left over, "the broken ears after the man / That the main harvest reaps," so long as she will "loose now and then / A scatter'd smile" in his direction. The courtly lover asks no more. Phebe then examines her emotional response to Ganymede, one filled with contradictions, and decides to write him "a very taunting letter," which Silvius agrees to deliver. He is ecstatic to be of service.

So we have it all now, three pairings across the spectrum of love relationships—with a fourth to come, which we learn of by report. The attraction between Orlando and Rosalind, with its paradoxical mixture of

*From Marlowe's *Hero and Leander*.

joy and anguish, would be called today "romance," marked by love at first sight and the compelling desire, though thwarted, just to be with each other. Touchstone's desire for Audrey, on the other hand, is calculatingly lustful, a factor not absent from any love affair certainly, but here it is quite blatantly the only attraction in evidence. The devotion of Silvius for Phebe imitates and parodies the tradition of courtly love: eyes that wound, pleas for pity, and a dedication to service, amply rewarded by so little as a "scatter'd smile." Phebe's infatuation for the abusive Ganymede adds yet another dimension to Shakespeare's survey of the subject in its many guises. And, aside from these relationships, moved as they are by passion, we have examples of other, calmer bondings—the affection between Rosalind and Celia, and the loyalty between Orlando and Adam.

Further, the phenomenon of love is the subject of a wealth of commentary as the various figures respond to the pairings in the plot. Jaques contemplates the lovers scornfully—they seem to leave him sad and cynical. Touchstone, on the other hand, is merry and lecherous. The most interesting, of course, is Rosalind, who in the character of Ganymede is ruthlessly practical. She is certainly the most intriguing of Shakespeare's comic heroines, a character endowed with the best of both worlds. As a young woman in the throes of love, she has all our sympathy, while at the same time we can heartily agree with Ganymede's dismissal of her condition as "merely a madness." She demonstrates, through the artifice of her disguise, the ideal balance between mind and emotion, good sense and desire. Because she is in love herself, she can scoff at Orlando's state without losing our sympathies, which might otherwise be alienated by the game she plays. The role she assumes to cure his distress permits her to act out all the follies of a lover without appearing subject to them herself. She can be at once frivolous and wise, coy and genuine, unsettled and poised, vacillating and constant, playing the part without suffering the censure of frivolity. She is truly a masterful creation.

4.1 Act Four opens with a discussion of melancholy between Rosalind and Jaques, but they are interrupted by Orlando, who is late for his appointment. In a delightful instance of her double role, Rosalind is genuinely upset by his tardiness. In her own person she may well be inclined to forgive him and leap into his arms; but as Ganymede playing Rosalind, she can be more "changeable, longing and liking, proud, fantastical, apish, shallow, [and] inconstant," as she had warned him she would. She chides him for his lack of devotion. "You a lover!" she scoffs, declaring that no true one would "break an hour's promise." She continues to berate him with more talk of horns but suddenly changes her tone, inviting him to "woo me, woo me." Orlando gallantly says that he would rather kiss her first, but she puts him off with more witty banter and then announces that she "will not have him." Orlando responds that therefore he will die. He is playing his part in the charade here, not the first nor the last young man to proclaim that he would willingly give his life for his mistress. Taking him at his word, Rosalind assumes the posture of a worldly-wise cynic who scoffs at the whole notion of romantic love, ending with the practical counsel, "men have died from time to time and worms have eaten them, but not for love."

Rosalind then arranges for a mock wedding with Celia presiding. This accomplished, she asks Orlando how long he will keep her. He replies with the predictable "for ever, and a day," at which she scoffs again, explaining that lovers change once married: "Men are April when they woo, December when they wed. Maids are May when they are maids, but the sky changes when they are wives." She offers a graphic picture of what her disposition will be after the wedding: jealous, clamorous, giddy, perverse, and unfaithful. So much for romance! Orlando then announces that he must leave for dinner with the duke, a foreshadowing of the postnuptial priorities of a man of the world. Rosalind replies with a plaintive "alas, dear love, I cannot lack thee two hours," and dismisses him mockingly—"my friends told me" about men like you—but not before pledging him to be punctual next time.

Once he has left, Celia is sharp with Rosalind, accusing her of dirtying "her own nest," but the poor girl is in genuine distress: "I tell thee Aliena, I cannot be out of the sight of Orlando. I'll go find a shadow and sigh till he come." The somewhat unsympathetic Celia replies simply, "and I'll sleep." This is a charming instance of Rosalind's two roles converging. When she says that she begrudges Orlando his two hours with the duke, she really means it! But we forgive her peevish response to his departure, assured that she is in the role of Ganymede playing Rosalind and would certainly not behave so unpleasantly in her own person. Or would she?

4.2–3   There follows a brief interlude with Jaques and some lords who have killed a deer for supper. They indulge in banter and sing a song, here again on the theme of "the horn, the horn, the lusty horn." But we quickly return to Celia and Rosalind, who complains that Orlando is late again. Silvius comes up to deliver the letter from Phebe, which he has been persuaded "bears an angry tenor," but Rosalind reads it aloud to reveal that it is rather a love letter. She has harsh words for Phebe but accepts the fact that love has made Silvius "a tame snake," and she poses a stern trial for his devotion. She will not have Phebe, she says, unless he pleads for her, certainly the ultimate test of his courtly dedication to his lady's service.

As Silvius leaves, Oliver approaches the two, who acknowledge their disguised identities. It will be recalled that Duke Frederick sent him on a mission to bring back Orlando, dead or alive, but this is a radically changed Oliver. He bears an offering from Orlando, a "bloody napkin [handkerchief]," and explains that his brother has saved him from the attack of a lioness in the forest and as a consequence the two have reconciled. In the fight, however, Orlando was slightly wounded and sends the "napkin" as his excuse for missing his appointment. On hearing that the blood is Orlando's, Rosalind faints. She quickly recovers and anxiously insists that she was only "counterfeiting" her distress, acting her part in the charade she is playing with him. Oliver is unconvinced but accompanies her to her cottage.

5.1 Act Five opens with an encounter between Touchstone and William, a simple, slow-witted shepherd who is a rival for Audrey's hand. Touchstone toys with him, talking rings around the uncomprehending man, and finally dismisses him with threats of bodily harm—"therefore tremble and depart." At a word from Audrey, William leaves with a lighthearted, "God rest you merry, sir."

5.2–3 We turn next to Orlando and Oliver, who confesses that he has fallen in love with Aliena and is so enthralled that he intends to turn over all his wealth to his brother, content to "live and die a shepherd" with her. Rosalind enters and confirms the match: "They are in the very wrath of love, and they will together. Clubs cannot part them." They are to be married the following day, but the thought of such happiness so saddens Orlando that he cannot continue his game with Rosalind. She claims to have some skills in magic and promises that next day she will

produce the real Rosalind for him. The company is then approached by
Silvius and Phebe, who is upset that Rosalind has read her letter to him
but has accepted the challenge, having apparently persuaded the poor
man to plead for her. She asks Silvius to say "what 'tis to love" and in
what surely is the ultimate act of "service," he describes it in the courtly
tradition: sighs, tears, service, fantasy, passion, adoration, duty, and trial.
The scene assumes a tone of ritual as all profess their love, Silvius for
Phebe, Phebe for Ganymede, Orlando for Rosalind, and she, cryptically,
"for no woman." She promises that the desire of each will be fulfilled the
following day, including Phebe's, and pledges to her, "I will marry you, if
ever I marry woman, and I'll be married tomorrow."

5.4   Shakespeare's comedies invariably end on a note of reconciliation, hope, and joy, and this one is no exception. The banished court enters, followed shortly by Silvius, Phebe, and Rosalind, still in the guise of
Ganymede. She pledges all present to abide by the various promises made
and then departs with Celia. Touchstone and Audrey approach, and he
confirms his intention to marry, though in characteristically ribald terms.
He surveys the various lovers in the company and in mock humility excuses himself for pressing "in here sir, amongst the rest of the country
copulatives" with his prospective bride, "a poor virgin sir, an ill-favored
thing sir, but mine own." His blatantly sensual vision of love cuts across
the romantic and courtly versions voiced by the others. Touchstone has
been described as "the scapegoat of Arden," since all of the least attractive
qualities of love are heaped upon him, leaving the other relationships unsullied by sex. On the other hand, his unscrupulous pursuit of Audrey reminds us of the basic passion that lies just below the surface of the
idealized devotion the others profess for one another.

Jaques is more interested in Touchstone's chance remark about quarrels "upon the seventh cause" and is favored with an elaborate discourse
on courtly behavior. Rosalind and Celia now appear as themselves, led on
stage by the figure of Hymen, the Greek god of marriage. It was quite
common for ancient Greek plays to end with the appearance of a god, a
deus ex machina who descends to straighten out a mess that muddled humans have created. But Hymen is a purely ceremonial figure here, whose
only function is to preside over the marriages with precise poetry and due
decorum. There is more ritual and song as the four couples are joined in a
ceremony with overtones of a *masque*.

To tie up some loose ends of the plot, another Jaques enters, this one the briefly mentioned brother to Oliver and Orlando, who carries some happy news. Duke Frederick, who was leading an armed force to root out Duke Senior, encountered "an old religious man" upon entering the forest and has been converted to a monastic life, surrendering the dukedom to his brother. The restored duke assures all who have remained loyal that they will "share the good of our returned fortune," but for the moment, he declares, they will celebrate the marriages with "rustic revelry."

Jaques has the last word, however. He declines to join in the revelry or to return to court with the company. Instead he will seek out Frederick, since from such converts, he says, "there is much matter to be heard and learn'd." Before leaving, he has a word for each of the bridegrooms. To Orlando he bequeaths a love that his "true faith doth merit." Oliver, he observes, will not have to live on love alone, since he need not give up his "lands" to marry Celia and will have "great allies" in his friends and relatives. Discarding all of Silvius's elaborate language of courtly love, all that business of service, adoration, fantasy, and trial, Jaques cuts to the quick, awarding him "a well-deserved bed." To Touchstone he bequeaths only "wrangling," and predicts that his "loving voyage" will last but two months, a safe estimate from what we have observed. His melancholy, or realistic, description of the couples is not permitted to dampen the joyous mood, however, and the play ends with an episode of music and dance.

Epi.   Rosalind reappears to deliver the epilogue. It is unusual for "the lady" to do so, as she acknowledges; but her assumption of the role serves to emphasize that she is indeed the chief figure of the play, as complex and attractive a comic character as ever Shakespeare created for the stage.

Thus Shakespeare's Forest of Arden is a place where love can blossom, in contrast to Duke Frederick's court where hatred thrives and breaking ribs is sport for ladies, and from which citizens are banished simply because they are well liked. But Arden is not the ideal pastoral setting of the tradition. Deer are slaughtered here, lions lie in wait for human prey, and foresters must endure "winter and rough weather." It has its magic nonetheless. Oliver sheds his jealousy under the shade of its trees; upon entering it the duke undergoes a conversion, abandoning his court for a hermit's cave; and Orlando and Rosalind, whose love is doomed by court custom, find one another in a woodland glade.

Love can flourish in the forest, but Shakespeare describes it as a passion of many colors. Orlando is faithful to his absent Rosalind, to be sure, and Oliver willingly surrenders his wealth just to be with Aliena; but Silvius suffers the tortures of the rejected courtly lover pining away for his disdainful mistress, and Phebe's sudden infatuation for Ganymede is destined for disappointment. Touchstone is little more than a lustful predator, intent only upon satisfying his desires in pursuit of the simple, innocent Audrey. For every winner there is a loser—even the witless William understands that. But no such thoughts can dim the joy of the final celebration of music and dance, after which the entire party, save only for Jaques and the shepherd pair, will return to the court, where things will now be different, it is implied, where love, purified and blessed by the forest, will prevail. Though not for Touchstone, we may be assured.

TWELFTH NIGHT
or
WHAT YOU WILL

❧

LIKE MANY of Shakespeare's plays, this one contains a plot and a sub-plot; and again, as in the case of Beatrice and Benedict in *Much Ado About Nothing* and Falstaff in *Henry IV*, the subplot seems to take over the poet's pen and provide most of the comic element, even supplying the title. The twelve days after Christmas were a traditional time of festival, culminating in a night of unrestrained revelry, of masqueing and merriment. There is nothing in the play to indicate that it takes place at this time of year—the title simply announces that the spirit of holiday will prevail throughout.

The plot is an involved love story. Twins, a sister Viola and a brother Sebastian, survive a shipwreck but are separated. Each thinks the other drowned. Viola, disguised as a young man, Cesario, joins the service of Duke Orsino, who takes her into his close confidence. He is in love with Olivia, who spurns him; and he employs Cesario to woo her in his name. But Olivia falls in love with Cesario, a development complicated by the fact that the disguised Viola has fallen in love with the duke. When Sebastian enters the scene, Olivia thinks he is Cesario and pledges him to marriage; and when the twins are brought face to face, revealing Viola's identity, the duke takes her as his wife and Olivia embraces Sebastian in her stead, concluding the play on a note of love and harmony.

The subplot pits the spirit of irrepressible and irresponsible merriment, represented by Sir Toby Belch, the maidservant Maria, and Sir Andrew Aguecheek,* against the influence of solemn sobriety, embodied in the stuffy person of Olivia's steward, the dour Malvolio. He is tricked into believing that his mistress is in love with him, and in the end is humiliated mercilessly, resulting in a momentary triumph for the spirit of Twelfth Night over puritanical self-righteousness.

1.1   The first scenes introduce two of the principal characters in the love story. Duke Orsino of Illyria is the rejected suitor of his neighbor, Olivia, and he plays the part to the hilt, sighing at the sound of music and comparing himself to the "hart [deer]" beset by the "cruel hounds" of his desires. He is prostrate, the *courtly lover* suffering the pangs of unrequited devotion. The lady, he is told, having just lost her brother, is determined to mourn him for seven years, during which time no one will be permitted to "behold her face at ample vision."

1.2   Next we find Viola, rescued from a shipwreck by a solicitous captain who is native to the area. She also mourns the loss of a brother, who she fears has drowned in the storm. She learns that they have landed in Illyria, that it is ruled by Duke Orsino, and that he seeks the hand of Olivia, who spurns him. Viola finds the captain worthy of trust and enlists his aid to disguise her as a man so that she can join Orsino's service. She will play the part of a eunuch, or castrato, she says, so as to account for her high voice.

1.3   We then move to Olivia's estate where we meet two of the revelers of the play, the lady's uncle, Sir Toby Belch, and her maidservant Maria. Sir Toby is to be imagined as a Falstaffian figure, elderly, fat, red-faced from the effects of wine, and careless in his appearance. Maria is cautioning him that Olivia is upset about his late hours, his drinking, and the company he keeps, one Sir Andrew Aguecheek, whom he has introduced to his niece as a prospective suitor. Sir Toby defends his companion who, he says, has an income of "three thousand ducats a year" and is besides a musician and the master of "three or four languages"—two claims that promptly turn out to be gross exaggerations. Maria insists otherwise. The man, she contends, is a fool, a quarreler, a coward, and a

---

*Pronounced *egg-you-cheek*. An "ague" is an acute fever, marked by shivering and shaking.

drunkard, a description that serves as a cue for the entrance of Sir Andrew himself.

Aguecheek, we discover, is a dim-witted fop, the brunt of jokes by those more quick than he and easily led on by stronger spirits. Still, he is somehow endearing in his ingenuous way. His simplemindedness is immediately apparent when Sir Toby introduces him to Maria and urges him to "accost" her. Aguecheek takes the word as her name and addresses her courteously as "Good Mistress Accost," and further explanations fail to dislodge this conviction. So much for his linguistic abilities. Further banter concludes with his announcement that he intends to abandon his suit and return home. But Sir Toby insists that "there's life in't" yet, and he is easily persuaded to remain. The two engage in a lighthearted exchange about Sir Andrew's dancing skills, and they bounce off stage to "set about some revels."

1.4   Some days have passed, and in Orsino's court Viola, as the eunuch Cesario, is firmly entrenched in the duke's affections. As he puts it, "I have unclasped / To thee even the book of my secret soul." Orsino prevails upon her[*] to plead his suit with Olivia, who refuses to see him. She agrees to do so, though with great reluctance, for as she admits in an *aside*, "whoe'er I woo, myself would be his wife." She has fallen in love with Orsino!

1.5   The long final scene of Act One opens on Feste, the clown or fool. A common figure in medieval and Renaissance court circles, the jester entertained the nobility with songs, riddles, and the clever play of words, often at the expense of the very lords he served. We meet him again in Lear's Fool and Touchstone in *As You Like It,* though Shakespeare is endlessly inventive, giving him a different role wherever he appears. Here he remains generally outside of events, almost as a *chorus* commenting wittily on the antics of those involved, though by his very nature he is sympathetically attuned to the spirit of Sir Toby.

Maria chides Feste for his long absence, implying that he is attached to Olivia's household. He seems as much a minstrel as a jester, however, wandering wherever there is money to be had. Maria proves herself a worthy opponent in an exchange of wit, playing here on the double meanings

---

[*]Although Viola is known to everyone in the play as Cesario, we shall use the feminine pronoun, since after all we know who she is.

of "color," "hanging," and "points." (For a full appreciation of the puns we will be forced to consult footnotes.) Olivia enters, somewhat out of sorts, and peevishly orders her attendants to "take the fool away," to which he quickly responds, "do you hear, fellows? Take away the lady." Following a clever chain of logic, he concludes that she is indeed the fool for mourning the death of her brother, whose soul is now in heaven, and again directs the others to "take away the fool."

Here too we first encounter Olivia's steward, Malvolio, who haughtily counsels her, "I marvel your ladyship takes delight in such a barren rascal." She values him as a loyal servant but has taken his measure: "O, you are sick of self-love, Malvolio, and taste with a disapproving appetite." We can imagine him as an aloof, sour-faced, impeccably dressed figure, the stereotypical English butler, a solemn, unbending presence concerned only with order and decorum, one who looks upon Feste's playful banter as an idle waste of time. He is scornful of the fool, since in his mind the jesting of such clowns has no place in a properly run household.

Maria enters to inform Olivia that a young gentleman from Orsino's court begs to speak with her, and she dispatches Malvolio to dismiss him. Sir Toby comes reeling in, "half drunk," as Olivia observes, and when he leaves, she sends Feste off to care for him. Malvolio returns to report that their visitor refuses to leave without speaking with her. When asked what sort of man he is, the steward replies that he is youthful, "not yet old enough for a man, nor young enough for a boy," that he is "well-favored," and that he "speaks very shrewishly [sharply]." Surprisingly, Olivia agrees to see him. Why? Well, she presides over a troublesome household, having to contend with a wayward jester, a drunken uncle, a ridiculous suitor, a solemn steward, and a mischievous maid; perhaps the description promises a diversion from this discordant company. In anticipation of the young man's entrance, the ladies draw their veils.

Viola enters and asks to have the lady of the house pointed out, confessing that she has prepared a speech and is loath to waste it on the wrong person. Shakespeare occasionally slips into Viola's lines a reminder of her double identity—as here with "I swear that I am not that I play"—remarks that are meaningless to those she is addressing but significant for the audience. Later she will use the device at greater length when she declares her love to Orsino without him knowing it. Viola and Olivia engage in yet another exchange of clever banter, the staple of Shakespearean comedy, until Viola asks to see the lady's face. She raises her veil, thus readily breaking her seven-year vow; and Viola launches into what appears to be her prepared speech, praising a beauty that, she says, it would be cruel of the lady to carry "to the grave / And leave the world no copy." Olivia replies with proper modesty but declares irrevocably that she cannot love Orsino. The lady ends the interview, bidding Viola to tell the duke that he is to send no more surrogates to plead his suit. But she unexpectedly adds an exception: "Unless, perchance, you come again / To tell me how he takes it." Olivia finds that she has inexplicably fallen in love with Cesario: "How now? / Even so quickly may one catch the plague?" She sends Malvolio to return a ring she claims the visitor has left, and to tell the youth that he is welcome to return the following day. It is not entirely clear what it is about Viola that has won her heart—perhaps the clever dialogue, perhaps the praise. But Shakespeare would not have us trouble ourselves about why people fall in love. It just happens, and invariably in these plays at first sight. He simply sets up a complex set of affections, rich in comic possibilities: Olivia is in love with the disguised Viola, who loves Orsino, who in turn loves Olivia.

2.1 To complicate matters further, Viola's twin brother, Sebastian, appears on the scene. He too has survived the shipwreck, saved by a seaman, Antonio, who wishes to accompany him as his servant. Sebastian declines because, as he says, "my stars shine darkly over me," and he fears his troubles will spill over onto his friend. In explaining his desire to travel alone, he reveals that he has lost a sister, whom he believes drowned in the storm, and that he will seek out Duke Orsino's court. In brief lines, Antonio, left alone, confesses that he has developed a strong affection for the young man. Despite the fact that he has enemies in the country, he is determined to follow him, since, as he says, "I do adore thee so / That danger shall seem sport." Some commentaries on the play find in the various relationships, especially Orsino-Cesario, Olivia-Viola, and Antonio-Sebastian, strong overtones of homosexuality. But Shakespeare frequently disguises his heroines as young men for comic effect, a device easily accommodated on a stage where the female parts were performed by boy actors anyway. In his age, when the sexes, particularly in the upper classes, were so severely separated, strong same-gender bonds were quite common, men often referring to their affection for one another in

terms of "love." Besides, it would be contrary to Shakespeare's purpose to
burden a comic plot with the heavy weight of what his era condemned as
perverse passion. His audience was meant to laugh at these antics, not
frown on them.

The comic confusion with which the play ends calls for a willing *suspension of disbelief* on the part of the audience, who are asked to accept the
fact that the brother and sister can be mistaken for each other. We are certainly content to do so, and Shakespeare now and again provides us with
reasons to accept the resemblance. Here we learn from Sebastian that they
are twins, "both born in an hour," and do indeed closely resemble one another. Thus Shakespeare introduces yet another situation ripe with comic
possibilities—the twins will be together in Orsino's court, each thinking
the other drowned.

2.2   In the short scene that follows, Malvolio overtakes Viola and attempts to give her Olivia's ring. Viola does not deny that the ring is hers
but refuses to take it, so Malvolio, highly indignant, throws it on the
ground and turns abruptly to leave. She picks it up and immediately realizes its significance—"I am the man"—a development further complicated, as we have seen, by her love for Orsino—"my master loves her
dearly, / And I, poor monster, fond as much on him." It is too confusing,
she concludes: "O Time, thou must untangle this, not I; / It is too hard a
knot for me t'untie." In seeing or reading these plays, we often come
upon lines that seem quintessentially Shakespeare, and these are two that
no one else could have written. The sound of them alone, with the repetition of the hard "n" and "t," conveys the agitation in Viola's mind. The
lines reflect, further, her uniqueness among Shakespeare's comic heroines,
highlighting the degree to which she differs from a Rosalind in *As You
Like It* or a Portia in *The Merchant of Venice.* She does not command the action or manipulate others as they do; indeed she doesn't really *do anything*
except act as messenger and serve as the butt of one of Sir Toby's pranks.
She falls in love with the duke but must remain mute about it; Olivia
falls in love with her and must be rejected. A still center to the events
swirling about her, she never takes control of them. They determine her,
not she them, and her predicament is so conflicting that, as she says, only
time can "untangle this, not I."

2.3   Meanwhile, at Olivia's estate the revelers are up late. Sir Toby
and Sir Andrew, joined now by Feste, enjoy their dancing, singing, and

drinking until Maria intrudes, warning them to tone down their "cater-wauling" or Olivia will have Malvolio turn them "out of doors." Sir Toby, however, will not be subdued, and in due course Malvolio himself appears to admonish them sternly:

> My masters, are you mad? Or what are you? Have you no wit,
> manners, nor honesty but to gabble like tinkers at this time of
> night? . . . Is there no respect of places, persons, nor time in you?

He warns that his mistress is distressed at the uproar. If they do not mend their manners, "she is very willing to bid you farewell." Here is a face-to-face confrontation between the opposing spirits of revelry and sobriety, and Sir Toby will not back down. The steward's demeanor only incites the group to renewed energy as they mock him with more riotous song and dance. The knight finally turns angrily on Malvolio, first with a reminder of his social position—"art any more than a steward?"—and then with a challenge of all that he stands for: "Dost thou think, because thou art virtuous, there shall be no more cakes and ale?" So much for sobriety! Malvolio warns Maria imperiously that he will inform her mistress of her part in the revels—somewhat unjustly, since she has been trying to quell the disturbance—and he stalks off.

Maria vows indignantly to make a fool of him. She brands him "a kind of puritan," charging that he is "but a time-pleaser; an affectioned ass" who is so well "persuaded of himself, so crammed, as he thinks, with excellencies, that it is his grounds of faith that all that look on him love him." The condemnation of Malvolio as a "kind of puritan" had a particular meaning for Shakespeare's audience. An increasing number of devout English at the time were convinced that the reformation of the Church of England had not gone far enough. They looked upon the priesthood, the elaborate ceremony, and the lavish decorations of the church as hindrances to individual salvation, a harmful barrier imposed by improper authority between them and a God whom, they insisted, all had a right to worship as they saw fit. These reformers, who varied considerably in their religious practices, were known collectively as Puritans, a body of Christians characterized by independence, strong beliefs, hard work (the "Puritan work ethic"), sober demeanor, strict moral behavior, and a singular lack of humor.

Shakespeare, though well aware of the spiritual associations of the word, carefully avoids any reference to the religious controversy. Maria characterizes Malvolio in explicitly secular terms, criticizing him for qualities closer to a modern definition of "puritanical" (with a lowercase "p"). He is insufferably overbearing in the conviction of his own rectitude, and in his self-righteous insistence on propriety and sober behavior, he considers himself morally superior to the irresponsible revelers who openly violate the order of the household. To give him credit, they are less than ideal guests with their carousing into the night, as on this occasion when Sir Toby announces that "'tis too late to go to bed now," so they might as well go on until dawn. Shakespeare presents the extremes: on the one side the spirit of unrestrained mirth, on the other the puritanical insistence on sobriety and self-control. Neither is offered as a model of moral behavior. Sir Toby is, after all, a drunkard, an irresponsible, aging playboy given to unruly excess, mindless of the sensibilities of others; and Malvolio is a humorless pedant, an imperious prig whose self-important ego simply begs to be punctured. If there is an ideal figure in the house, it is probably Olivia, who puts up with them both. She is clever enough to trade quips with Feste and at the same time show concern for Malvolio despite his stuffy self-regard.

In the play, however, the two spirits are unalterably opposed, and Maria has a scheme to bring down the haughty steward. She will prepare a letter in Olivia's hand, which she can imitate, designed to persuade Malvolio that his lady is in love with him, and she will place it where her companions can watch as he comes upon it. As she leaves, they exult in her inventiveness. Sir Andrew, however, is still complaining about the lack of progress in his suit of Olivia, and Sir Toby continues to encourage him, advising that he "send for more money." This counsel calls to mind the passage in *Othello* where Iago urges Roderigo, another foppish figure, to "put money in thy purse."

2.4 At Orsino's court the duke calls for more music and an "old and antique song," one which, he says, had somewhat relieved his passions. Feste is sent for, and Orsino engages Viola in a discussion of love, the only topic of conversation, it seems, he is capable of. He describes his state in terms of the courtly love tradition, a suitor who is "unstaid and skittish," "giddy and unfirm," unable to contemplate anything but his beloved. Orsino is a comic figure, but a part of Shakespeare's fun with him arises from the distinct impression that he relishes the role of the rejected lover, indeed enjoys the theatrical effects of the part. A modern audience would find him in love not so much with Olivia as with love itself. But there is a danger in playing him too much as the shallow dandy, else we begin to wonder what in the world Viola sees in him. He is entertaining in his affectations surely, a figure of fun, but he should not be seen as utterly ridiculous or the whole affair will lose our sympathy.

Orsino asks Viola-Cesario if she has ever been in love and wonders what sort of woman might have caught her eye. One, she replies carefully, "of your complexion" and "about your years." "Too old," he counsels, but then says that a woman should "take an elder than herself," since a young man's fancies are "more longing, wavering, sooner lost and won / Than women's are." Feste enters, interrupting the confidences, and upon request sings the "old and antique song." It proves to be the tale of a courtly lover "slain by a fair cruel maid" who has rejected him, a theme wonderfully attuned to Orsino's perception of his own pitiable state.

Dismissing the court, Orsino take up the thread of his conversation with Viola, asking her to press his suit with Olivia once more. She replies that any further efforts would be fruitless, asking him to consider how he would answer if a woman loved him as much as he does Olivia. He replies that such devotion is impossible, for the heart of a woman could never match the scope of his passion. It is too small "to hold so much," he claims, and besides, women's hearts "lack retention." He seems to be contradicting his contention, only just expressed, that men's fancies are "sooner lost and won / Than women's are," but then a man in his state of mind is not expected to be consistent in his reasoning. Viola, of course, is speaking of herself, and she continues with a touching revelation of her love for him by inventing the tale of her father's daughter who loved a man but never declared herself to him and as a result pined away in solitude, "like Patience on a monument, / Smiling at grief." Orsino, moved by the story, asks if her sister died of her love, to which Viola replies evasively, "I am all the daughters of my father's house, / And all the brothers too." She is willing, however, to try again with Olivia.

2.5 In Olivia's garden, preparations are under way to ensnare Malvolio in his own conceit. Fabian, a servant in Olivia's household, has a grudge against the steward and joins the conspirators to enjoy his humiliation. Maria approaches, places the letter on the ground where Malvolio will see it, and quickly steals off. The three men conceal themselves. As frequently staged, their hiding places are transparently obvious, often no more than a slim pillar or tree trunk. Thus, while Malvolio remains unaware of their presence, they remain in full view of the audience, who delight in an incensed Sir Toby who at times must be restrained from physically attacking the steward and spoiling the scheme.

Malvolio, strolling in the garden, is rehearsing to himself an imagined scene once he has married Olivia. He sees himself holding court and calling for Sir Toby, who he fancies will appear and meekly bow to him. The concealed knight is furious: "Shall this fellow live?" Malvolio then practices a speech, chiding him for his drunkenness and the "foolish knight" he carouses with.

Malvolio's fantasy is interrupted when he spies the letter, which he picks up and sees that it is in Olivia's hand. It is a love letter, addressed to M. O. A. I.," which he concludes to be himself since all of the letters, slightly rearranged, are in his name. So he breaks the seal to find that it urges him to seize the moment. "Some are born great," he reads, "some achieve greatness, and some have greatness thrust upon 'em," and on this occasion it is clearly "thrust" upon him. The letter goes on to describe how he is to behave so as to signal that he returns the writer's affections. He is to "be opposite with a kinsman, surly with servants"—no problem there—and further to appear clad in yellow stockings and "cross-gartered." And above all he is to smile. He leaves, exultantly convinced of Olivia's love. The eavesdroppers are convulsed in laughter, all praising Maria's cleverness, Sir Toby even suggesting that he will marry her. She enters and joins in the merriment, revealing that her mistress abhors cross-garters and the color yellow, and in her melancholy state will not appreciate a smiling steward. The trap is set.

3.1   But there are other matters to pursue before it is sprung. Viola approaches Olivia's estate, where she encounters Feste, providing an occasion to demonstrate that she has a pretty wit as well. She gives him a coin for "expenses," to which he replies with one of the clever devices of his trade: "Would not a pair of these have bred, sir?" He leaves to announce her, and she contemplates the jester's skill, "a practice / As full of labor as a wise man's art." When she is admitted to Olivia's presence, the two engage in a careful exchange somewhat at cross-purposes. Viola pursues Orsino's suit, but Olivia keeps turning the conversation back to Cesario's feelings for her. She apologizes for the trick of the ring and asks what Viola thought it meant, to which Viola replies simply, "I pity you." The game goes on, Olivia protesting, "be not afraid, good youth, I will not have you," but soon thereafter confessing, "I love thee so that, maugre all thy pride, / Nor wit nor reason can my passion hide." Viola replies cryptically that she has but one heart, and "no woman has, nor never none / Shall mistress be of it save I alone." Viola leaves as Olivia pleads with her to come again.

3.2 Sir Toby and Fabian hatch yet another plot, this time at the expense of Aguecheek, who protests once again that he will abandon his suit and return home. It is no use, he says, since Olivia pays more attention to "the Count's servingman" than she ever did to him.[*] Fabian, now a partner in the scheming, argues that Olivia does so "only to exasperate" him, and if he would challenge the youth to a duel, she would be won by his show of valor. Sir Toby urges him to write an insulting letter, which honor would require the young man to answer, and the pliable Aguecheek rushes off to find pen and paper. Sir Toby reveals why he wants to keep the simpleton on the hook—he has already fleeced him of "some two thousand strong, or so" and hopes for more in time. Even so, they cannot pass up a promising opportunity for further mischief. Sir Toby is resolved to "by all means stir on the youth for an answer," confident that neither of them have much skill at swordplay.

Maria approaches and invites them to witness the fruits of their scheme against Malvolio, who seems to be smiling a lot since last seen.

3.3 Meanwhile, Antonio has followed Sebastian to town, anxious, he says, for his friend's safety. Sebastian wants to do some sight-seeing, but Antonio urges that they seek lodgings first. He confesses that the streets are dangerous for him because at one time he had engaged in a "sea fight 'gainst the Count his galleys," and he fears that if recognized he will "pay dear." Antonio gives Sebastian his purse, should he wish to make some purchases, and they agree to meet later at "the Elephant." They go their separate ways.

3.4 Olivia, meanwhile, is excited that Viola-Cesario has agreed to return, and she calls for Malvolio to make preparations. Maria remarks

[*]"Count" and "duke" are used interchangeably in the play.

that the steward has been acting strangely of late, showing a tendency to do "nothing but smile," and she goes to summon him. He enters, ridiculously garbed in cross-gartered yellow stockings and smiling broadly, which makes his dour features roughly resemble the cracked surface of a dried-out, sunbaked lake bed. Confident of Olivia's affections, he quotes passages from the letter as she looks on bewildered at his behavior and Maria struggles to contain herself. Hearing of Viola's arrival, Olivia dashes off, telling Maria to entrust Malvolio, whom she believes to be seriously distracted, to the care of Sir Toby, declaring that she "would not have him miscarry for the half of my dowry." Malvolio, left alone, gloats over his good fortune, construing her every word as a mark of devotion. He ends the *soliloquy* on a note of triumph: "Nothing that can be can come between me and the full prospect of my hopes."

The revelers come upon him and immediately adopt the fiction that the steward is possessed by the devil, thought to be a common cause for insanity at the time. Maria cautions, "la, how hollow the fiend speaks within him!" and Sir Toby urges, "what, man, defy the devil!" Malvolio says little, still ridiculously attired in his garish stockings and smiling grotesquely, and finally leaves with a parting shot, "go hang yourselves all!" They are delighted with their success and determined to pursue the scheme further, Sir Toby proposing that "we'll have him in a dark room and bound"—considered proper therapy for a madman in that era.

But first Aguecheek hurries in with his letter challenging Cesario, which is full of comic contradictions, ending "thy friend, as thou usest him, and thy sworn enemy." They all praise his wording and persuade him to ambush his adversary, who will be leaving shortly. Sir Toby decides to deliver the challenge verbally so as to frighten the youth with accounts of Aguecheek's "rage, skill, fury, and impetuosity." They leave as Viola appears, pursued by Olivia, who urges her to come again and then returns dejectedly to her house. Sir Toby and Fabian intercept Viola and deliver the challenge, emphasizing the skill and daring of Aguecheek—"souls and bodies hath he divorced three"—and when she, now terrified, attempts to retreat to the safety of the house, they bar her way. She asks what she has done to offend the knight. Sir Toby, now adopting the role of concerned go-between, agrees to inquire, leaving her under the guard of Fabian, who confirms the ferocity of her "skillful, bloody, and fatal opposite." Thoroughly enjoying himself, Sir Toby confides in Aguecheek that the man he has challenged has proven himself a fierce and accomplished swordsman, and the timorous knight decides to have nothing to do with him. Sir Toby informs him that it is too late to back down since, once having been challenged, the young man insists on satisfaction. The ensuing scene is all the schemers could have desired. The two opponents, each in deathly fear of the other, are forced to draw their swords and thrust feebly at each other while they try desperately to avoid a fight.

Before anything can happen, however, this ludicrous scene is interrupted by the intrusion of Antonio. Thinking Viola is Sebastian, he leaps to her defense. But yet another interruption stops him as the duke's officers come upon them and, recognizing Antonio, arrest him. Forced to submit, he asks Viola to return the purse he had given Sebastian. Bewildered, she offers him what small sum she has, only to find herself abused for rank ingratitude. Antonio claims indignantly that he had rescued Sebastian "out of the jaws of death," and now it appears to him that his devotion has been betrayed. He is led off as she, having caught the reference to Sebastian, begins to hope that her brother is alive, conjecturing that Antonio has mistaken her for him, since, as she says, she imitates his "fashion, color, ornament." Without explanation, productions often have Sebastian and Viola dressed in identical costumes, one film version suggesting that she had salvaged a trunk of her brother's clothing from the shipwreck. In any event, Antonio feels himself abandoned by the man he "adores." Others will be equally confused by the resemblance, to our continued delight.

4.1   The next to be perplexed is Feste. Coming upon Sebastian, he informs him that Olivia wishes to see him and is disconcerted by the young man's uncomprehending response. The bewildered fool utters the *theme* of these encounters: "Nothing that is so is so." Then come the two knights, and Aguecheek, thinking there is safety in numbers, attacks Sebastian, only to receive a sound beating for his cowardly audacity. Sir Toby draws his sword but is stopped by the appearance of Olivia, who, thinking Sebastian to be Cesario, invites him to her house, where she promises to tell him of the "fruitless pranks / This ruffian hath botched up." Utterly confused but intrigued by the lovely Olivia, he willingly follows her.

4.2   But Sir Toby has further "fruitless pranks" to perform. He and his fellows plan more ways to torment Malvolio, who has been imprisoned in a dark cellar with but one small window. Maria and the knight disguise Feste as "Sir Topas the curate" to further play with Malvolio's mind. Approaching the window, Feste, disguising his voice, adopts the role of an exorcist intent only upon purging the fiend from the spirit of the steward, who plaintively pleads his sanity. Feste withdraws, and Maria and Sir Toby, thoroughly enjoying themselves, persuade him to return, this time as himself, and plague the steward more. By now, however, Sir Toby has tired of the charade. He decides that "we were well rid of this knavery" and seeks a way that Malvolio may be "conveniently delivered" so as not to reflect too badly on his credit with his niece. Feste returns to the task, reveals himself to Malvolio, and pretends to converse with Sir Topas, who warns him to "maintain no words" with the possessed steward. The fool agrees to provide Malvolio with "some ink, paper, and light" so that he can inform Olivia of his abuse.

4.3   A puzzled Sebastian contemplates a pearl that Olivia has given him and wonders what has become of Antonio. Having found her supposed Cesario far more agreeable than heretofore, she wastes no time. Appearing with a priest in tow, she asks if he is willing to accompany them to church, there to "plight me the full assurance of your faith." She promises that the ceremony will remain secret until he is willing to reveal it. Sebastian, either captivated by her beauty or thoroughly confused by the swift developments, readily agrees, and off they go to church.

5.1   The final act is one long scene filled with abrupt entrances and exits, bringing the comedy to an end. It starts tamely enough at Olivia's estate with Fabian asking Feste to show him Malvolio's letter, only to be interrupted by the entrance of Orsino and his entire court, including Viola. The scene unfolds in a marvelous example of Shakespeare's skill at creating comic suspense. We anticipate disclosures we know are bound to come, only to have them interrupted by intrusions that leave resolution hanging. Here the expected revelation of Malvolio's letter is suspended by a playful exchange between Orsino and Feste, who extracts a second coin from the duke and this time tries for a third. Orsino has come for a final, personal effort to win Olivia, but that encounter is in turn delayed by the appearance of Antonio in the keeping of the duke's officers. Orsino recalls him as a "notable pirate," and the officer gives an account of his offenses. Things look bleak for Antonio until Viola vouches that he has rescued her from the encounter with Aguecheek. Confusion reigns as Antonio complains that he has been denied his purse but confirms that he has been in the company of Sebastian "for three months before," a claim that Orsino dismisses, since Viola has been with him continually for a like period.

Olivia and her attendants arrive before the contradictions can be explored, and she angrily accuses Viola-Cesario of violating her promise. But before this mistake can be resolved, Orsino finally presents himself to Olivia, who rejects him outright. Disappointed, he declares that her "nonregardance" leaves him no choice but to abandon his suit, and he turns to leave, calling Viola after him—"Come, boy, with me." Olivia, taken aback by her Cesario's willingness to leave, asks where she is going. Viola replies, "after him I love / More than I love these eyes, more than my life." Desperate by now, Olivia cries out, "Cesario, husband, stay," and produces the priest, who affirms that the two have been joined "by the holy close of lips, / Strengthened by interchangement of your rings." Orsino is incensed, accusing Viola, "thou dissembling cub!" of betraying his trust.

But yet again, before these misconceptions can be untangled, Aguecheek staggers in, his head bloodied, calling for a surgeon for Sir Toby, who has been injured as well. They have encountered Sebastian again and, still thinking him the unwarlike Cesario, challenged him, to their distress. The aged knight hobbles in, and Sir Andrew attempts to console him—"I'll help you, Sir Toby, because we'll be dressed together"—only to receive a scathing rebuke. Sir Toby finally blurts out his true feelings toward the ridiculous Aguecheek: "Will you help? An asshead and a coxcomb and a knave, a thin-faced knave, a gull!" So concludes the mindless revelry of Twelfth Night, the now squabbling celebrants limping off to lick their wounds, their hilarity reduced to this painful end.

Finally! Sebastian enters and the twins are on stage together for the first time. The close resemblance between brother and sister is an effect more easily achieved on a live stage than on film, where close-ups are expected. But if they are of the same height and coloring, and costumed alike, we will accept the illusion, having long since quite willingly suspended our disbelief.

All stand amazed as Orsino voices their confusion: "One face, one voice, one habit, and two persons, / A natural perspective, that is and is not!" The brother and sister engage in a touching reunion as Viola finally reveals her identity. But her revelation creates further complications, leaving momentarily unresolved the fate of Sebastian's marriage to Olivia and Viola's love for Orsino. A resolution is again postponed by the arrival of Feste bearing Malvolio's letter. Olivia trades puns with Feste and then has Fabian read the steward's complaint about the injury done him. She sends the fool for him and proposes a resolution to their tangled relationships. She readily accepts Sebastian in place of Viola and, observing Viola's devotion to the duke, suggests that he wed her and henceforth "think me as well a sister as a wife." Orsino agrees, declaring to Viola that "you shall from this time be / Your master's mistress." This sudden transference of affections draws substance from the twins' close resemblance in appearance and temperament. They are so much alike that Orsino's abrupt love for Viola is but a short step from his affection for Cesario, and the shift in Olivia's passion from the one she thought a man to the man himself is not unimaginable.

But a cloud hangs over this bright scene of love and reconciliation. The humiliated Malvolio enters, his yellow stockings and cross-garters trailing about his ankles, and demands an explanation for his abusive treatment. He is convinced that it was all Olivia's doing. Handing her Maria's letter, he asks why she plotted to render him "the most notorious geck [dupe] and gull / That e're invention played on." Reading the letter, she replies that the handwriting is Maria's, not hers. Now that the trick has been exposed, Fabian confesses to the plot, revealing in the process that Sir Toby has married Maria. Feste has a word here as well, justifying is own role in the trickery. He reminds Malvolio of his earlier insult—"I marvel your ladyship takes delight in such a barren rascal"— and observes philosophically that "the whirligig of time brings in his revenges." Malvolio picks up on his remark and in an impassioned outburst threatens, "I'll be revenged on the whole pack of you!" He stalks out, having cast a pall over the festive gaiety of the occasion. Feste ends the play with a song in keeping with the subdued mood, its theme the absurdity of life and the dim prospects for those who must endure a rain that "raineth every day."

As mentioned earlier, the women of *Twelfth Night* do not have the stature of a Rosalind or a Portia. Indeed, the men they fall in love with raise questions about their judgment—Viola with the shallow Orsino, Olivia with the effeminate Cesario, and Maria with the drunken Sir Toby. But Shakespeare never claimed that love makes sense. Indeed, as we leave the theater we are inclined to conclude that it is quite the opposite—in Olivia's words, a "very midsummer madness."

These matters are overshadowed, however, by the play's representation of the unresolved conflict between mirth and melancholy, between the impulse for unrestrained revelry and the stern demands of an ordered society. In the end both suffer defeat, the two knights no longer now a carefree couple but wounded and angrily at odds, and Malvolio so disgraced that he vows vengeance on "the whole pack of you." Shakespeare is eerily prophetic here, for within a generation after his death all the theaters of London were closed and the Puritans had imposed an austere, colorless rule upon the country, one that temporarily eclipsed the mindless merriment of Sir Toby and Aguecheek. For a time, during what historians call the Interregnum (1642–1660), there was indeed a scarcity of "cakes and ale" in England.

MUCH ADO ABOUT NOTHING

❦

IN THE PLAY, Don Pedro, Prince of Aragon, returning from a successful campaign against his rebellious brother, Don John, finds hospitality for his forces in the estate of Leonato, the Governor of Messina. There Don Pedro encourages the love affairs of two of his young officers, Claudio with Leonato's daughter Hero, and Benedick with his sharp-tongued niece Beatrice. Don John, who has been returned to favor by his generous brother, is jealous of Claudio and plots to discredit Hero in his eyes. He succeeds, but the sentinels of Dogberry, the ridiculous chief constable of Messina, discover the deception. Don John is apprehended and the two couples reconciled, to the joy of all.*

Much Ado About Nothing actually has two plots, which advance on parallel lines until they converge in a single surprising moment. The first is the courtship of Claudio and Hero—an old tale really, retold in countless works before Shakespeare took it up. It is assumed that he had been working on a play based on that troubled affair before he conceived of the second plot, the "merry war" between Beatrice and Benedick, which is entirely his own invention, as are the antics of Dogberry and his inept "watch." It has been suggested that Shakespeare was captured by the comic possibilities of two lovers engaging in a wooing ritual that involved the exchange of a steady stream of insults, and that what he had intended as a subplot quite took over his pen, evolving into what are agreed to be the most appealing episodes of the play. Generations of theatergoers, at any rate, may have forgotten the old tale and remember the

---

*The presence of the "Dons" in the party reflects the fact that in Shakespeare's time the southern part of Italy and the island of Sicily were ruled by Spain.

play only as the turbulent courtship of Beatrice and Benedick. The Claudio-Hero affair is troubling—he is not the most sympathetic of romantic figures—while the "merry war" is a sheer delight.

1.1 The curtain rises on Leonato, the governor of the Sicilian town of Messina, announcing to his daughter Hero and his niece Beatrice that Don Pedro, Prince of Aragon, returning from a military campaign, will pay a visit. He will be accompanied by some of his younger officers who have distinguished themselves in the action. Beatrice questions whether a certain "Signior Mountanto" will be in the party—a reference to Benedick as a mere fencer or amateur sportsman rather than a true soldier*—and she goes on to deride his martial prowess, promising to "eat all" that he has killed in battle. It is revealed that Don Pedro's forces had also stopped at Messina on their outward journey, and that on that occasion Beatrice and Benedick had to all appearances taken an immediate dislike for one another. She continues in the same vein, questioning his "stomach [valor]," his wit, and his constancy.

The guests arrive and the two are brought face to face. Beatrice initiates the exchange: "I wonder that you are still talking, Signior Benedick: nobody marks you," to which he responds sharply, "What, my dear Lady Disdain! Are you yet living?" They continue to trade insults until Benedick calls a halt—"I have done"—but she has the last word, accusing him of "a jade's trick," that is, simply refusing to respond further. It would appear that although Benedick can hold his own in these encounters, Beatrice generally gets the better of them.

The party moves off to Leonato's house, leaving Benedick alone with Claudio, who confesses that he has fallen in love with Hero and asks his friend's advice. Benedick, the confirmed bachelor, brazenly derides his choice. In a revealing remark he praises Beatrice, whose beauty, he says, exceeds Hero's "as the first of May doth the last of December." Don Pedro reappears and Claudio confides in him as well, but the conversation soon turns to Benedick's determined bachelorhood. Speaking of women in general, he declares, "because I will not do them the wrong to mistrust any, I will do myself the right to trust none; and the fine [conclusion] is this, for which I may go the finer, I will live a bachelor." Don Pedro takes

---

*Not to be ignored is the erotic allusion: a "montant" is an upward thrust of the sword.

the declaration as a challenge: "I shall see thee, ere I die, look pale with love."

Benedick departs, and Claudio returns to the subject of his suit. Although it may not be evident to a theater audience, a reader will notice that at this point in the scene the speeches begin to appear in verse. Shakespeare almost invariably composed comic episodes in prose and serious scenes in poetry, better suited to express anger, love, or despair. Here, in contrast to the lighthearted banter with Benedick, Claudio turns serious in describing his affection for Hero. He was attracted to her, he says, on their outward journey to the war. Now that the campaign is over and "war-thoughts / Have left their places vacant," he finds that "in their rooms / Come thronging soft and delicate desires." Claudio seeks Don Pedro's help in pursuing his suit, and the prince readily agrees, adding his own twist to the cause. At the masked revels planned for that night, he will pass himself off as Claudio, win the heart of Hero, and then, unmasking, turn her over to him.

This curious arrangement calls for comment on several counts. A modern audience may well wonder that Hero is not to be consulted in the matter, indeed appears to be little more than a prized possession to be passed among the men at their will. But in Shakespeare's time the family elders customarily *arranged for the marriage* of their daughters. Thus in the present instance Don Pedro, as Claudio's commanding officer, stands somewhat *in loco parentis* to him, and the young man appeals to him to make the necessary presentations to Hero's father to gain approval for the match. The prince's variation on the custom is simply a gesture in keeping with the carefree spirit of the visit. It may seem equally curious that the two young people have yet to exchange a word—indeed, Hero has spoken but one line thus far—in contrast to Beatrice and Benedick, who have already sparred with one another at some length. But, again, Shakespeare's lovers always fall in love at first sight; he makes the connection without fuss so as to get on with the play and exploit the relationship for all its comic potential. Further, if Don Pedro's offer to stand in for Claudio seems strange, note that the young man is only acting in the tradition of the distraught *courtly lover,* afflicted with fear and trembling at the thought of rejection. Claudio, the renowned warrior, is reduced to jelly in the presence of the one he desires and so welcomes the prince's offer to do his wooing for him. Lastly, this little plot is only the first in a play that abounds in disguises, misunderstandings, and overheard conversations that provide occasion for no little deviltry and much fun. Shakespeare is setting his characters up for comic action, and though the arrangement may seem somewhat contrived, we shall have no complaints once that fun begins.

1.2 Don Pedro's device bears immediate comic fruit in a misunderstanding. Leonato learns of the prince's intent from his brother, Antonio, who heard it from one of his servants, who in turn misheard the conversation. Thus Antonio is under the impression that Don Pedro will woo Hero for himself, and Leonato, excited by the prospect of his daughter wedded to a prince, directs that she be informed of his supposed intentions. So the disguises, misconceptions, and eavesdroppings have begun.

1.3 The following scene introduces the dark side of the play in the person of Don John, listed in the Dramatis Personae as Don Pedro's "bastard brother," though he is not so identified in the text until much later. Don John had rebelled against his brother, precipitating the military campaign from which the party is returning, and the prince has generously restored him to favor despite the fact that his brother had "stood out" against his legitimate rule. Don John immediately identifies himself as a malcontent who wants only to create trouble for the prince. His reasons are unspecified—perhaps envy of his legitimate brother—but his motives are largely irrelevant. He defines himself at the outset—"it must not be denied that I am a plain-dealing villain"—and that will suffice for Shakespeare's purposes. In the comedies he is no more inclined to explore the motives of a villain than he is to explain why people fall in love. He is and they do, so let's get on with the play.

Don John's follower, Borachio, has also overheard the conversation between Don Pedro and Claudio. But apparently his ears are sharper than Antonio's man, since he heard the plan clearly: the prince will "woo Hero for himself, and having obtained her, give her to Count Claudio." Don John sees an opportunity to avenge himself on Claudio, his "brother's right hand," whom he resents because "that young upstart hath all the glory of my overthrow."

2.1 The long first scene of the second act sees one scheme played out and another hatched. It opens with Beatrice's witty derision of men and marriage, a companion piece to Benedick's diatribe in the opening scene of the play. The conversation initially concerns Don John, but Beatrice quickly shifts the subject to Benedick. Whatever the topic under discussion, each of them always manages to steer the talk around to the other. Like Benedick, she delights in her single state and is grateful that God has not sent her a husband, "for the which blessing I am at him on my knees every morning and evening."

Antonio, still under the impression that Don Pedro is wooing Hero for himself, advises her to "be ruled by your father" in the matter, which arouses the spirited Beatrice to denounce the whole tradition of arranged marriages:

> Yes, faith, it is my cousin's duty to make curtsy and say, "Father, as it please you": but yet for all that, cousin, let him be a handsome fellow, or else make another curtsy and say, "Father, as it pleases me."

Leonato, anxious perhaps that Beatrice's independence of mind may be catching, reminds Hero to do as she has been told, precipitating yet another display of wit from his niece on the follies of marriage.

The revelers enter dressed for a masked ball, which creates situations in which individuals feel released from social inhibitions, free to indulge in behavior that would customarily be taken amiss. Shakespeare prepares us for the confrontation between Beatrice and Benedick with a parade of couples, some of whom are aware of the identity of their masked partners while others are not. The first pair, Don Pedro and Hero, obviously know one another, but the masking allows them to pretend they do not. Hero finally finds her tongue and takes liberties she would not otherwise with the prince, displaying some of Beatrice's spirit and wit. Borachio and Margaret seem not to know each other, but their meeting sets up the affair between them that is important in later scenes. Ursula recognizes Antonio, though it is not clear whether he knows her as well—we may assume so.

In the exchange between Beatrice and Benedick, he is aware of her identity. Hiding his own, he passes on some insulting remarks about the quality of her "wit," which he pretends to have heard from a source he refuses to name. Beatrice concludes that the slights originated with Benedick and proceeds to ridicule him as "the Prince's jester, a very dull fool" whom "none but libertines delight in." His later remarks clearly indicate that he believes her ignorant of his identity, but is she? Immediately after heaping scorn on the supposedly absent Benedick, she glances about the room and concludes with an overtly erotic remark: "I am sure he is in the fleet [among the dancers]; I would he had boarded me." Does she take advantage of the masking game here and, fully aware of his identity, confess her true feelings toward him; or does she utter the wish that "he had boarded" her somewhat wistfully, as an *aside* to herself? In any event, the remark fails to register on Benedick, who is smarting from her ridicule of him as "a very dull fool." His reply is singularly noncommittal: "When I know the gentleman, I'll tell him what you say." Beatrice as usual has the last word, and they join the dancers.

Meanwhile, Don John approaches Claudio, and under the pretense that he is addressing his friend Benedick, informs him that Don Pedro is wooing Hero for himself. The impressionable young man readily accepts the news—much too readily it may seem—and, once more in verse, contemplates the inconstancy of lovers, concluding, "Farewell, therefore, Hero!" He encounters the real Benedick who, unaware of Don Pedro's scheme, thinks also that "the Prince hath got your Hero," and jokes lightly about his friend's distress. The distraught Claudio dashes off, and Benedick's thoughts turn to Beatrice's recent reference to him as "the Prince's jester." Since he was masked at the time, he wonders how she "should know me, and not know me," but in any case he promises revenge. Don Pedro joins him, and Benedick repeats his indignation that Beatrice, "not thinking I had been myself," has insulted him. This seems to bother him inordinately and he goes on at length, listing her imagined faults, concluding finally that he could never marry a woman who "speaks poniards, and every word stabs." When he sees her approaching with Claudio, both apparently unmasked by now, he asks mockingly to be sent on a mission to distant corners of the globe and then dashes off, exclaiming, "O God, sir, here's a dish I love not! I cannot endure my Lady Tongue!"

Don Pedro observes to Beatrice that she has "lost the heart of Signior Benedick." She responds that he had indeed "lent it me awhile" and that she had given her own in return, "a double heart for a single one," but that in the end he proved false. This exchange, and her earlier wish that he "had boarded" her, are hints that beneath her acerbic exterior she entertains a strong affection for him. Having been once stung, however, presumably on the army's outward march to the war, "my Lady Tongue" is keeping him at a distance with her wit. There are no comparable hints of Benedick's affections, except for his earlier praise of her beauty and, of course, the fact that she is seldom from his thoughts.

Don Pedro clears up the misunderstanding about his role by relinquishing Hero to Claudio, again without a word from her, and he then engages in a flirtatious exchange with Beatrice, asking her if she will have him. Is he serious or is this just lighthearted banter? She assumes the latter—he is after all a prince, well above her station, "too costly to wear every day"—and so she declines, upon which all agree that she is indeed a "merry" one.

Don Pedro, in pursuit of his design to see Benedick "pale with love," and impressed perhaps by Beatrice's remark that she had once given her "heart" to him, confirms his promise to "get" her a husband. Once she has wandered off, he enlists the others, including Hero, in a scheme to bring Beatrice and Benedick "into a mountain of affection th'one with th'other." Thus Don John's desire for revenge is thwarted because of the honesty of the interested parties, though we cannot escape the impression that Claudio, for all his martial prowess, is a rather shallow youth, too easily subject to mistrust in matters of love. In balance, however, here again he is typical of the *courtly lover*, who sallies forth resolutely to slay Turks by the score but is quickly reduced to despair by the slightest evidence of disregard from the lady he worships. In the end, Don John's scheme to defeat love is replaced by Don Pedro's to encourage it.

2.2   Don John is not to be dismissed so easily, however. It is Borachio, his loyal follower, who conceives a plan to satisfy his villainy. He proposes to trick Margaret, Hero's maid, into appearing at her mistress's window that night, where they will indulge in amorous conversation during which he will address her as Hero. If Don John can bring Don Pedro and Claudio to view the scene at some distance, they can be persuaded that Borachio is actually making love to Hero, thus discrediting her and subverting the marriage. Don John is so pleased with the scheme that he promises to pay Borachio a thousand ducats if he can bring it off. It is immaterial that the bastard brother has nothing to gain by the success of the plot; he is the figure of the satanic spoiler, for whom the sight of love and happiness is distressing and who bends every effort to destroy it.

2.3   Meanwhile, Benedick contemplates the impending wedding with dismay, wondering how a good man and valiant soldier like Claudio could have possibly been reduced to marriage, how a resolute bachelor who "laughed at such shallow follies in others, [could] become the argument of his own scorn by falling in love." For Benedick, it appears, Claudio's fall amounts to a betrayal of the sacred bond of bachelorhood. He declares that he will never be made such a fool until he meets the impossibly perfect woman, one who is rich, wise, virtuous, mild, noble, "of good discourse," and "an excellent musician." This haughty speech sets him up nicely for his own fall.

Don Pedro and the others enter, Benedick conceals himself where he can overhear the conversation, and the charade begins. First we are entertained with a song about the inconstancy of men, and then the trap is set. They talk of the great love Beatrice bears for Benedick, praise her highly, and regret that she is reluctant to reveal her affection, fearful that he would reject her with the same scorn that she outwardly shows for him. She is said to be resigned to silence rather than risk that scorn, since, as she reasons, she would do the same to him: "I should flout him, if he writ to me, yea, though I love him, I should." They consider telling him but agree that it would be fruitless, and after enjoying a few uncomplimentary remarks about him, they depart. The scheme achieves all they could have desired. Benedick emerges from hiding exultantly convinced that Beatrice loves him and that he loves her in return. At this point she enters to call him to dinner. Unaware of his change of heart, of course, she does so with her usual disdain, but the amorous Benedick happily construes her words, finding in them evidence of her "pain," and he determines to "take pity of her."

3.1   In a companion scene, the women gather and Beatrice conceals herself. They speak of Benedick's love for her and praise him highly, but decide not to tell her of his affections for fear that "she'll make sport at it." Sadly, they conclude, he must be left to suffer, to "consume away in sighs, waste inwardly," rather than "die with mocks." They leave and Beatrice emerges, breaking into rhyme:

> And, Benedick, love on, I will requite thee,
> Taming my wild heart to thy loving hand.
> If thou dost love, my kindness shall incite thee
> To bind our loves up in a holy band.

The chief difference between the two scenes is that the men speak in prose and the women in verse—and one wonders why. Since poetry is the language of the emotions, are we to conclude that women feel more

deeply than men? And since prose, in Shakespeare, is the language of
comedy, are we meant to be merely amused by Benedick but to sympathize with Beatrice? Who is to know!

3.2   There follows the first of two episodes, the other in 3.4, during
which the participants in the plot have their fun with the victims, both
in prose appropriately, and the audience enjoys the dialogue because of
Shakespeare's artful introduction of *dramatic irony*. In the case of
Benedick, the men know what has happened to him, but he doesn't know
that they know. The same is true of Beatrice and the women. Benedick
enters, complaining of a toothache, but his friends, aware that the pain
lies elsewhere, joke about his new appearance—his hair brushed, his
beard shaven, his person deodorized, his face washed and painted. Tiring
of their jests, he leaves with Leonato, apparently to request the hand of
Beatrice, and Don John enters, intruding on the fun with his dark plot.
He informs Claudio and Don Pedro that Hero is "disloyal" and promises
to prove the charge if they will accompany him to her window that night.

They seem all too willing to accept the accusation, but such charges
had to be taken seriously in an age when illegitimacy raised questions of
political and commercial inheritance. If she were "disloyal" before marriage, doubts could be raised about the children of the union, doubts
which in that day precipitated the rise and fall of dynasties. Richard III,
in Shakespeare's play, questions the legitimacy of both Edward IV and his
children, and so gains the throne. The man, of course, could have as many
bastards as he wished to acknowledge, like Gloucester's illegitimate Edmund in *King Lear*; but if an offspring claimed a title, his mother must
have been unsullied in fact and in reputation. To modern ears, Claudio
and the Don may seem too easily taken in by the plot, but their concerns
were quite in keeping with contemporary custom.

3.3   We are introduced here to Dogberry and his inept "watch." He
is in the rich tradition of Shakespeare's clowns, characters, it is said,
whom he created to employ the comic talents of Will Kemp, a member
of his theater company for many years. Kemp often played the court
jester in the plays, an entertaining figure who sings songs, poses riddles,
and comments wittily on the characters and their predicaments, somewhat in the role of a comic *chorus*.

There is nothing choric about Dogberry, however. Although he and
his watch play an important part in the action, he consistently spouts

nonsense rather than common sense. He is comic chiefly in two respects. He preens himself in his office of master constable, a position in which he is hopelessly incompetent. And he mangles the language. His incompetence is seen in the instructions he issues to the watch for the preservation of peace and order in Messina. For example, he instructs them to apprehend vagrants. But when asked what they are to do if the suspect refuses to "stand," he tells them to ignore him, since "if he will not stand when he is bidden, he is none of the Prince's subjects," and their orders are "to meddle with none but the Prince's subjects." In the end the "watch" has little to do but watch, so they retire to a nearby church bench to await the end of their tour of duty. Dogberry mangles the language in this exchange by instructing his constables to "comprehend all vagrom men," and exhorting them to "be vigitant," but his *malaprops* reach heroic proportions when he speaks with his social betters, as with Leonato in 3.5.

As it turns out, the watch, by doing nothing, perform a signal service in overhearing a drunken Borachio brag to Conrad about his deception, which, he claims, has had the desired effect. Claudio, seeing Margaret exchange endearments with Borachio from Hero's window, has become convinced that his future bride is "disloyal." He intends to shame her at the wedding on the following day. The watch suddenly come to life, arrest the two, and march them off to the master constable.

Shakespeare chose not to dramatize the assignation between Borachio and Margaret, leaving it to the audience to imagine the scene. Don John promises to show Hero's "chamber-window entered," but Borachio's remarks both before and after the event refer only to an amorous exchange in which Margaret is said to "look out" and "lean out" of the window. In any event, Shakespeare left it to Borachio's narrative to record the event, perhaps because he felt the scene too difficult to dramatize convincingly, or because he sensed that it would intrude upon the comic flow of the play.* By placing Borachio's drunken account in the context of the sedentary constables, whose presence adds a certain antic effect, he prevents the action from becoming too dark. In the end, the watch, by simply watching, serve justice and the plot.

---

*Kenneth Branagh's film version of the play, on the other hand, leaves nothing to the imagination.

3.4   At Leonato's estate, Hero is worrying about her wedding dress, and Margaret offers some earthy advice. She is a stock character in Shakespeare, the worldly-wise maid who speaks plainly and in somewhat ribald terms to her young and innocent lady. We see her again as Emilia in *Othello* and the good-hearted nurse in *Romeo and Juliet*. Beatrice enters, and in a companion scene to 3.2 the women have their fun at her expense. She is visibly suffering, as is Benedick. With a delightful pun, Margaret proposes a remedy—the *cardus benedictus*, a medieval cure-all distilled from the thistle, which, she says, can be medicinal if laid close to the heart.

3.5   Dogberry and his assistant, Verges, interrupt Leonato on his way to the church, asking him to interrogate their prisoners. The humor here arises from Dogberry's exaggerated sense of self-importance. In the presence of the governor of Messina, he pretends to a vocabulary he does not have, resulting in such constructions as "comparisons are odorous" and "comprehend two auspicious persons." In the process he never does get around to telling an increasingly exasperated Leonato why they have been "comprehended." Every time Verges interrupts to do so, Dogberry silences him for talking too much. He is the superior officer, reminding his subordinate that "when two men ride a horse, one must ride behind," and he wants all the credit for the arrest himself. But he never reveals the crime! And the audience waits in vain for him to just spit it out!

4.1   Claudio denounces Hero at the altar and explains why: "She knows the heat of a luxurious bed." Don John and Don Pedro confirm the indictment, and Hero falls into a faint, whereupon the heartless accusers simply walk off. Beatrice fears Hero is dead. Her father, stunned by the allegation, declares her better off so, since "death is the fairest cover for her shame." The friar, who keeps his head, doubts the charge and counsels that they should let it be thought that she is indeed dead until it can be shown that Claudio's accusation is false. If it proves true, he concludes, she can enter into "some reclusive and religious life, / Out of all eyes, tongues, minds and injuries." All depart, leaving the stage to Beatrice and Benedick.

The two declare their love for each other. Under normal circumstances, such a moment of mutual avowals would be joyous, filled with sweet and tender reminiscences of their love's history, but there is nothing normal about this relationship. As we have seen, there have been hints all along that their "merry war" was but a protective cover for hidden affection, and so it seems as they circle each other warily, each uncertain how a declaration will be received. Further, they meet in the shadow of the harsh scene just ended, in which one loving couple has been torn asunder by scandal, dimming the joy of another coming together. Under the circumstances, Beatrice and Benedick do not immediately fall into one another's arms. Shakespeare drains the scene not of sentiment, surely, but of sentimentality, quite in keeping with the characters we have come to know. As Benedick aptly remarks to her on a later occasion, "thou and I are too wise to woo peaceably."

Beatrice is still brooding over Hero's shame, and when Benedick pledges the familiar lover's vow that he will do anything for her, she has a ready answer: "Kill Claudio!" In a single, startling moment, Shakespeare merges plot and subplot. Benedick is totally taken aback and at first refuses, whereupon she dismisses him angrily, questioning his manhood and love for her. So at the very outset Benedick's affections are put to a severe test by a conflict between loyalty to his old comrade-in-arms and devotion to his newfound love. Beatrice is unrelenting. Finally persuaded by her conviction, he agrees to challenge his friend.

4.2 For the balance of the play, the dark dimensions of the Claudio-Hero tale overshadow the lighthearted gaiety of the earlier scenes. But Dogberry continues to entertain. Here he interrogates the prisoners in his customary bumbling way, and but for the presence of the sensible sexton, nothing would have come of it. In the end, when Conrad calls him "an ass"—quite appropriately we might agree—he is more incensed by the affront to his "place" than the severity of their crime.

5.1 The final act opens on the two elderly men, Leonato and his brother Antonio, lamenting Hero's shame. Her father has had a change of heart, however, refusing now to believe his daughter guilty, and he determines to challenge Claudio to defend her honor. When he and Don Pedro appear, Leonato issues his challenge, but it is an even more incensed Antonio who taunts Claudio: "Come follow me, boy, come, sir boy, come follow me, / Sir boy." The epithet "boy," thrown in the teeth of an adversary, is apparently an insult answerable only in a duel; but the two younger men refuse to respond to the taunts, and the frustrated elders leave.

Benedick joins them, and Don Pedro and Claudio attempt to restore the old camaraderie with jests about the behavior of the old men. But Benedick will have none of it and solemnly challenges Claudio. Don Pedro, in a vain effort to lighten the mood, begins a witty discourse on Beatrice, but Benedick will not be moved from his purpose. He repeats his challenge—"Fare you well, boy, you know my mind." "Boy" has more bite here. Benedick departs, leaving them to ponder his resolve. Both he and the elders continue to maintain the fiction of Hero's death.

As this long scene continues, Dogberry enters with the prisoners guarded by the watch. Despite the master constable's incoherent ramblings, a repentant Borachio is finally able to confess to his deception, stunning Don Pedro and Claudio. Don John, we have learned, has fled Messina, lending credence to his complicity. The elders return and a contrite Claudio, burdened now with both grief and guilt, offers to do anything to compensate for his unjust accusations: "Impose me what penance your invention / Can lay upon my sin." Leonato's "penance" is mild enough. He asks them to proclaim Hero's innocence to all Messina and requires Claudio to "hang her an epitaph upon her tomb." In a surprise move, he then proposes that Claudio marry his brother's daughter, not failing to mention that "she alone is heir to both of us." * If this offer seems somewhat too patriarchal for modern taste, it is, as mentioned earlier, quite in keeping with the custom of the time. Claudio readily agrees, and the wedding is set for the next day. Leonato then turns his attention to Margaret, but Borachio assures him that she was entirely innocent of the plot. After badly bungling some obsequious compliments to Leonato, Dogberry marches off his prisoners, and this is the last we see or hear of any of them.

5.2 Benedick, though still under the burden of his challenge to Claudio, turns his mind to wooing, and he consults the earthy Margaret for help. He is, he admits, hopelessly inept at poetry, the language of love, so when Beatrice appears he resorts to wit. He informs her that he has issued the challenge. That matter put aside, they digress into an exchange of confidences about what first attracted the one to the other. Such an exchange is, of course, customary with lovers, but again with

---

*Although she is Leonarto's niece, Beatrice is not Antonio's daughter. There's apparently another brother somewhere, even if Shakespeare doesn't mention him.

these two there is a difference, and they trade insults as much as affections. Benedick holds his own and even has the last word as Ursula brings news of the startling turn of events and they rush off to find Leonato.

5.3–4 Claudio tearfully fulfills his promise to "hang an epitaph" on Hero's tomb, and the following morning the company assembles at Leonato's house for the wedding. The ladies enter, masked, and upon their unmasking all are reconciled, though not without another verbal duel between Beatrice and Benedick. Each agrees to wed, but only, they both insist, to relieve the other's pain, and we suspect that the "merry war" will continue after the marriage. Theirs will not be an easy union, but it will never be dull, and he can always stop her mouth with a kiss. The play concludes in a spirit of reconciliation and harmony, as do all of Shakespeare's comedies, with only Benedick's remark about Don John's punishment to cast a brief shadow over the general joy. But that's for tomorrow. Today they will dance.

The play pursues one of Shakespeare's favorite themes—things are not what they seem. Hero, for example is not the fallen woman that Claudio becomes convinced she is. The charge against her is the "Nothing" of the title, and it has been suggested that Shakespeare engaged in subtle word play in naming the work. That "Nothing," it is said, is a variation of "noting," that is, watching, as when Don Pedro and Claudio spy on Hero's supposed assignation with Borachio. They make much ado about "noting" her affair, though there is "nothing" to it.

Then too, the insulting banter between Beatrice and Benedick, so acerbic on the surface, is actually a mating dance between headstrong lovers, who must be tricked into acknowledging their true feelings toward each other. Clearly they steal the show. Producers often cut portions of the dialogue, as does Kenneth Branagh in his delightful film version, but they are reluctant to tamper with the "merry war."

A MIDSUMMER NIGHT'S DREAM

❧

THIS IS A FAIRY TALE, a delight to children who can watch those of their own age in roles with delicious names like Peaseblossom and Mustardseed. It is a love story as well, though a singularly convoluted one, and also a comic burlesque. Three worlds intersect in the play. The first is aristocratic Athens, where the noble Duke Theseus prepares to wed Hippolyta, queen of the Amazons, and young lovers pursue one another in passionate defiance of ancient law. The second world is Fairyland, where the powerful king and queen squabble over possession of a changeling boy. The third is that of everyday workmen who are apprehensively preparing a play they hope to perform at the duke's wedding festivities. Their play, based on the popular tale of Pyramus and Thisbe, is a spectacle of ludicrous excess that in a way offers a comic commentary on the other two worlds, those of romance and fantasy. At the outset, each of the three worlds is internally contentious, and its anxieties are resolved by various means only when it comes in contact with one of the other worlds, so that the final curtain closes on a celebration of love and reconciliation.

The opening lines of the play contain the first of many allusions to the "moon," all of which serve at least two purposes, one a matter of practical stagecraft, the other more thematic. Shakespeare wrote his plays for performance on a *stage* open to the skies, and in the absence of adequate lighting they began and ended in broad daylight. In these artful allusions he asks his audience to imagine that most of what they see takes place on a moonlit night. More to the *theme* of the play, he works on the anxious belief of his audience that strange things happen by the light of the moon, when shadows are a refuge for unworldly creatures and the human eye sees everything through a silver veil, never quite able to distinguish between what is and what is not. An alerted fancy imagines fairy figures reveling in song and dance or hidden monsters lurking to pounce on unwary wanderers. Reason is an uncertain guide in moonlight, so Shakespeare asks us to dismiss it for a time and lose ourselves in fancy, so that we may witness the unseen and rejoice in the imagined.

1.1 The play opens on the real world as Theseus, the Duke of Athens, awaits impatiently his marriage to Hippolyta, complaining that the nuptials are still four days off. Theseus may or may not have been an actual historical figure. He, or someone very like him, is credited with the founding of the great city-state of Athens, and his name is associated with that achievement in Greek mythology. One tale records the war between Athens and the Amazons, a tribe of fierce woman warriors, whose queen, Hippolyta, Theseus took in marriage after defeating them in battle.*

Theseus calls for "merriments" to pass the time. But before light-hearted entertainment can begin, he finds he must deal with Egeus, an Athenian nobleman who introduces the tangled love story of the play. Two young men of the city, Lysander and Demetrius, are in love with Egeus's daughter Hermia. Complications arise because although she favors Lysander, Egeus intends for her to marry Demetrius. This Demetrius is a somewhat inconstant youth. Before turning his attentions to Hermia he had wooed her close friend, Helena—with some success it appears, since she now dotes on him while he wants nothing to do with his former love.

Among the upper classes of Shakespeare's time, it was a father's prerogative to *arrange suitable marriages* for his daughters, and they were expected to conform obediently to the parental wishes. This may have been a social custom in Renaissance England, but in ancient Athens it is apparently the law of the land. As Egeus argues, "I beg the ancient privilege

---

*We find Theseus and Hippolyta again in *The Two Noble Kinsmen*, which Shakespeare adapted from Chaucer's "The Knight's Tale," which he in turn took from the Italian Boccaccio, and so on. It is an ancient tale.

of Athens: / As she is mine, I may dispose of her," and Theseus agrees, pronouncing the penalty for a daughter's disobedience, "either to die the death, or to abjure / For ever the society of men" by entering a convent. The duke is in something of a dilemma here. As a man about to marry, he has a profound sympathy for the young lovers, but as the ruler he has an obligation to uphold the law. Hoping perhaps to strike a compromise, he moves off with Egeus and the favored Demetrius, advising "I have some private schooling for you both."

Lysander and Hermia, left alone, affirm their love and lament the obstacles to it. Lysander proposes that they leave Athens and seek refuge in a distant town with his "widow aunt, a dowager / Of good revenue." There they can escape "the harsh Athenian law" and marry. They agree to meet on the following night at a spot familiar to them both in the nearby woods.

Helena enters, despondent over her loss of Demetrius, and asks Hermia the secret of his attraction to her. She has no idea, she replies, having done everything she can to discourage him: "I frown on him; yet he loves me still,"and "the more I hate, the more he follows me." It's all a mystery, really, this passionate attraction to those who reject us. The lovers then confide in Helena their plan to meet in the woods and make their escape from Athens. As they leave, Helena ponders the fickle nature of love and decides to inform Demetrius of the plan, if only to gain his attention for a brief moment, to "have his sight thither and back again." Thus it is with affairs of the heart, Shakespeare seems to say, love is complicated enough, and society only makes it worse. But this complex mix of affections is considerably more complicated than the familiar lovers' triangle.

1.2   While there is a conflict between lovers and the law among the noble classes of Athens, the anxieties of those further down the social scale are of a different order, as we discover in the following scene. A group of common workmen—"rude mechanicals," the fairy Puck later calls them, a term by which they were known in Shakespeare's time—have met to rehearse a play they hope to perform before the duke at the wedding festival. These "mechanicals," a carpenter, a weaver, a tinker, a tailor, and others, are the comic or farcical figures of the work, appealing in their unsophisticated simplicity, amusing in their anxiety over the reception of their play, and hilarious in their bumbling performance of "The most lamentable comedy, and most cruel death of Pyramus and

Thisbe." The principal comic figure is Bottom, the weaver, who is very full of himself. As Peter Quince, the carpenter who is managing the project, announces the various parts, Bottom insists on playing them all and gives a brief demonstration of his talents in each role: as Thisbe he will "speak in a monstrous little voice," and as the lion he will roar so well that the duke will demand that he "roar again." At this last suggestion the company become fearful that if the lion is too realistic, he will frighten the ladies, and that, warns Peter Quince, "were enough to hang us all." Bottom finally agrees to restrict his talents to the role of Pyramus, then he fusses over what color beard to wear. Like many of Shakespeare's comic figures drawn from the lower classes, his speech is subject to *malaprops*, as when Peter Quince announces a rehearsal the following night and Bottom voices his confidence that they will do so "obscenely and courageously."

The "mechanicals" are obviously out of their depth in this theatrical enterprise, but they are brimming with optimism that their "lamentable comedy" will be well received. The self-important Bottom is the most assured of them all, supremely confident in his own abilities, however lacking they may seem to us. He is an unself-conscious buffoon but endearing in his well-meaning simplicity. Indeed, these are all good-natured, down-to-earth, workaday men, innocent of the sophistication of a courtly society. Part of our sympathy for them arises from a concern that they will be cruelly mocked by a cultured audience. After all, we laugh at them, so how will the haughty duke respond?

2.1   Next we enter Fairyland, the domain of Oberon and Titania, who preside over another kingdom entirely. Although hidden from mortal eyes, it is no less contentious than the world of humans. A fairy in the service of Titania encounters Puck, who serves Oberon, and we learn that the king and queen are at odds over "a lovely boy, stol'n from an Indian king," a "changeling," that is, a mortal child taken by fairies. The queen has added him to her train, and Oberon wants him for his. The fairy recognizes Puck as that "Robin Goodfellow" known for his mischievous pranks on unsuspecting humans, and he acknowledges himself "that merry wanderer of the night" who entertains Oberon with his harmless tricks. Puck is responsible for many of the inexplicable things that go wrong in everyday life: despite vigorous churning the cream refuses to make butter, "night-wanderers" are led astray, and the "three-foot stool" collapses when sat upon. Such things do happen, went the common wisdom of the day, so some mysterious being must be making them happen.

Oberon and Titania enter, each attended by a court. He greets her ominously: "Ill met by moonlight, proud Titania." They trade barbs, each accusing the other of attendance in Athens because of affection for the betrothed couple, Oberon for Hippolyta, whom the queen dismisses derisively as "the bouncing Amazon, / Your buskin'd [booted] mistress and your warrior love," and Titania, he responds bitingly, because of her love for Theseus. Theirs is a lovers' quarrel, not unlike a heated exchange between any mortal couple in which each accuses the other of infidelity when the real question is who will rule in the union, an issue raised by dispute over the changeling child. "Am not I thy lord?" demands Oberon, to which Titania replies, "then I must be thy lady" and should be respected as such. This quarrel, we discover, is not to be taken lightly, for it has destructive consequences for the world of humans. Because of their "brawls," Titania reveals, the wind has "suck'd up from the sea / Contagious fogs" that flood the land, leaving fields unplowed and corn rotting on the stalk.* "The seasons alter," bringing frost and ice in summer so that the mortal world "now knows not which is which"—all evils, she says, that arise "from our debate, from our dissension." Puck's pranks are one thing, but a quarrel in the royal family quite another, where discord can result in widespread misery for human beings.

Oberon replies curtly that it's all her fault for denying him the changeling boy. Titania's answer reveals that the spirit and the mortal worlds do mix, preparing us for the later episode of "Bottom's dream." The child's mother "was a votress [worshipper] of my order," Titania explains, whose company she had often enjoyed. So when the mother died in childbirth, she adopted the boy and "for her sake I will not part with him." After further demands and denials, she departs.

Oberon will have his revenge. He summons Puck, directing him to secure "a little western flower, / Before milk-white, now purple with love's wound: / And maidens call it 'love-in-idleness.'" † If the juice from this flower is dropped on sleeping eyelids, he explains, the sleeper will

---

*Effects not unlike the consequences of El Niño.
†Said to be the pansy.

awake to fall in love with the first creature to come in sight. He will apply the juice to Titania's eyes, he says, causing her to dote upon a "meddling monkey, or a busy ape," and he will refuse to remove the spell until she surrenders the boy. His thoughts are interrupted by the approach of humans, however, and he stands by invisibly to observe them.

It is Demetrius searching for Lysander and Hermia, himself pursued by the desolate Helena. She pleads her love for him, only to be spurned in the harshest terms: "I am sick when I do look on thee." He dashes out, and she resolves to follow him even if she must "die upon the hand I love so well." The fairy king, taking pity on her, decides to come to her aid. When Puck returns with the "little western flower," Oberon confirms his intent to punish Titania by filling her with "hateful fantasies" if he can catch her asleep in her customary resting place. Shakespeare embellishes the moment with some inspired scene-setting, asking his audience to imagine a place that the bare stage can only suggest:

> I know a bank where the wild thyme blows,
> Where oxlips and the nodding violet grows,
> Quite over-canopied with luscious woodbine,
> With sweet musk-roses, and with eglantine.

Not forgetting the lovesick Helena, Oberon instructs Puck to drop the juice on the sleeping eyes of Demetrius, whom he will know by his "Athenian garments," and arrange matters so that she will be the first creature he sees on awakening.

2.2   The next scene finds Titania's fairies singing her to sleep, casting a spell to ward off all harmful things. She lies down, presumably on the "bank where the wild thyme blows," and Oberon steals upon her to administer the juice of "love-in-idleness." As he leaves, Lysander and Hermia enter, intent upon their escape, but they are lost and decide to rest before continuing. Lysander suggests that they sleep side by side, but with maidenly modesty Hermia urges him to "lie further off yet; do not lie so near." They sleep as Puck enters. Spying Lysander, dressed like Demetrius in "weeds of Athens," he applies the juice to his eyes and glides away. Helena enters, still pursuing Demetrius, and when he dashes off she drops in exhaustion, wondering again at his attraction to Hermia. She sees the sleeping Lysander, who awakens and immediately falls in love with her, but Helena is upset by his unwelcome attention, convinced that he is mocking her: "Good troth, you do me wrong, good sooth, you do, / In such disdainful manner me to woo." She stalks out with Lysander in pursuit, as Hermia awakens to find herself deserted.

An audience will notice that most of the lines in this scene are rhymed couplets, and indeed this is Shakespeare's most heavily rhymed play. He was less inclined to use this lyric style in later works, employing it only on appropriate occasions. It just happens that this scene is filled with such occasions: songs, spells, speeches by supernatural figures, and declarations of love. Shakespeare found rhyme appropriate for moments of great emotion. He used it also to lend dignity to royal decrees, mystery to incantations ("Double, double, toil and trouble"), ominous weight to curses and prophecies (see *Richard III*), authority to blessings (see the close of this play), and, as mentioned, passion to declarations of love. *A Midsummer Night's Dream* has some of the flavor of a *masque* to it, with supernatural figures in stately procession and scenes enlivened by song and dance, all features of that more stylized form of theater which is customarily rhymed throughout. The lilting lines add an air of unreality, of sweetness and melody, to a play that, after all, is something of a dream.

3.1   Titania is still asleep on stage. (There is a lot of sleeping in this play, providing ample time for dreams.) The "mechanicals" enter to begin their rehearsal, still concerned about the reception of their play, particularly by supposedly fainthearted ladies, which is a bit ironic in light of the fact that Hippolyta is the queen of fierce Amazon warriors. The would-be players are apprehensive that their audience will be too literal-minded and mistake their fiction for reality. Bottom is uneasy about drawing a sword to kill himself and proposes that they add a prologue explaining that it's not actually a sword and he is not really Pyramus. They decide to take the same precaution with the lion. Further, they fear that the audience will be unable to imagine the scene on the basis only of allusions in their lines, and so they designate actors to play the parts of a moon and a wall. Shakespeare reflects wittily on the fragile artifice of the stage, reminding us that we must catch the allusions in his lines as well—"Ill met by moonlight, proud Titania" and "I know a bank where the wild thyme blows"— to imagine what the bare stage of the Globe Theater cannot provide. So the actors decide, as we learn later, that Snout will play the Wall and Snug the Moon, thus eliminating two roles from the original script. So, we also learn later, they end up with only three speaking parts—plus the lion, of course.

As they begin their rehearsal, Puck, who comes upon them, sees an opportunity for a useful prank. Bottom exits momentarily to return with the head of an ass on his shoulders—such is the power of the fairies. His companions flee the puzzled Bottom in terror, and Titania awakens to fall immediately in love with him. She dotes on this absurd creature and appoints members of her court—the whimsically named Peaseblossom, Mustardseed, Cobweb, and Moth—to serve him. In modern productions they are often played charmingly by young children. They lead him off to Titania's "bower."

3.2 A short time later, Puck delivers a long account of his success to Oberon, who is delighted. But they are interrupted by Demetrius still in pursuit of Hermia, who is distressed over the absent Lysander, even accusing Demetrius of murdering him. She rushes out, leaving him despondent and prone to sleep. Oberon chides Puck for applying the magic juice to the wrong Athenian and sends him to find Helena. In an effort to remedy matters, Oberon squeezes drops of "love-in-idleness" on the eyes of the sleeping Demetrius. The charmed Lysander follows Helena into the grove, pleading his case and waking Demetrius, who, seeing her, immediately protests his love. The affections of these four young people are now incredibly muddled. The two men under the influence of the charm have shifted their affections from one woman to the other. But Helena, who initially doted on Demetrius, is now furious with them all, convinced that they are playing a monstrous trick on her: "O spite! O hell! I see you all are bent / To set against me for your merriment." The two men, oblivious to Helena's anger, square off to fight for her. A bewildered Hermia comes upon them and rushes up to Lysander, who now rejects the advances of his former love with a sharp rebuff: "The hate I bear thee made me leave you so."

Helena concludes that Hermia is in league with the men to humiliate her. In an extended speech she reproaches her, recalling their long, intimate friendship in which they were like "two lovely berries moulded on one stem; / So, with two seeming bodies, but one heart." Hermia, who has no idea what is going on, stands by as the two men squabble over Helena, and she pleads once more with Lysander, only to be rejected

scornfully yet again: "Away, you Ethiope!" and "Out, tawny Tartar, out!"
The epithets reflect the fact that the two women are customarily played
by actresses quite different in appearance. Hermia is dark in complexion
and hair coloring, while Helena is fair, blond, and the taller of the two.
The women then turn on one another, as Helena infuriates Hermia with
insulting references to her small stature: "You puppet you!," "she is
something lower than myself," and "though she be but little, she is
fierce." Helena, now the favorite, has to be protected from the "fierce"
Hermia, whom Lysander dismisses once more: "Get you gone, you
dwarf." The men leave, glaring at one another, determined to fight it out
over Helena, and the women, now hostile rivals, follow them off, exchanging harsh words.

What a mess! The charmed men are ready to kill each other over Helena, who is furious at them both, and the two women, once so close, come
near to blows. Love, as mentioned earlier, is complicated enough in a lawful society, but once the fairies, however well intentioned, intervene, it
becomes impossibly muddled. Oberon steps forward and reprimands
Puck: "This is thy negligence." He determines to undo the damage, but
first he takes the precaution of sending Puck off to prevent the two men
from harming each other. He instructs him to anoint Lysander's eyes with
an herbal antidote to the flower's juice so that he will return his affections
to Hermia, his original love.

Lysander and Demetrius are rushing about the forest in search of each
other. Puck keeps them apart by imitating the voice of each until both,
exhausted, lie down to sleep. The women enter and, unaware of the men,
fall to sleep as well, as Puck steals upon Lysander and applies the antidote. He leaves with a mocking judgment on the whole episode—"Jack
shall have Jill, / Naught shall go ill; / The man shall have his mare again,
and all shall be well"—or, as he remarked earlier, "Lord, what fools these
mortals be!"

4.1 Titania enters, attended by her train of fairies and, as Oberon
looks on, leads a bemused Bottom to her bower. Unaware of his grotesque
appearance, he acts as himself, but at times he seems as much an ass as a
man. He delights in the presence of the fairies, addressing them with
gentle courtesy, asking Peaseblossom to scratch his head. When Titania
inquires what he will have to eat, he responds, "I could munch your good

dry oats" or enjoy "a bottle of hay." Titania is enthralled—"O how I love thee! How I dote on thee!"—and she embraces him as closely as the "female ivy" does "the elm," as they both fall asleep. The stage before us is now draped with sleeping figures, the four Athenians first and now these two, as Oberon and Puck approach.

Oberon is satisfied. He had encountered Titania, he says, while she was gathering flowers to adorn Bottom's head, and asked her again for the changeling child. Now caring little about anything but her affection for Bottom, she readily agreed. Taking pity, Oberon decides to release her from the spell. As he does, she awakens, wondering at her infatuation for the strange creature. Puck removes the ass's head, and the king and queen dance in reconciliation. Amity has returned to one of the three worlds.

Oberon also expresses the wish that when the Athenians awake they will "think no more of this night's accidents / But as the fierce vexation of a dream." But for them there is still the matter of Athenian law to contend with. Theseus and Hippolyta, on a morning hunt, come upon the sleeping couples and awaken them. The duke reminds Egeus that Hermia's decision is expected that day. The men kneel to the duke and, rising, give a bewildered account of the night's events. Lysander, now released from the spell, admits that he and Hermia had planned to escape Athens, whereupon an enraged Egeus condemns him: "I beg the law, the law upon his head." Demetrius speaks up—and it may escape notice that he has *not* been released from the spell—describing how his love for Hermia had mysteriously "melted as the snow" as his affections turned once more to Helena. A compassionate Theseus overrides the demands of Egeus, now that the couples seem to have resolved their tangled relationships satisfactorily. So much for the law—we thought it stupid anyway. The duke proclaims that there will be a triple wedding that day. He leads the party back to Athens as the lovers ponder over the experience: "Are you sure / That we are awake? It seems to me / That we sleep, we dream."

The lovers follow Theseus out, leaving to all appearances an empty stage. I once attended a stunning performance of *A Midsummer Night's Dream* in London, during which the stage was covered to about knee height with a fine mist during this scene. As a result I had completely forgotten, as had apparently most of the audience, that Bottom was still asleep there. After an exquisitely timed pause, he suddenly popped up out of the mist, an inspired staging that reduced the audience to helpless, weeping laughter. He thinks he is still awaiting his cue at the rehearsal, and is convinced that everything that happened since that moment has been a dream, "Bottom's dream," as he calls it, "because it hath no bottom." Attempting to recapture it, he mixes the senses abominably: "The eye of man hath not heard, the ear of man hath not seen . . . what my dream was."

4.2 Meanwhile, the "mechanicals" are wondering what has become of Bottom and mourn his loss to their play, which, it seems, cannot go forward without him. The loss is significant, says Snug, since they are confident that the duke would have rewarded him with "sixpence a day during his life," a tidy pension, for his performance. Bottom has been about, however, and enters to announce that the "play is preferred" and they must prepare. Thisbe is to "have clean linen," and all are cautioned not to eat garlic or onions.

We are now out of the woods, so to speak, and the action moves to the court, where reason prevails and the couples anticipate a happy life together. But there is still the matter of "the lamentable comedy" of Pyramus and Thisbe; and we wonder how the well-meaning efforts of the simple tradesmen will be received by these sophisticated gentry.

5.1 Act Five is all one long scene. As it opens, Theseus and Hippolyta are discussing the lovers' strange tale, and the duke is skeptical. After all, he says, these are lovers, who by their very nature are subject to fantasies. In famous lines he places no faith in "these antique fables, nor these fairy toys" concocted by "the lunatic, the lover, and the poet," who alike "are of imagination all compact [made up]"—especially the poet, he declares, who "turns [things unknown] to shapes, and gives to airy nothing / A local habitation and a name." Shakespeare's whimsy surfaces as he identifies himself, the poet, with lunatics and lovers, but the analogy is apt. The down-to-earth duke concludes that such overwrought imaginations are not to be entirely trusted.

The young couples enter, and Theseus calls for entertainment to while away the hours until they retire. The choices are not promising. Philostrate, the Master of Revels, ticks off the possibilities, none of which please, finally coming to "a tedious brief scene of young Pyramus / And his love Thisbe, very tragical mirth." Philostrate does not recommend it—a play, he remarks contemptuously, "some ten words long . . . but by ten words, my lord, it is too long." But the magnanimous Theseus decides to hear it, graciously confident that "never anything can be amiss / When simpleness and duty tender it." Hippolyta has her doubts, but he counsels her that there is more value in "tongue-tied simplicity" than in the "saucy and audacious eloquence" of more learned, worldly men.

The play opens on Peter Quince as Prologue, and the pattern of the scene is set. The "mechanicals" will carry on while the sophisticated courtly audience exchange clever remarks ridiculing the clumsy performance of the simple workmen. The lovers may sacrifice a bit of our sympathy with their haughty witticisms, but in fact we laugh as well at the extravagant histrionics and overblown rhetoric of the performance. Theseus remains gracious throughout, advising the others to be indulgent, though he adds a witty remark of his own here and there. To appreciate the exchange after Prologue's lines, the reader must examine the punctuation, or "points" of the speech. Peter Quince stops at all the wrong places, breaking up sentences and running them together to produce such bumbling absurdities as "all for your delight, we are not here."

The entire cast troops on stage, and Prologue carefully explains the plot in lines that include some heady alliterative flourishes: "Whereat with blade, with bloody blameful blade, / He bravely broach'd his boiling bloody breast." Wall appears, his role to just stand there and form a "v" with his fore and middle fingers to represent the "chink" through which the lovers speak. Then comes Bottom as Pyramus, who with melodramatic excess takes three lines to ensure that everyone knows it is nighttime. He curses Wall for separating him from his love, and Theseus remarks that since Wall can speak, he ought to curse back. Bottom hears him but takes no offense, simply stepping out of character momentarily to explain that the line was a cue for Thisbe. It is not clear how much of these exchanges the actors hear, but in any case the remarks go right over their heads. They seem never to suspect that they are the objects of courtly wit. Anxious that their play not be misunderstood, they take pains to conduct their audience step by step through the plot. Thisbe enters, and after an passionate exchange through Wall's fingers, the lovers agree to meet at "Ninny's tomb." Hippolyta has had enough: "This is the silliest stuff that ever I heard."

The comic effect of the scene arises from the fact that the "mechanicals" are deadly serious about the performance and in their amateurish simplicity present a hilarious burlesque of a play. Lion enters, careful to explain to the ladies that he is not a real lion but only Snug the joiner, so they have nothing to fear. Moon is next, but by this time wit is flying back and forth among the observers. He tries twice to start his speech, finally abandoning the prepared lines and announcing in exasperation, "all I have to say is . . ."

Thisbe arrives at "Ninny's tomb," is frightened by the lion, and flees, dropping her mantle which the lion then smears with blood. Pyramus appears, finds the bloody mantle, and, thinking Thisbe dead, stabs himself in despair. Actors, of course, delight in death scenes, and Shakespeare, in a parody of their excesses, has Bottom take an unconscionably long time in killing himself: "Now, die, die, die, die, die," with a separate stagger for each "die." Thisbe enters, and Hippolyta wonders impatiently if she will outdo him: "I hope she will be brief." Thisbe's speech, though not as long as his, is quite long enough, and as she stabs herself her final "adieu, adieu, adieu" offers opportunity for more histrionics. The play is over, or so the court hopes, and Demetrius observes that Wall is left to bury the dead, but Bottom pops up to assure him that the wall no longer stands. He offers Theseus an epilogue or a "Burgomask," a rustic dance; the duke, having had quite enough of the play, opts for the dance.

This "most lamentable comedy" of Pyramus and Thisbe is in some ways a parody of the larger play itself, Shakespeare having fun with his own creation. The "wall" of Athenian law separates both pairs of lovers, who engage to meet, again by moonlight, at a rendezvous where they become separated, both by misadventure in an encounter with creatures of the forest, one couple fatally by a lion, the other benignly by a fairy spell. The "tragical mirth" of Pyramus and Thisbe ends up comically tragic, and the "lamentable comedy" of the Athenian lovers concludes in joy for all.

The revels now over, Theseus announces, "lovers, to bed; 'tis almost fairy time," and indeed as the Athenians retire the empty rooms are immediately filled with woodland spirits. Puck is first, his lines and those to follow all in lilting rhyme. He describes the many terrors of the night—hungry lions and wolves, screech owls, and Hecate, goddess of the underworld—dangers, he says, that he has been sent to ward off so that "not a mouse / Shall disturb this house." Oberon and Titania enter in stately procession and dispatch their attendant fairies to various rooms to bless the brides' beds, ensuring that the children born of these unions will be without blemish. The fairies hurry off to their various duties, leaving Puck on stage for a brief epilogue. The audience, he cautions, is to imagine that they have only "slumber'd here" for a time and that the visions they have seen are "but a dream."

So these three worlds, so often distant from one another, are seen as interdependent, sharing a single realm of wonder and delight. The anxieties and tensions of each are relieved through the mediation of one of the others. The lovers' discord is resolved by the fairies' magic potion; the quarrel between the fairy rulers is settled by the introduction of a "mechanical" in their midst; and the simple workmen's fears about their performance are relieved by an outwardly courteous reception.

Was that night in the woods "but a dream," as Puck would have it? Well, yes, in so far as any play works upon the imagination to produce pleasure and mystery. Life itself, Shakespeare tells us over and over, may be an imagined realm, no more or less substantial than the play itself. It is "a walking shadow" to Macbeth; men and women are "merely players" to Jaques in *As You Like It*; and Prospero tells us that "we are such stuff as dreams are made on." The boundaries between the real and unreal, the actual and imagined, life itself and the artifice of the stage, are ill defined in human consciousness; and a life richly lived passes back and forth across the line with ease. So separate worlds in which fairies sing, and workmen dance, and lovers woo, Shakespeare seems to say, are all really one, as is the realm that lies between our dreaming and awakening. Yes, we have been in a dream, as Puck tells us, but that world is not so different from the one we return to as the curtain falls.

THE TAMING OF THE SHREW

❧

AS ORIGINALLY WRITTEN, *The Taming of the Shrew* finds little favor with modern gender-sensitive scholars, who are less than pleased with its principal male figure, Petruchio. He has all the marks of an irredeemable chauvinist. To make matters worse, the high-spirited Kate, after resolute resistance, ultimately acknowledges him as her lord and master. In the play, Petruchio comes to Padua to "wive it wealthily," as he puts it, and there finds the troubled Minola family. The father, Baptista, has two daughters, Bianca, a beautiful and modest young woman, who is beset with suitors, and her older sister, Katherina, an obstinate, sharp-tongued, and quick-tempered "shrew," who has none. Baptista announces that the younger sister may not marry until the older is provided for, and Bianca's suitors persuade Petruchio to wed the difficult Kate so that they may woo her beauteous sister. He readily agrees, attracted, it would appear, by the challenge of "taming" her. The two do indeed marry, and by a series of clever and hilarious devices Petruchio succeeds in subduing Kate so effectively that in the end she publicly acknowledges his superiority as her "lord," "king," and "governor." While the sentiment is in keeping with the custom of Shakespeare's time, it does not always appeal to modern sensibilities.

The play, however, seems to be more popular with theater audiences than it is with scholars. Over the years it has been adapted for stage and screen in a variety of forms, among them Cole Porter's delightful *Kiss Me Kate*, an episode of "Moonlighting" with Cybill Shepherd as Kate and Bruce Willis as Petruchio, and the film *10 Things I Hate About You*, a teenage comedy. Stage productions of the original take resourceful liberties with Kate's final speech in an effort to make it less offensive to modern sentiments on the subject.

Ind.1   The play opens with two scenes that form the "Induction," or preface, to the main plot. As a preface it is puzzling, however, since at first glance it seems to have little relevance to the actual play except to introduce the comic tone of the action. The characters in the episode take no further part in the play, except to act as a silent audience to the performance.

Christopher Sly is a quarrelsome drunk who refuses to pay for his drinks and simply falls asleep in a stupor. A lord enters, fresh from the hunt, and, observing the inebriated Sly, decides to make use of him in an entertaining diversion. He instructs his servants to carry Sly off to bed, dress him in some ducal clothing, and when he awakes persuade him that he is a lord who has been asleep for many years and has only just emerged from a coma. They are to treat him with the deferential respect due such a lord, a charade that will provide silent amusement for all.

When a traveling troupe of players arrives, the lord seizes an opportunity to embellish on his scheme. They will perform for the supposed nobleman and are warned to take no notice should he exhibit strange behavior, else he will be offended. For further comic effect the lord orders that "Barthol'mew my page" be dressed as a lady and play the role of a grieving wife who is overjoyed at her husband's recovery from his long illness. This is a disguise easily arranged for an Elizabethan play, in which the female parts were customarily performed by adolescent boys anyway.

Ind.2   Sly awakens to find himself surrounded by obsequious serving men, eager to cater to his every desire. He at first insists on his true identity—"Am not I Christopher Sly, old Sly's son of Burton-heath . . . and now by present profession a tinker"—but he is soon persuaded that the life he remembers was but a dream. He is particularly intrigued by the news that he has a lady, "the fairest creature in the world," and he calls to have her brought forth, along with "a pot o'th' smallest [cheapest] ale." The disguised page enters, and after some confusion about what they should call each other, Sly being ignorant of such niceties, he decides to take full advantage of the situation: "Madam, undress you and come now to bed." He is deterred, however, by the page's warning that any excessive exertion might cause a recurrence of his "former malady." So he must content himself to wait and pass the time by watching "a pleasant comedy," though he has no idea whether the play is "a Christmas gambol or a tumbling trick."

So much for the "Induction"! It is an amusing interval, to be sure, but why is it here at all? It seems to have no direct connection to the play itself, and with the exception of four lines at the end of the first scene, the episode is never referred to again. Several explanations have been proposed for this puzzling fragment. It has been suggested that Shakespeare included an epilogue in which Sly, rendered unconscious again by liberal doses of "small ale" during the performance, is deposited once again in the tavern, but that those final lines were somehow mislaid on the way to the printer. Others propose that Shakespeare deliberately omitted the closing episode so as not to detract from the dramatic force of Kate's last speech.

But in the end it may be that Shakespeare is up to his old tricks, commenting wryly on the artifice of the stage, its ability to make dreams seem reality. In the "Induction" the lord plays the part of a serving man who persuades a lowly tinker that he is a nobleman. In the play, as we shall see, a wealthy merchant's son assumes a humble role, and his servant masquerades as the son, only one of a lengthy string of disguises on a stage crowded with characters who adopt false identities. And then there is the disguised page's mocking exclamation to Sly: "My husband and my lord, my lord and husband; / I am your wife in all obedience." Perhaps Shakespeare is simply signaling that we should take nothing we see seriously. The whole play is little more than a huge joke on a drunken tinker, and we should just sit back and enjoy the comic spectacle of the timeless struggle between men and women, caught up in the contradictory conflict between love and power.

1.1　The play itself opens on Lucentio, son of Vincentio, a wealthy merchant of Pisa. The young man has come to Padua, famed for its university, to undertake "a course of learning and ingenious studies." But his pragmatic manservant Tranio cautions that in his pursuit of philosophy he should not neglect to enjoy himself: "No profit grows where is no pleasure ta'en." They are interrupted by the entrance of a group of local citizens in the midst of a heated exchange.

Baptista, a merchant of Padua, is beset by two men, suitors for the hand of his youngest daughter, Bianca, one of whom is the young and quite presentable Hortensio, the other Gremio, a "pantaloon," or foolish old man. Baptista asserts his prerogative to *arrange for his daughter's marriage*. He puts them both off, insisting that Bianca may not marry until a husband is provided for his older daughter, Katherina. This presents something of a problem since Katherina appears to be vilely ill-tempered. Hortensio rejects the notion that he should wed her, and she heartily agrees, threatening, should he even try, to "comb your noodle with a three-legg'd stool." Despite the suitors' pleas, Baptista instructs Bianca to retire. He will, he tells them, engage tutors "fit to instruct her youth," and asks if they can recommend "cunning men" for the position. Katherina, who has been largely ignored in the discussion, stalks off as Gremio taunts her ironically: "Your gifts are so good here's none will hold you." The two suitors, rivals for Bianca's hand, now have a common cause—to find a husband for Katherina—and they set off to secure one.

Lucentio and Tranio, who have overheard the exchange, are left on stage, and the appearance of Bianca, who has spoken only once, seems to have had a profound effect upon the young man: "Tranio, I burn, I pine, I perish, Tranio, / If I achieve not this young modest girl." Lucentio has fallen in love at first sight, as do all Shakespeare's comic lovers, and indeed at sight only, for he has yet to exchange a word with her. He describes his affliction in terms of the traditional *courtly lover*, who will "perish" if he does not find favor with his mistress. The practical-minded Tranio reminds him of the chief obstacle to his desires, the unmarried "elder sister" who is "so curst and shrewd," but Lucentio's only concern is gaining access to Bianca. Recalling Baptista's intent to obtain "cunning schoolmasters" for his daughter, he decides that, since no one in Padua knows him as yet, he will adopt a disguise and enter her service in such a role. Meanwhile, Tranio will play the part of his young master, set up a suitable household, entertain dignitaries, and pursue his studies, as if he were Lucentio. They implicate Biondello, another servant, in the scheme and depart.

The scene concludes with a brief exchange between characters from the "Induction," who have been silently watching the action. Sly has been nodding off during the performance. He finds the whole thing tedious and wishes " 'twere done"—Shakespeare perhaps having fun at the expense of his own creation. This is the last we hear of these figures, but if they are left on stage their presence has an intriguing effect.* The theater audience watches as a stage audience watches what we never quite forget is a troupe of players putting on a play, one in which, as will become evident, several characters adopt false identities. Artifice within artifice within artifice within a play that is itself but an artifice! Perhaps Shakespeare simply takes delight in demonstrating his mastery of stagecraft, reminding us that this outrageous tale of male supremacy is but an absurd fiction, intended only for our enjoyment.

1.2　In the next scene we are introduced to Petruchio and his clever servant Grumio (not to be confused with the old man Gremio), who have arrived from Verona to visit the young man's good friend Hortensio. Petruchio directs his man to "knock me here," meaning, in the idiom of the time, "knock on Hortensio's door for me," but the mischievous Grumio insists on taking "knock me" literally and refuses, reasoning that it would be improper for a servant to "knock" his master, a bit of impertinence that earns him a playful tweaking of his ear. Hortensio comes out to greet his friend warmly. Petruchio announces that, his father having died and he inheriting, he has decided to see a bit of the world, "haply to wive and thrive as best I may," as he puts it. Hortensio sees him as a prospective husband for Katherina, but he is reluctant to visit upon his friend "a shrewd ill-favor'd wife," no matter how convenient it may be for him. Petruchio is lightheartedly unconcerned about whom he marries so long as she be "rich enough." He has come, he says, "to wive it wealthily in Padua, / If wealthily, then happily in Padua."

Petruchio may seem a distastefully mercenary young man, intent only marrying for material gain, but in fact he is not the only one to voice the priority of wealth in marital choices. As we shall see, Baptista quizzes Petruchio about his ability to provide for Katherina, and later Gremio and Tranio (in the guise of Lucentio) barter for Bianca's hand in the most blatantly materialistic terms. The social setting of the play is the burgeoning merchant class of Shakespeare's time, and he may be indulging in a subtle mockery of their predilection for assigning a monetary value to everything, including human relations. So Petruchio is no

---

*An alternative, one adopted by the BBC television production with John Cleese and Sarah Badel, is to omit the Induction entirely.

worse than any of them in his intent to "wive it wealthily" with a woman of his own class, however ugly, or old, or "rough / As are the swelling Adriatic seas" she may be. Hortensio, seeing a way out of his own predicament, offers to help Petruchio win a wealthy wife, but again honestly acknowledges to his friend that Katherina "is intolerably curst, / And shrewd, and froward [outspoken]." Petruchio, perhaps intrigued by the challenge, is determined to meet this "Katherine the curst," and Grumio, speaking from long experience, voices the opinion that he will be more than a match for her, since "scolding would do little good upon him." Hortensio reveals his passion for Bianca and asks help in disguising himself as a music tutor so that he may "unsuspected court her by herself." Grumio provides the theme of Shakespeare's comic plots in which young lovers scheme to outwit parental authority in matters of love and marriage: "See, to beguile the old folks, how young folks lay their heads together."

Gremio enters with the disguised Lucentio, who has managed to worm his way into the aged "pantaloon's" confidence by passing himself off as a man of letters, suitable to tutor Bianca and, as he pledges, to woo her for him in the process. Hortensio informs Gremio that he has secured a suitor for Katherina who will eliminate the bar to Bianca's marriage, but the old man is skeptical that anyone in his right mind would undertake such a thankless task: "But will you woo a wildcat?" Petruchio replies that he has endured fearsome noises before—the roar of lions, storms at sea, and artillery in battle—hence "a woman's tongue" holds no terrors for him. Tranio enters in the guise, it will be recalled, of Lucentio, and announces that he too is a suitor for Bianca's hand. After some initial hostility from the others, he is informed of the situation with the daughters, and Petruchio is introduced as the man who will "achieve the elder [and] set the younger free." The four suitors, bonded by their common interests, march off fraternally to the local tavern to "quaff carouses to our mistress' health."

2.1 The second act opens on a turbulent scene. The two sisters are alone, and Katherina has managed somehow to bind Bianca's hands. She pleads to be released, but her sister demands angrily that she choose from among her suitors. Bianca mockingly offers to surrender to Katherina whichever she fancies if she will just untie her hands, and she receives a slap in the face for her impertinence. Baptista comes upon them, releases Bianca, sends her off, and demands to know why Katherina treats her sister so harshly. Why indeed! She is jealous. She rages at her father for his partiality toward Bianca, who, she claims, "is your treasure" and "must have a husband" while she remains unmarried. So she will "go sit and weep" until she can devise a revenge for the inequity. In his comedies Shakespeare does not indulge in deep psychological studies. Bianca is Baptista's pampered favorite, and Katherina has grown "shrewish," it is implied, because she thinks herself unloved. That is all we know, really, and for Shakespeare's purposes, all we need to know. Katherina is in a jealous rage because her favored sister has a steady string of suitors and she has none. But all that's about to change.

The various suitors troop in. Petruchio presents himself as a prospective husband for Katherina and establishes the posture he will assume in pursuit of her. He has heard, he says in mock innocence, "of her beauty and her wit, / Her affability and bashful modesty, / Her wondrous qualities and mild behavior." He then introduces Hortensio, disguised as Litio, the music tutor, come to instruct the daughters; and Gremio offers Lucentio, as Cambio, to teach them letters. Tranio presents himself as Lucentio, son of Vincentio of Pisa, a stranger in their midst, come also to seek the hand of Bianca. Thus we have a stage full of impostors:

Tranio is acting the part of his master, Lucentio.

Lucentio pretends to be a man of letters, one Cambio.

Hortensio is disguised as a music teacher named Litio.

Petruchio is himself—or is he?

Hortensio-Litio is sent in to give Katherina a music lesson while Petruchio and Baptista negotiate a marriage settlement. The monetary arrangements agreed to, the father wonders if the young man will be able to secure his difficult daughter's love. In a key passage, Petruchio confesses that he is not easy to live with either. He is "as peremptory," he admits, "as she is proud-minded." But he voices confidence that all will be well, for "where two raging fires meet together, / They do consume the thing that feeds their fury." Only time will tell whether this is wisdom or folly.

Hortensio reenters with his lute wrapped around his neck. Katherina, he complains, took offense at his instruction and cracked him over the head with the instrument. Petruchio is rapt in admiration: "Now, by the

world, it is a lusty wench. / I love her ten times more than e're I did."
They all depart, Baptista promising to send Katherina to see Petruchio,
and he is left momentarily alone on stage. In a short *soliloquy,* he unfolds
his courtship strategy, which turns out to be one of obstinate perversity.
If she rails, he will compliment her on the sweetness of her voice; if she
frowns, he will praise her complexion, "clear / As morning roses newly
wash'd with dew"; and if she refuses to speak, he will admire her "pierc-
ing eloquence." Will it work?

When Katherina enters, Petruchio addresses her as "Kate." When she
objects to being so called, he launches into a speech which is full of compliments but pointedly repeats "Kate" no less than eleven times in six
lines, ending with a declaration that he is "mov'd to woo thee for my
wife." * This initial encounter is followed by an extended verbal skirmish
in which she insults him wittily as a "joint-stool," an "ass," a "buzzard,"
and a "fool," all of which he deflects with equal wit. After a final sexual
pun on "tale" = "tail," she turns to leave and he reaches out to prevent her,
receiving in response a sharp slap to the face. The lines here, particularly
the references to "arms" and her later "let me go," seem to indicate that
during the following exchange he continues to hold her under physical
restraint. He launches into a series of perverse compliments, praising her
as "passing gentle" and "pleasant, gamesome, passing courteous," all the
while wrestling with her. She persists in replying sharply until he finally
announces that he has reached agreement with her father, so "will you,
nill you, I will marry you." Petruchio concludes provocatively that he was
"born to tame you, Kate, / And bring you from a wild Kate to a
Kate / Conformable as other household Kates." So the battle lines are
drawn in this skirmish between the sexes.

This is all enormously entertaining, of course, but these two make a
decidedly unromantic pair. Kate is an ill-tempered, spiteful woman, and
though we may catch glimpses of the reasons for her abrasive disposition,
she remains a character difficult to like. Petruchio is a brash, abusive,
overbearing bully, intent only, it would appear, on imposing his will
upon his wife and reducing her to a state of abject obedience. Only an ardent feminist could sympathize with Kate's behavior, or an adamant
chauvinist with Petruchio's, and most of those watching will be hard

*Since Petruchio calls her "Kate" throughout, henceforth so shall we.

pressed to apologize for the temperament of either. They do seem well matched, however, and we wish them well, not just *him* but *them*. We hope Petruchio is not mistaken in his confidence that when two fires meet, they "consume the thing that feeds their fury." Could the union of these two dampen the fiery disposition of each and reduce them to loving amity?

Baptista enters, accompanied by Gremio and Tranio in the guise of young Lucentio. Kate rages at her father for matching her with a "lunatic, / A madcap ruffian and a swearing Jack [of base birth]." A smiling Petruchio assures the others that despite her outward behavior Kate is in reality as "modest as a dove." The two have agreed, he says, that she will continue to act the shrew in public while she dotes on him in private: "I tell you 'tis incredible to believe / How much she loves me." Kate is rendered speechless by the brazen effrontery of his claim, so Petruchio announces his departure for Venice to purchase wedding garments and unceremoniously drags her out as he leaves.

After some expressions of wonder at this development—couched, it will be noted, in the language of commerce—the three men get down to the business before them, bartering for the hand of Bianca. Gremio, with some satisfaction, lists his many possessions, promising that his wife will inherit them on his death. Tranio, speaking as Lucentio, tops his bid with an account of Vincentio's wealth, to be inherited similarly. Vincentio is described as very wealthy indeed, but it is never quite clear how much of Tranio's claim he fabricates simply to outmatch Gremio. At any rate, Baptista declares Tranio the highest bidder, but the careful merchant requires "the assurance" of the father himself before the contract can be sealed. The wily Tranio must now take steps to provide himself with a "father."

3.1 The two disguised "tutors," Hortensio as Litio, the music teacher, and Lucentio as Cambio, the man of letters, pay courtship to Bianca. The scene works well if, as they compete for her attention, we imagine Lucentio as a very attractive young man and Hortensio as something less. They clash initially, one calling the other a mere "fiddler" and "preposterous ass," the other replying that his rival is a "wrangling pedant." Bianca, who seems to enjoy the contention, decides to hear Lucentio while Hortensio tunes his instrument. In his "lecture" the young man reveals his identity and declares his intent, and Bianca, intrigued, keeps putting Hortensio off by insisting that his lute is not in tune. She finally submits to Hortensio's tutelage, which consists of a declaration of love cleverly couched in terms of the musical scale. She has already been captured, however, by Lucentio, who got there first, and so she rejects the musician's advances. A servant enters, calling her to help prepare her sister for the wedding, and she departs, leaving Hortensio somewhat discouraged.

3.2 The wedding day has arrived, but there is no sign of the groom. Kate is both furious and disconsolate. She rages against him as a man "who woo'd in haste and means to wed at leisure," one who "never means to wed where he hath woo'd," leaving her humiliated as the bride abandoned at the altar. She rushes off weeping as Biondello enters with a curious tale. Petruchio is indeed coming, but not equipped like a prospective bridegroom. He is outlandishly dressed, mounted on a swaybacked derelict of a horse, and accompanied by Grumio in similar mean apparel. (The costume designer of a production is allowed wide latitude to drape Petruchio in the gaudiest outfit fancy can imagine, and his entrance in the mockery of a wedding garment will entertain the audience as much as it shocks the stage company.) Baptista and Tranio plead with him to dress more appropriately, to which he replies, not implausibly, that "to me she's married, not unto my clothes," and they depart in search of Kate, leaving Tranio and Lucentio on stage. Tranio reports on his success in bidding for Bianca and the added complication of engaging someone to play Lucentio's father, whom Baptista had insisted must confirm the contract struck. Lucentio chaffs at the hovering presence of his rival, Hortensio, and decides to marry the apparently quite willing Bianca in secret so as to bypass such complications. Tranio will continue to search for a bogus father nonetheless, since Shakespeare is reluctant to pass up the comic possibilities of yet another impersonation.

Gremio comes upon them with an account of the wedding of Kate and Petruchio, during which, he reports, the groom comported himself like "a devil, a devil, a very fiend." He swore at the priest, knocked him down, called for wine, and having drunk it off, "threw the sops all in the sexton's face." The wedding party now approaches, led by the boisterous Petruchio, who suddenly announces that he cannot stay for the feast. He thanks them all for attending the ceremony in which, as he puts it, he gave himself away "to this most patient, sweet, and virtuous wife." Rejecting all entreaties, including Kate's, he insists that he must return to Verona immediately. She declares she'll stay in Padua, else she'll look like a fool for not showing "the spirit to resist." But in a speech that can be expected to make any modern woman bristle, he insists that she accompany him since she is now his property, his "goods," his "chattels." She is as much his now, he claims, as are "my household stuff, my field, my barn, / My horse, my ox, my ass, my any thing." Then, on the pretext that they "are beset with thieves" who plot to keep his wife from him, he and Grumio draw their swords to protect her. With Kate in tow, they retreat off stage.

However crudely expressed and offensive to modern ears, Petruchio's characterization of Kate as his "goods" and "chattels" is quite in keeping with the accepted status of wives in Shakespeare's time. In an age that fervently believed in a *universal order* of all things, the husband was acknowledged the unchallenged master of a family, presiding over his household as does the king his subjects and the sun the heavens.

Along with the husband's prerogatives in the family, however, came the obligation to provide for their welfare. Baptista performs this duty by negotiating with his daughters' suitors to ensure that they will be financially secure, though in this community of merchants it may sound like he is bartering off a house or a horse to the highest bidder. The daughter, of course, is expected to accept her father's choice of a husband with modest obedience, though in Shakespeare's comedies this is rarely the case. The plays are filled with loving couples who plot to defy parental authority as Lucentio and Bianca do here, though in the present instance their scheme is an ironic confirmation of the father's choice. Tranio, in the guise of Lucentio, has already negotiated successfully for the hand of Bianca, but, as it turns out, Lucentio wins her anyway. Baptista's choice of a husband for the cantankerous Kate is another matter, however, for while she must submit to her father's wishes, she does so with fierce reluctance.

4.1   We find ourselves at Petruchio's estate in Verona. Grumio has been sent ahead to prepare the household for the arrival of the master and his bride, who have endured a long, cold ride from Padua. He converses with another servant, Curtis, and the two exchange witticisms involving wordplay on popular catches and proverbs of the time, with which, we may assume, Shakespeare's audiences were familiar. Grumio complains of Petruchio's behavior on the journey. On one occasion Kate's horse slipped on some muddy ground and fell on her. Petruchio, apparently ignoring her, flew into a rage and began beating Grumio for his carelessness in allowing the horse to stumble. He relented only when Kate scrambled through the mire and "prayed that never prayed before" for him to stop. Curtis's reply offers a key to Petruchio's subsequent behavior: "By this reckoning he is more shrew than she." In the scenes to come he will act the irascible tyrant of his household, violently demanding and impossible to please, though never directing his anger at Kate, indeed insisting all the while that he is concerned only for her health and comfort. There are several hints that this is not his normal demeanor, but we are never entirely sure. He did admit earlier that he is "as peremptory as she proudminded."

Grumio lines up the household staff—all men, so Kate will be denied the comfort of a woman companion—and checks to ensure that everything is in readiness. The couple arrive, and Petruchio begins immediately to abuse what he calls his "logger-headed and unpolish'd grooms." Shakespeare is able to call upon his well-stocked vocabulary of insults (see also Hal and Falstaff in *Henry IV, Part 1*) as Petruchio roars out his displeasure with everything: To Grumio—"You peasant swain! You whoreson malt-horse drudge!"—for failing to meet them on the road. To another—"Off with my boots, you rogues! You villains, when?"—whom he kicks for supposedly turning his foot in the process. To yet another whom he strikes for spilling some water—"You whoreson villain, will you let it fall?" This one is also a "a whoreson beetle-headed, flap-ear'd knave!"

While carrying on this tirade, however, Petruchio is the very picture of courtesy toward his wife: "Sit down, Kate, and welcome"; "Come, Kate, and wash, and welcome heartily"; and "Come, Kate, sit down, I know you have stomach. / Will you give thanks, sweet Kate, or else shall I?" As a result she finds herself in the unfamiliar role of peacemaker. All she wants is something to eat and a place to rest, but Petruchio seems determined to deny her even those simple comforts. Meat is brought, but he rages that it is burnt and throws the dishes at the servants, explaining to her that overcooked meat "engenders choler, planteth anger," as if to imply that his behavior so far has been perfectly normal and she has yet to see him really angry. They retire to the bridal chamber; but, as Curtis reports, she is denied rest because he continually "rails, and swears, and rants," apparently about his inept servants.

Petruchio now appears on stage alone and in a *soliloquy* reveals that his rough behavior is a conscious design to "tame" his wife. He compares the process to the training of a falcon, one deprived of food until it learns to "know her keeper's call." Kate has had no meat and she'll have no sleep, he says, since he'll find fault with the bed and dismantle it, all the while insisting that he acts "in reverend care of her." "This is a way," he concludes, "to kill a wife with kindness [and] curb her mad and headstrong humor." And if anyone knows a better way "to tame a shrew," he says, he will be pleased to hear of it.

4.2   Back in Padua, Tranio (as Lucentio) and Hortensio (as Litio) observe Lucentio (as Cambio), who seems to be having his way with Bianca by reading to her from *The Art of Love*. The two men share their disappointment and vow to abandon their efforts to win her. Hortensio, revealing his identity, decides to "be married to a wealthy widow" who favors him. Tranio then informs Bianca that they have both "foresworn" their suits, leaving Lucentio a clear field. Biondello enters with news of an elderly man approaching them, identified simply as a "pedant [tutor or schoolmaster]," one old enough to pass as a father. Tranio, directing the young couple to leave, undertakes to enlist him to play the part of Vincentio and give his approval of the contract with Baptista. He meets the "pedant," who has come from Mantua, he says, to spend a week or two in Padua. Tranio warns him that it is death for a Mantuan to be found within the walls of the city, but as a courtesy, he says, he will lodge the man in his house, letting it be known abroad that he is Vincentio, his father. Yet another impostor!

4.3   The scene shifts back to Verona, where Kate is complaining to Grumio that she is "starv'd for meat [and] giddy for lack of sleep" because Petruchio has continued his tantrums—all, she says, "under name of perfect love." She begs Grumio to find her something to eat. Now complicit in his master's strategy, he taunts her by suggesting dishes and then rejecting them for one reason or another, finally settling on "mustard without the beef." Enraged by his insolence, she beats him until interrupted by Petruchio, accompanied by Hortensio, who has joined his friend in Verona. Petruchio carries a dish of meat for her but threatens to send it back unless she thanks him for it. In an *aside*, he urges Hortensio to consume the dish while he distracts Kate with the news that they will return to her father's house after she has been properly dressed by a tailor he has engaged.

A haberdasher enters with a new hat for Kate, and Petruchio angrily discards it as "a knack, a toy, a trick, a baby's cap," despite her protest that it is quite proper for a "gentlewoman." Petruchio now adopts a more direct strategy: "When you are gentle, you shall have one too, / And not till then." It backfires on him, however. In a ringing declaration of her independence, Kate responds defiantly, "I trust I may have leave to speak, / And speak I will. I am no child, no babe," and concludes "I will be free / Even to the uttermost, as I please, with words." Petruchio is perhaps temporarily taken aback by her resolute spirit, but he is rescued by the appearance of the tailor. The former scene is repeated here, though at more length, as Petruchio angrily finds fault with the gown while Kate insists it is perfectly proper. She knows what is going on by now, suspecting that her husband's irascible behavior may not arise entirely out of "perfect love." She turns sharply on him—"Belike you mean to make a puppet of me"—but Petruchio deflects the challenge by pretending that she has addressed the tailor, not him. In the end both the tailor and his gown are dismissed, and, in an aside, Hortensio is sent to assure him that he will be paid.

Kate therefore must return to her father's house in her wedding gown, now somewhat the worse for wear. Petruchio lectures her sanctimoniously on the virtues of "honest mean habiliments," philosophizing grandly that " 'tis the mind that makes the body rich," not its clothing. He orders that horses be prepared for the trip and remarks offhandedly that it must be about seven o'clock. Kate corrects him, replying innocently that it is actually "almost two"—for which she is sharply reprimanded. Petruchio now initiates a new stage in his "taming," complaining bitterly that whatever "I speak, or do, or think to do, / You are still crossing it." Knowing that Kate wants very much to return to Padua, he declares that they will not leave until "it shall be what o'clock I say it is." Petruchio raises the level of his campaign, no longer pretending that he acts out of "perfect love." Kate, reduced to exhaustion by lack of sleep and food, and dressed in her tattered wedding gown, is confronted with a husband who demands she acknowledge that his word is law, even when what he says is patently absurd.

4.4 In Padua, Tranio has persuaded the visiting "pedant" to impersonate Vincentio. They meet Baptista and Lucentio-Cambio and strike an agreement with assurances of Vincentio's wealth and Bianca's dowry. Lucentio-Cambio is dispatched to fetch Bianca so that the contract may be sealed, but he encounters Biondello, who informs him that Tranio has arranged for a priest to be available to him. Lucentio, confident that Bianca "will be pleas'd, then wherefore should I doubt?" determines to marry her without delay.

4.5 On the road to Padua, Petruchio pursues his latest strategy for "taming." He remarks that the moon shines brightly, and when Kate quite sensibly draws attention to the fact that it is actually the sun, he flies into a petulant rage, threatens to turn back, and complains once again, "evermore cross'd and cross'd, nothing but cross'd." To satisfy him, she agrees it is the moon, but he then changes his mind, calling it the sun, and in exasperation she agrees again, "what you will have it nam'd, even that it is, / And so it shall be so for Katherine."

The party meets an elderly gentleman on the road, and Petruchio tests his newfound authority again, directing Kate to greet the approaching "gentlewoman." Well versed in the rules of the game by now—for it has become a game—she deliberately overplays the part, praising the old man as a "young budding virgin, fair, and fresh, and sweet." Petruchio corrects her for addressing "a man, old, wrinkled, faded, wither'd" in this manner; and she apologizes to the bewildered stranger for her mistake. The stranger turns out to be the real Vincentio, Lucentio's father, on his way to Padua to visit his son. On learning his identity, Petruchio greets him warmly and invites him to accompany them on the journey.

5.1 In Padua, Lucentio and Bianca steal off to be married. The party from Verona arrives, and Vincentio knocks on his son's door, only to be confronted by the "pedant," who continues to insist that he is Lucentio's father. Vincentio is incensed and grows even angrier when Biondello enters and refuses to recognize him. The "pedant" calls for help when Vincentio begins to beat his servant as Baptista and Tranio come upon the scene. Tranio, sticking to his role as Lucentio, also denies the identity of the real father and calls an officer to have him arrested. Lucentio and

Bianca, now married, enter, and he explains the whole series of impersonations, asking his father's forgiveness. A bewildered Baptista asks if they are indeed married, and Vincentio calms him with the assurance that "we will content you," presumably about money matters. He reserves the right to deal later with Tranio, however, who will pay for having him arrested.

Petruchio and Kate have been watching, much amused by the scene. She playfully urges that they "follow to see the end of this ado." Petruchio again asserts his authority, this time, however, with obvious affection, insisting that they kiss first. She resists coyly at the impropriety of kissing in public but gives in willingly at the end as they embrace with every appearance of mutual passion. Is it possible that despite all the contention between the two they have actually fallen in love? Perhaps. One possibility is that they were attracted to one another from the very first, and all that followed was Petruchio's clever device to cure her of her petulance. In another interpretation, the initially unloved Kate finally finds someone she believes can love her, persuaded perhaps by the pains Petruchio has taken to win her. His efforts can be seen not so much as a design to subdue her but as a strategy to remedy her sour disposition and permit her to love him in return. However these scenes are enacted, it appears that by some mysterious chemistry they have emerged from their battles a truly loving couple.

5.2 We now come to the troublesome final scene. It is a wedding feast hosted by Lucentio for the three couples—himself and Bianca, Petruchio and Kate, Hortensio and his wealthy widow. There is a great deal of witty banter back and forth across the table, some of it rather sharp between Kate and the widow, ending only when Bianca rises and invites the ladies to retire. The men, left to their own devices, conceive of a wager over "whose wife is the most obedient," to be won by the husband of the wife who will return when summoned. Bianca and the widow refuse, to the embarrassment of their husbands, but Kate enters in response to Petruchio's call. He directs her to return and bring the other women in as the men express their wonder at the transformation. The women reenter and, to emphasize their newfound harmony, Petruchio voices a distaste for Kate's hat and directs her to discard it. She does so readily, to more expressions of wonder. Bianca and the widow grow peevish with their husbands, who chide them for failure to come when summoned, and Petruchio directs Kate to "tell these headstrong women / What duty they do owe their lords and husbands."

This brings us to her controversial speech. Kate reprimands the women for their "scornful glances" intended, she says "to wound thy lord, thy king, thy governor." "Thy husband," she goes on, "is thy lord, thy life, thy keeper, / Thy head, thy sovereign," who in return for his labors on their behalf asks only for "love, fair looks, and true obedience." They do him wrong, she chides, to "seek for rule, supremacy, and sway, / When they are bound to serve, love, and obey," and she concludes in a sequence of rhymed couplets, urging them to accept their duty to "do him ease." Petruchio is delighted—"Why there's a wench! Come on, and kiss me, Kate"—and they depart joyfully for bed. The sense of the final scene is that the marital strife of Lucentio and Hortensio has only just begun, but that the struggle between Petruchio and Kate, played out in their turbulent courtship, is at an end. Each now has respect for the fires in the other, and though it will not be an easy union, it will never be dull.

Kate's description of the dominant role of the husband is entirely in keeping with the accepted social structure in the medieval and Renaissance family, but such an explanation cannot render her words any more agreeable to twenty-first-century sentiments in such matters. Directors have employed a number of ingenious devices to make the speech more palatable—cutting it drastically, or assigning some of its more offensive lines to Petruchio, or eliminating it altogether. Others have disassembled the speech and distributed lines to various characters here and there in other parts of the play. A popular device is to have the actress deliver it with heavy irony, as if the spirited Kate is saying to the men, "if you can believe this rubbish, you're all fools." Perhaps the most satisfactory alternative for productions that remain faithful to the original text will imply that Kate and Petruchio are performing a pre-planned charade, broadly winking at each other as they have fun at the expense of the other couples. These two, both strong-willed, high-spirited, and consummately clever, having found each other in a perfect loving match, revel in their good fortune and join in playing an enormous joke on their friends. Skilled actors and actresses can project any of these alternatives with ingenious stage business, so that modern audiences, rather than bristle at the message, can delight in the wit of it.

THE TEMPEST
(A Romance)

❧

THIS IS the most enchanting of Shakespeare's plays, though not solely because the chief figure is a wizard and spirits haunt its air. Its appeal derives from unsurpassed poetry that gives rise to a rich array of conflicting responses from the audience: joy at the flowering of love, regret at the loss of innocence, satisfaction at evil contained and justice done, wonder at the supernatural, laughter at a delusionary drunkard, offense at ugliness, and sorrow at the spectacle of slavery. But no such list can explain the spell that Shakespeare casts, which has for centuries challenged the skill of actors and producers.

The challenge, perhaps, is that the play is so insubstantial. We reach for it only to grasp a handful of air, since there is not much in it that might be called plot. It opens dramatically enough with a ship caught in the terrors of a storm at sea, but soon it settles down to a sequence of incidents and encounters which, since a godlike power controls them, promise little in the way of suspense. All aboard the ship are delivered unharmed at four different locations on the shores of an island where the wizard Prospero holds sway over their destinies. We learn that he is the unjustly deposed Duke of Milan, stranded years before on the island with his infant daughter Miranda, and that the ship holds his enemies—his treacherous brother Antonio and Alonso, the king of Naples, who conspired to bring about his overthrow. Skilled in the magic arts, Prospero works his charms, luring each of the groups to the cave where he has lived for a dozen years with the maturing Miranda, served by the half-human Caliban and a dutiful spirit, Ariel. Once they are assembled there, justice and mercy prevail in a scene of reconciliation, after which all depart the enchanted island and return to the real world.

The plot, then, is unlikely to enthrall us, even though along the way we are treated to a tender love story, rich and ribald humor, unearthly music, murderous schemes, supernatural charms and apparitions, and, as mentioned, a storm at sea. There is excitement enough, surely, but the charm of the play seems to lie elsewhere. Shakespeare weaves a tale of love and innocence in the isolated Eden that dwells deep in the imagination of us all. He plays upon the painful paradox of our feelings toward the earthly Paradise by reminding us that no matter how strong our desire to return to that first shining time, we are always painfully aware that we could never flourish there. In that sense, then, *The Tempest* is a celebration of innocence, but one with a shadow cast over its joys by the sad knowledge that innocence, like the play itself, must fade in the end.

1.1 The tempest of the play occupies only the first scene—a brilliant theatrical device, nonetheless, to capture the attention of the audience and keep them in their seats. The storm serves several purposes: It provides a highly dramatic opening to the play, a ship in danger of foundering in high seas and howling wind. It introduces us briefly to some of the chief characters of the play, the lords of Italy in peril of their lives. And it has a comic effect, the nobility rushing fearfully on deck, only to be ordered below by common seamen. The imperious lords are indignant at the slights to their social standing, and they vow to have the struggling boatswain hanged for his insolence should they manage to survive—which ironically they will do only as a result of his labors.

1.2 The scene shifts to a nearby island, where Prospero and his daughter Miranda are watching the imperiled ship from the entrance to the cave where they live. Miranda is distressed at the sight and begs her father to calm the storm if he has caused it "by [his] art." She has "suffered," she says, for the "brave vessel, / (Who had no doubt some noble creature in her!)." He acknowledges that the storm is his doing but insists that no harm will come of it, adding mysteriously, "I have done nothing, but in care of thee." Prospero then lays aside his "magic garment" and his strange powers to assume the role of a father preparing to tell his daughter for the first time the story of their lives.

Shakespeare now has the formidable task of narrating the whole background of the play without losing the attention of the audience, and he does so by characterizing Prospero as a parent anxious to relate family history to a daughter who, though respectful, has little interest in the account. As he talks, her eyes stray to the stricken vessel and he must continually recapture her attention: "Dost thou attend me?" "Thou attend'st not!" and "Dost thou hear?" It is as if the playwright admits to the audience that this is pretty dull stuff, but insists that it is necessary if we are to proceed. After all, he seems to say, I gave you a storm at sea, now bear with me awhile.

Miranda's innocence is touchingly ironic. While her father is telling her a tale of political intrigue, treachery, and attempted murder, all matters entirely outside her experience, she weeps in pity for the very men, those "noble creatures" on the ship, whose wickedness he is describing. In brief, some dozen years before, when she was just three years old, Prospero had been the Duke of Milan until his brother Antonio, in collusion with the king of Naples, had deposed and replaced him. Antonio, fearful of the consequences of assassinating his popular brother, had set him and his infant daughter adrift on a leaky bark, "a rotten carcass of a butt." But "a noble Neapolitan, Gonzalo" provided them with provisions, garments, and, of particular importance, Prospero's books, which contain the secret of his powers. They survived, to be stranded on this isolated island; and now, he tells her, "by accident most strange, bountiful Fortune" has brought all his enemies within his reach. He must seize the opportunity or else his "fortunes / Will ever after droop."

His tale told, Prospero once more dons his magic robes and, reducing Miranda to sleep, summons Ariel, the lively spirit through whom he works his spells. "Ariel appears aloft," according to the stage directions, an effect that modern cinematography can produce with ease, but on Shakespeare's bare *stage* his appearances and disappearances must have presented a challenge. The part would have been played by a boy gifted with acrobatic skills and a voice appropriate to his many songs.

Ariel reports that he has raised the storm as Prospero directed and deposited the ship, its crew, and its passengers unharmed about the island. When his master proposes further tasks for him, Ariel complains peevishly that he had been promised his freedom, and in Prospero's angry reply we learn of the spirit's history: An earlier inhabitant of the island, "the foul witch Sycorax," had also been stranded there with her son Caliban. Sycorax, who possessed certain magical powers of her own, had employed Ariel until he refused "to act her earthy and abhorred commands."

She had angrily locked him into "a cloven pine" and then died, leaving him imprisoned until Prospero arrived to free him. He warns Ariel sternly that if there are further complaints he will "peg" him again in the "knotty entrails" of an oak for another twelve years. Ariel fearfully submits, and Prospero, mellowing somewhat, promises to release him in two days, meanwhile instructing him to remain invisible, revealing himself "to no sight but thine and mine."

It appears that Miranda is unaware of Ariel's existence, since it is not until the spirit's departure that Prospero awakens his daughter. They set out in search of the only other inhabitant of the island, the child of "the foul witch Sycorax," Caliban, who lives in a hole in the rock. Prospero calls him forth in the most abusive terms, "what ho! slave! Caliban! / Thou earth, thou!" and "come, thou tortoise." He emerges uttering malignant curses on them both, and Prospero threatens to punish him with cramps, side-stitches, and pinches if he is not obedient. Caliban complains that the island is his by rights and recalls that Prospero was kind to him when the wizard first arrived. "Then I loved thee," he remembers, "and showed you all the qualities o'th'isle," responding to Prospero's kindness at the time with the only simple gift he had to bestow. Now, he complains with more curses, he is no more than a slave, confined to the hole he inhabits.

Prospero replies angrily that he had at first treated Caliban "with human care" until the day when he tried "to violate the honor of my child." The unrepentant creature relishes the memory, declaring gleefully that had he not been prevented he would have "peopled else / This isle with Calibans." He acknowledges that Prospero taught him language and the learning that goes with it, but he spits back, "my only profit on't / Is, I know how to curse." Learning has been nothing but a burden, he claims; he was better off ignorant. An exasperated Prospero ends the confrontation by ordering him to perform his duties with a threat of cramps and aches should he neglect them. A cowed Caliban must submit, since, as he acknowledges, his master's "art is of such power" that it would even enslave his mother's god, Setebos.

Caliban is often played as a subhuman or half-human being, an ugly, filthy, misshapen creature whose most prominent posture is a crouch. He is a step below human and a step above beast; and the ambiguity of his nature evokes an audience reaction that is decidedly mixed. In his human nature he can love, and learn, and worship, and we may deplore Prospero's treatment of him as an abject slave. As a beast, however, he lusts after an innocent Miranda and has no remorse about doing so, hence we can appreciate her father's anger and at the same time regret the harsh measures he takes to keep him in check.

The ultimate end of Prospero's spells is to kindle love, and Ariel works his purpose with music. He charms Ferdinand, the young son of the king of Naples, with a lyric song about his father, whom the prince believes drowned, and leads him to the cave. On first seeing him, Miranda thinks him a spirit. After assurances from her father that he is indeed human, she is touched to tears by the marvel before her. She moves out of the cave to address what she perceives as "a thing divine—for nothing natural / I ever saw so noble." Ferdinand is stunned as well by her appearance, and, thinking her "the goddess / On whom these airs attend," asks, "O you wonder! / If you be maid, or no?" She replies modestly, "no wonder, sir, but certainly a maid." It is a wonderfully touching scene as the two fall in love at first sight.

But Prospero is gruffly abrupt with the young man, and despite his daughter's pleas—"This / Is the third man that e'er I saw . . . the first / That e'er I sighed for"—accuses him of spying on them. Miranda pleads again—"There's nothing ill can dwell in such a temple"—but Prospero is adamant, branding Ferdinand a traitor and threatening to imprison him. The prince draws his sword but finds himself charmed into immobility, a paralysis that Prospero attributes to his guilty conscience. Ferdinand is led quietly away, uttering the *courtly lover's* vow that he will gladly surrender his liberty "might I but through my prison once a day / Behold this maid."

Prospero, in an *aside*, reveals his intent: he means to create obstacles to their love, "lest too light winning / Make the prize light." In another sense this test of Ferdinand will be a form of purification. Since he comes from a world steeped in sin and is by association "possessed with guilt," he must be cleansed through trial. Prospero knows too well the depths of treachery to which the lords of Italy will descend to feed their pride, depths to which Ferdinand is not immune.

2.1 The second act finds us in the company of those lords. Chief among them are Alonso, the king of Naples, his brother Sebastian, and

Prospero's brother Antonio, who usurped the dukedom with the king's help. They are accompanied by old Gonzalo, the "noble Neapolitan" who aided Prospero in his escape. All are depressed by the shipwreck—all, that is, except Gonzalo, who is annoyingly cheerful, attempting to comfort the king by emphasizing the good fortune of their survival. As Gonzalo goes on about the beauties of the island, Sebastian and Antonio, in a series of asides, ridicule his optimism, which clearly irritates them. When, for example, the old man observes that "here is everything advantageous to life," Antonio responds, "true, save means to live." It is evident that these two are cynical men-of-the-world, hardened and unfeeling, but uneasy when separated from court life. Their talk is all of Europe and Africa, Naples and Milan; and they comfort themselves with court chitchat about the king's poor choice of a son-in-law. Alonso is so weighed down with grief at the supposed drowning of his son that he is hardly listening, and Sebastian is ruthless in blaming him for the loss: "The fault's your own."

To distract the king, Gonzalo launches into a utopian vision, his concept of an ideal commonwealth, one without government, commerce, letters, husbandry, or labor, a place with "no occupation, all men idle, all: / And women too, but, innocent and pure." It is a description of the original Eden, but also, curiously enough, an image of Prospero's island itself, populated as it is by an idle man and a woman, "innocent and pure," whom nature sustains in "all abundance." There is a difference, of course, in that they are served by a resentful slave and a spirit of the air, both anxious to be free of Prospero's dominion. It is a fallen Eden, therefore, but no less of an Eden for that.

Aside from its resemblance to Gonzalo's utopia, the island community reflects yet another imagined construct of Shakespeare's time, the belief in a *universal order* to all existence, which was embodied in the figure of a great *Chain of Being*. Because of his supernatural powers, Prospero, "the god o'th'island," presides at the top of the chain. Below him comes Ariel, a creature of the spirit world, and then Miranda, who in her innocence is an image of Eve before the Fall. Further down the chain is a link to the lower realms, the half-human Caliban, possessed of speech and reason but ruled by animal instinct. At the bottom are the trees and plants that provide nature's "abundance," and finally the rock in which he lives. With his godlike powers, Prospero rules over all. By his art he holds evil in check, protects innocence, nurtures love, and dispenses justice. He is also, of course, a father, a duke, and a learned man; but when he dons his "magic garment," he resembles most a benign deity.

Gonzalo's fanciful vision is subject to more ridicule by Antonio and Sebastian, who are blind to the beauties of a place so alien to their nature. They have no eyes for Eden. Yet while we reject their cruel disdain for what they haughtily presume to be a touch of simplemindedness in Gonzalo, we are troubled by our old ambivalence about that lost Garden. When they say that Eden is not for them, they seem to be voicing our own hidden thoughts, and we must agree that a place where all men are idle and all women pure is no more appropriate for us than for them. Perhaps this explains why Shakespeare does not visit on them the punishment their treachery so richly deserves—what they say has too much of the ring of painful truth to it.

Ariel appears "aloft" and with some enchanting music reduces the lords to sleep—except Antonio and Sebastian, who seem impervious to the charm. While the others drowse, Antonio persuades his friend to kill the king, his brother, and seize the crown, in much the same way he had won Milan from Prospero. They draw their swords to do away with Alonso and Gonzalo, but before they can act Ariel awakens the sleepers; after some confusion they set out in search of Ferdinand. It is a somewhat ludicrous scene in which the treacherous nobles plot to secure a crown that, given their present circumstances, is all but meaningless. Yet it is their very nature to plot and scheme wherever they are. Hence even here, marooned on an isolated island with no apparent means of rescue, these creatures of the court cannot resist the urge to engage in intrigue.

2.2   The following scene introduces two more of the ship's passengers cast ashore on the island, the jester Trinculo and the drunken butler Stephano. These two, along with Caliban, provide the comic element of the play, which thus far has offered much to charm but little to laugh at. The scene opens on Caliban cursing Prospero still, and complaining about the spirits that pinch, bite, and prick him for "every trifle" of neglect or disobedience. He hears what he thinks is one of them approaching and hides foolishly under his "gaberdine [cloak or poncho]," much as would a small child who covers his eyes and claims he can't be seen. The intruder, however, is Trinculo, who trips over the concealed Caliban and pauses to consider what sort of creature he is. Trinculo's remark that "he smells like a fish," along with later similar references, influenced early productions to costume Caliban as half human and half fish. On the other hand, he must be recognizably human since Miranda refers to Ferdinand as "the third man that e'er I saw." For the most part, Caliban's companions give few hints of his appearance, addressing him as "moon-calf" or simply "monster." Trinculo, seeking shelter from a threatening storm, crawls under the "gaberdine" with him in such a way that their legs protrude at opposite ends, explaining Stephano's subsequent misconception that he has discovered a creature with four legs.

Stephano enters, reeling drunk, and coming upon the strange sight, speculates the profit if only he could transport the four-legged monster back to Naples for display. He lifts a corner of the gaberdine, uncovering the head of Caliban, to whom he gives a drink from his bottle. Trinculo emerges, and after a fond reunion Stephano explains that he survived the storm by riding ashore "upon a butt of sack [a barrel of wine]," which he has carefully preserved. Caliban, in awe of the two, approaches; heightened by the wine himself, he assumes from their resemblance to Prospero—who is the only man he has ever seen—that they too have supernatural powers. Since it has been his unhappy fate to fall under the sway of the godlike Prospero, he imagines that by placing himself in the service of a new god he can gain release from slavery. The natural man, not unlike ourselves, has need of a god to worship. Since Prospero displaced his Setebos but in the end proved false, Caliban seeks salvation in another, who he has faith will be on his side this time. He prostrates himself before Stephano, declaring, "I will kiss thy feet" and begging him to "be my god."

When Prospero first appeared, Caliban gave him all he had to offer, a knowledge of the island. But that god failed him, and now he lays his same small gifts before the new object of his worship: "I prithee, let me bring you to where crabs grow; / And I with my long nails will dig thee pig-nuts . . . Wilt thou go with me?" Stephano is briefly taken aback by this display, but in his drunken state he finds it agreeable to be rendered such homage and consents to the role. Caliban is pathetically exultant, crying out "freedom, high-day! high-day, freedom! freedom, high-day, freedom!" We pity him for his simple faith that merely by changing gods he can gain release, since we know that, as Trinculo puts it, he has made "a wonder of a poor drunkard" who will fail him as have the others he has loved and worshipped. If he is once more abandoned, where is he to turn?

It seems that all the "pains" Prospero took to teach Caliban language have only raised him to a level of superstitious simplemindedness. He was better off unknowing, when alone on his island he was free to worship his uncouth Setebos. If we had the chance, we might ask Prospero to consider his slave Caliban, whom he has only made wretched by endowing him with knowledge. And we might ask him to consider his daughter as well: Is she not happier in her innocence? Why expose her to the corrupt world? What good is all this learning anyway? Have your books made you content?

3.1   The third act opens on Ferdinand who is engaged in Caliban's task, hauling logs; but he finds pleasure in his labors since they are sweetened by thoughts of Miranda. He undergoes the traditional trial of the courtly lover, willing to undertake any quest or bear any burden to win his lady's favor. Miranda appears, but she proves no chivalric maiden content to be admired from afar. She offers to help in his task, but he refuses, again in the tradition, protesting that it would be a "dishonor" for her to do so or for him to permit it. Prospero, standing unseen nearby, murmurs, "poor worm thou art infected." He is pleased at their growing love, but this does seem a curious way to express his pleasure. Is love a disease?

Ferdinand asks her name and then plays upon it with a lilting phrase, "admired Miranda!" the first word pronounced with three syllables, *ad-mir-ed,* as was the poetic custom. He then compares her to women of his experience, praising her as one "so perfect, so peerless" that she is "created / Of every creature's best." She replies with true modesty and in her innocence, casting aside reserve, declares, "I would not wish / Any companion in the world but you." Ferdinand then resorts to the stock phrases of the courtly lover—at first glance his heart flew to her service and he is now her slave—but she cuts through all this fanciful language and asks simply, directly: "Do you love me?" He professes he does, and she, discarding "bashful cunning," declares, "I am your wife, if you will marry me; / If not, I'll die your maid." Prospero, still unseen, is delighted. All seems to be going according to plan.

The response of any audience to this tender scene is curiously mixed.

As the two declare their love, Miranda shares the ambivalence of our own feelings as we watch the scene unfold: "I am a fool / To weep at what I am glad of." Shakespeare here, as elsewhere, works upon our awareness of the tragic contradiction of our nature. Miranda has lost her pure, untainted vision of life—for that we foolishly weep. But she has gained love with its promise of happiness, fulfillment, and deeper understanding—for that Prospero is glad, and we too must rejoice at the gain while we sigh at the loss. It is a conflict of emotions that may explain why we shed tears at a wedding. In one sense, it would be better for her not to hear that she is "so perfect, so peerless." On the other hand, well, he seems a nice young man. Prospero's earlier, puzzling remark takes on meaning now—the "worm" has indeed "infected" Eden, a cause for both joy and sorrow.

3.2   The next scene finds us back with the comic trio, who are by now thoroughly besotted with wine. Stephano relishes the worship of Caliban, while Trinculo wittily mocks the spectacle. If, he says, there are only five inhabitants on the island, as he has been told, and "th'other two be brained like us, the state totters." Caliban has taken a dislike to the jester—"I'll not serve him, he is not valiant"—and urges Stephano to punish him for his insolence, as he knows Prospero would him for a like offense. Ariel enters invisible, and while Caliban unfolds his plan to murder Prospero, the spirit, imitating Trinculo's voice, intrudes here and there with an abrupt, "thou liest." The result is a scene of antic confusion as the two turn angrily on the uncomprehending jester, who apparently does not hear the voice. If the trick seems familiar, it is because countless comics have adopted the device in the centuries since.

Caliban is finally able to propose his plan. They will kill Prospero, but, he insists, they must first "possess his books." Without them, he believes, the wizard is powerless. Once this is accomplished, he goes on, Stephano can mate with Miranda and populate the island. Stephano heartily agrees to the plan, announcing that he and she will then rule as king and queen, with the other two serving as "viceroys." He is drunk, of course, but his grandiose vision of ruling over a kingdom with no subjects is only slightly more ludicrous than Sebastian's plot to kill Alonso and assume the crown of Naples, now made meaningless by their isolation. The lords of Italy, it would appear, and their servants as well, are by their very nature treacherous, but their malicious streak seems also to have rendered them irredeemably stupid.

Ariel overhears all, of course, and will inform Prospero. For the moment he begins his unearthly music, unnerving Stephano and Trinculo. A troubled Caliban detects a flaw in his new god: "Are you afeared?" The "monster" reassures them that this is not an uncommon occurrence— "The isle is full of voices, / Sounds and sweet airs that give delight and hurt not." While asleep, he says, he has heard soaring music and seen wondrous visions, such that "when I waked / I cried to dream again." Drawn by Ariel's "sounds and sweet airs," they follow him out.

3.3 Meanwhile, the other party of shipwrecks has wearied of their search for Ferdinand, and a despairing Alonso concludes that his son has surely drowned. As Antonio and Sebastian secretly reaffirm their intent to murder the king, they are all surprised by the sound of music and the appearance of "several strange shapes" bearing a sumptuous banquet, which they spread out before the stunned company. The spirits courteously invite them to sit and eat, and then depart. After expressions of wonder comparing the spectacle to tales of strange creatures reported by travelers returning from distant places, they sit and prepare to feast. Suddenly Ariel appears in the shape of a harpy, the legendary Greek figure of retribution, half woman and half vulture, and with a gesture dissolves the banquet. Visible apparently only to the guilty, he addresses the three who conspired against Prospero, and angrily accuses them of their crime, declaring that he and his "fellows / Are ministers of fate" who have caused the shipwreck as punishment for their treachery. Prospero, who has been watching, praises Ariel for his performance and gloats that all his enemies "are now knit up / In their distractions" and in his power.

Gonzalo, apparently unaware of Ariel's visitation, is bewildered by the behavior of his companions. When Alonso, after some wild words, rushes off toward the sea intent upon drowning himself, the old man sends others to give chase and save him. Sebastian and Antonio have backed off fearfully with swords drawn, and Gonzalo can only conclude that "their great guilt" has finally poisoned them and begun "to bite the spirit."

4.1 The fourth act opens at the cave, where a mellower Prospero explains to Ferdinand that his earlier harshness was but a trial of the young man's love for Miranda, and that he "hast strangely stood the test." He surrenders his daughter, "a third of mine own life," to Ferdinand, but with the stern warning that he is not to "break her virgin-knot" before the wedding ceremony. The prince vows that nothing could possibly "melt [his] honor into lust," and Prospero, satisfied, plans to celebrate their betrothal with "some vanity of mine art."

At his command, Ariel and his fellow spirits entertain the couple with a play within the play. The performance is a type of *masque*, combining poetry, music, and dance in a highly formal mode of theater. In keeping with such productions, popular in court at the time, there is little action, with the characters, all mythological goddesses, delivering set speeches in rhymed couplets, in distinct contrast to the free flow of Shakespeare's poetry elsewhere.

Ferdinand, in awe at the spirits' performance, responds, "let me live here ever— / So rare a wond'red father and a wise / Makes this place Paradise." His words conjure up again the image of the island as an Eden ruled over by a benign god. But at the same time they reflect the ill-advised human desire to retreat into a world of fancy. The masque is, after all, an illusion, performed by spirits in an unreal place, and the wish to retire there poses dangers to reason. We live within the bounds of the real world—Eden is no longer for us.

The spell is broken as that world intrudes with Prospero's sudden thought of the "foul conspiracy / Of the beast Caliban and his confederates," and he summarily sweeps the spirits away. Ferdinand is distressed, but Miranda is somewhat less so, since, we may assume, she has been diverted by such entertainments before and knows that in time they all end. In one of Shakespeare's most memorable passages, Prospero comforts the young man. "Our revels now are ended," he tells Ferdinand, and the spirits he has just seen are now "melted into air, into thin air." And like the play, the world itself, with all its riches and glories, will some day dissolve as well, leaving "not a rack behind." Again like the play, he concludes, we ourselves are but a dream "and our little life / Is rounded with a sleep." The passage is a lovely evocation of the powers of the imagination—but it is not a happy thought.

Prospero asks the couple to retire to the cave and then summons Ariel. The spirit has led the three conspirators on a merry chase as they followed his music through thickets and thorn bushes, ending finally up to their chins in a stinking, marshy pool nearby. Prospero shakes his head in dismay at the thought of Caliban, "a devil, a born devil, on whose nature / Nurture can never stick." This blunt condemnation, which seems justified in the context of the play, is occasionally cited to confirm the image of Prospero as the colonial exploiter justifying his cruel treatment of the natives he enslaves, dismissing them as subhuman savages unresponsive to any "pains" he might take to civilize them. But he could just as well be said to sound like the Old Testament God, brooding over the wayward human race who ignore the many gifts he has bestowed upon them and perversely sink back into decadence and idolatry. Prospero's determination to "plague them all" echoes the sentiment of a wrathful Jehovah, preparing to unleash the Flood and start over again.

He prepares for the arrival of the conspirators by displaying his wardrobe on a line outside his cave, the richly wrought cloaks and costumes he had worn as Duke of Milan. The three enter, stinking of marsh mud, Trinculo and Stephano complaining about their discomfort, especially the loss of their bottles. Caliban, intent upon his scheme, leads them to the cave entrance and urges them to carry out the murder. Distracted by the splendor of Prospero's garments, however, they neglect to first dispose of their owner before celebrating their access to power by trying on the trappings of office. Caliban is furious at their behavior, entreating them to do the deed. But his pleas go unheeded as they load him down with the garments and prepare to depart, their original purpose now forgotten. Prospero unleashes his spirits upon them in the form of hunters and their hounds, and they flee back into the forest. He observes the ludicrous scene and remarks with satisfaction that "at this hour / Lies at my mercy all mine enemies."

5.1 At the opening of the final act, which is one long scene, Prospero repeats his satisfaction, "now does my project gather to a head." Ariel gives an account of the king and his company, who are all "confined together," the three villains in a "distracted" state, the others mourning their condition. Ariel observes that his master's "affections would become tender" could he see their suffering, as would his own, he says, were he human. Ariel's touch of compassion brings about a sharp change in Prospero. It is never quite clear what his original "project" was, that is, exactly what he planned to do with his enemies once they were at his mercy—but whatever it was, he now abandons it. Although still angry at his former oppressors, he declares that he will permit his "nobler reason" to prevail, since "the rarer action is / In virtue than in vengeance." "They being penitent," he promises, he will forgive their treachery, punishing them "not a frown further." He directs Ariel to release his enemies from their confinement and charm them to his cave. The "god o'th'island" is a deity of mercy as well as power and justice.

The long speech that follows is widely admired and variously interpreted. Prospero reviews his magic powers: by his "so potent art," he has "bedimmed / The noontide sun," called forth storms at sea, created thunder and lightning, "plucked up / The pine and cedar," and opened graves. But now, he says, he will abandon "this rough magic," break his staff, bury it "certain fathoms in the earth," and drown his books, the source of his power, "deeper than did ever plummet sound."

Evidence from both within and without the work gives reason to believe that *The Tempest* is the last complete play Shakespeare wrote, and many hear in this moving speech his farewell to the theater. Prospero's account of his miraculous powers is a recital of the many effects that Shakespeare had produced on the stage in one play after another over the years. Tiring of the demanding pace of London, it is said, he like Prospero wants only to surrender his poetic powers and retreat to Stratford-on-Avon, there to assume once again the role of a mere mortal. We are as reluctant to see Prospero surrender his powers as Shakespeare's audience must have been to hear that he would no longer work his magic on the stage.

Ariel returns, leading the lords of Italy into a charmed circle his master has etched upon the ground. There they stand, speechless and immobile, as Prospero moves among them with a word for each—pity for Gonzalo, scorn for the others. In keeping with his vow of mercy, he forgives them all, though not without some reservations about his brother Sebastian, "unnatural though thou art." As their senses return, Prospero retires to don his official robes as Duke of Milan and instructs Ariel to bring the ship's crew to the cave.

Prospero startles the group, now in full command of their senses, with his appearance. By now overawed by the series of mysterious events, they don't know what to think, "whether this be / Or be not, I'll not swear." Alonso accepts him for what he is, however, and asks that he "pardon me my wrongs." Sebastian and Antonio, it seems, are another matter. These two, who would not recognize Eden if they stood on it, see in Prospero only "the devil"; but he forgives them as well, even though they show no sign of repentance, which he had declared the condition for his mercy.

Alonso still mourns the loss of his son, and Prospero, feigning sympathy, counsels patience, which, he says, has comforted him in the like loss of a daughter. He then draws aside the curtain of his cave to reveal the couple playing chess. Unaware of those watching, Miranda accuses Ferdinand of cheating, "sweet lord, you play me false"; but at his protest she vows that whatever he may do, she will "call it fair play." The two come forth, Ferdinand to a joyful reunion with his father, Miranda to a startling revelation. She looks upon more human beings than she has ever seen and in her innocence exclaims, "how many goodly creatures are there here! / How beauteous mankind is! O brave new world, / That has such people in't!" Prospero, glancing perhaps at the cutthroats in the company, murmurs with sad and knowing irony, " 'tis new to thee."

Miranda's sense of wonder is so much like Caliban's when he first sees Trinculo and Stephano that we suddenly realize both of them project the image of innocence in the play, she as she is now and he as he was before the arrival of Prospero. There are differences, of course: she is comely, he ugly; learning is an ornament to her, to him a burden. Nonetheless the similarities are striking. She is appealingly unself-conscious and ignorant of the world, as was he in his natural state. She is pure, and he, as a child of nature, was equally untainted. Her desire for Ferdinand is as unrestrained as Caliban's was for her. Neither can detect evil, she seeing only goodly creatures in the lords of Italy, he a god in a drunken butler. And as learning has taught him only how to curse, we sense that she too will in time discard her untested faith in humankind. Knowledge and experience will in the end strip her, as they have him, of innocence. I suppose the closest parallel in our lives to a condition of innocence is what we assume to be the state of mind of a young child seeing everything for the first time, which may help explain why we dote so over toddlers. Perhaps the sight of Miranda's wonder and the thought of Caliban's naiveté awakens our nostalgia for an imagined time when in childlike simplicity we too saw the world unsullied.

Happily there are at least a few "goodly creatures" among those assembled before the cave. A penitent Alonso sees Miranda as "a goddess," and old Gonzalo calls down the blessing of heaven upon the couple, exclaiming that the gods have miraculously wrought good out of evil: "Was Milan thrust from Milan, that his issue / Should become kings of Naples?" As we know, however, it is Prospero, who has worked this miracle—he is the "god" here.

Ariel leads the members of the ship's crew to the cave, where they reveal that all are safe and the vessel ready to sail, which leaves but one loose thread of the plot to tie up: the fate of the trio of pathetic conspirators. Ariel leads them in as well, and Caliban is the subject of some comment; to one he is "a plain fish," to another "as strange a thing as e're I looked on." Prospero, acknowledging "this thing of darkness" as his own, orders Caliban to trim the cave and to do it well if he is to be pardoned, an order he submits to with unaccustomed civility. He will "be wise hereafter," he says, and "seek for grace." He knows now the folly of bowing to every new god that comes along and admits that he was an ass for worshipping a drunkard and a dull fool.

Some have found in Caliban's new willingness to serve, his admission of error, and his desire to "seek for grace" a sign of his redemption, the side of him that is human assuming dominance over the bestial. If so, it is ironic that when everyone finally departs for Italy, leaving the island once more to him, his humanity will avail him little. Again he was better off ignorant. But it is perhaps best to go no further here than to observe that the apparent change in Caliban is in concert with the general tone of reconciliation that marks the end of the play. Prospero invites the company to his cave for the night, proposing that they set sail for Naples the next day. There they will attend the wedding of Ferdinand and Miranda, after which, he says, he will retire to Milan, "where / Every third thought shall be my grave." He directs Ariel to provide "calm seas, auspicious gales" for the voyage, and then sets the spirit free with a regretful "fare thou well."

Epi. The epilogue to *The Tempest* is unusual. In several of Shakespeare's comedies a figure appears at the close to offer a witty finale, asking the audience to deal gently with the play and applaud those who have labored to entertain them.* In *The Tempest*, however, Prospero comes forth

---

*As in *A Midsummer Night's Dream, As You Like It, Twelfth Night,* and *All's Well That Ends Well.*

with a different appeal entirely—he asks the audience for permission to leave "this bare island" and return to Italy: "As you from crimes would pardoned be, / Let your indulgence set me free." It is attractive to think of Prospero, speaking for Shakespeare himself, who, weary from his labors, is asking his audience to set him free from the toil of the theater so that he may retire honorably to Stratford-on-Avon and live out his years there.

But there is another reading of this curious appeal, one that grows out of the fabric of the play itself and may help explain the spell it weaves. Indeed, the play almost requires Prospero to seek our permission to leave the island—because in truth we don't want him to go. In bringing before us the aged magician, now stripped of his powers, Shakespeare makes us aware of what he has done for us. By the miracle of his art we have been blessed to dwell for a time in this imagined Eden, and when a weary Prospero appears to ask our consent to his departure, we suddenly realize that should he leave, so too must we and return to our fallen world. So we would have him stay! We have sat through these hours like so many Ferdinands enchanted by the masque, and say with him, "let me live here ever" in this "Paradise" of our imagination.

Were we allowed words to respond to Prospero's appeal, we might plead with him thus: *Stay, you "god o'th'island," dismiss not Ariel, retain your staff and book, abjure not that rough magic and its power over evil, magic that prevents harm and works the flowering of innocence. Miranda will be forever pure in your bright Paradise, and always love her Ferdinand. Why must you retire to Milan with only thoughts of the grave? Your rejected charms cannot order things there, where the vicious lords of Italy hold sway over the affairs of men. Sebastian and Antonio will plot again, Milan and Naples conspire, and Caliban will surface in the race, unchecked by your so potent art. There the happy couple will be infected by the worm, the bloom of their love will fade, and on that harsh chessboard of life a tainted Ferdinand may well play his Miranda false. Stay, Prospero! Then we shall know that there is at least one sweet place of wonder and order and innocence in this corrupted world, one quiet corner of our minds to which we can turn when our mortality overwhelms us.*

But the aging figure who appears before us is no longer our benevolent, all-seeing god of the island. He comes as a man asking simply to return to the society of men. We are stunned into the sudden awareness that there never was such a god, nor was Miranda a goddess, as Gonzalo thought, nor was Ferdinand the "thing divine" Miranda saw. This island, this play, was but a trick of fancy, an insubstantial pageant now faded. It has vanished from our eyes as did Prospero's masque when the thought of Caliban intruded. It melted into air, into thin air when the curtain fell and returned us to our all-too-substantial world. We have lived in the Garden for a time, but Naples is that world. And though the great globe itself may be a dream, it is out there on that stage of life that we must dream our dream, not here in this land of fancies. It is sad to return to a place where evil thrives and a distant and unfathomable god works no magic to restrain it. It is sad to leave Eden. But return we must.

And so in the end we submit: *Go then, Prospero. Leave your enchanted isle to Caliban, who may in time forget the words you taught him, and who as he sinks back into his natural self and all that troublesome learning slowly dims in his thick mind, may finally forget how to curse. Ariel is kind here, his songs are sweet, they "give delight and hurt not"—and Caliban may dream.*

But not Miranda. No more of dreaming for "Admired Miranda."

No matter. Go, Prospero, back to your Milan.

We follow.

THE MERRY WIVES OF WINDSOR

🌿

LEGEND HAS IT that Queen Elizabeth was so captivated by the *Henry IV* plays that she asked for one about Falstaff in love. A monarch's request had the force of a command, so, it is said, Shakespeare composed *The Merry Wives of Windsor* in a white heat. The result, however, does not really show Falstaff in love. He seems to be moved more by his customary instincts, fun and gain, than any romantic passion. It must be said that he lacks some of his old zest, that satirically irreverent edge of the *Henry IV* plays—but he is a Falstaff nonetheless, though in this play all the jokes are on him.

The Merry Wives of Windsor is a feast of fractured English. Prominent are a hot-tempered Frenchman, Doctor Caius, whose woeful diction and imperfect grasp of meanings render him farcically comic, and a Welsh parson, Sir Hugh Evans, who affects a learned vocabulary distorted by a heavy accent. The dim-witted Slender is given to *malaprops*—"if there be no great love in the beginning, yet heaven may decrease it upon greater acquaintance"—and Mistress Quickly to questionable pronunciation, "alligant" for elegant and "fartuous" for virtuous. Aside from these, there are figures with marked linguistic idiosyncrasies: Corporal Nym, who cannot speak a sentence without the word "humor" in it, and the blustering Pistol with his pompous allusions to ancient history and mythology. We also find mention of places and events topical in Shakespeare's time—the bear "Sarkenson" and London's "Pickt-hatch." His audiences were presumably familiar with the terms, but a modern reader needs a generous set of footnotes to fully savor the wit of them. The play, then, rewards a bit of study and grows in delight after an additional attendance or two. We shall not attempt to explain this constant stream of linguistic jokes in the dialogue. More to the purpose, a survey of the comic characters and situations will prepare readers to better appreciate the verbal gymnastics of the play.

The plot involves schemes by Mistress Page and Mistress Ford to humiliate Falstaff, avenging his effrontery in pressing his amorous attentions upon them. There are subplots, one a competition of a trio of suitors for the hand of the lovely young Anne Page, and yet another design to humiliate, this time the host of the Garter Inn. They are artfully woven into the main action, however, and do not distract from the spectacle of "Falstaff in love."

1.1–2   The long first scene opens on three minor characters: Justice Shallow,* who has a grievance against Falstaff; Abraham Slender, his young cousin; and Sir Hugh Evans, a Welsh parson, who proposes that the young man marry Anne Page. Slender is a spindly youth, as his name implies, sporting evidence of an ineffectual effort to grow hair on his face. He immediately establishes his characteristic ability to muddle a thought, observing that his cousin Shallow's "successors [have] gone before him" and "his ancestors [have] come after." And the well-meaning Parson Evans demonstrates his tendency to garble the language—he will use his "benevolence to make atonements and compremises between" Shallow and Falstaff.

They stand before the house of George Page, a local merchant, who appears in response to Evans's knocking. Page and the parson attempt to make peace between Shallow and Falstaff, as well as between Slender and the fat knight, whose followers have relieved the young man of his purse. Falstaff comes upon them, accompanied by his disreputable entourage of Bardolph, Nym, and Pistol, and readily admits to his offenses, but without the slightest sign of regret. Slender then accuses Pistol of robbing him and in reply receives a challenge to a duel. Bardolph denies the crime, claiming that Slender was too drunk to know what was going on anyway.

---

*Shallow appears in *Henry IV, Part 2,* as do many of the other comic figures in this play—Mistress Quickly, Nym, Pistol, and Bardolph.

Mistress Page and her daughter Anne come forth and invite them all in to dinner, but before entering, Evans and Shallow urge Slender to make his intentions known to Anne. When she returns to repeat the invitation, they go in, leaving her alone with him. Slender is completely unnerved. He stammers that he is not hungry and then covers his embarrassment by babbling incoherently about his household staff and injuries in a dueling lesson, about barking dogs and bear-baiting. Anne patiently endures his ramblings and simply repeats that he is called to dinner. Page himself comes out and persuades him finally to join them.

While the others are eating, Evans directs Slender's servant, Simple, to deliver a letter to Mistress Quickly asking her, as a friend to Anne Page, to support the young man's suit. Mistress Quickly serves as a housekeeper to the French physician Doctor Caius (pronounced *Keys*).

1.3 Meanwhile, at the Garter Inn, Falstaff confides in the host that he is running short of funds and must dismiss his followers. The first to go is Bardolph, whom the host hires on as a tapster, or in modern terms a bartender. To repair his fortunes Falstaff intends to "make love" to Mistress Page and a Mistress Ford, wives of two wealthy Windsor merchants. Both ladies, he has learned, have control of their husbands' money, and, he boasts, "I will be cheaters to them both, and they shall be exchequer [treasurer] to me." He has composed letters to each of them, but when he orders Pistol and Nym to deliver them, the two men refuse to have any part in his disgraceful scheme. Falstaff promptly dismisses them from his service, and they conspire to avenge themselves by informing the husbands of his intentions.

1.4 At the house of Doctor Caius, Mistress Quickly tells John Rugby, his servant, to keep a lookout for him while she talks with Slender's servant, Simple, who has come with the letter from Parson Evans. When the Doctor approaches, Quickly hides Simple in a closet, fearful that he will come to harm if he is found with her. Caius is a hotheaded, ridiculously pompous master who orders his servants about with exaggerated gestures while abusing, as Quickly remarks, "God's patience and the King's English." He enters and, discovering Simple, calls for his rapier. Quickly attempts to defend the frightened youth as "an honest man," and Caius asks, quite reasonably, "what shall de honest man do in my closet?" Simple hastily explains that he has been sent to ask Quickly to put in a good word for his master "in the way of marriage" to Anne Page. As it happens, Caius has designs on the young woman himself. Concluding erroneously from the garbled explanation that his rival is Evans, not Slender, he challenges the parson to a duel over the matter. The host of the Garter, he says, will be his second.

When the men leave, Fenton enters. He is a presentable young man who gives Mistress Quickly money to intercede for him with Anne, whom he loves. Quickly assures him that the young woman loves him, though after he is gone she remarks that she "loves him not." The delightful Mistress Quickly chatters on about this and that, but beneath her scatterbrained exterior she conceals a streak of guile. Claiming that she is a close confidante of Anne Page, she manages to extract money from all three suitors, including her employer, Doctor Caius, and as the persuasive messenger from the wives to Falstaff, she receives a purse from him as well. It is a rich part for a comic actress.

2.1   The second act brings us to the main plot. Mrs. Page and Mrs. Ford have received identical letters from Falstaff, couched in flowery language with an insert of atrocious verse. They conspire to take revenge on him by leading him to believe that they welcome his advances. Their scheme will have to be kept from their husbands, however, for though Page is a good-natured man who has full confidence in his wife, Ford is subject to jealous fits.

As the women retire the husbands enter, accompanied by Pistol and Nym, who inform them of Falstaff's designs. They determine to be avenged on the fat knight as well, but will keep their knowledge secret from their wives. The women reenter briefly and go off with Mistress Quickly, who has come to see Anne, and they decide to employ her to carry their messages to Falstaff. The men continue to conspire until interrupted by the host of the Garter and Justice Shallow. The host is an outgoing, perpetually merry man—he calls everyone a "bully-rook [fine fellow]"—and he has devised a trick to play on Doctor Caius and Parson Evans, who are preparing for their duel. To prevent bloodshed he has told each of them to meet at a different place, and he expects their confusion to be the occasion for some amusement. Ford calls him aside and asks his aid in gaining access to Falstaff. He will introduce himself to the knight, he says, in the guise of a man named Brook.

2.2   Back at the Garter Inn, Falstaff has harsh words for Pistol, who has asked for money. Mistress Quickly enters with a message, and as she prattles on an impatient Falstaff has trouble persuading her to deliver it. Finally she swears that both wives are highly virtuous women (or "fartuous," as she puts it) but that his letters have put them into a state of high excitement—though, she assures him, neither has told the other. Mrs. Ford, she reveals, will be at home to receive him between ten and eleven, when her husband will be away. Mrs. Page replies that her husband "is seldom from home," but she asks Falstaff to send his page, Robin, to act as go-between. Falstaff sends them off, followed by Pistol, who has overheard the exchange and determines to make use of the knowledge.

Ford enters, disguised as Brook, and asks Falstaff for his help, enticing him with money and promising more. He has long been in love with Mrs. Ford, he confesses, but the virtuous woman has resisted all his advances and refused his presents. If, he explains, Falstaff can bed her, thus compromising her virtue, "Brook" will have an easier time with her. Falstaff readily agrees to the scheme, revealing that he has an assignation with her between ten and eleven that very day and that he intends to milk Ford of his wealth through her. The knight leaves, and Ford resolves fiercely to be revenged on both Falstaff and his wife for their plot to brand him a cuckold.

2.3 Doctor Caius, prepared for the duel, impatiently awaits Parson Evans in a field near Windsor. The host of the Garter approaches with others who have come, he says, to witness the fight. Caius rages that his cowardly opponent has not appeared, and they amuse themselves a bit at his expense, calling him names he does not understand, "Castilion-King-Urinal" and "Mounseur Mock-water [urine]." Accepting their translation, he takes them as compliments. The host, in an *aside*, urges his companions to make for nearby Frogmore, where they will find Parson Evans. As they leave, the host persuades Caius to accompany him to Frogmore, where, he says, the Frenchman will have an opportunity to woo Anne Page. Love prevails over war. Promptly forgetting his grievance, Caius readily agrees, gratefully promising to send the host noble guests from among his patients.

3.1 In a field near Frogmore we find Parson Evans and Slender's servant, Simple, who are waiting for Doctor Caius to appear. Evans sends Simple off in search of the Frenchman and tries to calm himself by singing a song, which turns out to be from Christopher Marlowe's poem, "Come live with me and be my love," a sentiment not entirely appropriate to the occasion. Simple returns with Page, Shallow, and Slender, followed shortly by the host and Caius. The parson and the doctor square off to fight but are disarmed before they can do each other damage. The host explains his little trick, urging them to be friends. After the others leave, Caius and Evans forget their enmity and join forces to be revenged on the host for their indignities. All this time Slender is oblivious to what is going on, muttering to himself inanely, "O sweet Anne Page."

3.2 Ford meets Mrs. Page and, seeing Falstaff's page, Robin, with her, concludes that he has been placed to act as a messenger between the women and the knight. All of those who have been involved in the aborted duel enter and discuss the various suitors for the hand of Anne Page. Her father favors Slender, but the mother prefers Doctor Caius. When the host mentions Fenton, Page dismisses him as a profligate ne'er-do-well who is known to have caroused with the irresponsible Prince Hal and Poins in London (another reference to the *Henry IV* plays). Ford invites them home with him, where, he promises, "I will show you a monster."

3.3 The wives, awaiting Falstaff at Ford's home, place a large clothes basket in readiness and hear from Robin, who is now a partner in the scheme, that the knight is at the back door. Mrs. Page hides and Falstaff enters, greeting Mrs. Ford seductively with a flood of flowery speeches. Playing along, she flirts with him openly—"O sweet Sir John"—and accuses him of really loving Mrs. Page. He dismisses her supposed rival scornfully as Robin rushes in to announce that she is at the door. Falstaff hides—though there is too much of him to hide well—as the wives engage in their charade. Mrs. Page chides her friend for her infidelity and urges her to be rid of any man who is with her, since Ford is approaching "with all the officers in Windsor." Falstaff pops out of hiding and pleads with them for help. They urge him to hide in the clothes basket, cover him with dirty garments, call in two burly servants, and order them to carry it out. Ford meets them at the door and, after an anxious moment, orders them to be about their business.

Ford storms in and directs his companions to search the house. While they are gone, Mrs. Ford reveals that she has instructed her servants to dump Falstaff into the Thames—and the two women decide to play further tricks on the fat knight. The searchers return, empty-handed of course, and Ford, properly contrite, asks his wife's pardon and concludes with an invitation to all for dinner. As they leave, Parson Evans reminds Caius of their intent to humiliate the host.

3.4   At the Page residence, Fenton declares his love to Anne. Because of his reputation for profligacy and riotous behavior, however, her father is convinced that he wants her only for his wealth. Fenton admits that such was his intent at first, but on meeting Anne he has fallen genuinely in love. They are interrupted by Justice Shallow, who urges Slender to press his suit. They address Anne as Mistress Quickly draws Fenton aside, but Shallow does all the talking until an exasperated Anne demands that he let Slender "woo for himself." The dim youth admits that he cares little one way or the other about marriage and refers her to her father, who approaches.

Page, who intends Slender for his daughter, rejects Fenton; and when the men leave, the young man pleads his love to Mrs. Page, who rejects him as well, preferring Doctor Caius. Anne has nothing but scorn for them both. The one is a "fool" and as for the other, "I had rather be set quick [alive] i'th'earth /And bowl'd [stoned] to death with turnips." The women leave and Fenton gives Mistress Quickly a ring for Anne, with money for her trouble. She has accepted payment for her services from each of them, and so in conscience acknowledges that she must "do what I can for them all three," but she "speciously [especially]" favors Fenton. She hurries off on another errand, however, bearing a message from the wives to Falstaff.

3.5   A wet and disgruntled Falstaff has made his way back to the Garter Inn, where he calls for "a quart of sack [sherry]." He complains about being thrown in the Thames and resolves never again to be part of such a scheme. Bardolph enters to announce Mistress Quickly, who reports that Mrs. Ford sincerely regrets the indignity he has suffered and asks him to return tomorrow between eight and nine, when her husband will be out birding. Despite his earlier resolve, Falstaff cannot resist the invitation, which he takes as a tribute to his charms; and he wonders where Brook could be, for as he confesses, "I like his money well."

Ford enters, again in the disguise of Brook, and Falstaff gives him a vivid account of his misadventure—how to escape Ford he hid in a clothes basket and was covered with "foul shirts and smocks, socks, foul stockings, [and] greasy napkins," and was then tossed unceremoniously into the Thames—suffering all, he insists, in devoted service to Brook. He will try again, however, between eight and nine the next morning, and expresses confidence that "Master Brook, you shall cuckold Ford." Ford is chagrined that he has been duped so easily and vows not to be fooled again.

4.1   Mistress Quickly finds Mrs. Page in a Windsor street and delivers an urgent appeal from Mrs. Ford to come at once. Before responding, however, the lady encounters Parson Evans and submits her son to a lengthy examination of his schooling, said to be Shakespeare's parody of his grammar school education with its deadening reliance on rote learning.

4.2   Falstaff comes again to Mrs. Ford but must conceal himself once more when Mrs. Page approaches. Again Ford is on his way, and means must be found for Falstaff's escape. He refuses another escapade in the clothes basket, so the wives suggest an alternative: they will dress him as a woman! The only garment they have large enough to fit him, however, is one left there by a "fat woman of Brainford." Fearful of Ford's wrath, Falstaff reluctantly agrees to the indignity and hurries off to don the disguise as Mrs. Ford confides gleefully to her friend that her husband abhors the Brainford woman, believing her to be a witch, and will react violently to the sight of her. They decide to repeat the charade of the clothes basket to see how Ford will react to it this time. Mrs. Ford is determined to demonstrate that "wives may be merry, and yet honest too."

Ford enters, accompanied by the others, and on meeting the servants with the basket at the door commands them to put it down. He makes a fool of himself by throwing soiled clothes frantically about the room. Frustrated by his failure, he orders another search of the house. At this point Falstaff descends the stairs in his ludicrous disguise. Ford is so aroused by the sight of the Brainford witch that he forgets his purpose there, grabs a stick, and beats him out of the house. As the men leave to search the house once again, the wives revel in their success and determine to continue their campaign to shame Falstaff.

4.3   In a brief, entirely unrelated episode, Bardolph informs the host of the Garter that the three "Germans" who are lodged with him are in need of horses to join their duke at court. They have, it seems, engaged the entire inn for a week, apparently in anticipation of a larger party, and to accommodate them the host has turned away all other guests (except for Falstaff, of course). He eagerly agrees to their request.

4.4　At Ford's house the ladies have entertained everyone with an account of their humiliation of Falstaff, and Ford again apologizes to his wife for mistrusting her. Now all of them conspire together to further disgrace the fat knight. They plot to entice him to a meeting by a certain oak tree in Windsor forest, where legend has it that the spirit of one "Herne the Hunter" appears with a cap of "great ragg'd horns" on his head and performs miraculous deeds of destruction. There Anne Page and the children of the town, dressed as wood nymphs and fairies, will attack him, presumably to protect the forest, and scare him off.

The Pages plan to make use of the occasion to further their plans for their daughter. Learning from his wife that Anne will be dressed in white, the father will have Slender take her off during the commotion to be married to him. The mother, however, reveals that Anne will actually wear a dress of green, and she will alert Doctor Caius to carry her off. Plots within plots!

4.5　Simple arrives at the Garter Inn to see Falstaff, who he understands is in the company of "the wise woman of Brainford." His master, Slender, has confidence in this woman's ability to foresee the future and has sent Simple to ask her if he will marry Anne Page, or as he puts it, whether he will "have her or no." Falstaff says he has just seen the woman off and tells Simple that she has confided in him that, yes indeed, Slender will "have her, or no." Simple returns happily to his master with the good news.

A disheveled Bardolph rushes in to inform the host that the "three German devils" have treated him roughly and taken off with his horses. A gleeful Parson Evans relates that these same three have performed a similar trick on other innkeepers in the area, and Doctor Caius enters to announce that there is no such person as "a duke de Jarmany" at court. It is unclear whether Evans and Caius have concocted this scheme to avenge themselves on the host or simply take advantage of his misfortune. Whichever the case, they delight in his distress.

Mistress Quickly now arrives to deliver the wives' invitation to Falstaff to meet in Windsor Forest.

4.6　Fenton, who has learned of the plans for that night, appeals to the host for help in thwarting the Pages' designs for their daughter. Anne loves him, he insists, and she has arranged to avoid both Slender and Caius so as to slip off and marry the young man. Fenton asks the host to provide a priest for the occasion and pays him a handsome sum for his aid.

5.1–4   In a series of short scenes, the stage is set for the final humiliation. Falstaff agrees to meet the wives and, in keeping with the legend, to wear a pair of horns.* Ford enters as Brook, and Falstaff gives him a vivid account of his disguise as the witch of Brainford and his subsequent beating, for which he is resolved to be avenged. Page informs Slender of his plan—he is to go off with the fairy in the white dress. Mrs. Page tells Caius to take the one in green by the hand. In Windsor forest Evans hides the children in a ditch near the oak tree.

Falstaff appears by the oak at the appointed hour, topped ridiculously with a cap of horns. The wives greet him seductively but are frightened off by a sudden noise. The fairies enter and perform an eerie dance about the tree, as Falstaff hides in fear. They discover him and, forming a circle around the terrified man, abuse him mercilessly at Mistress Quickly's urging: "Pinch him, and burn him, and turn him about."

The adults emerge from hiding and call for an end to the abuse. Falstaff is compelled to submit to some good-natured taunting, and he is properly chastened: "Well, I am your theme. . . . Use me as you will." He remains an enormously appealing figure, however, with his quick wit and endless store of jests, and Page invites him to drink with them at his home, where he can "laugh at my wife that now laughs as you."

Slender and Caius enter, complaining indignantly that they stole off as planned with two of the fairies, one in white, the other in green, whom they thought to be Anne Page, only to find that they were "great lubbering" boys in dresses. Fenton comes in with Anne to announce their marriage, which the Pages accept with goodwill: "Well, what remedy? Fenton, heaven give thee joy! / What cannot be eschew'd must be em-

---

*The frequent references to "horns" in the play are allusions to the old tale that they grew out of the forehead of a cuckolded husband, where they are on view to everyone but him. Falstaff is not the cuckold here, of course, but he is the only one unaware of the scheme to shame him.

brac'd." Mrs. Page repeats her husband's invitation to retire to their home, where, she predicts, they will "laugh this sport o'er by a country fire— / Sir John and all." He will be a welcome addition to the party— or, for that matter, to any party.

We may assume that Queen Elizabeth was pleased with the play.

Some critics are distressed at a much-diminished Falstaff, complaining that the boundlessly energetic knight of the *Henry IV* plays is reduced here to a figure of farce. Nonetheless *The Merry Wives* has remained a popular favorite for four hundred years and is regularly produced in numerous Shakespeare festivals in our own time. Indeed, it has been the comedy, not the history play, that has attracted the imagination of operatic composers in more recent times, including Otto Nicolai (1849), Giuseppe Verdi (1893), and Ralph Vaughan Williams (1929). We are grateful to the queen for ordering a "Falstaff in love."

THE COMEDY OF ERRORS

🌿

THIS IS THOUGHT to be Shakespeare's earliest comedy, and as such it is often dismissed as a product of his immature pen, but if its many performances at festivals are any guide, it has nonetheless proven popular with theater audiences over the years.* It is, to be sure, a farce, which makes for good fun but not much substance, and the improbable plot may test severely our willing *suspension of disbelief.*

Briefly, identical twin brothers, sons of a wealthy Syracuse merchant, Egeon, are separated soon after birth in a storm at sea. Divided in the same storm is another set of identical twins, sons of a poor woman, whom the generous Egeon had adopted, thinking to raise them as servants to his own. One of the merchant's and one of the poor woman's sons are preserved by the father and the other pair by the mother. The two parts of the family are rescued within sight of one another by separate ships, which sail off in different directions. Egeon raises his pair of boys in Syracuse while, unknown to him, the others grow up in Ephesus. On coming of age, his son becomes curious about his lost brother and, accompanied by his servant, sets out in search of him. The father too travels widely on the same quest, finally arriving in Ephesus where, again unknown to him, his son and servant have landed as well.

To complicate matters further, each set of twins has the same name. To avoid confusion, the early reading texts of the play identified the merchant's sons as "E[phesus] Antipholus" and "S[yracuse] Antipholus" and the servants as "E[phesus] Dromio" and "S[yracuse] Dromio." Some other

---

*The play was popularized in the highly successful Rodgers and Hart musical *The Boys from Syracuse* (1938).

means of distinguishing among them will have to be devised for a viewing audience, however, since the play requires that each of the twins appear on stage in the same costume. Indeed, in some productions the pairs have been played by just two actors until the final scene, though it's a busy night's work for them. Once we accept this improbable series of coincidences, we can settle in for an evening of delightful entertainment. The stage is set for a sequence of mistaken identities as the twins dash on and off, each Antipholus encountering his brother's Dromio, to the bewilderment of all four, and others in the cast taking one for the other in a tangled web of comic misunderstandings.

1.1 The Syracuse merchant Egeon arrives in Ephesus in search of his lost son, only to be promptly arrested and brought before Duke Solinus, who informs him that if he cannot raise a thousand marks, he will be condemned to die. The two cities are mutually hostile, each declaring that if a citizen of one is found in the other, he must pay a ransom or be executed. The duke asks Egeon why he is so foolhardy as to enter Ephesus, and the merchant offers an account of his trials: the birth of his twin sons, his adoption of the poor woman's twin boys, the shipwreck in which one of each is rescued with him and one of each with his wife, and his long search for his lost son. The duke is sympathetic but regretfully must uphold the law. In a generous gesture he frees Egeus for the rest of the day to allow him raise the required ransom.

1.2 Having provided the necessary background for the play, Egeon leaves the stage, not to reappear until the final scene. The tangled tale of the twins now gets under way as S. Antipholus arrives in Ephesus, accompanied by his servant, S. Dromio. The two Dromios, we discover, are not obsequious servants. Rather, like many such figures in Shakespeare, they are sharp-tongued clowns who engage their masters in lengthy exchanges of wit and are often beaten for their insolence.

The comic action of the play is set in motion by a tension between E. Antipholus and his wife, into which the men from Syracuse are drawn because of their resemblance to those in Ephesus. The misunderstandings arise over the possession and exchange of several objects—money, a gold chain, a piece of rope, and a ring—and the money is immediately in evidence. S. Antipholus entrusts his funds to S. Dromio and decides to take in the scene, only to be approached by E. Dromio, who has been sent by his mistress to fetch his master home to dinner. When asked about the money, E. Dromio pleads ignorance, receives a beating for his supposed insolence, and takes to his heels. S. Antipholus suspects his servant of cheating him and follows E. Dromio out.

2.1   The scene shifts to the home of E. Antipholus, where his wife, Adriana, complains to her sister Luciana that her husband is neglectful. They exchange views on the role of women in a male-dominated world until interrupted by E. Dromio. The servant relates his encounter with the man he assumes is Adriana's husband, who, he reports, has refused her call to dinner. She sends him back to try again, threatening to beat him if he disobeys. E. Dromio, caught in the middle of these misunderstandings, leaves reluctantly, after complaining to her that "you spurn me hence, and he will spurn me hither. / If I last in this service, you must case me in leather." Adriana continues to lament her husband's inattention. He "feeds from home," she complains to her sister, and while she awaits him patiently day after day, her beauty fading in his absence, she suspects him of betraying their marriage bed. He has, however, promised her a gift of a gold chain, perhaps as a token peace offering.

2.2   S. Antipholus discovers that his money is safe and encounters his servant, whom he upbraids for his "merry humor" in denying he had it. The bewildered S. Dromio insists that he has not seen his master since they parted and receives a beating for "flouting" him, not once but now twice. The troubles have begun as S. Dromio responds philosophically: "Was ever any man thus beaten out of season, / When in the why and the wherefore is neither rhyme nor reason?" He then thanks his master ironically, initiating a witty though entirely irrelevant exchange between the two involving a play on the word "bald." Adriana and Luciana come upon them, and the wife launches into a lengthy rebuke of her supposed husband's wayward behavior, concluding, "I live disdain'd, thou dishonored." Neither man has any idea what she is talking about, of course, but after several protests, which the women dismiss as so much "counterfeit," S. Antipholus agrees to accompany them home to dinner. S. Dromio is set on guard at the door with instructions to allow no one to enter.

3.1   We finally meet E. Antipholus, here in the company of the merchant Balthazar, whose shop is making a gold chain for his wife. He confirms that "my wife is shrewish when I keep not hours" and laughs at the claim of E. Dromio that he had beat the servant in the marketplace. After some banter on the subject, he tries to enter his house, only to find the door locked. There follows a long, heated exchange, conducted through the closed door, during which the Ephesus pair attempt to persuade S. Dromio and others inside to allow him entrance. His wife, who is even then dining with the man she believes to be her husband, dismisses E. Antipholus as an impostor, and the two Dromios exchange barbs. E. Antipholus is determined to break the door down, but Balthazar prevails upon him to be patient and return later "to know the reason of this strange restraint." They retire to a local tavern where the angry husband, out of spite, is determined to give the chain he intended for his wife to the "hostess" there (later identified as the Courtezan).

3.2   In the house, Luciana chides S. Antipholus for neglect of his wife. He protests—"Your weeping sister is no wife of mine, / Nor to her bed no homage do I owe"—eliciting a sharp response from the uncomprehending Luciana: "What, are you mad, that you do reason so?" He seems to have taken a fancy to her, however, and shocks her by proposing marriage: "Thee will I love and with thee lead my life." Taken aback, she leaves to find her sister.

S. Dromio enters in haste, to escape, he explains, a "kitchen wench" who claims he is betrothed to her. The two exchange witty remarks about the woman, who is apparently of considerable girth, comparing her various body parts to different nations. S. Antipholus, despite his proposal to Luciana, decides not to spend another day in Ephesus, convinced that "there's none but witches do inhabit here," and he sends his servant off to secure passage on a ship. Angelo the goldsmith approaches him to deliver the chain and receive payment for the work. S. Antipholus, of course, knows nothing of a chain, but he accepts it anyway and puts Angelo off with instructions to come back later for his money. The encounter only reinforces his conviction that he should leave Ephesus without delay.

4.1   Angelo is apparently in debt to a merchant who threatens to have him arrested for nonpayment. He pleads that he will discharge the debt as soon as he is paid for the chain, and he is relieved to see E. Antipholus approaching. Still angry with his wife, he decides to give her a "rope's end" instead of a chain and sends E. Dromio off to secure it. Confusion follows as Angelo asks payment for the chain and E. Antipholus tells him to deliver it to his home, where, he says, his wife will give him the agreed sum. Angelo insists that he has only moments before given him the chain, and when E. Antipholus denies having received it, the goldsmith has him arrested.

S. Dromio comes upon them and, thinking E. Antipholus his master, blithely announces that he has secured passage on a ship, only to receive the angry reply that he was sent for a piece of rope, not a ship. E. Antipholus then gives S. Dromio the key to his desk at home, instructing him to secure money for his bail. The puzzled servant doesn't know what to make of his master's curious behavior, but he knows the house, having dined there, and he leaves dutifully to carry out the order.

4.2 On learning that the man she believes to be her husband has made amorous advances to her sister, Adriana is upset with Luciana. S. Dromio enters, asking for the money to provide bail for the man he thinks is his master. Adriana gives the money to the man she thinks is her servant, and he hurries off.

4.3 Meanwhile, S. Antipholus is puzzled that everyone he meets in town seems to know and respect him. S. Dromio enters and offers him the money intended for the release of E. Antipholus, but before they can untangle the conflicting identities they are interrupted by the Courtezan. It was she who had dined with E. Antipholus after he had been denied entry to his home, and on that occasion he promised to give her the chain, asking for a diamond ring she was wearing in return. She approaches the men from Syracuse and asks for either the ring or the promised chain—and they dash off, reinforced in their conviction that the town is filled with witches. It is never quite clear what E. Antipholus intended to do with the ring, but the Courtezan decides to tell his wife that he had forced it from her. And now S. Antipholus has both the money and the chain.

4.4 E. Antipholus assures the arresting officer that he will have the money for his release as E. Dromio comes upon them, carrying a piece of rope. The master demands the money, but the servant insists that he was sent for rope, not ducats, for which he receives another beating. The women enter, accompanied by the ridiculous Dr. Pinch, described as "a conjuring schoolmaster." He immediately sets about to exorcise the demon they are convinced has possessed E. Antipholus, who insists that

he did not dine at home that day, having been locked out by his wife—
claims that E. Dromio confirms. Adriana in turn insists that she gave E.
Dromio money for her husband, but he continues to protest that he "was
sent for nothing but a rope." Thoroughly convinced now that both men
are daft, she calls in attendants who bind the pair and escort them off to
her house. Shortly thereafter the Syracuse pair enter with drawn swords
and Adriana, thinking her husband and his servant have somehow escaped their captors, beats a hasty retreat with her companions. S. Antipholus observes with some satisfaction, "I see these witches are afraid of
swords," and he determines not to spend another night in Ephesus.

5.1 The final act is one long scene in which matters grow even more
complicated before the anticipated face-to-face encounter between the
two pairs. As it opens, Angelo and the merchant are standing outside a
priory discussing the enviable reputation of E. Antipholus, when the
Syracuse pair come upon them, with S. Antipholus openly wearing the
chain. Angelo demands his money, and the merchant unfortunately
makes an insulting remark, causing all to draw swords. Bloodshed is prevented by the women, who return with reinforcements. The Syracuse
pair, outnumbered now, seek sanctuary in the priory.

The elderly abbess emerges, asking the cause of the disturbance.
Adriana replies that her husband is mad and must be bound. On learning
of his distemper, the abbess launches into a lengthy rebuke of the wife,
accusing her of nagging him to distraction. If, she counsels, "his sleep
were hind'red by thy railing" and "his meat was sauc'd by thy upbraid-
ings" and "his sports were hind'red by thy brawls," no wonder he has
gone mad: "Thy jealous fits / Hath scar'd they husband from the use of
wits." Adriana acknowledges the justice of the rebuke but nevertheless
asks the abbess to release her husband from sanctuary, promising that she
will take loving care of him. In Shakespeare's time it was a privilege of
the church that anyone could escape civic authorities by seeking refuge
on ecclesiastical property, and the poet is assuming that the same custom
prevailed in ancient Greece.

The abbess refuses, and the women decide to take their appeal to the
duke. As it happens, he appears at that moment, escorting Egeon to his
execution. Adriana makes her appeal and the duke calls for the abbess,
but they are interrupted by a messenger who reports that her husband

and servant have indeed escaped and are approaching with threats to do her harm. They burst upon the scene, E. Antipholus loudly demanding justice—and Egeon is stunned by the sight of them: "Unless the fear of death hath made me dote, / I see my son Antipholus and Dromio." He remains silent, however, as the duke attempts to sort out the various accusations. E. Antipholus gives a lengthy account of his own actions, after which claims and counterclaims fly back and forth about who had dinner where and who has the chain and ring, until the exasperated duke finally exclaims, "I think you are all mated [stupified] or stark mad."

Egeon finally speaks up, asking the Ephesus pair if they are not his son and servant. They reply that they have never seen him before. The desolate father pleads that, though his countenance may have changed, they must recognize his voice. Again they deny knowing him, E. Antipholus asserting that he has been living in Ephesus for the past twenty years, a claim the duke confirms.

At this point the abbess returns, accompanied by the Syracuse pair. All stand amazed, especially Adriana—"I see two husbands, or mine eyes deceive me"—and the abbess stuns them further with the revelation that she is Emilia, Egeon's long-lost wife. All the misunderstandings are resolved, S. Antipholus affirms his intentions toward Luciana, Egeon is freed, and the abbess invites the company into the priory for a celebratory feast. The spirit of recognition and reconciliation is captured in her joyous exclamation: "After so long grief, such nativity!" The brothers Antipholus do not seem to embrace in affectionate reunion, perhaps understandably after all that has happened, but the two Dromios immediately recognize a kinship of spirit and exit hand in hand.

The characters in this play, it must be admitted, are not especially memorable. E. Antipholus seems to have an emotional range of angry to very angry, and his brother is no less one-dimensional. S. Antipholus does fall in love with Luciana, but without much passion, and once he becomes convinced that "there's none but witches do inhabit" Ephesus, his chief concern is to get out of town—this, ironically, just as his many years of search have finally reached their goal. And the women are not very interesting; Adriana's constant whining and Luciana's advice about the proper role of a wife do not particularly endear them to us. The twin clowns are more appealing. They are disarmingly clever and, more than

anyone else, suffer the unjust consequences of the mistaken identities—
every time confusion arises they take a beating.

Yet once we have suspended our disbelief, it all comes together. There
are no distracting subplots, the whole action of the play takes place on a
single afternoon, and suspense mounts convincingly to the anticipated
disclosure at the end, tantalizingly delayed by episodes where characters
remain oblivious to the obvious. The confusion of identities makes for a
lot of fun, the more so perhaps because the play is untroubled by any design other than simply and solely to amuse.

THE TWO GENTLEMEN
OF VERONA

❧

THE "TWO GENTLEMEN" are *courtly lovers* who suffer from the traditional symptoms of the "love-sickness." They are careless of dress, melancholy of mood, and thoughtless of anything but their lady, desiring only to "serve" her. They relish solitude, eat little, sleep less, sigh a lot, sometimes weep, and melt at the sound of music. And one of them is fickle, abandoning one woman and attempting treacherously to steal another from his best friend. Shakespeare makes fun of the whole idea in a play further complicated by an imperious father who asserts his prerogative to force his daughter into an *arranged marriage*.

Act One   In Verona, Valentine informs Proteus that he has decided to broaden himself by joining the emperor's court in Milan, and he urges his friend to accompany him. But Proteus is tied to Verona by his love for Julia and cannot leave. He has written her a letter to be delivered by Valentine's servant, Speed, who apparently gave it to Julia's maid, Lucetta, to be passed on to the lady. When she discovers that her maid has been an unwanted go-between, Julia angrily tears up the letter and dismisses her, but then collects the scattered pieces so as to read it. Meanwhile, Proteus's father decides that his son has spent too much time idly at home and sends him off to Milan to join Valentine.

Act Two   In Milan, Valentine has fallen in love with Silvia, who cleverly lets him know that his affection is returned without actually saying it. Meanwhile in Verona, Proteus and Julia bid each other a sorrowful farewell, and she gives him a ring as a keepsake. His servant, Launce, has also taken leave of his family. They lamented his departure while, he complains, his dog Crab shed not a tear.

In Milan, Silvia is in the company of her two suitors, Valentine and the wealthy but foppish Thurio, who exchange insults to her amusement until Proteus enters, having just arrived from Verona. Valentine introduces him to Silvia and on her departure informs his friend that they have secretly arranged to be married in defiance of her father, who prefers Thurio. Left alone, Proteus finds that he too has suddenly fallen in love with Silvia, and he plots to prevent the marriage by disclosing their intentions to her father, the duke. Meanwhile, Julia decides to follow Proteus to Milan in the disguise of a young male page.

Act Three   Alerted by Proteus, the duke intercepts Valentine on his way to Silvia's chamber and banishes him from Milan. Proteus meets his friend and promises to help him by delivering his letters to Silvia. The chief comic characters of the play, the servants Launce and Speed, meet and Launce confesses that he has fallen in love with a milkmaid. In a parody of their masters' passion, they catalogue her qualities, ending with "she hath more hair than wit," "more faults than hair," but "more money than faults," the last of which recommends her highly. The trusting duke enlists the aid of Proteus in an effort to persuade his daughter to forget Valentine and accept Thurio.

Act Four   On their way into exile, Valentine and Speed are apprehended by a band of outlaws. They claim to be gentlemen banished for various crimes and, recognizing Valentine's qualities, invite him to be their captain. Proteus, having slandered Valentine, now plans to discredit Thurio as well. He advises Thurio to engage a band of musicians to serenade her, among whom is the disguised Julia, who overhears Proteus tell Silvia that both his Verona love and Valentine are dead. Silvia rejects him as a "subtle, perjur'd, disloyal man," and puts him off impatiently with a promise to give him her picture. She actually plans to escape and join Valentine, and persuades a Sir Eglamour to help her. Proteus unknowingly engages Julia to collect the picture and in exchange to present Silvia with the ring Julia had given him on his departure from Verona. When she does so, Silvia recognizes the ring as Julia's and inquires about her.

Act Five   Proteus encourages Thurio in his suit, but the duke enters to disclose that Silvia and Eglamour have gone in search of Valentine. Proteus pursues them, only to find that they have been captured by the outlaws, some of whom chase after the fleeing Eglamour. Accompanied by the still-disguised Julia, Proteus rescues Silvia and asks as a reward "one fair look," but she scornfully rejects him. Enraged, he attempts to rape her but is prevented by the sudden appearance of Valentine. Confronted by his friend, a penitent Proteus asks forgiveness, and Valentine, out of reverence for their old friendship, not only forgives his treacherous behavior but magnanimously surrenders Silvia to him! Julia faints, but quickly recovers and reveals her identity. Seeing her again, Proteus has a sudden change of heart, rejects Silvia, and renews his affection for his first love. The duke enters and, disposing of the cowardly Thurio, agrees to the marriage of Valentine and Silvia, and so they set out for Milan to celebrate a double wedding.

The ending of the play is much criticized. The plot complication arises from Proteus's infatuation with Silvia, and Valentine's sudden surrender of his claim to her love in the name of male friendship is difficult to excuse. She, it would appear, has no say in the matter and must submit to being bounced back and forth between the two men in what is generally regarded as a clumsy resolution.

LOVE'S LABOUR'S LOST

❧

THIS PLAY is a linguistic romp, an explosion of wit. A first-time modern viewer, however, may be hard pressed to keep up with the swift shuttle of its play on obscure words and allusions to the life and customs of sixteenth-century England. Shakespeare raids the English language with a squad of clever servants, bungling *malaprops*, and sophisticated courtiers competing in contests of wit, as well as an extravagant romantic and a pretentious scholar. *Love's Labour's Lost* is a swift and varied scherzo of a play, filled with long passages of one-line exchanges, often delivered at a dazzling pace. But this is not a concern—should one miss a turn of wit as it flies past, another will follow quickly upon it.

Act One   The youthful King of Navarre and three of his lords, Longaville, Dumaine, and Berowne, discuss his latest decree. Determined to make Navarre a center of learning, he has imposed three years of monastic discipline on his people and persuaded the lords to join him in a regimen of study, fasting, strict hours of sleep, and a suspension of the company of women. Two of the idealistic lords agree, but it is only with great reluctance that the more practical Berowne joins them. He reminds the king that a French princess is coming to settle a controversy between the two kingdoms, so the king must dispense with one provision of the pact almost immediately.

Constable Dull appears before them with young Costard under guard—both are given to malaprops. Costard was observed talking to a young woman, Jaquenetta, by a visiting Spanish lord, Armado, who ordered him arrested for violating the king's decree. The lords enjoy reading Armado's letter, with its tiresome digressions and overblown lan-

guage, and the king sentences Costard to a week's fasting under his ac-
cuser's supervision. As they leave, the flamboyant Armado enters, accompanied by his clever page Mote, who entertains his master with flashes of
wit. Armado confesses that he has fallen in love with Jaquenetta, and she
appears with Costard, both in the custody of Dull, who turns him over to
Armado and leads her off to serve her sentence as a milkmaid. The lord
ends the scene with a *soliloquy* on the contradictions of love and hurries
off to compose poems to Jaquenetta.

Act Two   The French princess arrives with her three attendants,
Rosaline, Maria, and Katharine, accompanied by an elderly lord, Boyet.
Having heard of the king's decree, she sends Boyet to announce their arrival and discusses the Navarre lords with her ladies, each of whom has
encountered one of them on an earlier occasion. Boyet returns with the
news that they may not enter the court but will be accommodated under
a tent in a nearby field. When the king approaches with his three young
lords, she greets them coldly as each singles out one of her ladies for conversation. He and the princess discuss the controversy between the two
kingdoms, to the satisfaction of neither. The lords, obviously captivated,
ask Boyet the names of the ladies, and he informs the princess that the
king is smitten with her as well.

Act Three   Armado enters with Mote, who continues to entertain
his Spanish master. The lord sends for Costard, whom he sets at liberty
and entrusts with a letter to Jaquenetta. As Armado leaves, Berowne engages Costard as well to deliver a letter of his to Rosaline. In a long soliloquy, Berowne confirms that he has fallen in love—and he can't believe
it: "What? I love? I sue? I seek a wife?" But he is forced to admit to it and
resigns himself to the *courtly lover's* fate, to "love, write, sigh, pray, sue,
and groan."

Act Four   Costard comes upon the French ladies and mixes up the
two letters, handing the princess the letter from Armado to Jacquenetta,
for delivery to Rosaline. After having a bit of fun over its preposterous
language, they retire, leaving the stage to a trio of comic figures—
Holofernes, a pretentious schoolmaster; Nathaniel, a curate; and Constable Dull. Holofernes thinks highly of his learning. He speaks in

elaborate, almost impenetrable prose sprinkled with Latin phrases, to the admiration of Nathaniel and the mystification of Dull. Jaquenetta approaches them with Costard, who has mistakenly given her Berowne's letter to Rosaline, and she asks them to read it for her. It is a sonnet filled with florid phrases, and Holofernes turns literary critic, dismissing it as having neither "poetry, wit, nor invention."

Drawing liberally on the convention of courtly love, each of the Navarre foursome composes a poem to his lady—the king to the princess, Berowne to Rosaline, Longaville to Maria, and Dumaine to Katharine. Berowne, in hiding, overhears the recitations of the others and emerges to rebuke them for violating their vows. His pretense of moral superiority is short-lived, however, as Jaquenetta come in with his letter to Rosaline, which unmasks his own straying. Since it appears that they have all broken their oaths, they ask Berowne to justify their apostasy, and he replies with an effusive praise of love, concluding, "it is religion to be thus forsworn." United now in their cause, they romp merrily off "to woo these girls of France."

Act Five   All six of the minor characters come together in a kind of comic ensemble, not unlike later operatic set pieces by Mozart and Rossini. Holofernes and Armado match one another in pomposity as Dull stands silently by, complaining in the end that he hasn't understood a word they're saying. The king has requested them to provide entertainment for the visiting ladies, and they decide to put on a parade of "The Nine Worthies," the most famous men of myth and history.

In the long final scene of the play the ladies emerge triumphant, as they invariably do in Shakespeare's comedies. They learn of the men's intention to woo them disguised as Russians and decide to conceal their own identities by receiving them masked. The lords have sent each of them favors to wear, and the ladies mischievously exchange them so that the men will single out the wrong one. They enter, bearded and outrageously costumed, and each devotes attention to the lady he thinks is his choice. After a lively exchange, the princess calls a halt to the foolery and the men depart. The women delight in their deception and, anticipating the men's return, decide to mock them further by describing what fools the Russians were. The men reenter as themselves and are thoroughly confused as the ladies subject them to more derisive wit, until

Berowne finally catches on to their trick. The comic characters arrive to put on their Nine Worthies entertainment, but the lords ridicule them so mercilessly that none of them is able to finish his prepared speech.

A messenger arrives with the news that the French king is dead. The princess, having persuaded the lovesick Navarre to resolve the controversy between them entirely in her favor, announces that they will return home. The men press their suits, but the princess mocks their lover's vows as no more constant than their original devotion to an ascetic pursuit of learning. They must demonstrate some proof of their sincerity, she claims, and the ladies impose harsh terms. The men may renew their suits in a year and a day, but under certain conditions: in the interim the king is to live a hermit's existence and Berowne is to perform community service, using his famous wit to cheer dying patients. The ridiculous Armado reports that he has agreed to an even more severe penance—to gain Jaquenetta he will "hold the plow for her sweet love three years." The play ends with a song and each group goes its own way, with all that labor of love quite lost.

Left in question at the end is whether the young men will be willing, or able, to undergo the trials the ladies have set for them. Given the short life of their earlier resolve, one would suspect not.

Shakespeare's plays are endlessly adaptable to any time or form. Kenneth Branagh has produced a film version of *Love's Labour's Lost* set in the 1930s. It is a musical, filled with songs from the period and Busby Berkeley production numbers.

TROILUS AND CRESSIDA

❦

THIS IS A TALE of the Trojan War, which was precipitated, it will be recalled, when the Trojan prince Paris seduced Helen, the wife of the Spar-
tan king Menelaus, and persuaded her to return with him to Troy.
Menelaus rallied the Greeks to avenge the insult, and an army under his
brother, Agamemnon, set sail, initiating what tradition tells us was a ten
years war. In *Troilus and Cressida*, Shakespeare assembled a cast including
many of the heroes on both sides celebrated in Homer's *The Iliad*. Among
the Trojans are the elderly King Priam; his sons Paris and Hector, who is
their most formidable warrior; Aeneas, a hero of Troy; the beautiful but
vain Helen; Andromache, Hector's loving wife; and Priam's mad daughter Cassandra. In the Greek camp, aside from Agamemnon and Menelaus,
we meet the elderly sage Nestor, the heroes Ulysses, Ajax, Diomedes, and
the most fearsome of them all, Achilles, who is accompanied by his dear
friend Patroclus.

The central concern of the play, however, is the love affair between
Troilus, the Trojan prince, and Cressida, the daughter of a Trojan priest
who has deserted to the Greeks. This is thus a story of love and war,
though in many ways it constitutes a parody of both. Its satirical edge is
provided by two minor figures. Cressida's uncle, the salacious Pandarus,
arranges for an assignation between the two lovers.[*] On the Greek side is
the cynical soldier Thersites, who mocks the martial ethic, heaping scorn
on all so-called heroes who pursue glory in war.

---

[*]Hence the word "pander," meaning to minister to base passions. In modern terms
he is a pimp.

Act One   A Prologue informs us that the play, like Homer's epic, concerns itself with events "in the middle" of the war. In Troy, Troilus professes his love for Cressida to her uncle, Pandarus, who is acting as an intermediary between them. Pandarus attempts to persuade his niece that Troilus is the most worthy of the Trojans, arousing her jealousy with an account of Helen flirting with him. The Trojan warriors troop across stage as Pandarus points them out, praising Troilus as the bravest of them all. When her uncle leaves, Cressida admits to her love for Troilus but is modestly reluctant to reveal it.

Meanwhile in the Greek camp their commander Agamemnon and the old sage Nestor attempt to raise the spirits of their troops, who are depressed by the long war. Ulysses gives his famous speech on the importance of order and degree, and they discuss the disorder in their ranks. The chief cause, they complain, is the withdrawal from battle of two of their greatest warriors, Achilles and Ajax, both of whom are disdainful of the Greek leadership. The Trojan Aeneas enters the camp with a challenge from Hector to meet any Greek champion in single combat. On the advice of Ulysses and Nestor, it is decided not to oppose Hector with the obvious choice, Achilles, since if he wins he will be even more insufferable, and if he loses the Greek cause will be damaged. They choose instead the "dull brainless Ajax."

Act Two   Thersites, a common soldier, rails at his dim-witted master, Ajax—"thou hast no more brain than I have in mine elbow"—and receives a beating for his insolence. When Achilles and Patroclus enter, the sharp-tongued Thersites complains to them about Ajax, whom he ridicules as a thick-minded fighting machine who "wears his wit in his belly and his guts in his head," and goes on to insult Achilles as well. Achilles brings word that Ajax is to fight Hector the following day.

In Priam's palace the Trojans are no less weary of the war. They debate returning Helen, the source of all their suffering, to her husband Menelaus, since, as Hector observes, "she is not worth what she doth cost / The keeping." His sister, the mad prophetess Cassandra, enters raving that if they do not return Helen, Troy will surely burn. Troilus argues against the proposal, and in the end Hector agrees with him.

Back in the Greek camp, Thersites, who has joined the service of

Achilles, entertains him by disparaging the Greek leaders, who at that moment are approaching. They have come to persuade Achilles to return to the field, but he will not even emerge from his tent to meet them. Ulysses is sent in as spokesman and returns to report that Achilles is determined to remain aloof from the war.

Act Three In Troy, Pandarus pays a visit to Paris and Helen to deliver a message from Troilus. The meeting provides an occasion for witty banter among them and a provocative love song from Pandarus. He arranges a lovers' tryst between Troilus and Cressida, during which she declares that she loves him in return. After an exchange of pretty speeches in which they vow never to be false to each other, Pandarus leads them off to a room he has prepared for them.

In the Greek camp Cressida's father, Calchas, who has defected from Troy, expresses a desire to be reunited with his daughter. He persuades the Greeks to release one of their captives, the prince Antenor, if the Trojans will agree to send her to join him. It is so agreed, and Diomedes is sent to escort her. Agamemnon instructs his followers to ignore Achilles, who becomes visibly upset at their indifference. Ulysses pauses to report to Achilles that Ajax is now highly praised by the Greeks while he, because of his isolation, has been quite forgotten. Confirming that Ajax will fight Hector, Achilles sends Patroclus to invite the Trojan to his tent "after the combat" and to secure a safe-conduct for him from Agamemnon. Apparently they anticipate that the fight will be a gentlemanly affair, harmless to the two warriors, and so it turns out to be.

Act Four Diomedes arrives in Troy to escort Cressida, who bids farewell to her lover. Both pledge to be true. Troilus promises to visit Cressida somehow once she joins her father. In the Greek camp, Ajax, awaiting Hector, has a trumpet sounded to indicate his readiness for battle, and it produces not the Trojan hero but Cressida, who enters accompanied by Diomedes. The Greeks greet her, and she unexpectedly turns vamp, flirting with them and kissing each in turn. Diomedes leads her off as the Trojans troop in, but Hector expresses himself reluctant to fight Ajax, who is his nephew. They clash, but Hector is only halfhearted in the fight, and it is finally called to a halt. The opponents embrace, each

praising the other, and Ajax invites Hector to visit Achilles in his tent.
When the two meet, the Greek hero is defiant, challenging Hector to a
contest of arms.

Act Five   Thersites delivers a letter to Achilles from the Trojan
queen Hecuba, asking him to refrain from battle out his love for her
daughter Polyxana. He reluctantly agrees. The warriors retire, except for
Diomedes, who has, he says, "important business," and Troilus, who has
made his way into the Greek camp. He asks Ulysses to guide him to
Calchas's tent, where he hopes to find Cressida. There they watch in hiding as Diomedes seduces her. Troilus is distraught at the sight—"O false
Cressid! False, false, false!"—and Aeneas arrives to conduct him back to
Troy. Thersites, a satirical *chorus*, comments bitingly on the principals'
behavior throughout these scenes, here: "Lechery, lechery; still wars and
lechery; nothing else holds fashion."

In Troy, Hector's wife and mother urge him to refrain from battle on
that day, but he insists it is his duty to go. Troilus accuses him of being
too merciful to his enemies, and he replies that he does so out of a sense of
"fair play." Hector, it seems, is vulnerable to occasional moments of humanity in battle, unlike the relentless Achilles. Cassandra enters, ranting
that Hector will die, but he dismisses the warning.

As the armies clash we witness a series of one-on-one encounters,
with Thersites ridiculing the spectacle as so much "clapper-clawing,"
that is, an undignified, brawling fistfight. Diomedes and Troilus meet
and exit fighting, while Thersites saves himself from Hector by pleading
that he is only "a very filthy rogue," too menial for the great warrior to
bother with. Patroclus is killed and Achilles, wrathful in his grief, prepares to return to battle as Ajax seeks out Troilus. Hector and Achilles finally meet, fighting until the Greek shows signs of fatigue, explaining
that he is a bit out of shape. Hector gallantly pauses, out of "fair play"
presumably, allowing his opponent to catch his breath and escape. Since
he has been unable to defeat the Trojan in single combat, Achilles mobilizes his followers, the Myrmidons, and returns to the battle. They attack
Hector en masse, overwhelming him, and Achilles prepares to display his
corpse to the enemy. Troilus announces Hector's death, and the disheartened Trojans retire. Pandarus appears and receives a tongue-lashing from
Troilus, but he has the last word: "Thus is the poor agent despised," he

complains philosophically, and leaves his legacy to "good traders in flesh."

The 1623 First Folio edition of Shakespeare's plays included *Troilus and Cressida*, but neglected to list it in the table of contents, raising questions ever since about whether it is a history, comedy, or tragedy. It was printed ambiguously in the Folio between the histories and tragedies but is commonly included as a comedy in modern anthologies, as it is here— though an account of the Trojan War may not seem entirely appropriate for comic treatment and its ending is certainly not a happy one. It is in many ways a bitter play, its most memorable character probably the cynical Thersites.

ALL'S WELL THAT ENDS WELL

❧

THIS IS A PLAY about unrequited love, a common theme in the *courtly love* tradition, but rather than a haughty maid spurning a suffering suitor, in this case the man rejects the woman, much to his discredit. Bertram is an insufferably proud young man, but he is not the first, nor the last, to ward off the advances of an infatuated woman. Helena is a wise and virtuous woman, but she is not the first, nor the last, to fall in love with a man so unworthy of her that her friends wonder what in the world she sees in him.

Act One His father newly dead, Bertram, the young Count of Rossillion, is summoned to the French court where, it is said, the king is seriously ill. He bids farewell to his mother, the countess, and Helena, the daughter of a famous physician, also recently deceased, and leaves in the company of an old lord, Lafew. Helena, left alone, confesses her love for Bertram and laments that she is too far beneath him in social rank to entertain any hope of his noticing her. Parolles comes upon her, and the two engage in a witty debate about the relative value of virginity. He is a stock character, the "braggart soldier," who talks a good fight but avoids battle (Pistol is another in *Henry V*). Bertram thinks well of him, however, and he accompanies the count to court. Helena decides to follow him, seeing the king's illness as an opportunity to realize her dream.

At court the king remarks on the war between Florence and Siena, a conflict his restless lords are eager to join. Bertram enters, and the king laments the deaths of his father and of the famous physician, who if he were alive, he says, might cure him. Meanwhile in Rossillion the countess learns that Helena is in love with her son. The kindly old woman has a special affection for her and offers to help as Helena sets out for Paris. There, using the knowledge and medicines left her by her father, she hopes to cure the king.

Act Two   In Paris the king bids farewell to his lords who are off to the war, and Bertram complains that he has been denied permission to join them. Helena arrives and strikes a bargain with the king: if her medicines fail, she will forfeit her life; but if they succeed, she will have her choice of a husband from among his attendant lords. He is quickly restored to health, and Helena selects Bertram, who is incensed at the insult to his standing: "A poor physician's daughter my wife! Disdain / Rather corrupt me ever!" The king insists, however, and they are married. Bertram, egged on by Parolles, is determined to desert Helena and join the French lords in the service of Florence. He directs her to return to Rossillion, bids her a curt farewell, and, spurning her request for a kiss, leaves with Parolles.

Act Three   Bertram writes to his mother, informing her that though he is married to Helena, he will not accept her as his wife. Helena enters with two gentlemen, who inform the countess that her son has gone to Florence and left with them a letter to his wife. She reads that she can never call him "husband" until she secures a ring he wears and proves that she has a child by him. She sadly regrets that she has caused him to endanger himself in the war and decides to leave Rossillion so that he can return home.

Bertram distinguishes himself in battle and is appointed the general of the Florentine cavalry, while in Rossillion the countess learns that Helena has left on a pilgrimage to the shrine of St. James of Compostela. Later in Florence an elderly widow, her daughter Diana, and a friend, Mariana, remark on Bertram's brilliant victories; and Mariana warns Diana about him. He has apparently taken a liking to her and sent the distasteful Parolles to solicit her on his behalf. Helena comes upon them and hears of both her husband's exploits and his unwelcome advances to Diana. The widow invites her to stay at her house with other pilgrims to St. James.*

*Of course, St. James of Compostela is in Spain, not Italy. But no matter.

In the Florentine camp the French lords attempt to persuade Bertram that his confidence in Parolles is misplaced. They insist he is "a most notable coward [and] an infinite and endless liar," and they devise a scheme to prove it. Parolles has been fretting about the loss of a drum in battle, and they plan to shame him into recovering it from the Sienese camp. Then, disguising themselves as the enemy, they will kidnap, blindfold, and interrogate him, confident that he will turn traitor and inform on the Florentine army to save himself. Bertram agrees, but first he will pursue Diana.

Meanwhile, Helena devises a scheme of her own. Revealing her identity, she persuades Diana to submit to Bertram's advances. Diana is to demand his ring as a token of his devotion and promise to allow him an hour's pleasure starting at midnight, under the condition that he not speak. Helena will take Diana's place in bed.

Act Four   The French lords learn that peace has been declared and hear that Helena is dead. Bertram joins them, having unknowingly bedded his wife, and they turn their attention to Parolles, whom they have captured. To save himself, he blurts out details of the Florentine forces, slanders the French lords, and dismisses Bertram as "a foolish idle boy." They remove his blindfold and release him, having successfully unmasked his cowardice. Meanwhile Helena persuades Diana and her mother to accompany her to the French court to confirm her story. Back in Rossillion the old lord, Lafew, hearing of Helena's death, proposes that Bertram marry his daughter. The king is expected shortly.

Act Five   The three women arrive too late to see the king, who has left for Rossillion. Helena, determined to follow him, prevails upon the others to continue on. The king arrives in Rossillion, lamenting the loss of Helena, but he forgives Bertram for his role in her death. The young duke agrees to the marriage to Lafew's daughter and gives him a ring as a gift for her. Lafew and the king immediately recognize the ring as Helena's, and they demand to know how Bertram came by it. Helena gave it to him, of course, during their hour of love; but, believing that he had received it from Diana, he invents a story about receiving it as a gift from a noble lady. The king insists it is Helena's and arrests Bertram, suspecting him now of complicity in her death. Diana arrives, claiming that the count had promised to marry her and that she had given him the ring "being abed"—another lie, but in a good cause. Bertram is forced to admit that he had it from her, another serious blot on his character since he had offered it as a gift to the noble Lafew's daughter. The king is more interested, however, in how Diana came by Helena's ring. When she refuses to say, he has her arrested as well.

There is yet another ring, of course—the one Bertram gave to Diana in anticipation of her favors. She produces it as proof of his promise of marriage, and he is forced to admit that he exchanged a six-generation heirloom for an hour's roll in bed. Confusion reigns until Helena herself appears, to reveal that it was she, not Diana, who slept with Bertram. Further, she has his ring, thus fulfilling both conditions he had imposed on her before she could call him "husband." An apparently contrite Bertram promises to "love her dearly, ever, ever dearly," and so all does indeed end well.

The women triumph, of course, as they so often do in Shakespeare's comedies. In *Measure for Measure* Mariana plays the same bed trick on a thoroughly unappealing Angelo, and the wayward Proteus is restored to Julia in *Two Gentlemen of Verona*. It happens over and over again, and we must always wonder if the prize is worth winning. It is difficult to fathom what these clever women can see in such men; but, as Shakespeare knew well, in matters of love a young maid's heart is wrapped in mystery.

MEASURE FOR MEASURE

❧

IF ONE ACCEPTS the four plays following this one as "romances," *Measure for Measure* may be properly called Shakespeare's last comedy, composed just before he undertook *Othello, Lear*, and *Macbeth*. He turned away from comedy, it is said, and *Measure for Measure* stands at the cusp of his transition. Critics find it a "problem play" or "dark comedy," its characters contradictory, their motivations dubious, and its themes obscure. Nevertheless it has proven a touchstone in modern ideological debate because of its ridicule of absolute values, its exposure of unprincipled male "hegemony," and its image of a woman's unsullied fortitude. It is a comedy about the balance between justice and mercy, and predictably, since it *is* a comedy, mercy prevails, but only after much discussion of the conflict between society's laws and human frailty.

Act One   The play opens with a relatively clear-cut decision. Duke Vincentio of Vienna is concerned that his city has become corrupt under his rule. As a consequence of either his leniency or indifference, respect for law has gone slack, and it is time, he has decided, to restore it. His plan is to retire for a time ostensibly for an interval of prayer and contemplation, and leave the reins of government in the hands of a deputy, Angelo, a self-righteous purist, single-mindedly devoted to upholding the laws of civil society.

Angelo's first steps are to condemn a young man, Claudio, to death for prematurely impregnating his wife-to-be, Juliet, and to order the razing of all the brothels in the suburbs. The focus of his efforts, and the central concern of the play, are the laws governing morality in Vienna, which strictly forbid fornication. These developments are the subject of

conversation among a pair of gentlemen and some of the comic figures of
the play: Lucio, identified only as a "fantistic" (given to fantasies); Mistress Overdone, who presides over one of the proscribed brothels; her servant, Pompey; and Claudio himself, whom they meet as he is being
paraded off to prison. He prevails upon Lucio to contact his sister, an as-
pirant in a convent, and ask her to plead for him.

The duke actually remains in Vienna, disguised as a holy friar. Lucio
persuades the sister, Isabella, to intercede with Angelo for her brother's
life.

Act Two   Escalus, an elderly lord, counsels Angelo to show leniency
toward Claudio, but to no avail. A constable, Elbow, brings a pair of prisoners, Pompey and Froth, before them. Elbow, like his counterpart Dogberry in *Much Ado About Nothing*, is long-winded, circuitous, and given to
malaprops—the prisoners are "notorious benefactors"—and Angelo, impatient with the interrogation, departs, leaving Escalus to deal with the
matter. After much comic accusation and denial, he dismisses the prisoners for lack of evidence.

Isabella appears before Angelo to plead for her brother. He is adamant
at first but finally agrees to reconsider the case and tells her to return the
following day. Attracted by her beauty, eloquence, and innocence, he has
fallen in love with her. The disguised duke visits the prison and learns of
Claudio's sentence. Isabella returns to renew her plea, and Angelo offers
to spare her brother if she will yield her "body to my will." She refuses
and leaves for the prison to inform Claudio that he must die.

Act Three   The duke, in his role as a friar, counsels Claudio to "be
absolute for death," advising him that life is a meaningless struggle ending in diseased old age, and that death, like sleep, is a welcome rest from
it. The young man is momentarily consoled, and as Isabella enters the
duke hides where he can overhear them. She tells Claudio of Angelo's
offer. At first he is indignant and insists that she reject it, but on further
thought he begs her to submit and save his life. Isabella is incensed—
"Take my defiance! Die! Perish!"—but the duke joins them and, sending
off a now contrite Claudio, proposes a scheme to Isabella. The plot grows
complicated here as he advises her to agree to Angelo's demands but to
impose such conditions that they can substitute another woman for her in

his bed without his being aware of it. He knows of a certain Mariana, whom Angelo had agreed to marry and then rejected some years ago. She remains faithful to him, he says, and will welcome the opportunity.

Later the disguised duke encounters Constable Elbow, who has re-arrested Pompey, this time as a "bawd," or what is called today a "pimp." Lucio comes upon them and, once Elbow has led his prisoner off, insists to the friar that if the case were left to the duke, he would not condemn Claudio to death since he "had some feeling of the sport" himself. The friar objects, but Lucio claims outrageously that he knows the duke well and is privy to his dissolute life. Escalus enters with Mistress Overdone, who has been arrested for operating a brothel. He confirms Angelo's determination that Claudio will die.

Act Four   The disguised duke persuades Mariana to exchange places with Isabella that night. In the prison the provost engages Pompey as an apprentice to the headsman, Abhorson, and they prepare to execute Claudio and another prisoner, the murderer Barnardine. Even though Isabella has agreed to Angelo's demands, the treacherous deputy orders that Claudio be executed anyway and his head brought to him. The friar, more or less taking charge, directs that Barnadine's head be delivered instead, but the prisoner insists he is too drunk to die and refuses to cooperate. The provost suggests they behead another condemned criminal who bears a closer resemblance to Claudio, and it is so agreed. The duke then informs Isabella that her brother is dead and she shall have her revenge on Angelo. He writes to the deputy announcing his return to Vienna and all gather at the city gate to meet him.

Act Five   The duke arrives and reaffirms his confidence in Angelo, rejecting Isabella's account of his duplicity. As she is led off to prison, Mariana comes forward to reveal that, in keeping with the friar's scheme, it was she who slept with Angelo, not Isabella. The duke orders the friar to be brought forth and departs, only to reappear shortly thereafter as the friar, escorting Isabella, who is under guard. Lucio accuses him of slandering the character of the duke. The friar replies that, quite the opposite, it was he who uttered the insults. Lucio angrily rips off the friar's hood, and the duke is revealed. He mercifully forgives everyone their "earthly faults" and announces four weddings: the contrite Angelo to Mariana,

Claudio to Juliet, himself to Isabella, and the devious Lucio, over his protests, to any woman he has got with child.

Measure for measure—or "tit for tat," that is—all are rewarded according to their individual merits, the prize being marriage, whether desired or not. Shakespeare also concludes *As You Like It* with four weddings, three of them similarly promising and one significantly less so. And mercy prevails over the law in Vienna. Noticeably absent is any suggestion that the law be changed, but it would have been impolitic for Shakespeare to propose such a measure in an England increasingly influenced by puritan morality. It was sufficient for him to imply that fornication, while objectionable in excess, as in the case of Lucio, has its place in human affairs.

THE WINTER'S TALE

❧

LIKE *The Tempest* and the three plays that follow here, *The Winter's Tale* has been identified as a "romance" since the end of the nineteenth century; but it is listed among the comedies in the First Folio edition of 1623. These five plays, all a product of Shakespeare's later years, are comic in the Aristotelian sense that they all end happily, though they are not especially amusing. *The Winter's Tale*, for example, features a blindly jealous husband, an unjustly accused wife, a child who dies stricken with grief, an infant abandoned to the elements, a man gored by a bear, a wrathful father, and a shipwreck at sea with all hands lost; and its chief comic figure, Autolycus, is an accomplished con man and cutpurse (pickpocket). Each of the "romances" concludes on a note of harmony and reconciliation, however, despite all the griefs and losses their characters endure: love in the end does conquer all.

Act One   Leontes, King of Sicily, is enjoying a visit of many months from a close companion of his youth, Polixenes, King of Bohemia. Leontes urges his friend to extend his stay. When Polixenes insists on returning home, Leontes asks his wife, Hermoine, to plead the case. She succeeds in persuading Polixenes to remain, but Leontes notices that they seem unusually intimate and is seized by a sudden fit of jealousy. He engages a Sicilian lord, Camillo, to poison Polixenes, but Camillo warns the king instead and escapes with him to Bohemia.

Act Two   Leontes accuses Hermione, who is visibly pregnant, of adultery, and in his anger orders that their son Mamillius be kept from her. Shocked by his accusation, she denies the charge, but Leontes confines her to prison, pending a trial. Antigonus, another lord, attempts to reason with Leontes, but the king is deaf to his counsel and sends two courtiers to consult the Delphic Oracle, whose prophecy, he says, "shall stop or spur me."

Antigonus's wife, Paulina, gains entrance to Hermione's prison to hear that she has been delivered of a baby girl. She undertakes to present the infant to Leontes, hoping to soften his heart; but, convinced that Polixenes is its father, he becomes even more incensed and orders it killed. Prevailed upon to relent, he instructs Antigonus to carry the baby to a remote, foreign shore and leave it to the mercy of the elements.

Act Three At her trial Hermione is accused of committing adultery with Polixenes and, for good measure, plotting with Camillo to murder Leontes. She defends herself stoutly but to no avail. The courtiers arrive with the prophecy of the Oracle: Hermione and Polixenes are innocent, and Leontes will remain without an heir until the abandoned baby is recovered. A servant enters to inform them that Mamillius, grieving over his mother's fate, has died. At the news Hermione faints and is carried off. Stunned by the prophecy and the death of his son, Leontes suddenly relents—"I have too much believed mine own suspicions"—but the damage has been done. Paulina reenters to announce that the queen is dead, and he vows to mourn for the rest of his days.

Meanwhile Antigonus abandons the baby, Perdita, at a remote spot on the Bohemian coast, but he leaves evidence of her identity and a bundle of gold and jewels. Before he can return to his ship, however, he is attacked by a bear.[*] A shepherd's son, identified as a "Clown," observes the bear mangle Antigonus and the ship founder in a storm.[†] He and his father rescue the baby and, discovering the gold, carry her off to their home.

Act Four A *chorus*, "Time," informs us that a period of sixteen years has passed and that Perdita has "grown in grace / Equal with wondering"

---

[*]As indicated by the best-known stage direction in the history of the theater: "Exit, pursued by a bear."

[†]Of course, the central European kingdom of Bohemia has no shoreline, but if Shakespeare wanted a shipwreck, he had need of a sea.

as a shepherd's daughter. King Polixenes and Camillo, who has remained in Bohemia since their escape, learn that the prince, Florizel, has been paying attention to the daughter of a certain shepherd, one who has grown surprisingly wealthy over the years. They decide to don disguises and question him. A notorious rogue, Autolycus, posing as a peddler, feigns injury; when the shepherd's son pauses to help him, Autolycus steals his purse.

The long final scene of the act, over eight hundred lines, begins with a springtime sheep-shearing festival at which Perdita has been selected queen. Prince Florizel, dressed as a shepherd for the occasion, declares his love for her, but she is hesitant, fearing that his father would disapprove of the match. A crowd of shepherds enters, accompanied by the disguised Polixenes and Camillo. The old shepherd chides Perdita for not acting the proper hostess, and in one of Shakespeare's delightful flower passages, she greets each guest with a gift of blossoms.* An interval of song and dance follows, enlivened by Autolycus, who has joined the festival to hawk his wares and cut purses. In the midst of the gaiety the disguised Polixenes advises Florizel that it would be proper for him to inform his father of his intention to wed Perdita. When his son refuses, the king reveals himself and orders him angrily back to court, threatening him with disinheritance and Perdita with death should she ever see him again.

A compassionate Camillo comes to their rescue. He has long been reconciled with the sorrowing Leontes and holds a place of honor and wealth in Sicily. He advises the couple to seek refuge there, where he will provide them with an introduction to court and a false story to explain their presence. Meanwhile the old shepherd and his son, anxious to mend their fortunes with the angry king, seek him out to show him the jewels and other items Antigonus left with the baby Perdita. On their way they encounter Autolycus, who, learning of the wealth they carry and hoping to gain favor with the prince, misleads them into believing that the king is aboard the vessel carrying the lovers to Sicily. The shepherds follow him trustingly and end up making the trip—though, as we learn later, the couple are so seasick that they fail to question them.

---

*Another, of course, is Ophelia's famous mad scene in *Hamlet*.

Act Five In Sicily, Paulina mysteriously pledges the mournful Leontes never to marry unless she picks his queen. He receives Florizel and Perdita, whom the prince passes off as a princess of Libya. Word arrives that Polixenes has also arrived and has ordered his son's arrest. Leontes offers to intercede for them.

Shakespeare chose not to dramatize the scene of reconciliation, leaving it rather to a trio of gentlemen to relate the event: The shepherds' evidence identified Perdita, and the reunited kings rejoiced at the union of their children; but the joy of the occasion was dimmed by Leontes's description of Hermione's death. Paulina reveals that she has commissioned a statue of the queen and invites the entire company to view the wonder. They accept and at its unveiling they praise its lifelike qualities, only to be stunned when it steps off its pedestal and embraces Leontes. Hermione is alive, having remained hopeful all these years that her daughter would be found, as the Delphic Oracle had implied.

Leontes's jealousy has been criticized as too abrupt and totally unwarranted. In contrast it requires almost five hundred lines and the insinuations of a malicious Iago to persuade Othello that Desdemona is unfaithful. But Shakespeare knew that jealousy, like love and hatred, can strike the spirit at any moment, and is often precipitated by "trifles light as air."

PERICLES, PRINCE OF TYRE

❧

THIS PLAY might well be named "The Travels of Pericles." He and his wife and daughter come ashore at half a dozen ports of call in the eastern Mediterranean, stranded by storms at sea, kidnapped by pirates, pursued by murderers, or otherwise assailed by man and nature over a period of some twenty years. *Pericles* is a "romance," however; so despite these travels and travails, the principals end up reunited with the promise of a happy future. There are so many persons and places in the plot that it is useful to jot down a list of them before proceeding:

Tyre. Ruler: Pericles. His wife: Thaisa. His daughter: Marina.

Antioch. Ruler: Antiochus. His daughter: Unnamed.

Tarsus. Ruler: Cleon. His wife: Dionyza.

Pentapolis. Ruler: Simonides. His daughter: Thaisa, who marries Pericles.

Ephesus.

Mytilene. Ruler: Lysimachus, who marries Marina.

Shakespeare employs a *chorus* to account for events during the time intervals between acts, in this case the fourteenth-century poet John Gower, who had told the tale himself in his *Confessio Amantis* (c. 1383–1393).

Act One   Gower: The King of Antioch has a secret incestuous relationship with his beautiful daughter. To keep her for himself he requires her suitors to solve a riddle he puts to them, with death as the penalty should they fail to do so. None has yet succeeded.

Pericles arrives to seek the daughter's hand and recognizes the riddle for what it is—the king's convoluted confession of his incest. Thinking it impolitic to announce their sin in public, Pericles gives an obscure answer. The king, seeing that he has solved the riddle, engages Thaliard to put him to death. Pericles flees back to Tyre. There, fearful that the king seeks his life and may invade the country to keep his secret, Pericles decides to leave for Tarsus and appoints the trusted Helicanus as regent during his absence. Thaliard, learning that Pericles has left and confident that he will perish at sea, returns to Antioch.

In Tarsus, King Cleon laments that his people are suffering from a severe drought. Pericles arrives with a fleet and offers him stores of grain to prevent starvation. The king greets him warmly.

Act Two Gower: Helicanus writes Pericles that Thaliard is still stalking him and advises that he leave Tarsus. The prince sets sail but his ship founders in a storm, and he is cast up on a foreign shore.

Pericles receives help from three fishermen, from whom he learns that he is in Pentapolis, ruled by King Simonides. His arms and armor having somehow survived the storm, he decides to present himself at court and compete in a tournament being held to celebrate the birthday of the princess, Thaisa. He triumphs in the tournament, is honored by Simonides, reveals his identity, and, with the encouragement of the king, marries Thaisa. In Tyre, Helicanus learns that the incestuous King of Antioch and his daughter have been killed by a lightning bolt.

Act Three Gower: Thaisa in time becomes pregnant. In Tyre the people are uneasy without a king and insist that Helicanus take the crown. The loyal lord writes to Pericles, informing him that his enemy is dead and urging him to return. The couple embark on a ship that is soon beset by a storm.

Thaisa gives birth to a baby girl in the midst of the tempest, but her nurse reports to Pericles that his wife has died in the process. The master of the ship insists that the storm will not subside until they are rid of the body, so Pericles sadly consigns his wife to the sea in a sturdy coffin. It is cast ashore in Ephesus where the lord Cerimon, who is skilled in medicine, restores her to life. Convinced that her husband has perished in the storm, Thaisa vows to devote herself to the worship of Diana.

Unable to reach Tyre, Pericles directs the ship to Tarsus, where a grateful Cleon greets him warmly. The prince leaves the infant, whom he

has named Marina, in the care of Cleon and his wife Dionyza, and returns
to Tyre to resume the throne.

Act Four   Gower: Several years pass as Thaisa remains in Ephesus
and Marina grows into a young woman in Tarsus, one so lovely and
skilled that she overshadows Cleon's daughter of the same age. The envious queen, Dionyza, decides to have Marina murdered.

She engages Leonine to kill her during a walk by the seashore. He is
interrupted in the act, however, by pirates, who seize her. Making his escape, Leonine decides to report her dead.

In Mytilene three dealers in prostitutes—Pander, his wife the
"Bawd," and their man Bolt—complain about the quality of women they
have in trade and decide to procure "fresh ones." They purchase Marina
from the pirates and, since she is a virgin, hope to get a good price for her
services, though she is determined to keep "untied [her] virgin knot."
Meanwhile, in Tarsus, Cleon rebukes his wife for killing Marina—and
apparently Leonine as well—and she scoffs at him for his cowardly concern. To satisfy Pericles, they have erected a monument to the dead girl.
He embarks for Tarsus to bring his daughter home to Tyre, only to hear
on his arrival that she is dead.

In Mytilene things are not going well in the brothel. The "bawds"
bring Marina customers, but she preaches virtue to them and sends them
off shamed. Lysimachus, the governor, is so impressed by her that he
gives her gold and is contrite as he leaves. Bolt is convinced that he will
have to rape her himself to make her serviceable, but she converts him as
well and persuades him to find her honorable employment where she can
use her considerable skills to teach others how to "sing, weave, sew, and
dance."

Act Five   Gower: Installed in "an honest house," Marina soon becomes widely admired for her beauty, ability, and charm. Meanwhile Pericles has come to Mytilene, and Lysimachus takes a barge out to meet his
ship.

Pericles is in such a deep depression, however, that he will speak to
no one, and Lysimachus tells Helicanus of a young woman he knows who
may help cheer him. Marina comes aboard and sings to him, but he will
have nothing to do with her until she tells him of her own sorrowful life.

The father and daughter are joyfully reunited, and Pericles in a dream has a vision of Diana, who tells him to worship at her temple in Ephesus. There he finds Thaisa and, learning that her father, Simonides, is dead, he decides to return with her to rule over Pentapolis. Marina, he says, will marry Lysimachus, and the couple will reign in Tyre.

In an epilogue, Gower informs us that when the people of Tarsus learned of the "cursed deed" of "wicked Cleon and his wife," they rose up and burned them in their palace.

This is a moral tale, with virtue triumphant over vice—except perhaps for Cleon, who seems a good sort but dies in the end. Marina's influence over her customers may seem a bit far-fetched to modern ears, but it was quite in keeping with an age that acknowledged the power, in John Milton's phrase, of "the sage / And serious doctrine of Virginity" (*Comus*).

CYMBELINE

❦

SHAKESPEARE pulled out all the stops with *Cymbeline*, loading its plot with every trick of the dramatic trade he had learned during two decades of writing for the London stage: scenes of battle during a Roman invasion of early Britain; an irate king who rejects his daughter for marrying a man of *her* choice rather than his; the man, a poor but noble innocent who is transformed into a jealous husband by a devious charlatan; a virtuous wife who, disguised as a man, exposes herself to danger in search of her husband; a wicked stepmother and queen, adept at poisons, ambitious for her arrogant, vile-tempered lout of a son; royal children kidnapped as infants and raised as rude rustics; a loyal servant who, ordered to kill his mistress, protects her instead; an angry Jupiter who descends from the heavens hurling lightning bolts; a soothsayer; several ghosts; and a headless corpse—all this and much, much more in "the two hours' traffic of our stage." There's never a dull moment.

With such a cast it is difficult to imagine the play as a comedy, and indeed in the 1623 First Folio edition it was listed among the tragedies, despite the fact that it has a happy ending. Modern editions include it as a "romance."

Act One Cymbeline, the King of Britain during the Roman era, is upset because his daughter, Imogen, has married "a poor but worthy gentleman," Posthumus Leonatus, without his permission. He had intended her for Cloten (rhymes with "rotten"), the son of his queen by a former marriage. Imogen is his only child, two sons having been kidnapped as infants some twenty years in the past, and the king's angry response is to banish Posthumus and imprison his daughter. The two bid each other farewell and exchange love tokens, for him her ring, for her a bracelet, and he leaves, sending his loyal servant Pisano back to serve his wife. Cloten, meanwhile, is furious that Imogen has refused him.

Posthumus finds refuge at a friend's house in Rome, where he meets the cynical Iachimo. The loyal husband praises the virtues of his wife, and Iachimo challenges him to a wager, betting a sum of gold against Posthumus's ring that he can seduce Imogen. The ingenuous Posthumus foolishly agrees, confident of her virtue. In Britain the queen asks for poison from a doctor, who, mistrusting her, delivers a strong sedative instead, and she gives it to Pisano for Imogen's use, claiming that it is a powerful medicine for any illness.

Iachimo arrives with a tale of Posthumus's carousing in Rome. Feigning sympathy, he urges Imogen to be avenged by carousing with him. When she rebuffs him, he apologizes for falsely reporting her husband's behavior, explaining unctuously that he did so only so that he could report her fidelity to him. He asks to secure a trunk of valuables in her chamber overnight; now placated, she agrees.

Act Two   When Imogen falls into a deep sleep that night, Iachimo emerges from hiding in the trunk. He takes careful note of the room's decorations, steals the bracelet from Imogen's arm, and observes a mole on her breast. Later, Cloten presses his attention on Imogen, who rejects him outright, responding that she values her husband's garments more than she does Cloten. He vows vengeance. Iachimo returns to Rome and, citing the evidence he has gained, especially the mole, convinces Posthumus that he has won their wager by seducing his wife. Posthumus surrenders her ring and vows vengeance as well. Everyone, it seems, hates the virtuous Imogen—the king, the queen, Cloten, and now her husband! Only the faithful Pisano remains loyal to her.

Act Three   Cymbeline receives the Roman general Caius Lucius, who has come to demand the annual tribute that the king's predecessor had agreed to pay Rome after Julius Caesar conquered Britain. Cymbeline, prodded by the queen and Cloten, refuses to pay, and Lucius warns him that his obstinacy can only result in "war and confusion." Meanwhile Pisano has received two letters from Posthumus, the one to him ordering him to murder Imogen, and the other to her revealing that he is with the

Roman army in Milford Haven, a Welsh seaport. She decides to go in
search of him and secures the aid of Pisano.

The scene shifts abruptly to the Welsh mountains, where an elderly
man and two youths whom he calls his sons occupy a cave and live off the
wild. The young men are restless, complaining that they know nothing
of the outside world. Despite the older man's counsel that it is not worth
knowing, they yearn for broader experience. Left alone, he confesses that
he is Belarius, a British lord whom Cymbeline unjustly accused of treason
many years ago. In retaliation, he kidnapped the king's two sons and has
raised them as outcasts, isolated from civil society.*

On their way to Milford Haven, Pisano reveals to Imogen that her
husband has commissioned him to murder her. Distraught, she urges him
to do so. But he is convinced that his "master is abused" by some villain,
and he refuses. He will tell Posthumus that she is dead, however, and he
proposes that she assume the disguise of a young page and seek to enter
the service of the Roman general, Lucius, while she searches for her husband. Pisano gives her the "medicine" he received from the queen, which
she thought poison but which is in fact only a strong sedative.

Cymbeline discovers that his daughter has fled, and Cloten threatens
Pisano, who to save himself shows him Posthumus's letter. Cloten requires him to secure one of Posthumus's suits for him. Stung by Imogen's
remark that she values her husband's clothing more than him, he refines
his plan of revenge. Dressed as Posthumus, he will kill him and rip up his
garments before her eyes, ravish her, and "foot her home again" in disgrace. Meanwhile, Imogen, in her disguise as a page, comes upon the cave
where the outcasts live and enters it in search of food. Returning from a
hunt, they discover her. The youths are immediately moved by a natural
affection for one they know only as a young man, but who is, of course,
their sister. They invite her courteously to join them.

Act Four   Cloten nears the cave in search of Imogen and Posthumus.
The three men leave on a hunt but she, feeling ill, stays behind, intend-
ing to take the "medicine" Pisano has given her. When Cloten comes
upon the three men, Morgan, recognizing him and suspecting that he is

---

*In the ensuing dialogue they refer to one another by their assumed names, and so
shall we. Belarius is "Morgan"; Guiderius, the elder son, is "Polydore"; and Arviragus,
the younger, is "Cadwal."

not alone, urges that they flee. Polydore remains, however, and after an exchange of insults he and Cloten exit fighting. Shortly Polydore greets his companions bearing Cloten's head, and Morgan urges him to dispose of it. They enter the cave to find Imogen, apparently dead, and lay the two bodies side by side in preparation for burial.

Imogen awakens and, seeing the headless body dressed in her husband's clothing, falls in a faint across it. When the Roman general Lucius comes upon the scene, he is attracted by the revived Imogen, who calls herself Fidele, and takes her into his service. Cymbeline, troubled already by a missing stepson and a queen who has taken ill, learns that he must contend with an invading army. Hearing the sound of battle, Polydore and Cadwal, still eager for experience, persuade Morgan to join in the fight.

Act Five Posthumus, who has landed with the Roman army, receives a message from Pisano that Imogen is dead. Regretting his jealous anger, he mourns her briefly and, disguising himself as a peasant, joins the British forces. In the ensuing battle the British are routed and Cymbeline captured. The three outcasts rescue him, and Posthumus joins them in holding a narrow pass against the Romans until the British, inspired by their courage, rally and return to achieve the victory. Posthumus, mourning Imogen's death, resumes his Roman dress and is captured and led off in chains. Imprisoned, he is visited by the ghosts of his family who plead with Jupiter to rescue him. The god appears above, angrily hurling thunderbolts, and rebukes them for questioning his will. He predicts a happy ending and leaves behind a tablet containing a cryptic message. The jailers arrive to take Posthumus to his execution, but he is saved by the king's order that he be freed and brought to the court.

In the long final scene, Cymbeline knights the outcasts for their part in the battle and learns that his queen has died, confessing to her treachery. Imogen, still in disguise, enters with the captive general Lucius, and the king, finding her vaguely familiar, takes her into his service. She asks Iachimo, who is among the Roman prisoners, how he came by the ring he wears. As he openly confesses to his villainy, Posthumus comes in raging at him for causing Imogen's death. Pisano inadvertently unmasks her, and the lovers are reunited. More revelations follow. Polydore admits to killing Cloten and is condemned to death. Morgan reveals their identity and the king, embracing his sons, forgives them all. Posthumus reveals that he was the unknown peasant who stood with the three against the Romans, and, caught up in the spirit of reconciliation, he forgives Iachimo. A soothsayer deciphers Jupiter's message and Cymbeline, unexpectedly freeing Lucius, agrees to pay the annual tribute to Rome in hopes that now they may live in peace.

Cymbeline is indeed a crowded "two hours' traffic of our stage," and we are not meant to judge the plot critically. Indeed, things happen so thick and fast, as we move from Britain to Rome to Wales, from castle to cave, that an audience is left breathless at the end. Imogen, like so many of Shakespeare's comic heroines, is superior to her witless husband and emerges as an entirely admirable figure. Jupiter is not an authentic *deus ex machina,* since he has no effect upon the course of action. But Elizabethan audiences delighted in ghosts and gods, so Shakespeare pleased them by adding a supernatural scene to this potpourri of a plot.

THE TWO NOBLE KINSMEN

❧

IN 1634, eighteen years after Shakespeare's death, a quarto edition of *The Two Noble Kinsmen* appeared in London, attributed to the poet and John Fletcher as co-authors. For the next two hundred years, however, it was considered a play by Fletcher, not Shakespeare, and even today some scholars exclude it from the canon of the poet's works.* Others find it sufficiently his to warrant inclusion, however, and so shall we. The sections that are Shakespeare's, it is said, are the last lines he wrote for the stage.

The play is a dramatization of Geoffrey Chaucer's "The Knight's Tale" from his fourteenth-century work *The Canterbury Tales*. The plot is generally faithful to the source, the prominent departure being the addition of the jailer's daughter, who is pathetically in love with Palamon of Thebes. It is a tale of *courtly love*, but Shakespeare paints the theme in darker tones than did Chaucer's saintly knight. If *The Two Noble Kinsmen* is a comedy, its humor has a satiric edge to it.

Act One   Theseus, Duke of Athens, is returning from a successful campaign against the Amazons, accompanied by their queen, Hippolytra, who is to be his bride. The procession is interrupted by three queens, who complain that Creon, King of Thebes, has left the bodies of their husbands in the open to rot after their unsuccessful assault on the city. They plead with Theseus to help them recover their remains so as to give them proper burial. He gallantly agrees and sends Hippolyta and her sister,

---

*The play did not appear in the First Folio edition of 1623. David Bevington, for example, excludes it from his comprehensive *The Complete Works of Shakespeare*, 3rd ed. (Glenview, Ill.; Scott, Foresman, 1980).

Emilia, on to Athens under the protection of his friend, Pirithous, while he marches on Thebes.

Two young men of that city, the cousins Palamon and Arcite, reject the corruption of Creon's reign but answer the call to arms against Theseus. In Athens, Hippolytra and Emilia discuss the close friendship between Theseus and Pirithous, and Emilia relates the tale of her childhood bond with another girl, now dead. Hippolytra remarks that the memory of such a friendship must prevent her from loving "any that's called man," and she agrees. In Thebes, the victorious Theseus notices the wounded cousins, whose courage in battle he had admired, and he orders them to be restored to health and imprisoned.

Act Two   The prisoners, Palamon and Arcite, having recovered from their wounds, pledge eternal brotherhood. Emilia enters a nearby garden visible from their prison window, and both immediately fall in love with her. Disclaiming their recent vows of friendship, they angrily dispute who shall have her. The jailer arrives with word that Arcite is to be released and Palamon shackled away from the window.

Later in Thebes, Arcite laments that his release amounts to a banishment from Emilia, and he envies Palamon his daily sight of her. He encounters a group of rustic comics on their way to the games in Athens and, hoping for a glimpse of Emilia, decides to disguise himself and enter the competitions. He is so successful that Theseus engages him as a servant to Emilia. Meanwhile the jailer's daughter, who has fallen in love with Palamon, arranges for his escape from prison and sets out to provide him with food and clothing.

Act Three   The Athenians engage in their annual ritual of "a-Maying" in the countryside, and Arcite rejoices at his good fortune in serving Emilia. When Palamon, still in shackles, confronts him, the two resume their feud over Emilia. They agree to a duel to the death, but in true chivalric tradition Arcite will first release his cousin from his shackles, provide him with food to restore his strength, and secure arms for both. The jailer's daughter, meanwhile, carries a file, food, and clothing for Palamon, but fails to find him. She becomes lost and seems to be losing her wits. She encounters a group of countrymen and, now quite mad, joins them in a rustic morris dance (a vigorous English traditional) to entertain the duke and his party.

Arcite brings Palamon provisions and arms, and in a ludicrous scene the two help each other don their armor, solicitously asking if a strap is too tight and if the gloves are a proper fit. Finally they square off to fight, only to be interrupted by the duke and his party. Learning their identities, Theseus condemns them to death, but his companions plead for mercy. Emilia also supports them, but on the condition that they leave her alone and never fight over her again. They both refuse, and Theseus proposes a solution to the impasse: they will be released to return in a month, each with three knights, and engage in a contest of arms, the winner to have Emilia, the loser to forfeit his head. The cousins agree and shake hands to honor the commitment.

Act Four   The jailer and his friends lament his daughter's distress, and she appears to them, raving about a ship that will carry her to Palamon. A month having passed, Emilia ponders over the relative merits of her two suitors and decides that she cannot choose between them. Word comes that they have arrived from Thebes and are prepared for the contest. Meanwhile a doctor holds out hope for the jailer's mad daughter, who, he says, is not really insane but subject only to "a most thick and profound melancholy" that can be cured.

Act Five   Before the battle, each of the principals prays to a god, Arcite to Mars, Palamon to Venus, each asking for victory. Emilia, who still cannot decide between them, prays to Diana, pleading only that the winner be the one that "best loves me." The doctor's remedy for the jailer's distracted daughter is to dress a young man who loves her in Palamon's clothes and have him propose marriage. In her deranged state of mind she wistfully accepts, and the doctor predicts that she will come to her senses under her lover's care.

Emilia refuses to view the battle and receives word that Arcite has triumphed. Theseus brings him in to receive the prize and, over the objections of Emilia, orders the execution of Palamon and his knights, as had been agreed. The knight contemplates his death and bids his companions farewell as the jailer enters. Palamon inquires after the jailer's daughter and is assured that she has recovered and is to be married. As the condemned men are led off, word arrives that Arcite's horse has bolted and fallen on him. He is carried in, fatally injured, and generously surrenders Emilia to Palamon, asking only for a final kiss from her before he dies. Theseus agrees to the marriage, observing that "never Fortune / did play a subtler game" than this.

Shakespeare (and Fletcher) transformed Chaucer's poem into a play, adding a morris dance and rustic humor to please his audience. Chaucer describes the combat between the knights in some detail while in the play we hear only the shouting of the spectators—Shakespeare's concession to the limitations of the Elizabethan *stage*. When deprived of the sight of Emilia, Chaucer's Arcite pines away in a true courtly love tradition until his appearance is so changed that he can enter her service unrecognized. Shakespeare leaves him hail and hearty, robust enough to win the games; but the play observes the tradition in the person of the jailer's daughter, who edges toward madness because of her unrequited love for Palamon.

The Histories

Not all the water in the rough rude sea
Can wash the balm off from an anointed king.
—*Richard II*

Small time: but, in that small, most greatly lived
This star of England.
—*Henry V*

The Royal Family

(with dates of their reigns and deaths)

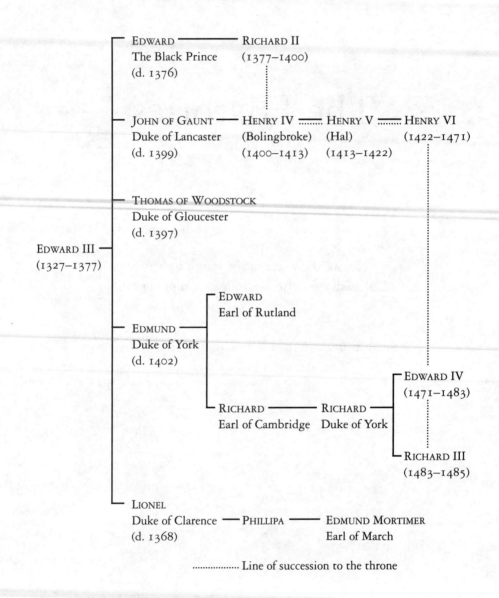

EDWARD ──────── RICHARD II
The Black Prince (1377–1400)
(d. 1376)

JOHN OF GAUNT ── HENRY IV ⋯⋯ HENRY V ⋯⋯ HENRY VI
Duke of Lancaster (Bolingbroke) (Hal) (1422–1471)
(d. 1399) (1400–1413) (1413–1422)

THOMAS OF WOODSTOCK
Duke of Gloucester
(d. 1397)

EDWARD III ──
(1327–1377)

EDWARD
Earl of Rutland

EDMUND ──
Duke of York
(d. 1402)

EDWARD IV
(1471–1483)

RICHARD ──────── RICHARD ──
Earl of Cambridge Duke of York

RICHARD III
(1483–1485)

LIONEL
Duke of Clarence ── PHILLIPA ──────── EDMUND MORTIMER
(d. 1368) Earl of March

⋯⋯⋯⋯ Line of succession to the throne

HISTORY

SHAKESPEARE'S earliest plays were histories, and it may be said that he cut his dramatic teeth on them. In the early 1590s, riding a wave of nationalistic fervor following the repulse of the Spanish Armada, he reached back into his country's chronicles and composed four plays on a chapter in England's troubled past, the War of the Roses, a destructive civil conflict that tore her people apart in the mid-fifteenth century. The first three of these plays, *Henry VI, Parts 1, 2, and 3*, are seldom if ever produced today. But he topped them off with *Richard III*, which features one of the most ingenious villains in stage history, signaling Shakespeare's arrival as a playwright.

When these early plays proved quite successful in their time, Shakespeare went back even further in England's chronicles and composed four more covering the twenty-odd years prior to the time frame of his earlier ones. These later works, in which one can trace the maturing of his dramatic art, record the rise to power of Henry Bolingbroke, Duke of Lancaster, who became Henry IV, and the reign of his son, Henry V, who became the most powerful king in Christendom when he joined the two crowns of England and France. These eight plays, if considered in historical sequence, dramatize the history of England from 1399 to 1485. The first, *Richard II*, opens the chronicle, relating the fall of that king and Bolingbroke's assumption of the throne. The two that follow, though entitled *Henry IV, Parts 1 and 2*, are largely the story of Bolingbroke's son, Prince Hal, who on his father's death succeeded him as Henry V. In *Henry V*, the king invades France, achieves a stunning victory at the battle of Agincourt, and finally joins the two crowns. He did not reign long but died at the height of his conquests, leaving a nine-month-old son who became Henry VI. During his minority, the English nobles, left to their own devices by the power vacuum created by an infant king, fell to wrangling among themselves, leading ultimately to the contest for the throne between the houses of Lancaster and York that is known as the War of the Roses, dramatized in the three *Henry VI* plays. The historical sequence ends with the brief, infamous reign of Richard, Duke of Gloucester, chronicled in *Richard III*.

The two tables below list the plays in sequence of composition and in historical chronology. The dates of composition are a matter of dispute among scholars and are offered only to clarify the sequence, which is not in dispute. The chronology is relatively accurate, complicated by Shakespeare's sometimes cavalier treatment of history.

IN SEQUENCE OF COMPOSITION

1589–1591	*Henry VI, Parts 1, 2, and 3*
1592–1593	*Richard III*
1595	*Richard II*
1596–1597	*Henry IV, Part 1*
1598	*Henry IV, Part 2*
1599	*Henry V*

IN HISTORICAL CHRONOLOGY*

1399–1400	*Richard II*
1400–1403	*Henry IV, Part 1*
1403–1413	*Henry IV, Part 2*
1413–1421	*Henry V*
1422–1471	*Henry VI, Parts 1, 2, and 3*
1483–1485	*Richard III*

In the pages that follow, four plays of this sequence are described in some detail. Brief summaries of the less frequently staged *Henry IV, Part 2* and the three *Henry VI* plays are placed in historical sequence in the text so as to provide the reader a convenient chronology of events (see also the chart of the royal family, page 354).

---

*During the 2000–2001 season at Stratford-on-Avon, all eight plays were staged in historical sequence under the general title "This England: The Histories."

A common *theme* threads its way through these histories—divine retribution for the killing of a king. The idea arose from a common belief of the time in the principle of *universal order*, which maintained that in the political scheme of things, even as God ruled the universe, so did the king rule his subjects—a part of the grand design emanating from the spirit and substance of the deity. In this way of thought, when Bolingbroke deposed Richard II and, it is suspected, had him killed, he committed the sin of disrupting the divinely ordained design. Shakespeare frequently implies that the ensuing disorders during the reign of Henry IV and the subsequent War of the Roses were punishments visited upon a people who dared to challenge that design. At the end of this troubled period, when the wicked Richard III assume the throne after murdering all other claimants, his harsh rule, it is implied, was God's final punishment on England for Bolingbroke's impious act. Only when Richard died in battle was the land finally purged of guilt. At his death Henry VII mounted the throne and established the Tudor line of English monarchs, under whose reign, say the chronicles, the kingdom entered a new era of peace and prosperity.*

Shakespeare was writing these plays during the long reign of the last of these Tudor monarchs, Queen Elizabeth I, who was Henry VII's granddaughter. Through him she could trace her line back to Henry V's French widow. As a playwright, Shakespeare was quite conscious that the prosperity of his acting company depended on the goodwill of the royal person. Most of this history he found in books such as Raphael Holinshed's *Chronicles of England, Scotland, and Ireland* (1577), a compendious account of those times that celebrated the legitimacy of the Tudor line. Since the book was unashamedly partial to those monarchs, its accuracy is open to question. Modern historians, for example, doubt that Richard III was all that wicked.

Shakespeare used the *Chronicles* as one of the sources for his plays, but he took as many liberties with Holinshed as the historian did with history. Prince Hal, for example, was not at the battle of Shrewsbury, nor was the French dauphin at Agincourt; but Shakespeare was writing plays

---

*These monarchs (and the years of their reign) were Henry VII (1485–1509), Henry VIII (1509–1547), Edward VI (1547–1553), Mary I (1553–1558), and Elizabeth I (1558–1603).

for the entertainment of an audience, and if it suited his dramatic purposes to place them at those battle scenes, he did so. Shakespeare's
achievement lies in his ability to bring to life figures drawn from dry-as-
dust historical accounts and recreate them as flesh-and-blood men and
women engaged in common human experiences—coming of age, high-
spirited gaiety, envy, hatred, despair, courage, cowardice, and the twin
passions of ambition and love. His kings are caught up in the conflict between the demands of their high office and the pull of personal desires,
his queens between the sometimes harsh dictates of the state and their
devotion to family. Although high public figures, they endure the trials
and experience the joys of ordinary beings, reaching into the arena of our
own lives.

RICHARD II

❧

THE PLAY is a chronicle of an English king too much impressed with the splendor of his office, who spends too lavishly on its trappings and ceremonies and wields its power irresponsibly. When confronted with a dispute between one of his favorites and Henry Bolingbroke, a nobleman of royal blood, he exiles them both. When Bolingbroke's father, the Duke of Lancaster, dies, Richard confiscates his title and lands to help pay for a campaign to subdue the Irish. As the king embarks for Ireland, Bolingbroke violates his exile and returns to England at the head of an army. He is soon joined by the disaffected nobles of the realm and confronts the king, whose supporters desert him. Richard submits and agrees to abdicate the throne in favor of Bolingbroke, who is crowned Henry IV. The deposed king is imprisoned and later murdered.

In modern terms, Richard II is a man with an exaggerated sense of his own importance, but he has some reason to believe himself inviolate, given his era's concept of the divine sanction of a king. The monarch, it was believed, is one of the visible signs of a *universal order*, ruling his land with the same authority as the Almighty does the universe, the sun the heavens, and the father his family. The king, it was said, had been anointed by God, and any who challenged his rule threatened to disrupt what was perceived as a divinely ordained pattern. To depose him was a sacrilege, risking the wrath of God, who, it was believed, was sure to exact retribution, not only on the usurper but on the offending kingdom itself. Bolingbroke stands out against this tradition, his ambition and actions suggesting a more modern, pragmatic image of the gaining and wielding of political power. He dutifully observes the surface ceremonies of the throne but has a practical grasp of the brutal realities that sustain or imperil it. Shakespeare places before us a weak but eloquent king, who represents the preservation of an ancient civil order proclaiming that the monarch draws his authority from God, and the usurper, who recognizes that a ruler draws his power from the people.

This is a play, however, and the choice is defined not as a matter of political theory but in terms of human sympathy. There is much to like and dislike in both Richard and Bolingbroke, and Shakespeare engages our sentiments first with one and then with the other as the play moves to its destined end. Again, he does not judge but leaves the troubling choices to us.

1.1   The play opens on a scene of formal ceremony, as the king presides over a tense confrontation in which Henry Bolingbroke, the son of the Duke of Lancaster, accuses Thomas Mowbray, Duke of Norfolk, of high treason. The royal court is the highest judicial body in the land and formalities are observed, with ritual questions and ritual replies intoned before the moment of accusation arrives. There is much ceremony in this play, expressed in language traditionally employed in the public enactment and definition of the king's role; and Shakespeare often uses rhymed verse in such scenes to enhance the formal dignity of the occasion. But he also rhymes speeches that probe beneath the public display to explore the human passions it conceals.

The royal family relationships are of importance in the history plays, where the names of those both living and dead are frequently invoked. Both Richard and Bolingbroke are grandsons of Edward III, but by tradition the line of succession to the throne passed down from eldest son to eldest son. Richard's father, the Black Prince, was the eldest of Edward's sons, but he predeceased the old king by a year, hence the crown descended legitimately to Richard.* Since the king is at this time childless, Bolingbroke stands next in line behind his aged father, the Duke of Lancaster, hence has a legitimate claim to the throne once the duke dies. Richard may thus consider his cousin a possible threat to his reign, and though he declares that he will judge the case impartially, he is not likely to forget their kinship.

---

*Richard actually inherited the crown at age eleven in 1377. The time frame of the play, however, is much later, generally from 1398 to 1400, at the end of his twenty-three-year reign.

Bolingbroke and Mowbray exchange insults, and the former throws down his "gage [glove]," a challenge to a duel in "all the rites of knighthood." Mowbray picks it up to signify that he accepts. Bolingbroke accuses Mowbray of misusing the king's money and plotting the murder of Thomas Woodstock, the Duke of Gloucester, another of Edward III's sons. Mowbray denies the charge and then throws down his own gage, which Bolingbroke in turn takes up. The king, attempting to avoid bloodshed, directs the Duke of Lancaster to reason with his son while he tries to persuade Mowbray to abandon his challenge. But honor is now at stake and neither succeeds, since Mowbray must defend his "fair name" and Bolingbroke insists that to withdraw his accusations now would "wound [his] honor." Richard, declaring that "we were not born to sue, but to command," orders them to prepare for a contest of arms, where justice will be determined by "the victor's chivalry."

This medieval custom of "trial by combat" was based on the belief that God plays a direct role in human affairs and that in any controversy he will favor the righteous cause. Richard is faced by two noblemen, one of whom accuses the other of treason, which the other denies. In the absence of evidence on either side, the trial comes down to a matter of one man's word against another's. Since the challenges stand, the king agrees to a contest of arms, the outcome of which, the tradition holds, will reflect God's judgment in the case.

Some ugly human facts lie just beneath the surface of this ritual. As we learn in the next scene, it is generally believed that Richard himself was responsible for the murder of Gloucester (or Woodstock, as he is frequently called) and that Mowbray dutifully carried out the king's order for the assassination. Richard therefore is stung by Bolingbroke's accusation against Mowbray, which indirectly implicates him in the crime.

1.2 In the following scene the Duchess of Gloucester invokes the family honor in demanding that Lancaster, called John of Gaunt, avenge the murder of his brother. But Gaunt is of the old tradition, believing in the sanctity of the crown. It is God's quarrel, he insists, and if the king, God's deputy, is wrongfully responsible for Gloucester's death, "let heaven revenge, for I may never lift / An angry arm against His minister." The duchess, disappointed that family loyalties have so little weight in matters concerning the king, replies that she will retire to her castle, stripped bare now, she says, of its furnishings, presumably by Richard. There, she mourns, "desolate, desolate, will I hence and die."

1.3   In the next scene we are at the lists in Coventry, an arena where the trial by combat is to take place, and the participants again follow the medieval ritual prescribed for such events. The opponents are called forth. Kneeling before the king, both declare their loyalty to the crown; the accusation and denial are formally announced by heralds, and the two men prepare for the contest. Richard suddenly interrupts, however, and after a brief conference with his council declares that there will be no fight. Rather, he proclaims, the two will be banished from the kingdom, Mowbray for life, Bolingbroke for ten years, both "upon pain of life" should they return. Mowbray responds with a moving speech in which he laments that his exile will deprive him of his "native English language," ending with a poignant regret that the sentence condemns him to "speechless death, / Which robs my tongue from breathing native breath." Richard, insisting that the ceremony be played out in full, requires them both to swear on his sword that they will not in the future conspire together against him. They comply.

Richard then glances at the grieving Gaunt and in sympathy reduces Bolingbroke's exile from ten to six years. When the duke is not consoled, Richard reproaches him, observing that as a member of his council he had agreed to the banishment of his son. He replies sorrowfully, "you urg'd me as a judge, but I had rather / You would have bid me argue like a father." Gaunt here embodies the conflicting loyalties that trouble public figures. As a member of the king's council he agrees to Bolingbroke's exile as a necessary measure to remove a potential threat to the crown, but as a father he grieves at the loss of a son. He submits since, as he had explained to the Duchess of Gloucester, he cannot oppose the will of "God's substitute, / His deputy anointed in His sight."

Bolingbroke later laments his banishment privately to his father. The old duke attempts to resign his son to exile, advising philosophically that "all places that the eye of heaven visits / Are to a wise man ports and happy havens." He urges him to imagine that his destiny lies in "the way thou goest, not whence thou com'st." Bolingbroke puts no faith in imagining, however, asking "who can hold a fire in his hand / By thinking on the frosty Caucasus?" And so they part.

1.4   In the next scene we catch a glimpse of the private Richard, surrounded by his closest confidants—Aumerle, another "cousin," the son of the Duke of York; and Bagot, Green, and Bushy, none of whom are members of the old aristocracy but friends whom the king has raised to prominence and in whose company he can be more himself. He confides in them his concern that Bolingbroke has been cultivating the favor of the people, as if England were his "and he our subjects' next degree in hope."

"Well, he is gone," Green replies confidently, and they turn their attention to the rebellion in Ireland. Richard is determined to lead the campaign against the rebels personally, but he notes that the treasury is bare as a result of "too great a court / And liberal largess." Hence he proposes to "farm our royal realm"—that is, rent out his lands for revenue. Further, if "that come short," he will distribute "blank charters" among his friends, who in his absence can collect additional taxes at will from those able to pay. Bushy enters with the news that Gaunt is mortally ill and asks to see the king. Richard callously anticipates Gaunt's death as yet another source of revenue and agrees to see the dying duke, though with a mocking prayer that "we may make haste and come too late!"

These scenes convey the impression of Richard as a king who insists on ceremonial deference to his position but frivolously wastes his country's wealth on court pleasures, so much so that he must resort to onerous taxation and wrongful seizure of his subjects' lands to support the crown. The staging, the dress, and the behavior of the characters can project the impression of the dissolute and extravagant court that Richard's is said to be.

2.1 We can have little sympathy for Richard at this point, and his encounter with old Gaunt will alienate us even further. The dying duke hopes that his final counsel will persuade Richard to mend his ways, for as he says, "they breathe truth that breathe their words in pain." But his brother, the Duke of York, doubts the king will listen and advises him to save his breath. Gaunt's lament at the state of England contains one of the most moving passages in literature expressing love of one's native land. "This royal throne of kings, this scept'red isle," he complains, "is now leas'd out—I die pronouncing it— / Like to a tenement or pelting [paltry] farm."

The royal party arrives, and Gaunt begins with a play on his name— he is thin and wasted with grief—and then launches into a condemnation of Richard's rule. "A thousand flatterers sit within thy crown," he charges, rendering him unfit to wear it. "It were a shame," he rages on, "to let this land to lease," leaving him no longer king but now "landlord of England." Richard replies angrily that were Gaunt not "brother to great Edward's son" he would have him executed, but the duke turns the remark back on him, accusing him openly of having already spilled "Edward's blood" in murdering Gloucester. Gaunt departs and dies, whereupon Richard seizes all his "plate, coin, revenues, and moveables" to help pay for the Irish wars. York finally speaks out, and with the authority of "the last of noble Edward's sons" counsels against the confiscation of property. He points out that Bolingbroke is now the rightful heir of all the lands and title of the Duke of Lancaster. As the king leaves, York warns him that in appropriating Lancaster's lands, "you pluck a thousand dangers on your head, / You lose a thousand well-disposed hearts." Richard is unmoved. Despite York's rebuke, he is so confident of his uncle's devotion to the ancient traditions that he appoints him governor of England during his absence in Ireland.

When the royal party departs, the noblemen left behind guardedly voice their discontent with Richard's circle of flattering friends and the heavy taxation of the old nobility. Northumberland finally reveals that Bolingbroke, at the head of an army and accompanied by a group of disaffected English lords, is even then preparing to land at Ravenspurgh, on England's northeast coast. They rush out, eager to join him.

2.2   After Richard's departure for Ireland, the queen confides in Bushy that her parting from her husband has left her with the fear that "some unborn sorrow ripe in Fortune's womb / Is coming towards" her.* Green arrives to give substance to her ill-defined fears, announcing that Bolingbroke has landed and that several powerful nobles have joined him. York enters, complaining that he has no money to raise an army, and he directs Richard's lords to "go muster men." As we have seen, York is torn between his loyalty to the crown and his conviction that Bolingbroke has been wronged, but he has no doubt where his duty lies and is determined to oppose the invasion. Richard's lords have no intention of

---

*Shakespeare again adapts history to his dramatic needs. Richard II's queen, Isabel of France, was ten years old at the time. But if a play about a king requires that he have a mature queen, Shakespeare will provide one.

mustering men, however—Bushy and Green flee to the refuge of Bristow (Bristol) Castle, and Bagot leaves for Ireland.

2.3 The scene shifts to Bolingbroke, now the Duke of Lancaster. He is accompanied on the march by Northumberland, who addresses him with all the deference due a monarch, obsequiously assuring him that the long journey has been made light by the pleasure of his company. His son, Harry Percy (later Hotspur), approaches and is introduced with all proper courtesy to Bolingbroke. Berkeley enters and is so indiscreet as to address Bolingbroke as "my Lord of Hereford," his old title, for which he is duly reprimanded. York appears, and when a kneeling Bolingbroke addresses him respectfully as "my gracious uncle," he cuts through all this ceremonial posturing about names and titles, "tut, tut! grace me no grace, nor uncle me no uncle." York, with no soldiers to back him up, attempts to shame his nephew into submission by accusing him of returning from exile in disobedience to the king and of aspiring to the throne. Bolingbroke resorts to a legal quibble—he was banished as Hereford but returns as Lancaster—and protests that he comes only to claim his rightful inheritance. York is skeptical of his nephew's motives—as the audience may be too—but as his "power is weak and all ill left," he has no choice but to open the castle at Berkeley to the rebel forces. Bolingbroke accepts but asks his uncle to accompany him to Bristol, where he intends to deal with Richard's lords—"the caterpillars of the commonwealth," as he calls them.

2.4 Richard is returning from Ireland, but tardily; and the Welsh, who are his chief supporters, grow tired of waiting and disband their forces. Salisbury foresees the king's fall, drawing on the imagery of universal order to express his disquiet:

> I see thy glory like a shooting-star
> Fall to the base earth from the firmament.
> Thy sun sets weeping in the lowly west,
> Witnessing storms to come, woe, and unrest.

3.1 Bolingbroke, who has moved swiftly to occupy Bristol, confronts Bushy and Green. Maintaining the posture of loyalty to the crown, he accuses them of misleading "a prince, a royal king" and of encouraging "a divorce betwixt his queen and him," thereby breaking "the possession

of a royal bed." The accusation emphasizes the image of Richard as an ineffectual king so preoccupied with his "lascivious" court that he neglects
his public, and private, duties. However much Bolingbroke may protest
his modest motives, the political reality of his position is that once he sets
foot on the path to rebellion he must pursue it to its ultimate end. In
open defiance of Richard's sentence he has returned from exile, returned
moreover at the head of an army. Should he fall short of deposing the
king, he can expect swift and fatal retribution. He condemns the two
lords to death and declares his devotion to the queen.

3.2   In the next scene Richard suddenly comes alive as a dramatic
figure, gifted with a new eloquence, inspired, it seems, by adversity. Returning from Ireland, he steps once again on English soil and kneels to
gather a handful of it, speaking of his love of country as movingly as had
Gaunt. He imagines a more personal bond, however: the reunion of "a
long-parted mother with her child," and he urges "my earth" to resist the
"treacherous feet" whose "usurping steps do trample thee." In this scene
and the one to follow, Richard defines with impassioned eloquence the
claim of Renaissance monarchs that they are anointed by God as his
deputies on earth and are protected on the throne by the power of the
Deity. Both he and the loyal Bishop of Carlisle prophesy divine retribution in punishment for any who challenge the king's sacred authority.
Richard's lofty vision of the kingship is progressively undercut by reports
that his earthly powers are shrinking as his followers desert him, and his
mood swings wildly between defiance and despair. He may indeed have
God on his side, but Bolingbroke has soldiers.

At first Richard confidently proclaims his supremacy: "Not all the
water in the rough rude sea / Can wash the balm off from an anointed
king." When Salisbury enters to tell him that the Welsh have deserted,
he falters momentarily, but quickly recovers: "I had forgot myself, am I
not king? / Awake, thou coward majesty!" Scroop approaches, and even
before he can speak, Richard seems to submit: "Say, is my kingdom lost?
why, 'twas my care." On hearing that his subjects have turned against
him and that his close friends have been executed, he sinks into despair
and reminds himself of his mortality. Aumerle asks where York's forces
are, but Richard waves the thought aside: "No matter where—of comfort
no man speak. / Let's talk of graves, of worms, and epitaphs." He contin-

ues in this vein—"for God's sake let us sit upon the ground / And tell sad stories of the death of kings"—and concludes with the admission that, for all his majesty, he is but a man: "I live with bread like you, feel want, / Taste grief, need friends." On learning that York is powerless and has yielded to the rebels, he dismisses his followers and prepares to move "from Richard's night, to Bolingbroke's fair day."

3.3 Bolingbroke, approaching Flint Castle with his forces, learns that the king is in residence there. Maintaining his posture as a loyal lord seeking only his just inheritance, he sends Northumberland to speak for him. The king appears above on the battlements of the castle and sternly rebukes Northumberland for failing to kneel to him, reminding him of the divine sanction of the crown. God, he proclaims, will punish those who threaten him, sending "armies of pestilence [that] shall strike / Your children yet unborn, and unbegot." The stolid Northumberland, unfazed by the outburst, insists on Bolingbroke's loyalty, claiming that his presence "hath no further scope / Than for his lineal royalties" and promising that, once these are returned to him, Bolingbroke will dismiss his army.

Richard quickly agrees to "his fair demands"—and then, in a private *aside* to Aumerle, laments that he must do so. The very act of restoring Lancaster's holdings to Bolingbroke seems to break his spirit, and it is he himself who first voices the possibility of relinquishing the crown. In a long and moving speech he contemplates exchanging all the glories of a king for a monastic life ending in "a little grave, / A little little grave, an obscure grave." He simply gives up, asking Northumberland, "what says King Bolingbroke? Will his Majesty / Give Richard leave to live till Richard die?" When requested to descend to "the base court" and speak with Bolingbroke, Richard dramatizes his fall—"down, down I come"— and compares himself to Phaeton, the youth from Greek myth who drove Apollo's sun chariot across the sky and was killed when he lost control of the horses, who plunged the sun toward earth. In a face-to-face encounter, he submits to the will of Bolingbroke, and the party sets out for London.

The scene has a powerful visual impact. Richard at first appears above. Northumberland from below refuses to kneel and speaks for Bolingbroke, itself an affront, since the inferior lord should be pleading for himself. Then the king enacts his fall by descending to meet his adversary on equal ground in "the base court." It is said that he surrenders too readily, that his submission is a sign of his essential weakness as a king and a man, and we are perhaps dismayed at his lack of resistance to the bully Bolingbroke. He wallows in self-pity and overdramatizes his defeat rather then facing it with dignity. On the other hand, for all of Bolingbroke's protestations of loyalty, it is clear that he has his eye on the crown, and Richard is aware of the realities of his position. He is a king in the ancient tradition, but the old reverence for the monarch will no longer protect him from the new breed of power brokers embodied by Bolingbroke.

3.4   The following scene, set in the garden of the Duke of York's castle, is justly admired both for its lyric lines and the richness of the imagery from the medieval belief in universal order. The queen and her attendants conceal themselves and overhear the dialogue between the gardener and his man, who voice the sentiments of the common people toward the controversies dividing the mighty. In lines that define the garden as a microcosm of England, the gardener compares his management of plants with the governing of a kingdom. He issues instructions for tending it in horticultural terms weighted with political significance: oppression, execution, commonwealth, and government. The men know that Richard's lords have been executed and "the wasteful king" taken. And they regret that he has not governed his kingdom as dutifully as they trim their garden, failing, for example, to prune "over-proud" fruit trees. It was a lack of diligence, "the waste of idle hours," the gardener concludes, that has brought the king down. The queen emerges from hiding and, stunned by this news, rebukes the gardener for bringing it. He does not resent her curse but out of pity intends to plant "a bank of rue" where her tear fell.

4.1   Bolingbroke is soon confronted with the same situation that faced Richard in the opening scenes of the play—one lord accusing and another denying a charge of treason. Bagot (who apparently never made it to Ireland) accuses Aumerle of implication in Gloucester's murder and of speaking against Bolingbroke. Aumerle denies the accusation and throws down his gage, whereupon various lords in attendance throw theirs down as well, demonstrating their allegiance to one or the other man until—in what appears to be a parody of the custom—the stage is littered with gloves. Bolingbroke is confronted with a serious division among his nobles and announces that there will be no immediate contest, declaring that the issue will "rest under gage" until a later date. Nothing more is said of the controversy, though Aumerle's subsequent conduct lends substance to Bagot's allegations.

York enters to announce that Richard has agreed to relinquish the throne. The loyal Bishop of Carlisle protests this passing of the crown. He utters prophetic warnings that God will punish England for the deed, and in his words Shakespeare foreshadows the civil wars to come, characterized as just retribution on a land that commits such a sacrilege: "The blood of English shall manure the ground, / And future ages groan for this foul act." Northumberland, with nice irony, compliments the bishop on his speech and promptly arrests him for treason.

Bolingbroke then directs that Richard be brought forward to renounce the throne publicly.* But the king, it appears, will not go quietly. While a perplexed Bolingbroke looks on, he seizes the stage and dramatizes his fall, even compelling his dumbstruck adversary to participate in the theatrics. He first complains that he has been brought into the presence of his successor too soon, before he has "learn'd / To insinuate, flatter, bow and bend my knee." Then he suddenly seizes the crown itself and impulsively thrusts it at Bolingbroke, who grasps it in a startled reflex, resulting in a dramatic visual image of the two holding it between them. Richard rhapsodizes on the spectacle by depicting himself and Bolingbroke as "two buckets" in a well, the one low and full of tears, the other mounted "up on high." The stolid Bolingbroke responds unimaginatively, "I thought you had been willing to resign." Richard replies with more poetry, a play on the word, "care," but Bolingbroke, sensing that he is being cast in a supporting role in this drama, returns to business: "Are you content to resign the crown?" This Richard does in a moving recital of his surrender. But more is demanded, as Northumberland insists that he read aloud a long list of his crimes against England. He pleads that his eyes are too full of tears to do so, but he will admit to one crime—he is indeed a traitor for conspiring with them "t'undeck the pompous body of

---

*The so-called "deposition scene" was omitted from editions of the play until after Elizabeth's death, for fear that she might be unduly sensitive to the portrayal of a monarch dethroned.

a king," an act, he says, that has reversed the political order of the kingdom, making "glory base, and sovereignty a slave; / Proud majesty a subject, state a peasant."

In a final dramatic gesture Richard asks for a mirror, and an exasperated Bolingbroke calls for one to be brought. Gazing on his reflected face, Richard questions if it is the same one that had looked out on others from the throne, that "like the sun did make beholders wink." Declaring that "a brittle glory shineth in this face," he dashes the mirror to the ground and, turning to Bolingbroke, advises him to take note how soon sorrow can destroy a face. Richard then turns to leave. When asked where he wishes to go, he replies defiantly, anywhere "so I were from your sights." Bolingbroke, by now angered by his theatrical display, curtly orders him taken to the Tower.

The royal party departs, leaving behind a group still loyal to Richard. Carlisle repeats his solemn prophecy that "children yet unborn / Shall feel this day as sharp as thorn," and Aumerle confides in them that he has devised a plot against the usurper. So at the moment of Bolingbroke's triumph, a conspiracy is already afoot to dethrone him, only the first that will trouble his reign.

5.1 Richard, escorted by Northumberland to the Tower, meets his grieving queen, who cannot understand his docility. "The lion dying," she protests, "thrusteth forth his paw / And wounds the earth, if nothing else, with rage." But Richard persists in his mood of paralyzing self-pity, counseling her to "think I am dead" and asking that when in time to come she sits at night with others exchanging stories, "tell thou the lamentable tale of me." Northumberland informs him that he will be held at Pomfret Castle rather than the Tower, and Richard, looking straight at his captor, predicts that Northumberland will in time become discontented and rebel against the new king as he has the old. The queen asks to accompany her husband to Pomfret, but Northumberland refuses, remarking dryly, "that were some love, but little policy," and leads the mournful Richard off to prison.

Shakespeare arouses a set of conflicting sympathies. On the one hand, Richard wrongfully confiscates his uncles' property at their deaths and is probably responsible for speeding one of them to his grave. But these are dynastic matters resulting from a struggle for power within the royal

family. As a king, he does not appear to rule tyrannically. The old gardener does not charge him with cruelty, only idleness and the failure to
"lop off" those grown "over-proud." Richard's heartless response to the
dying Gaunt loses our sympathy, but our sentiments are surely changed
by the painful spectacle of his fall from power, scenes in which he vents
his grief in soaring poetry.

On the other hand there is Bolingbroke, who is unjustly banished—a
sentence, it would appear, that hastened his father's death. He returns, he
says, only to claim what is rightfully his. He is a stolid, unimaginative
figure with none of Richard's eloquence, but he has a common touch, the
ability to win the peoples' hearts, which Richard, with his exalted vision
of his place, totally lacks. We may question, however, Bolingbroke's
method of seizing power, a coup d'état in which he simply gathers sufficient force to topple the legitimate government and place himself at the
head of the state. The traditional system of passing the crown from eldest
son to eldest son at least ensured a relatively peaceful transition of power,
sparing the people civil disorders.

5.2   In the Duke of York's house, he is describing to his wife Bolingbroke's earlier triumphal return to London from Wales, the victor
leading the procession grandly to the enthusiastic shouts of the fickle
public, Richard riding behind, a pitiful figure upon whom the people
threw dust from the windows above. York is saddened by the memory of
the fallen king, who, he says, endured the ordeal with patience, "his face
still combating with tears and smiles." But the old duke confirms his belief that "heaven hath a hand in these events" and declares his allegiance
to the new king, "whose state and honor I for aye allow."

York's allegiance is soon tested. Learning of his son Aumerle's complicity in a plot against the throne, he calls for his boots and horse, determined to report the treachery to the king. His duchess attempts to deter
him, pleading that he threatens the life of his own child, but to no avail.
The duke dashes off, followed closely by his wife and son in a race to see
who can reach the king first.

5.3   At the royal castle, Bolingbroke is asking if anyone can tell him
of his "unthrifty son" who is now heir to the throne. He is reported to
spend his time in the taverns and "stews" of London, where he voices contempt for the responsibilities of his position. The king here introduces
the audience to Prince Hal, who will be the central figure of Shake-

speare's next three plays, suggesting that he may have had those to follow well in mind as he composed *Richard II*.

Bolingbroke's inquiries are interrupted by Aumerle, who arrives in advance of his father and falls on his knees, asking pardon before disclosing his crime. Since he is the son of York, he is also a cousin to Bolingbroke, and this may account for the king's response, granting pardon on the condition that the crime was only intended, not committed, though he is naturally curious about what it was. York bursts in to reveal the plot and Aumerle's involvement in it, demanding that his son be punished for his treachery. Before the king can respond, the duchess rushes in. Falling on her knees as well, she begs forgiveness for her son. Bolingbroke, perhaps embarrassed or exasperated by the spectacle of these three kneeling before him, may well be pondering that if this is what it means to be a king, perhaps it was a mistake to seek the crown. He tries twice to raise the duchess from her knees, but she refuses until he forgives her son, which he finally does—perhaps more to escape this ludicrous scene than out of any loyalty to family ties. He condemns the other conspirators to death, however, and expresses the hope that in the future Aumerle will prove loyal. Bolingbroke, it would appear, is more lenient with his cousin than Richard was with him.

5.4   In the following scene Shakespeare constructs a defense for Henry IV (Bolingbroke), who, it was believed, ordered Richard's death, even as Richard had ordered Gloucester's. In a reenactment of the well-known account of Henry II's outburst against Thomas à Becket, the king is heard to say, "have I no friend will rid me of this living fear?" Exton, a lord seeking favor with the king, interprets the remark as a sanction for the murder of Richard.

5.5   Meanwhile, in Pomfret castle, Richard contemplates his state, striving to "compare / This prison where I live unto the world." Having little to do, he muses on his thoughts, his only subjects now in his solitary kingdom. He hears music, but it only reminds him that he has "wasted time, and now doth time waste me," prompting the thought that Bolingbroke's time has come and his is past. A groom manages to gain entrance, a man who cared for the royal horse, the "roan Barbary" on which Bolingbroke rode during his triumphal march through London. Though a minor figure, he gives us a brief, final glimpse of the commoners' loyalty to the crown. The keeper enters, dismisses the groom, and offers Richard food. When the keeper, on Exton's orders, refuses to taste it first, as was the custom to avoid poisoning, Richard flies into a rage. Finally! "Patience is stale, and I am weary of it," he cries, and strikes out at the keeper. Exton and others enter and Richard struggles with them, according to contemporary accounts killing some, but he is finally overcome. In his dying breath he foretells the blight his murder will inflict on England: "Exton, thy fierce hand / Hath with the king's blood stain'd the king's own land."

5.6 Back at court, the king receives news of the death of the conspirators and pardons only the Bishop of Carlisle, whom he banishes to a monastic life. The bishop has been an enemy, but he speaks with the voice of a biblical prophet, a figure whom monarchs are superstitiously reluctant to tamper with. Exton enters, anticipating praise for his service, but he receives instead a rebuke. The king absolves himself of blame for Richard's murder while acknowledging openly that "though I did wish him dead, / I hate the murtherer, love him murthered." He pledges himself to a crusade to the Holy Land in hopes of cleansing England of the sin of killing a king anointed by God.

Richard troubles us—he does, and yet does not, deserve his fate. He utters some of Shakespeare's most moving evocations of despair, but he seems to embrace his downfall, relishing the drama of it. He submits with "for God's sake, let us sit upon the ground"; engages in theatrics at his deposition, brandishing the crown and shattering the mirror; and utters a pathetic appeal to the queen to tell "the lamentable tale of me." Not until the very moment of his death, when patience becomes "stale," does he rise to the righteous rage of Shakespeare's tragic heroes who defy their fate and achieve a splendid dignity in their dying. He has, it seems, placed all his faith in the inviolable sanctity of the crown, and when earthly powers range against it, he has no spiritual forces to fall back on. It is as if he feels himself abandoned by God, and so he simply surrenders to despair—too readily, it seems, too meekly—when he discovers that the mantle of divine sanction in which he has wrapped himself offers no protection against the swords and lances of Bolingbroke.

Richard II is certainly compelling theater in itself, and it provides the narrative starting point for the plays that follow it in historical sequence. Its themes reecho in the three that carry the action to the death of Henry

V and the four that, though composed earlier, pursue the chronicle forward to the ascension of Henry VII, the first of the Tudor monarchs. The terrible prophecies of England's future suffering voiced by Richard and Carlisle are realized in the strife-torn reign of Henry IV. His death was followed by the all-too-brief ascendancy of Henry V, that "star of England" who blazed across the sky of history and then, cometlike, was gone as soon as he appeared. His death ushered in the time of devastation for England, the shattering War of the Roses and Richard III's short reign of terror, at the end of which, it was said, the burden of retribution was finally lifted and the nation cleansed of the sin of murdering "God's minister."

HENRY IV, PART 1

TWO PLAYS, *King Henry IV, Parts 1 and 2*, follow *Richard II* in historical sequence. They chronicle the troubled reign of Henry Bolingbroke, Duke of Lancaster, who deposed Richard and replaced him on the throne as Henry IV, only to have his years in power torn by the constant rebellion of disaffected nobles, especially the fiery Percys, the earls of Northumberland who guarded the Scottish border. The central figure of the plays, however, is the king's son, the Prince of Wales, or Duke of Hereford, or Harry of Monmouth, or Hal, as he is variously called, the young heir to the throne who prefers to spend his time carousing in the taverns of London rather than assume the responsibilities of his high office. There, in Eastcheap's Boar's Head tavern, he savors his youth in drink, song, wit, and trickery with Sir John Falstaff in the company of the common people of England. One of the central *themes* of the plays is therefore a young man's coming of age, his reluctant emergence from frivolity and self-indulgence to accept the obligations of maturity.

Henry IV, Part 1 opens where *Richard II* ends, with the king reaffirming his intention to join a crusade to the Holy Land. His resolve is short-lived, however, since England is beset with wars on her Scottish and Welsh borders. A rebellion brews as Hotspur, son of the Earl of Northumberland, momentarily unites Welsh, Scot, and northern English nobles against the king. Meanwhile Prince Hal is unconcerned, content to carouse with his friends at the Boar's Head while his father contends with his enemies. Not until they challenge the king at Shrewsbury does Hal emerge from his life of carefree frivolity, accept the responsibility of his position, join his father's forces, slay Hotspur in battle, and begin to enter into manhood.

1.1 As the play opens, Henry IV renews his vow to lead an English army to "the sepulchre of Christ," but news of the defeat of royal forces and the capture of Edmund Mortimer, the Earl of March, at the hands of the Welsh under Owen Glendower, causes the king to set his plan aside. There is trouble in the north as well, where the Scots under the Earl of Douglas are also in rebellion, but the news from that front is more encouraging. Young Hotspur, the son of the Earl of Northumberland, has defeated the Scots and taken a number of high-ranking prisoners. The report of Hotspur's victory turns the king's thoughts to his own son. He envies the earl, he says, whose son "is the theme of honor's tongue," while "riot and dishonor stain" the name of the prince. From the outset, then, Hotspur is set up as a *foil* to Hal, one whose presence on the stage will serve to highlight certain qualities of the chief figure of the play. The two are similar in many ways, both apparently about the same age, the sons of warlike fathers, even bearing the same name, Henry.*

This short scene introduces two themes that will emerge in this and later plays. First, the kingdom is beset by rebellions within, so much so that any thought of campaigns abroad must be set aside. These troubles seem to confirm the dark prophecies of the Bishop of Carlisle in *Richard II*, who warned the newly crowned Henry that he had placed a curse upon the land by deposing the rightful king—and as a consequence, "the blood of England shall manure the ground / And future ages groan for this foul act." The second theme is the wayward behavior of the prince. And just where is he, anyway, while his father is contending with these dangerous enemies?

1.2 We learn directly. He is at home with his companion, Sir John Falstaff, who is sleeping off a night of indulgence. Picture Falstaff, who may be the best-known comic figure on the English stage, as a man approaching sixty, fat, white-haired, and red-faced, with a mouth that is always ready for a joke or a cup of "sack" (sherry). He is a thief who lives by his wits, a thoroughly inappropriate associate for the Prince of Wales but a delightful companion prepared at any moment to dance, sing, drink, or engage in trickery, either innocently for a laugh or seriously for gain. The

---

*Indeed, there are enough Henrys in the play to cause possible confusion—the king, the prince, and the Percys, father and son. But Shakespeare uses titles and familiar names so as to distinguish them from one another.

relationship between the two is immediately evident as Falstaff struggles out of sleep and asks Hal the time of day. The prince answers this perfectly natural question with a string of insults, to which Falstaff, now fully awake, replies with barbs of his own: "I prithee, sweet wag, when thou art king, God save thy grace—majesty I should say, for grace thou wilt have none."

They go on in this vein for some time, exchanging good-humored insults, each enjoying the other's wit. It is clear that they delight in the play on words, as in Falstaff's mocking "here apparent" and "heir apparent," and the pun on the two meanings of "suits" from the worlds of law and apparel. Poins enters. He is a "gentleman-in-waiting" to the prince, a member of the royal court, not one of the commoners we meet in later scenes, but he enters fully into the spirit of the group, immediately exchanging insults with Falstaff. There is no love lost between the two, and their barbs tend to have more bite to them. Poins has a plan to rob pilgrims on the road to Canterbury, a scheme that receives Falstaff's prompt approval but about which Hal has his doubts: "Who I? rob? I a thief? not I, by my faith." A disappointed Falstaff departs, and Poins reveals his true intent—it is to be a trick on their friend! As he explains, they will agree to meet at a designated spot on the road, but the two of them will fail to appear. Falstaff and his crew will rob the pilgrims, after which Hal and Poins, disguised in "buckram," * will surprise the robbers and relieve them of their spoils.

And what is the purpose of this complicated scheme? As Poins explains, "the virtue of this jest will be the incomprehensible lies that this same fat rogue will tell us when we meet at supper," and the fun they will have once they reveal what actually happened. Hal agrees, for this is the very essence of their sport. They listen to Falstaff harangue them with outrageous tales about his courage, his martial prowess, or his sexual conquests, catch him in an outright lie, and then revel in his wit as he invents further lies to work his way out of the original falsehood. It's all in good fun. But what sort of behavior is this for the Prince of Wales, conspiring to rob his father's subjects on a holy pilgrimage? It may make for a good jest, but it hardly befits the heir to the throne to turn thief.

What can Hal be thinking? In a brief *soliloquy* closing the scene we

*A stiff canvas overall.

learn his thoughts, and it appears that he is quite calculating about his association with the less reputable levels of London society—the thieves, whores, and drunkards of Eastcheap. The speech leaves the impression that he knows exactly what he is doing. "I know you all," he says, "and will awhile uphold / The unyoked humor of your idleness." He compares himself to the sun, a common image in an age that believed in *universal order*—the king rules his country, it was said, as the sun rules the heavens. He will allow himself to be covered for a time by "base contagious clouds" so that when he emerges from the "foul and ugly mists" he will "be more wond'red at." Shakespeare strives here to rescue Hal from the reputation of a mindless, irresponsible playboy intent only on his own pleasures. Admittedly his self-justification may seem a bit contrived, his inner thoughts too much at variance with the outer Hal. But let us withhold judgment, awaiting more on this theme in later episodes.

1.3 We return to the king's court, a shift in setting that will be the pattern in the early acts of the play as we move back and forth between the castle and the tavern. Henry confronts his angry nobles, the brothers Northumberland and Worcester, and young Hotspur, all of whom were influential in helping him to the crown. The king complains that they have refused to release the Scottish prisoners to him. This is a matter not only of honor but of gain as well, since the Scots will be given their freedom only after the payment of a substantial ransom. The Percys were fighting in the name of the king, hence the prisoners are by right his. By refusing to surrender them, they would be in open defiance of the monarch. Henry dismisses Worcester, who is apparently too angry to show proper respect, and hears out Northumberland, who denies that they refused to turn over the prisoners. Hotspur explains that even before the smoke of battle had cleared, when he was catching his breath after an exhausting fight, a member of the king's court came by demanding the prisoners. The image is that of a court fop, "neat and trimly dressed / Fresh as a bridegroom . . . perfumed like a milliner," who took snuff to ward off the stench of the battlefield. Hotspur was so incensed by this "popinjay," he claims, that he sent him on his way, no offense intended.

Henry replies that this is all very well, but he still does not have the prisoners. He suspects they are being withheld on the condition that he ransom Edmund Mortimer, the Earl of March, who was captured by Glendower. The king adds insult to injury by accusing Mortimer of trea-

sonously surrendering to the Welsh, a charge that Hotspur heatedly denies. Henry rebukes him and stalks off, threatening, "send me your prisoners, or you'll hear of it."

Hotspur is enraged, particularly since Mortimer is his wife's brother.
Worcester returns to feed the flames of his anger with the information
that Richard II, before embarking for Ireland, had declared Mortimer
next in line to the throne. Mortimer is the grandson of yet another son of
Edward III, the Duke of Clarence (he had seven sons), so if Richard did
indeed designate him heir, he represents a threat to the king, whose suspicions about collusion are strengthened by the fact that, while a captive
of Glendower, Mortimer has married the Welshman's daughter!* Hotspur
rages on about the injustice done "Richard, that sweet lovely rose"
(whom he had actually helped unseat), about the prisoners, and about his
hatred of Henry. His exasperated elders finally calm him down, and they
devise a plot against the king. They will free the prisoners without ransom and enlist Douglas in a powerful alliance of Scots, Welsh, and northern English nobles to challenge Henry.

Thus, in both this scene and the one preceding it the characters hatch
plots, and the contrast between them is striking. In the first, Hal conspires in a frivolous scheme to trick Falstaff, one which, as we shall see,
results in the prince robbing his own father. In the latter, the nobles conspire in a serious plot to dethrone the king. The contrast between the two
young men is also telling. Hal wastes his time in a meaningless jest while
Hotspur places himself at the center of momentous events. In this, our
first view of Hotspur, we find him a valiant soldier, whom the king, on
hearing of his victory, had called "the theme of honor's tongue." He is impetuous, loyal to his family, quick to anger—as befits his name—and he
does not suffer fools gladly. As an obvious foil to Hal, we may ask, what
qualities of the prince is he meant to lend emphasis to, by comparison or
contrast?

2.1–2 We may pass over the first scene of Act Two, which is omitted from some productions. Gadshill is on reconnaissance to spy out po-

---

*Both Shakespeare and his source, the historian Richard Holinshed, confuse Mor-
timer with his nephew, another Edmund. Mortimer did marry Glendower's daughter,
but he was not the Earl of March. His nephew held the title, and it was he whom
Richard named heir. But no matter!

tential victims.* Later that night the thieves wait in ambush at Gad's Hill
and Falstaff complains about the absence of Hal and Poins. Gadshill arrives with the news that they will be robbing not pilgrims but men carrying money for the king's "exchequer" (treasurer). Everything goes as
planned. Falstaff and his crew carry out the robbery. Hal and Poins, disguised in buckram, surprise them and they run off, leaving the money
behind. As Poins says, it is a trick that will be worth "argument for a
week, laughter for a month, and a good jest for ever."

2.3   From this relatively harmless prank, we turn now to the ominous conspiracy against the king. Hotspur reads a letter from an unnamed correspondent who is lukewarm toward the plan. His wife enters
and demands to know what is going on. He hasn't shared her bed for two
weeks, and she tells him that he talks in his sleep "of sallies and retires, of
trenches, tents, / Of palisadoes, frontiers, parapets" and all the other elements of medieval warfare. Hotspur ignores her, asking a servant about
packets dispatched and horses collected. She insists that if he loves her he
will confide in her, to which he replies that he does not love her and then
calls for his horse. He relents, however, and affirms his love, but insists
that she ask no further: "I must not have you henceforth question me /
Whither I go, nor reason whereabout. / Whither I must, I must." This
seems excessively stern, but the men of the time seemed intent upon protecting their women from the harsh realities of their dangerous world, as
if to preserve some small corner of innocence in it. The incident calls to
mind Portia, who wounds herself in order to persuade Brutus to reveal
the conspiracy against Caesar (*Julius Caesar*). Lady Percy is somewhat
more practical, threatening to break *Hotspur's* finger if he doesn't tell.

2.4   Back at the Boar's Head tavern, Hal and Poins await the arrival
of Falstaff. This long comic scene defines the relationship between Hal
and Falstaff, so it will be of value to follow it in somewhat more detail
than those to follow. The prince has been mingling with the tavern's
"drawers" (waiters) and relates to Poins rather contemptuously how they
make up to him, calling him "a Corinthian, a lad of mettle, a good boy."
He arranges to have some fun with Francis, one of the drawers, and tells
Poins to place himself in the next room and call for service while he talks

---

*Gadshill is both a character in the play, as here, and the site of the robbery, Gad's
Hill. I have no idea why.

to the lad. Francis is indentured to the tavern owner, and to violate his apprenticeship would be a breach of contract punishable by law. Hal tempts him with the outrageous reward of a thousand pounds for a bit of sugar he had given the prince earlier, and the unspoken implication that Francis might secure a place in his household. Poins keeps calling for service, to which the bewildered drawer answers, "Anon, anon" (I'm coming, I'm coming), while Hal pours out his wit, thoroughly confusing the boy. The innkeeper finally enters to send Francis about his business while Hal and Poins enjoy a good laugh at the jest. It is a cruel joke, one that shows Hal in a rather unattractive light, hence it is sometimes omitted from productions.

Hal is in good humor. He mocks first Francis and then Hotspur, the first indication of his awareness that he is being compared unfavorably to young Percy. His mockery has the flavor of an overly sophisticated college man ridiculing a slow-witted but well-known athlete, the stereotypical "jock." He pictures "the Hotspur of the north" as a thickheaded warrior who kills so many Scots before breakfast and then complains of his "quiet life." Hal ends with the impulse to put on an extemporaneous play about Hotspur, which, though it never takes place, prepares us for the one that does. This, it appears, is the way they pass the time at the Boar's Head, staging short satirical pieces about public figures, a medieval version of "Saturday Night Live."

Falstaff enters, grumbling about "cowards," calling angrily for "a cup of sack," and accusing Hal and Poins of running away from the scene of the robbery. They had the money, he complains, but unknown assailants attacked and took it from them, while Hal and Poins, cowards both, took to their heels. The fun of the scene arises from his outrageous account of the mounting odds he then faced at Gad's Hill. As he speaks the assailants increase from two to four, then seven, nine, and finally eleven whom he claims to have personally "peppered" while Hal and Poins egg him on. They finally catch him in an outright lie—he could not have known his opponents were dressed in "Kendal green" if it was so dark that he could not see his hand before him—and they taunt him to explain himself. He bristles importantly, exclaiming that he would never speak "upon compulsion." Hal, momentarily checked, explains what actually happened, demanding again that Falstaff explain himself. He postures once more, precipitating a fusillade of mutual insults, Hal calling him, among other things, a "sanguine coward," a "bed-presser," and a "huge hill of flesh," and Falstaff responding in kind with a string of expletives. Shakespeare has the richest vocabulary of insults of any writer in the English language, and he displays it at its most colorful in the exchanges between these two.

The purpose of the prank is to force Falstaff to work his way out of his extravagant lies, and Poins prods him: "Come, let's hear, Jack—what trick hast thou now?" And, indeed, Falstaff is never at a loss for a "trick." He claims he knew all along that one of those in "Kendal green" was Hal and, as he puts it, on "instinct" he refrained from attacking "the true prince." It is indeed an outrageous conceit; but it is readily accepted by all in the frolic spirit of the group of friends, as Falstaff celebrates, "by the Lord, lads, I am glad you have the money," and enlivens the scene with a call for a "play extempore."

The general hilarity is interrupted by news of a court messenger at the tavern door. Falstaff volunteers to "send him packing," the customary response, it would appear, to all messengers from that quarter, and in his absence Hal wittily shames the other members of his party. The knight returns with news of the impending rebellion and Hal's summons to court the following day. Anticipating a stormy interview between the prince and his father, Falstaff proposes a "play extempore" in which he will take the part of the king and Hal will "practice an answer" for his behavior. This they do, with Falstaff in mock solemnity chastising Hal for the dissolute company he keeps—all reprobate, he says, with the sole exception of "a goodly portly man" with "a cheerful look, a pleasing eye, and a most noble carriage." "There is virtue in that Falstaff," he declares, and urges Hal to banish the rest of his company but "him keep with."

So the mock interview with Hal's father becomes an exchange about the character of Falstaff. The prince interrupts and insists that they change places—he will play the king and Sir John his son. Hal immediately raises the issue, "there is a devil haunts thee in the likeness of an old fat man, a tun of man is thy companion," and he continues with a litany of insults, all in the spirit of playful mockery but with an underlying edge to them. Falstaff defends himself, cleverly turning his faults to virtues. If to drink "sack and sugar," "to be old and merry," and to be fat are considered wicked, he replies, then much of the world is wicked as well. It is an engaging argument, and he again advises Hal, as the player king, to banish all his corrupting associates with the exception of sweet, kind, true, and valiant, though admittedly old, Jack Falstaff. To banish Falstaff, he declares, would be to "banish all the world." Hal regards him silently and, acknowledging perhaps the truth of what he says, replies, "I do, I will." It is a line that can be delivered in various ways—solemnly, sadly, or in jest—depending on the production's concept of Hal. It is difficult to take as other than serious, however, reflecting his deep ambivalence about his behavior. The sentiment takes us back to his soliloquy in which he justifies his waywardness as preparation for a time when he, like the sun, will emerge from behind clouds and be all the more admired for his reformation.

The tense moment of Hal's "I do, I will" is relieved by Bardolph's sudden entrance to announce that the sheriff has arrived to investigate the robbery. Hal tells Falstaff to hide. Asserting his royal authority, he dismisses the sheriff, only to discover that his old friend has fallen peacefully to sleep in his hiding place. Hal marvels at the sight and resolves to appoint him commander of "a charge of foot" in the wars to come, as well as to return the stolen money "with advantage."

What are we to make of this relationship? Is Hal genuinely fond of Falstaff—one perceptive scholar thinks so, remarking that to love him was the equivalent of a liberal education—or is he simply using the old man for his pleasure, delighting in the decadence of Eastcheap, slumming as it were? Their outward encounters are contentious. They play tricks on each other and exchange a constant barrage of insults, with Falstaff referring contemptuously to Hal's status as the "Prince of Wales" and he replying with an array of barbs about his companion's age, girth, cowardice, and love of sack. It is often the case, however—or so I have found—that the closest male friendships are marked by just this kind of insulting banter exchanged between those who know each other so well they can delight in the wit of mutual abuse precisely because of the strong bond between them. It's all in fun, no offense taken, and provides occasion for much lively laughter. Hal is drawn to the irrepressible joy of Falstaff's company, the broad humanity of the man, and it must be acknowledged that an evening with fat Jack is much to be preferred to the solemn ceremony of the king's court. But over all this merriment in the Boar's Head is cast the shadow of Hal's high position, and Shakespeare implies that he is all too conscious of it, always aware that he must in

time abandon his youthful indiscretion and accept the burden of his appointed place in the kingdom. His status is like that of a carefree under-
graduate of our own day, one who knows that graduation will eventually
come and he will have to enter the responsible world, a reality he would
rather forget but cannot, sparking him to revel all the more in his brief
time of "loose behavior." And who would deny him that time?

On the other hand, the impression of Hal as coldly calculating in his
attitude toward Falstaff is not an attractive one. At some time in the future, it would appear, he fully intends to abandon them all, fat Jack and
his whole dissolute band of thieves, and is simply using them now for his
own amusement. Is this friendship? Is this love? The irony of these scenes
is better appreciated when it is known that at the close of *Henry IV, Part
2*, Hal, after his coronation as Henry V, does indeed banish Falstaff from
his company, a rejection that leads, Shakespeare implies, to the grieving
death of the old man.

3.1   The third act returns us to the real world. The conspirators
gather in Wales to complete their plans against the king, and we are
given a closer look at Hotspur. The conference opens but rapidly deterio-
rates when Glendower, who considers himself a man of destiny, describes
the disturbances in heaven and on earth at his nativity. Hotspur replies
mockingly that the disturbances would have occurred if his "mother's cat
had been littered" at the time. The Welsh, in these days, were considered
by the more sophisticated English to be a backward people, given to superstitious beliefs and ceremonies inherited from ancient Celtic mysteries. Hotspur considers himself a practical man of the world, above such
primitive notions, and he continues to taunt Glendower—his ally!—in
this impolitic way until they almost come to blows.

Mortimer calls them back to the business at hand: an agreement on
the division of England once victory is theirs. Hotspur, still bristling, deliberately challenges the boundary between his lands and Wales, further
infuriating Glendower. When the Welshman finally agrees begrudgingly
to the change, Hotspur shrugs it off—"I do not care." It's just his nature,
he says, to drive a hard bargain. When Glendower leaves, Mortimer reproaches Hotspur for being unnecessarily contentious. He replies that he
has been forced to sit through a whole evening listening to the Welshman's superstitious ramblings and is quite out of patience with the man.

Mortimer warns Hotspur that Glendower is no one to trifle with, and Worcester admonishes him that he is "too wilful blame" (quick to anger), that his short temper too often gives the impression of "defect in manners, want of government, / Pride, haughtiness, opinion, and disdain." Hotspur tosses off the advice cavalierly—"Well, I am schooled"—and they greet the ladies as they enter. The balance of the scene is a charming account of Mortimer and Hotspur bidding farewell to their wives, each in his own manner.

This, then, is Hotspur, a foil to Hal. He is a valiant and daring soldier mindless of danger, but impetuous, hot-tempered, and impolitic. Although he is the highly respected leader of the rebel forces, his inflated sense of honor and abrasive manner undermine his better qualities.

3.2 At the royal palace the king finally confronts his son. This is a scene familiar to any age: the hardworking father, who has labored all his life to provide a decent living for his family and opportunities for his children to prosper, chides his wayward son who ignores the doors opened to him and seems interested only in amusing himself in riotous pranks with dissolute companions. The king minces no words, opening with a variation of the familiar "Where did I go wrong?" He can only believe that God gave him such a son "to punish my mistreadings," which voices either the common sentiment of an irate and disappointed father or a particular sense of guilt about the manner in which he gained the throne. He then gets down to cases, asking Hal if he thinks it appropriate for a prince to exhibit

> such inordinate and low desires,
> Such poor, such bare, such lewd, such mean attempts,
> Such barren pleasures, rude society,
> As thou art matched withal.

Hal replies rather lamely that some of the reports about him are exaggerated.

Henry then launches into a long speech describing his concept of proper behavior for a king. This is a pervasive theme of the history plays, in which Shakespeare explores the idea of kingship, placing before us figures who exemplify the best and the worst qualities of a monarch. When we come to *Henry V*, it will be evident that Shakespeare is preparing the ground in this play for his portrayal of the ideal Christian king, though we may wonder how this account of the Prince of Wales carousing with thieves, whores, and drunkards will contribute to that figure. For the moment at least, Shakespeare develops the theme of kingship in Henry's advice on how to *gain* the crown.

The king complains that his son fails in his duties as prince by neglecting his "place in council," which his younger brother fills in his absence. He then upbraids Hal for associating with "vulgar company" and gives an account of his own courting of the common people. He appeared infrequently, he says, but when he did "I could not stir / But like a comet I was wond'red at," on which occasions he assumed a posture of "such humility / That I did pluck allegiance from men's hearts," this while "the skipping king [Richard II] ambled up and down / With shallow jests and rash bavin [fiery] wits." He admonishes Hal for being too much in the public eye, again invoking Richard II who was so much on display, "whereof a little / More than a little is by much too much." Hal is today much as Richard was then, he claims, having lost his "princely privilege / With vile participation" in the company of the dissolute companions.

Two observations may be made about this advice. First, it seems to indicate that Henry had his eye on the crown from the start, confirming Richard II's complaint about his "courtship of the common people" during the former reign. The second is the implication that a political leader of a country degrades his office by appearing too often in public, mingling so much with ordinary citizens that the sight of him is no longer an "extraordinary gaze," a familiarity that renders the people "glutted, gorged, and full" with his presence. This advice certainly runs counter to modern perceptions of those in public office, who strive to assume the posture of ordinary citizens, no different from those they serve. Shakespeare is not endorsing Henry's philosophy of political power. He simply offers it as an alternative, one with the force of reason and practice. We shall have to wait and see how much of it Hal chooses to accept.

The prince is dutifully chastened: "I shall hereafter, my thrice gracious lord, / Be more myself." But the king is not finished. The enraged and disappointed father contrasts Hal with other sons of other fathers who can point with pride to the accomplishments of their offspring. He throws the name of Hotspur in Hal's face as a son who can make a father proud, a young man who gained "never-dying honor" in defeating Douglas, even though he now conspires against the crown.

The thought of Hotspur precipitates accusations that are too much for Hal to bear. The distraught father suggests that his own son may be "under Percy's pay, / To dog his heels and curtsy at his frowns, / To show how much thou art degenerate." All the rest Hal has probably heard before, but this charge strikes at his soul and convinces him that he has much to make up for. He vows that he will some day prove himself by redeeming his honor "on Percy's head" and then "be so bold to tell you that I am your son." Hotspur, he says, "is but my factor," who when they meet "shall render every glory up" to him when he defeats the famed youth. It is a claim that calls to mind the idiom of the American frontier, where a man who outdrew the fastest gun in the West earned the title of fastest gun in the West. The king seems satisfied and decides that Hal will have a "charge and sovereign trust" in the war. The armies gather toward the battlefield as Henry issues orders for the convergence of his forces.

Thus in three successive scenes in the play we encounter three figures who shape the character of the future Henry V. Each of us can recall individuals whom we recognize in retrospect to have had a lasting influence on our lives—a parent, a teacher, a coach, a favorite uncle, a longtime friend, or an opponent in a contest of mind or body—and it is these three who leave their mark on the king that Hal is to become.

3.3 At the Boar's Head, Falstaff is in a characteristic mood. He repents his ways and vows to reform his disordered life—but the notion passes quickly. Some joking about Bardolph's face—he has a severe complexion problem—is interrupted by the Hostess, who demands that Falstaff pay his considerable debts. Knowing that the best defense is a good offense, he accuses her of picking his pocket. Hal and Poins enter, and the room is soon in an uproar as they march about in carefree parody of the coming war. There is much witty banter about Falstaff's debts and his picked pocket, and Hal reveals that he has returned the stolen money, much to his friend's distress. The prince informs Falstaff that he has procured him "a charge of foot" in the army; the knight, well aware of all the marching involved, ruefully wishes it had been "of horse." In a sharp change of tone, Hal is suddenly all business, issuing orders and arranging a rendezvous.

4.1   At Shrewsbury, on the eve of battle, Hotspur learns that his father has been taken ill and cannot join forces with him, but he and Douglas remain confident. Vernon enters, a character who, though minor, plays an important role in shaping our perception of Hal. Shakespeare has the task now of transforming the fun-loving, somewhat dissolute youth of our acquaintance into a warrior who can convincingly confront the formidable Hotspur in battle. He can, of course, dress the prince in armor and place a sword in his hand, but to our minds he is still the carefree Hal of the Boar's Head. Shakespeare works the change through the secondhand reports of those who have seen him in this new guise, here Vernon answering Hotspur's inquiry about "the nimble-footed madcap Prince of Wales." Vernon replies that he saw Hal mount his horse, vaulting "with such ease into his seat, / As if an angel dropped down from the clouds" onto "a fiery Pegasus" (the famous winged horse of Greek mythology). Hotspur is not entirely pleased with this admiring image of the prince, but as for himself, he says, he is "on fire" for battle.

As they depart, Vernon has more bad news—Glendower will be delayed. There is no open suggestion that the Welshman's tardiness arises from resentment at the treatment he received from Hotspur during their earlier conference, but we may draw our own conclusions.

4.2   Falstaff is marching his "charge of foot" to join the king's army. He begins a long speech with the confession that he has "misused the king's press damnably." A brief description of the raising of medieval armies will clarify the monologue that follows. When the need arose, the king declared a "press"—a "draft" in modern terms—of able-bodied men for the campaign; and he appointed captains to announce in each town the names of those conscripted. It was a system open to corruption, as Falstaff so graphically illustrates, since anyone so pressed, if he had the means, could buy himself out of the duty or designate a servant to replace him. The result was a tidy profit for the captain but an army composed of the least desirable and least able elements of society, since it was often necessary to conscript vagrants and empty the prisons to fill the ranks. Each of the captains was also provided with funds—"coat and conduct money," it was called—with which to equip his troops with uniforms and supply them on the march. Falstaff has also pocketed these funds, for as he observes, "there's not a shirt and a half in all my company."

The prince overtakes the company and with a look of dismay observes, "I did never see such pitiful rascals." Falstaff, as ever, covers up his mischief with bluster: "Tut, tut, good enough to toss, food for powder, food for powder—they'll fill a pit as well as better." Hal is too pressed for time to remonstrate with him, however, and hurries on to the battle. This brief scene displays some of the least attractive qualities of "fat Jack."

4.3–4 In the rebel camp the impetuous Hotspur wants to force the battle immediately while others argue for delay. Sir Walter Blunt, an envoy from the king, arrives with a conciliatory message from Henry, who hopes to satisfy their grievances and promises a "pardon absolute" for all involved in the rebellion. Hotspur suspects the king's intentions, however, and he replies angrily with an account of the support he and his father gave Henry to help him gain the crown, followed by a litany of complaints: Henry refused to ransom Mortimer, disgraced and plotted against him, banished his uncle and father from the court, and "broke oath on oath, committed wrong on wrong." Blunt, taken aback by the fury of Hotspur's response, leaves to report to the king, and they agree to another parlay.

The Archbishop of York, who is sympathetic to the rebellion, learns that Northumberland is ill and Glendower tardy (Mortimer is absent as well), fears the worst, and issues orders to muster an army should the rebels be defeated. Hotspur, it appears, stands deserted by three of his powerful allies.

5.1 The fifth act opens on another meeting, this time between the rebels and the king. Worcester and Vernon enter, and Henry asks them if they are willing to dismiss their forces and "unknit / This churlish knot of all-abhorred war." In imagery drawn from the belief in universal order, he compares the role of noblemen loyal to the king to the regular path of planets that rotate in an "obedient orb" about the sun and "cast a fair and natural light." Those in rebellion, he goes on, are like meteors that flash unpredictably across the sky, raising fears that the disturbance in the heavens foreshadows dire events on earth. Worcester replies that he has joined the rebellion reluctantly, but he goes on later to give his reasons: the king's duplicity in seeking the crown, and later his treacherous treatment of those who helped him to it.

Hal speaks up with a gesture out of the old chivalric tradition. He praises Hotspur extravagantly, then proposes that to avoid bloodshed the two of them should engage in single combat to determine the victor. The pragmatic king promptly dismisses the offer—he has no desire to risk his crown in a fight between his untried son and a seasoned warrior like Hotspur. He repeats his offer of pardon, promising that if the rebels will abandon their cause, each "shall be my friend and I'll be his." The scene ends with more witty banter between Hal and Falstaff, followed by the latter's famous soliloquy on honor. Falstaff contemplates his role in the impending battle and concludes that his best course of action is to avoid it.

5.2 Worcester and Vernon discuss whether they should disclose the king's proposal of amnesty to Hotspur. Worcester argues that Henry will not honor it; and even if he should pardon Hotspur, he would never forgive the older conspirators. They decide to remain silent.* The rebels prepare for battle, and Hotspur asks again about Hal. Vernon gives another glowing account of the prince, venturing to say that if Hal does "outlive the envy of this day, / England did never owe so sweet a hope, / So much misconstrued in his wantonness." Hotspur concludes the scene with a speech to his soldiers, urging "let each man do his best." It is pale in comparison to Hal's stirring orations in *Henry V*, but then Hotspur is very much a man of action, unskilled, as he acknowledges, in words.

5.3 So the battle begins. Douglas encounters Sir Walter Blunt "disguised as the king" and kills him, shouting to Hotspur that the battle is won, only to discover his victim's true identity. In a time when kings sought renown in battle, it was the custom to equip several of his nobles with his arms and armor. This practice achieved two purposes: it was an extra insurance policy for the monarch, and it heartened his soldiers, who fought all the more vigorously in what they thought was the royal presence. Hotspur counsels Douglas on the practice—"the king has many marching in his coats"—but the doughty Scot is not accustomed to such subtle devices. Feeling tricked, he rages that he will kill them all.

When they have gone, Falstaff comes up and contemplates Blunt's body with more trenchant remarks about honor. The prince enters and, having lost his sword in the action, demands Falstaff's. He refuses but of-

---

*As well they might. In *Henry IV, Part 2*, the rebels accept a similar offer and dismiss their forces, only to be promptly arrested and executed for treason.

fers to give Hal his pistol, which turns out to be a bottle of sack. Fat Jack cannot pass up an opportunity for a jest even in the heat of battle.

5.4   There is much coming and going in the following scene, an apt portrayal of the confusion of any battlefield. The prince is wounded but refuses to leave the field. He departs with others, leaving the stage to Douglas and the king. The Scot complains that kings "grow like Hydra's heads," but he has finally found the real one. They fight, to Henry's disadvantage, and Hal returns to rescue him, forcing Douglas to flee. The prince is now redeemed in his father's eyes, having answered the accusations Henry hurled at his son during their stormy interview. "Oh God!" Hal exclaims, "they did me too much injury / That ever said I heark'ned for your death."

The king moves on and Hotspur enters, to bring about the moment of confrontation toward which the play has been leading.* After some high words they fall to fighting. Meanwhile Falstaff enters, only to be confronted by the fierce Douglas. These two fight until Falstaff falls down, playing dead, and the Scot passes on. The visual impact of the scene is impressive. At stage right Hal and Hotspur are locked in mortal combat for the "garland" of fame. At stage left we see another encounter that is a mockery of the whole idea of valor and honor. Hal is the victor, left standing alone over the apparent corpses of two of the three men who have had the most pervasive influence on his formative years. His reaction to the sight of them is revealing. He respects Hotspur. "Fare thee well, great heart!" he says, and in "fair rights of tenderness" lays a plume from his helmet over the eyes of the corpse. He exhibits no strong feeling, however, as he greets the body of Falstaff with a familiar jest: "Could not all this flesh / Keep in a little life?" He bids his old friend a curt farewell and moves on.

But of course Falstaff is very much alive. He pops up and, ever resourceful, seizes an opportunity for gain. He stabs the corpse of Hotspur with his sword, hoists him on his back, and starts off determined to claim

---

*Shakespeare again adapts history to his dramatic needs. Hal did not fight at Shrewsbury. If he had, the outcome of the encounter would probably have been other than in the play, since at the time of the battle he was a youth of sixteen and Hotspur a seasoned warrior some twenty years his senior. But if the play required a suitable foil for the central figure, one of about his age, Shakespeare had no reservations about supplying one.

credit for his death, only to be met immediately by Hal and his brother. Falstaff brazenly announces that he has killed Percy and proclaims that as a reward for his bravery, "I look to be either earl or duke." A stunned Hal, shaking his head at the outrageous lie, nonetheless agrees to "gild it with the happiest terms I have." His willingness to surrender credit for defeating the man whom he had called his "factor," whose death would "render every glory up" to his vanquisher, implies that such "glory" doesn't mean much to him. Falstaff drags the body off, vowing to "live cleanly" once he is rewarded. He repeatedly resolves to repent and mend his ways—but always on the condition that he have sufficient funds to do so.

5.5 Victory is proclaimed, casualties counted, and the traitors led off to their death. Hal asks his father for the right to dispose of Douglas, whom he has taken prisoner, and the king readily agrees. Hal liberates the Scot, claiming admiration for his valor in battle, but the prince may well be looking ahead to a time when Douglas's goodwill might prove a valuable political asset. The troubles are not over, however. Still to be contended with are Northumberland and the powerful Yorks in the north, as well as Glendower and Mortimer in Wales. Henry IV rules uneasily over a contentious kingdom.

Thus Shakespeare offers the tale of a young man coming of age, leaving behind the frivolities of his youth and accepting the responsibilities of maturity, and he places before us the three men most influential in shaping what Hal is to become: From Falstaff he gains the ability to relate to the common man. In Hotspur he sees an example of vibrant energy and martial valor. His father impresses upon him the need for dedication and responsible leadership. But they are not what we would call today absolute role models, since Hal rejects certain qualities in each, adopting only those that eventually merge to form his character. And each exhibits traits that are canceled by the others. Hotspur has a highly developed sense of honor, one so tightly strung that the merest slight can ignite a towering rage in him, while Falstaff has little use for honor and exchanges insults with Hal in riotous good humor. The king insists that in his high office he must remain aloof from his subjects, but Hal's visits to the Boar's Head tavern enrich him with a common touch, the ability to mingle with ordinary men and women without loss of respect or dignity. Falstaff, for all his good humor, is a self-indulgent profligate, a petty thief with no thought for the consequences of his acts, while Hotspur and the king are examples of men who accept the burdens and dangers of their role in the world. But Hotspur is headstrong and impulsive, the king careful and calculating. So Hal discards something of each—Falstaff's irresponsibility, Hotspur's exaggerated sense of self-worth, and Henry's humorless distance. And he takes something from each—Falstaff's broad humanity, Hotspur's daring and courage, and his father's sense of duty to his place in society.

HENRY IV, PART 2

THIS PLAY is only infrequently staged, and, if at all, in conjunction with *Part 1*. This brief summary is placed here to provide continuity in the historical chronology of the sequence. In truth, however, it is as much a repetition as a continuation of the earlier work. While it does advance the narrative, it mirrors many of the themes and events found in *Part 1*. Having devised a successful formula for a popular play, Shakespeare apparently decided to give the audience more of the same. Falstaff is even more in evidence, and as Hal's father once more contends with rebellious nobles, the prince continues to develop, eventually turning his back entirely on his frivolous youth.

Ind.   Rumor, acting as a *chorus*, quickly reviews events to date.

Act One   The Earl of Northumberland hears of Hotspur's death and the defeat at Shrewsbury. He plots to continue the rebellion in league with the Archbishop of York. Falstaff attempts unsuccessfully to borrow money and is confronted by the chief justice, who demands to know why he had failed to appear before him as ordered. Falstaff pleads that he was called to military service and is even now on the march to quell the uprising in the north. The play, like its earlier companion, alternates comic and serious scenes, here returning to the archbishop and his followers, who discuss strategy and leave to gather their forces.

Act Two   In Eastcheap, Hostess Quickly demands that officers of the law, Fang and Snare, arrest Falstaff for failure to pay his debts. When he appears with Bardolph, swords are drawn on both sides, but the entrance of the chief justice prevents bloodshed. The hostess and Falstaff are reconciled, and news arrives of the approach of the king. Meanwhile Hal and Poins pass the time in a witty exchange, largely devoted to Falstaff. They plot to eavesdrop on him while he is at supper in the Boar's Head tavern.

Lady Percy, Hotspur's widow, persuades Northumberland to abandon the rebellion and take refuge in Scotland. As in *Part 1*, he will absent himself from the impending battle.

Back in Eastcheap, Falstaff is making merry with the hostess and Doll Tearsheet when his ancient, Pistol, enters. He is a swaggering, quarrelsome braggart, a comic figure who reappears in *Henry V*. Hal and Poins enter undetected as Falstaff speaks contemptuously of both, calling Hal a "shallow young fellow" and Poins a "baboon." They reveal themselves and demand an explanation, to which he replies outrageously. So, as in *Part 1*, Hal plays tricks on Falstaff while armies gather to overthrow his father, and again he is called away to his duties.

Act Three   In a brief scene the king laments the disorder in his land and is assured that he has sufficient forces to defeat the rebels.

In *Part 1* Falstaff admitted to misusing "the king's press damnably," and here we see him at it again. The local magistrates, Justices Shallow and Silence, have collected a group of recruits for him to enlist in his company. These men are identified by their names—Mouldy, Feeble, Shadow, and Wart—as totally unfit for military service, but Falstaff accepts them anyway. After he and the justices leave, two of them bribe Bardolph to release them from service. He accepts the money and passes it on to Falstaff, who promptly dismisses them.

Act Four   The fourth act opens on a parlay between the opposing sides, a repetition of a scene in *Part 1*, though it has a different outcome. The king's forces are led by Prince John, Hal's younger brother. His emissary, Westmoreland, meets with the archbishop, who hands him a list of grievances against the king. The prince meets with the rebels and, promising that the king will remedy all their complaints, he proposes that both sides dismiss their soldiers. The trusting rebels discharge their forces, but the prince keeps his in readiness. On hearing that the rebel armies have been dispersed, he orders their leaders arrested and executed for treason, and he directs his soldiers to hunt down and destroy the retreating forces. During the chase Falstaff captures Coleville of Dale and turns him over to Prince John. As in the encounter with Hal after Shrewsbury, he expects that his deeds will be rewarded. On his way back to London, he says, he will stop over at Gloucestershire, where he senses that there is profit to be had in Justice Shallow's admiration for him.

In London the king is sick. He complains again that Hal neglects his duties and still keeps riotous company. He receives news that the rebellion has been crushed but suffers a sudden attack and retires to his bed. Hal comes upon him sleeping and, thinking him dead, picks up the crown, places it on his own head, and leaves. The king awakes and calls out, bringing his courtiers and finally Hal himself. As in *Part 1*, the father rages at his son, this time accusing him not of treachery but of wishing his death because of a heartless ambition for the throne. Hal defends himself, and the king, finally convinced of his devotion, gives him dying advice.

Act Five Falstaff is working on Justice Shallow for a loan. Meanwhile Hal, now king, encounters the chief justice, who had imprisoned him on one occasion and fully expects to be dismissed from office. But Hal praises him for his devotion to duty and reappoints him. Falstaff continues to carouse with Justice Shallow until Pistol arrives with news of the king's death. The knight, expecting preferment from his young friend, urges all to make haste to be on time for Hal's coronation.

They arrive as the royal procession approaches, and Falstaff calls out joyfully to Hal: "My king! my Jove! I speak to you, my heart." But the king dismisses him coldly—"I know thee not, old man"—and instructs the chief justice to banish him. Thus Hal finally puts his misspent youth behind him and accepts the responsibilities of his office. Falstaff is still pathetically optimistic, but Justice Shallow more realistically asks him to return the thousand pounds he lent him.

During the final encounter between Hal and his dying father, the politically astute king, worn out by the rebellions that have plagued his reign, advises his son "to busy giddy minds with foreign quarrels." His counsel sets the stage for the play to follow, when Henry V undertakes the conquest of France and Shakespeare portrays a charismatic king who unites the contentious factions of England under his leadership.

HENRY V

OVER THE YEARS this play has been greeted with both high praise and dismissive blame. Dover Wilson wrote of it in 1947, "*Henry V* is a play which men of action have been wont silently to admire, and literary men, at any rate during the last hundred and thirty years, volubly to contemn." To illustrate, Wilson cites William Hazlitt, who thought Henry "a brute and a hypocrite," and William Butler Yeats: "He has the gross vices, the coarse nerves, of one who is to rule among violent people. . . . He is as remorseless and undistinguished as some natural force."* Wilson argues that this was certainly not the perception of those who first saw the play, for whom Henry V was a national hero of almost mythic proportions, nor of those who flocked to Laurence Olivier's film version produced in 1944, when the Allied forces were engaged in another invasion of France.

Henry V is a play about war; and in the latter decades of the twentieth century a sizable segment of our culture considers warfare inherently "immoral," unjustified under any circumstances. It is said to be barbarous, and those who declare or engage in it are condemned as little better than barbarians themselves. The play, it is said, glorifies war, hence is objectionable on moral grounds. And Henry himself is little more than a glory-hungry adventurer, a Machiavellian schemer, callous to the suffering of those who fall victim to his ambition. On the other hand, some see him as the inspiring leader, calling forth the best in his subjects—their courage, resolve, and willingness to sacrifice in a righteous cause. When he addresses his soldiers as "we few, we happy few, we band of brothers,"

---

*John Dover Wilson, ed., *King Henry V*, in *The New Shakespeare* (Cambridge, England: Cambridge University Press, 1968 reprint), pp. vii, xv–xvi.

he stirs memories in older audiences of wartime unity and of a few to whom so many owed so much. So who or what is this Henry V—the remorseless brute force, intent only upon his own glory, or the courageous king who, by strength of character and firm belief in the justice of his cause, unites his people and leads them through fire and rain to their triumphal hour?

In reading or viewing *Henry V*, one can find confirmation for either response, and this of course is Shakespeare's genius. Armed conflict in its many forms is, sadly, one of the more common of human experiences; and he presents it in all of its complexity, in both its brutality and glory, its suffering and rewards. And, as in his dramatization of all human experience, Shakespeare does not take sides. He simply places before us the contradictory spectacle of human folly and nobility and leaves judgment to us. He gives us experience whole; and his comprehensive vision is well illustrated by the two film versions offered in the past half-century, Olivier's, and Kenneth Branagh's more recent production. The first, as mentioned, appeared in the midst of World War II, when unity of purpose and martial prowess were valued as essential to victory. Branagh's version was filmed in the post-Vietnam era, when sentiments are less sympathetic to such qualities. I shall be citing the contrasting treatment of scenes in the discussion to follow, and so will remark here only that both films are superb and were widely acclaimed when they appeared, and that both are true to Shakespeare's vision of war.

The play is an account of Henry V's assertion of a long-standing claim of English monarchs to the throne of France. On the advice of his council, he determines to pursue the claim, mobilizes his army, and, landing in France, lays siege to the port city of Harfleur. By the time the city surrenders, however, the English forces have been so depleted by sickness and casualties that the king decides to campaign no further that year. Instead he will conduct a symbolic march through his ancestral domain of Normandy to the English port at Calais, return home, refit his forces, and renew the campaign the following year. En route he is confronted at Agincourt by a French army vastly superior to his sadly depleted ranks. He nonetheless defeats the French resoundingly, continues his march, and later returns to complete the conquest. Shakespeare passes over the four years of campaigning that follow the battle and moves directly to the peace negotiations, where Henry claims the hand of Katherine, the French princess, and unites the two crowns.

1.Cho. Each of the five acts of the play opens with a *chorus* addressing the audience directly. The figure has several functions. He provides a setting for the scenes to follow, fills in the historical events during the lapse of time between acts, and celebrates the king. Here he has yet another role. The audience, he says, must excuse the inadequate efforts to present such grand events—the march of armies, the swirl of battle between vast forces, and the majesty of monarchs—within the poor confines of "this wooden O," the Globe Theater. The chorus appeals to the audience to make up for the limitations of the *stage* by an exercise of their imaginations. "Piece out our imperfections with your thoughts," he asks: When a single soldier appears, think of him as a multitude, and when there is talk of horses, see them, "printing their proud hoofs i'th'receiving earth." It is a request that applies as well to anyone reading or watching Shakespeare's plays, especially readers, who are called upon to engage their "imaginary forces," erect a stage in the mind, and people it with characters moving and talking within its confines.

1.1 The play opens on two high-ranking English clerics—minor characters, as it turns out, but important in setting the stage for the appearance of the king. They are troubled because Henry has revived his father's proposal to appropriate valuable church lands. After some talk of the king's many virtues and his miraculous change of character since his wild youth, the Archbishop of Canterbury reveals that the church has offered a substantial sum to support an enterprise "which I have opened to his grace at large, / As touching France." With that, they leave to attend the audience with the French ambassador.

1.2 Before the ambassador is heard, Henry confers with his council concerning the English claim to the French throne. His chief adviser on the matter is the archbishop, whom he cautions to be careful in his counsel—"take heed how you impawn our person, / How you awake our sleeping sword of war"—since his advice will surely result in the shedding of much blood. Canterbury, in a tediously long, legalistic, and pedantic speech, elaborates on the Salic Law. Briefly, the English claim to the French crown is based on descent in the female line, and the Salic Law prescribes that it can only be inherited in the male line. Canterbury argues that the Salic lands where it applies do not include France, hence Henry has a legal and moral right to the throne. Having listened patiently—or perhaps impatiently—to this lengthy argument, the king asks directly, "may I with right and conscience make this claim?" The question triggers yet another long-winded speech from the archbishop, urging Henry to revive his great-grandfather Edward III's claim to France and assert his right in the same "warlike spirit" of that king and his son, Edward the Black Prince. Henry's nobles add their voices to the design; and Canterbury offers "a mighty sum" to finance the expedition, to which the king agrees, proclaiming that with their help, "France being ours, we'll bend it to our awe, / Or break it all to pieces."

In the interpretation of Henry's character, the critical question of this exchange is, "Who is manipulating whom?" The two film versions contrast strikingly in their effect. In the 1944 Olivier production, the two clerics are fumbling, comic figures, and the king endures the archbishop's ramblings in a respectful but long-suffering manner. In the Branagh film, the clerics are shadowy, hooded figures conferring in conspiratorial whispers in a darkened room, and Canterbury's argument, much abbreviated, is delivered in solemn tones to a tense court. In the one case it appears that Henry has threatened church lands in order to extract funds for his expedition—in the other that the clergy make the offer to distract the king from his intent by encouraging him to undertake a campaign abroad. In Olivier, the king is blackmailing the clergy. In Branagh, they are bribing the king. Shakespeare's play can support either version.

The scene continues with the entrance of the French ambassador, who bears a gift from the dauphin, the heir to the French throne. The uneasy envoy asks if he may speak plainly, and the king replies with an image that invokes the concept of *universal order*. He assures the ambassador that his passions are as subject to his "grace"—that is, his reason—as are "our wretches fettered in our prisons." It is a harsh image, but in comparing the faculty of reason with the crown, and his passions with fettered prisoners, it links the human body and the body politic.

The ambassador delivers the dauphin's message, which dwells on Henry's reputation for youthful frivolity, and a gift of tennis balls, which mockingly implies that he should continue to devote himself to boyish games and leave such weighty matters as statecraft and warfare to grown men. The king responds with a heated speech in which he answers the affront on two levels, as an insult to him personally and, since he is king, to England as well. He begins calmly enough, admitting that in his youth he had little care for the throne and its responsibilities, hence "did give ourself / To barbarous license." He uses the royal "we" here, but as he grows more incensed at the insult, changes to the personal "I," promising to "rouse me in my throne of France . . . with so full a glory / That I will dazzle all the eyes" of its people. He then turns the insult to advantage, holding the dauphin responsible for the suffering to follow, in which "many a thousand widows / Shall this his mock mock out of their dear husbands; / Mock mothers from their sons, mock husbands down." He concludes with a rallying cry to his followers: "I am coming on, / To venge me as I may, and to put forth / My rightful hand in a well-hollowed cause." Having vented his anger, he resumes the regal plural: "We have now no thought in us but France," where "we'll chide this Dauphin at his father's door."

One can read these speeches as the hollow rhetoric of a devious man driven by ambition, coldly manipulating the occasion by feigning anger at the insult, or as the response of one genuinely stung by the mockery of the gift and mindful that he must defend his honor in the presence of his nobles. Henry is, after all, a newly crowned and untested monarch, and the taunts about his misspent youth are not without substance. He may indeed be posturing somewhat when he turns the incident to his advantage, for, as we shall see, this is not the only occasion when he shifts blame for the suffering of the war onto others. In either case, Shakespeare is careful to show that the decision to invade France is made before the ambassador enters, so as to avoid the impression that Henry is going to war over a petty insult.

The scene introduces yet another critical *theme* of the play—the justice of the cause. Does the king genuinely believe it "well-hollowed," as he says, or is he simply catering to the religious sensibilities of his people by assuring them that God is on their side? These assurances may ring false to modern ears, all too accustomed to wars in which both sides march under the banners of the same God, or when professional football players pray for touchdowns. But Henry V lived in a different era, when

Christians believed in a God intimately involved in human affairs and were convinced that if the cause could not survive the scrutiny of divine justice, it was doomed to failure.

It may seem puzzling at first that the king seeks the advice of an archbishop rather than perhaps a chief minister, his royal family, or his nobles, who in this scene are largely spectators to the exchange. The Archbishop of Canterbury was then, as he is now, the clerical head of the English church, and in Henry's time he was the personal representative of the pope in England. The king, therefore, needs not only the funds but also the blessing of the church, to satisfy both the conscience of the nation and, we may assume, his own as well. Conscience is always a critical factor in battle, where a soldier is called upon to take life. Modern nations continue to seek God's sanction in armed conflict, but conscience is also a factor in the debate among politicians and philosophers over the distinction between just and unjust wars. Henry's question, "may I with right and conscience make this claim?" is a timeless one, and the customs and beliefs of his time require that he ask it of an archbishop.

2.Cho.   The chorus paints a picture of "the youth of England" eagerly preparing for war and reveals a French plot to subvert the cause by bribing three members of the king's court to assassinate him. This method of simply informing the audience of the conspiracy, rather than enacting it, is admittedly a somewhat contrived way to introduce *dramatic irony* into the play, but Shakespeare is condensing time here and, as we shall see, setting up the action to come. We are transported to the port city of Southampton, where the army is preparing to embark for France.

2.1   But first we have a glimpse of "the youth of England," though they do not seem particularly "on fire" for war. These are the comic figures of the play, the characters from London's Boar's Head tavern who caroused with the king during his madcap youth, and they seem more concerned with a personal dispute than the one with France. Pistol has stolen Mistress Quickly from Nym, and there is bad blood between them. The two threaten to come to blows until separated by Bardolph and interrupted by the Boy, who brings word that Falstaff is grievously ill. Shakespeare has decided to kill off Falstaff, here described as dying of grief at the king's rejection. It is not clear why he chose to remove him from the scene—perhaps because he thought the popular knight would draw too much attention from the central character, or perhaps simply because Will Kemp, who played the part, had left the company. Pistol now becomes the chief comic figure, but he is very different—a pompous blowhard with none of Falstaff's redeeming humanity. He postures ridiculously as a warrior, full of high words and hostile gestures, but he is quick to back down when threatened by Bardolph. Shakespeare at times contrasts the heroic image of Henry V with figures that undercut his grand speeches. We are left with the impression that if these are representative of the eager "youth of England," hopes for the expedition may be less than promising.

2.2 The scene now shifts to Southampton, where we learn that the king is aware of the conspiracy against him, thus adding another layer of dramatic irony to the encounter—we now know that he knows. Henry enters, accompanied by the three men who even at that moment are planning his death, and it becomes clear why Shakespeare has taken pains to inform the audience of the plot. We can enjoy watching the king toy with them, first asking if they think his army strong enough for the task, to which they reply with obsequious assurances. He then orders the release of a man who had "railed against" him, eliciting objections from the three, who advise that he shows too much mercy to malcontents. The king insists, however—here laying on the irony with a heavy hand—and though they "in their dear care / And tender preservation of our person, / Would have him punished," he will release the man. He then hands them what he says are their commissions, but which turn out to be death warrants. They appeal for mercy but he refuses, recalling their recent advice.

The charade over, he turns on them bitterly in a long speech, one that explores another important theme of the play, indeed of all the histories: the nature of a king. In picturing Henry V as the ideal Christian monarch, Shakespeare examines the burdens and rewards of any high office in the worlds of politics, commerce, or for that matter in the church and education. Henry condemns the traitors for their betrayal, but he is especially harsh with Lord Scroop, who had been a trusted counselor and dear friend as well. Scroop, he says, "knew'st the bottom of my soul, / That almost mightst have coined me into gold." He had seemed the ideal confidant—dutiful, learned, nobly born, and religious. Hence his treason has "infected / The sweetness of affiance" and his revolt "is like / Another fall of man." Scroop's treachery is traumatic for Henry because in his eyes it infects all men. Never again will he be able to trust another as he has his friend, for all now bear the taint of his betrayal. In assuming the mantle of a king, Henry must henceforth deny himself the comforting bond of close friendship, for to him now every man seems fallen.

Despite their further pleas for mercy, Henry confirms the sentence, this time in more official terms. He shifts again to the royal "we," declaring that they must die because their plot, had it succeeded, would have reduced the entire kingdom to "desolation." He seeks no vengeance for himself, he declares, but condemns them rather for threatening "our kingdom's safety," leaving them subject "to her laws." In one speech he is a man raging against a broken friendship, in the other a monarch sentencing a traitor to his country. In this instance the desires of one and the duties of the other may not be in conflict, but they will often clash.

Henry recovers quickly from his disappointment and anger, turning the episode to advantage. He proclaims that the discovery of the conspiracy is a sign of divine sanction, that in bringing the treason to light God has given promise "of a fair and lucky war." Putting the incident behind him, he returns his soldiers' attention to the task at hand with the promise that he will be "no king of England, if not king of France."

2.3 Falstaff's companions mourn his death briefly, but they too soon turn their attention to France. Soldiers of that day were ill paid or not paid at all, and they joined the armies in hope of profit through looting. As Pistol puts it, they go like leeches, "to suck, to suck, the very blood to suck!"

2.4 The scene shifts to the French court, which is well informed of Henry's warlike preparations. The French take measures to defend themselves, but the dauphin is scornful of the English, who, he scoffs, are "idly kinged" by "a vain, giddy, shallow, humorous youth." Saner heads prevail, however. The old king recalls earlier invasions by Edward III and his son, the Black Prince, especially the battle of "Cressy [Crecy]," where the English defeated the French forces and captured "all our princes." Shakespeare plays with history here, characterizing the French king, Charles VI, as a seasoned and sensible monarch who takes the English threat seriously. In fact he was quite mad, during one phase, the story goes, imagin-

ing himself made of glass and forbidding anyone to touch him for fear he
would shatter. If the dynamics of play require a more respectable foe for
Henry, however, Shakespeare will provide one.

Exeter enters, bearing his king's claim to the French throne. He is
but the first of many envoys who will pass between the two forces, each
given to long, elaborate, and sometimes tedious speeches setting out demands and counterdemands of the opposing monarchs. The play tends to
lag on these occasions, but Shakespeare is simply adapting to the limitations of the Elizabethan stage, where it was easier to show scenes before
battle than the battle itself. Modern cinematography can display Agincourt in all its grandeur and brutality, but the "unworthy scaffold" of the
Globe can offer only a few figures in contrasting colored uniforms hack-
ing away at each other with purposely dull swords. Scenes of battle are
therefore brief and only suggestive in Shakespeare, and we must heed
the counsel of the chorus to "piece out our imperfections with your
thoughts."

Exeter, in brief, lays out Henry's claim. He concludes that, should the
king refuse, France, not England, will bear responsibility for "the widows' tears, the orphans' cries, / The dead men's blood, the pining maidens' groans, / For husbands, fathers and betrothed lovers" who will die in
the war. Exeter also bears a personal response to the dauphin from Henry,
who has not forgotten the tennis balls, a message of "scorn and defiance,
slight regard, [and] contempt." Shakespeare is clearly setting the French
prince up as a *foil* to Henry.

3.Cho.   The chorus opens Act Three urging the audience to imagine subsequent events: the embarkation of the English and their landing
on the French coast at Harfleur, where they lay siege to the port. He asks
them to imagine further the cannon blowing a breach in the town walls,
and in what follows to "eke out our performance with your mind."

3.1   The next three scenes offer contrasting views of warfare. Sand-
wiched between two of Henry's stirring speeches is a comic scene that
gives us a glimpse of the response of the common soldiers to battle. In the
first of these the king rallies his forces, urging them to renew their attack
through the breach. War, he declares, requires different qualities of men
than does peace—they must "imitate the actions of the tiger" and "bend
up every spirit / To his full height!" He calls upon them to remember

their warlike fathers, to "dishonor not" their mothers, and to show the traditional courage of Englishmen. He sees them "stand like greyhounds in the slips" and leads them in the charge to the cry of "God for Harry, England, and Saint George!"

3.2   Some of Henry's soldiers, it would appear, hardly "greyhounds" straining to begin the race, want nothing to do with the breach. The Boar's Head tavern warriors, while urging others forward, do everything to avoid the battle, wishing themselves back "in an alehouse in London" rather than where they are. Captain Fluellen comes upon the group hanging back from the action and, beating them with the flat of his sword, compels them to join the charge. The Boy hides, however, and in a long speech condemns his companions as cowards and thieves. "They will steal anything," he says, "and call it purchase."

We then encounter the captains. The fact that Henry has been able to attract the service of these four is a tribute to his ability to unite his country in a common effort. The Welshman (Fluellen), Englishman (Gower), Irishman (Macmorris), and Scot (Jamy) represent the main ethnic divisions of the kingdom, historically at one time or another hostile to the crown. Richard II, for example, led a campaign to subdue the Irish, and Douglas and Glendower joined Hotspur's conspiracy against Henry IV. These are all good men, devoted to the king, but Fluellen is distressed at the laying of the mines, which were placed in tunnels under the walls of cities and exploded to create a breach in the defenses. He is the chief figure among the captains, comic in the degree to which he prides himself a student of warfare. A familiar soldier in the armies of the world, he is single-mindedly pedantic about the military profession and complains bitterly that the mines have not been properly placed, or, as he puts it, in keeping with "the disciplines of the war." In contrast, Macmorris is a simple man of action, disgusted that the attack on Harfleur has been called off. When Fluellen attempts to engage him in a discussion "touching or concerning the disciplines of war," he replies impatiently, and quite reasonably, that this is no time for talk. Fluellen makes an unfortunate remark about Macmorris's "nation," and the two almost come to blows, prevented only by the town's call for a parlay.

3.3   In Henry's speech to the governor of Harfleur, Shakespeare gives us yet another dimension of warfare—its terror. In this age a city under siege, once all possibility of relief was past, could either surrender or hold out in hopes that the enemy would tire of the operation and with-draw. The besieging army offered the city two alternatives, either surren-der and submit to a relatively benign occupation, or continue to resist under the threat of a brutal sack. This latter was a common tactic of war-fare in which the victorious soldiers were given full license to murder, rape, plunder, and burn at will.

Henry offers these alternatives to the governor: either open the gates and submit, in which case he will keep his soldiers under control, or re-sist further. If the English are forced to fight their way in, however, Henry threatens to release his army from all restraints. He paints a horri-fying picture of what happened in the sack of a medieval city once the "blind and bloody soldier" was let loose upon the populace—daughters violated, old men murdered, and infants mercilessly "spitted upon pikes." Would the good Christian king have carried out his threat? We never learn, since the governor, despairing of relief from the French army, surrenders. But we should not think Henry above such barbarism. His army suffers the fate of large forces of his time compelled to remain in place for long periods of time. Medieval armies had inadequate means of supply and no concept of sanitation, with the result that they lost many more of their number from disease and desertion than from enemy action, and the English forces were sadly depleted by the long siege of Harfleur. Henry therefore uses his ultimate weapon, terror, and succeeds in forcing the city into submission. Given the condition of his forces, however, "the winter coming on, and sickness growing / Upon our soldiers," he decides to abort the campaign for that year and march north to Calais, a port on the French coast under English control.

In the scenes that follow, Shakespeare is faithful to the historical ac-count. Briefly, the king intends to conduct a symbolic march through his ancestral possessions in Normandy. Between him and his destination, however, flow several major rivers, and the French, who finally take to the field, begin their resistance by contesting the bridges over the chief of them, the Somme. The English are compelled to turn their line of march eastward, upriver along the south bank of the Somme, in search of a lightly defended bridge, thus taking them deeper and deeper into France. By the time they force a crossing and resume their march northward, the French have mobilized their army and placed themselves between the En-glish and Calais, forcing an engagement.

3.4 Audiences may justifiably complain that, as if they are not troubled enough with Shakespeare's English, they are now asked to contend with a scene in French! It is quite charming, really, when seen on stage. The French princess, Katharine, who has heard of plans to marry her to the king of England, is receiving a lesson in his language. Her lady-in-waiting is drilling her in the English words for parts of the body—the hand, fingers, nails, arm, elbow, neck, chin, foot, and dress. Into the midst of this harsh account of hostile armies maneuvering for battle, Shakespeare drops an image of innocence and civility.

3.5 The French nobles, meanwhile, prevail upon their king to mobilize the army and take the field to oppose the English, who, they complain, are challenging "the honor of our land" and must be answered. The failure to confront the invading English, the dauphin rages, has raised questions about French courage. "Our madams mock us," he exclaims, and threaten to "give / Their bodies to the lust of English youth" so as to produce a heartier breed of Frenchmen. The king finally agrees to rally the French forces, and we hear another reference to the condition of the English army, whose soldiers, according to the constable, are "sick and famished in their march."

3.6 A bridge over the Somme is finally secured by the English after a brush with the French. Pistol approaches Fluellen on behalf of Bardolph, who was caught stealing a "pax" (cross) from a church and has been sentenced to hang.* Fluellen, a stickler for rules, rejects Pistol's plea, declaring that he would recommend hanging were Bardolph his brother, "for discipline ought to be used." Gower recognizes Pistol, and Shakespeare uses the occasion to criticize false veterans, who, the captain claims, abound in England. When Henry enters, Fluellen informs him of Bardolph's crime and sentence. If the king regrets the death of an old companion from his Boar's Head days, he shows no sign of it. He had forbidden looting on the march through Normandy, since, as he puts it, "when lenity and cruelty play for a kingdom, the gentlest gamester is the soonest winner." Bardolph violated his orders and so must pay the penalty.

---

*Pistol holds the military rank of "ancient," a position roughly below a commissioned and above a noncommissioned officer in a modern army. Iago is Othello's "ancient."

The French herald, Montjoy, arrives with a defiant message from his king: he asks Henry to name his "ransom." In medieval times when a nobleman entered combat, he did so partially protected by an upper-class insurance policy. He was worth more alive than dead, since, if he was captured, it was a matter of honor for his family or his country to pay for his release. Montjoy's mention of ransom in the presence of English soldiers is a calculated affront to undermine their loyalty to the king, but Henry turns the taunt to advantage by declaring that his "ransom is this frail and worthless trunk." He then admits that they do not seek a battle but declares defiantly, "as we are, we say we will not shun it."

3.7 Meanwhile the French are supremely confident, and with good reason: they outnumber the march-weary English five to one. We are in the tent of the French high command, where they are wiling away the hours until dawn with talk of their armor, their horses, their mistresses, and their contempt for the English. The dauphin dwells extravagantly on the virtues of his horse while the others listen impatiently, wishing he would shut up.* Shakespeare completes his characterization of the dauphin as a foil to Henry V in his depiction of the French prince as an overbearing and superficial dilettante, annoying in his pretentiousness and shallow in his concerns, a representative of the old chivalric aristocracy but with none of their dignity. When he finally leaves, Orleans, a loyal courtier, disputes with the constable about the dauphin's character. The constable is the commander of the French armies, and his low opinion of his prince carries weight. As a soldier he has some sympathy for Henry's plight, and he does not underestimate the qualities of the English: "They will eat like wolves, and fight like devils."

4.Cho. The chorus introduces Act Four with some of Shakespeare's superb scene-setting lines:

> Now entertain conjecture of a time
> When creeping murmur and the poring dark
> Fills the wide vessel of the universe. . . .
> The country cocks do crow, the clocks do toll,
> And the third hour of drowsy morning name.

---

*Again Shakespeare plays with history. The dauphin was not present at the battle.

In contrast to the effete dauphin, Henry is described as moving among his soldiers—he "bids them good morrow with a modest smile, / And calls them brother, friends, and countrymen," raising their spirits with "a little touch of Harry in the night." The chorus, again apologizing for the limitations of the stage, draws the curtain on the English camp.

4.1   We now see the king making his way through every level of his army, bestowing on each "a little touch of Harry." In the course of his encounters we hear more of the troublesome question introduced in the first scenes of the play: the justice of his cause. He first exchanges brief remarks with his brothers, Bedford and Gloucester. Erpingham, who represents the nobility, approaches the royal family confidently, declares his loyalty, and is encouraged by Henry. The king then borrows his cloak, and we are meant to understand that in his ensuing encounters he goes unrecognized. The effectiveness of his disguise is immediately confirmed by Pistol, who is obsessively class-conscious and asks pompously if he is an "officer" or "base, common, and popular." Henry assures him that he is a gentleman, and the conversation turns to Fluellen, whom Pistol disparages. On learning that this stranger is a kinsman of the despised captain, Pistol insults him as well. As they part, Pistol gives his name, upon which Henry remarks archly, "it suits well with your fierceness." A pistol is a very small, and at the time undependable, weapon.

The king then overhears an exchange between Fluellen and the English captain, Gower, in which the Welshman chastises his companion for talking too loudly. Gower responds that the French are not concerned about making noise, to which Fluellen replies pedantically that just because "the enemy is an ass and a fool," there is no excuse for them to ignore "the laws of the wars." Henry appreciates his by-the-book captain, acknowledging that though he is "a little out of fashion, / There is much care and valor in this Welshman."

This air of levity is dispelled, however, when Henry comes upon the common soldiers of his army, Bates and Williams, who are less than eager for the night to end. They are quite realistically worried about being killed in battle. Henry tries to lift their spirits by reminding them of the mutual loyalty between themselves and the king: "Methinks I could not die any where so contented as in the king's company; his cause being just, and his quarrel honorable." The skeptical Williams replies, "that's more than we know," and goes on to confess his real concern: the fate of his soul should he be killed.

The conversation turns on the critical question of the "just cause." It may have seemed that Henry's earlier questioning of the Archbishop of Canterbury on the subject was simply a device to secure political and ecclesiastical cover for his ambitions, and that his later proclamations of the justice of his cause were so much pious rhetoric for public consumption. But in this encounter between the disguised king and his common subjects we discover how critical the issue is to all. Williams is concerned about eternal judgment, and he comforts himself with the thought that if the king's cause is unjust, his soldiers will not be called to account "at the latter day" for their actions. "I am afeard there are few die well, that die in a battle," he broods, "when blood is their argument." He concludes that "it will be a black matter for the king" if their cause is not just. Stung by the thought, Henry launches into a long speech refuting it, arguing that "every subject's duty is the king's, but every subject's soul is his own." Williams is swayed by the argument and in the end acknowledges that if he does not die well, "the king is not to answer for it."

Shakespeare addresses here an issue that since the beginning of civilization has troubled philosophers, politicians, and now lawyers. In the twentieth century nations undertook the quixotic task of regulating the conduct of war, and in the wake of World War II the victorious Allies set up a tribunal at Nuremberg to try the defeated German leaders. In that trial the laws of God—which cause Williams and Bates to fear for their immortal souls—were replaced by the laws of man, which, it was hoped, would make humans equally fearful to repeat the atrocities of the defendants, who were tried for "crimes against humanity." Henry's soldiers seek to exonerate themselves from guilt by arguing that they are subjects of the king, "who to disobey were against all proportion of subjection." Modern soldiers attempt to excuse their actions by citing their military obligation to obey the orders of their superiors, a defense employed by, among others, Adolf Eichmann at his trial in Israel. It is a defense rejected today, as it is by Henry. Thus Shakespeare, in his many-sided vision of warfare, raises issues that persist in the history of human conflict.

Henry then somewhat imprudently raises the question of ransom, observing that the king has rejected the French demand, and Williams gives us a glimpse of the common soldier's down-to earth skepticism on the issue: "When our throats are cut, he may be ransomed, and we ne'er the wiser." Henry bristles at his mistrust, but they agree to postpone their "quarrel" until after the battle. Exchanging gloves, each pledges to wear it in his cap so that they will recognize each other when the time comes.

The soldiers leave and Henry, musing on their words in a long *soliloquy*, contemplates the difference between king and commoner. There is not much to distinguish between them, he concludes, and it can all be reduced to a single distinction—ceremony. This is the only instance in the play where we are afforded insight into his private thoughts. On every other occasion he is a public figure, acting in the capacity of a monarch— speaking in court, encouraging his followers, weighing matters of state, directing his armies, and even wooing Katharine. On the one hand, the speech may sound a false note, like the politician who complains about the burdens of office and loneliness at the top, but promptly files for re-election. On the other hand, the king is speaking only to himself here, in words that attest to his appreciation for the common man (a lesson learned from Falstaff no doubt), and his sympathy for the peasant's daily toil is a sentiment not often attributed to the rich and powerful. Certainly the French aristocrats give no thought to such matters.

Erpingham enters to call him to council, but Henry dismisses him and kneels to pray. His first thought is of his army, "O God of battles, steel my soldiers' hearts, / Possess them not with fear," but the bulk of his prayer deals with another matter entirely. He begs God not to punish him—"Not to-day, O Lord, / O not to-day"—for his father's "fault" in seizing the crown. He pleads the measures he has taken to expiate the crime, fearful that God is still angry at the deposition and death of Richard II, at the removal of his anointed minister in the kingdom. He feels his cause is just but fears that God may use the occasion to show his displeasure at his father's disruption of divine order in the body politic.

4.2   The day of battle dawns and we are in the French camp, where the cream of that nation's chivalry are arming for the confrontation. In contrast to the solemn tones of the preceding scene, the French appear to be already celebrating their victory, as well they might. They greatly outnumber the English and are fresh, while their enemy, after conducting a difficult siege, has been trudging for days through hostile territory. They heap scorn on "yon poor and starved band," mocking their "ragged curtains [banners]," their "rusty beavers [helmets]," and their unkempt horses, whose neglected bits are "foul with chawed-grass." This boasting would have delighted Shakespeare's audience, who were well aware of the outcome of the battle.

4.3   But there are more speeches before the armies engage. Westmoreland, perhaps watching the French preparations with anxiety, remarks wistfully that he wishes the English had ten thousand more men, and Henry seizes the opportunity to deliver a speech to raise the spirits of his army, claiming that there are quite enough Englishmen present for the purpose. "O, do not wish one more" he declares, and even rather grandly offers a passport home to any who "hath no stomach to this fight." He dwells on the fellowship of those who serve in a common cause, "we few, we happy few, we band of brothers," and looks beyond the battle to a time when they will share the glory of that day's victory, when those left at home "shall think themselves accursed they were not here." He imagines a time when veterans of the battle will show their scars and say with pride that they had "fought with us upon St. Crispin's day." Westmoreland is satisfied, replying with the wish that the king and he alone "could fight this royal battle," hyperbole perhaps excusable given the emotions of the moment.

We are not quite finished with speeches, however. Montjoy reappears and taunts the king with yet another request that he name his ransom. Henry is exasperated—"Good God! why should they mock poor fellows thus?"—and he goes on to defy the arrogant French, declaring that his men may not look like much, but "our hearts are in the trim." Once more he predicts victory.

4.4   The next 180 lines or so depict scenes during the battle. Modern film versions can dwell on the spectacle at length, but on the Elizabethan stage, of course, there was little enough of it to see. Historical accounts describe the French organized into three lines, and the English, mostly longbowmen, in several ranks behind rows of pointed stakes placed at an angle in the ground to discourage direct cavalry assault. The French first line attacked and was thrown back by a hail of English arrows. The second line followed but became entangled in the retreat of the first, in the confusion creating a killing zone that the English archers took full advantage of, slaughtering thousands of the enemy as they stumbled about on a field thick in mud from an overnight rain. The third French line, after making a show of attacking, thought better of it, and they were forced to concede the victory to the English. During the main action, a French force raided the English camp, guarded only by defenseless boys, whom they killed.*

The play's only scene of individual combat is a comic one in which Pistol, in a parody of the custom of ransom, takes a French soldier prisoner and is promised two hundred crowns for his release. As Pistol leads his captive off, the Boy has more disparaging remarks about his companion, from which we learn that Nym too has been hanged for stealing. He heads back to the camp, which he complains has been left unguarded.

4.5–6   The next scene appears to take place between the attacks of the French first and second lines. They are shamed by the failure of the assault and are full of high words. They will "die in harness" and "offer up our lives." "Let life be short," they proclaim, rather than submit to the disgrace of defeat. The battle hangs in the balance, and on the English side Henry receives a touching account of the deaths of Suffolk and York, who were the only English nobles killed in action. The king is alarmed at what appears to be preparation for another attack by the French and orders that all those held prisoner by the English are to be killed.

4.7   We receive from Fluellen and Gower an account of the French raid on the English camp and the massacre of the boys, but the two then digress into an disagreement over the comparison between Henry and Alexander the Great. Defending the king, Gower argues that he never killed his closest friends, as did Alexander, but Fluellen reminds him of Falstaff. Henry appears and, enraged by the slaughter of the innocent boys, gives the order to "cut the throats" of French prisoners in retaliation.

This murder of the prisoners is a matter of historical record. Under modern international jurisprudence, Henry would probably be held accountable for a "crime against humanity." Shakespeare offers two different motives for the order, however. In the first instance, the French are seen preparing for an attack, and the exhausted English need every available man on the line of battle, thus killing the prisoners releases their

*Readers interested in the battle should consult John Keegan, *The Face of Battle* (New York: Viking, 1976), pp. 79–116.

guards for service to repel a force threatening annihilation. Pistol's capture of the French soldier provides background for Henry's order. The ancient is not the only Englishman who is more concerned about protecting his investment than he is with participating in battle.

In the second instance, the king responds angrily with a brutal act abhorrent in any age. Henry's two speeches leave his motive ambiguous. In the one case he is the commander of an army in a life-or-death battle and makes a tactical decision in the face of a threat to survival. In the other he is a vengeful warrior responding mindlessly to one atrocity with yet another. Both versions appear in the early printed editions, and it interesting to speculate which one was spoken on the stage at the Globe Theater.

In any event, the French herald enters, declares to Henry that "the day is yours," and asks leave to collect their dead and wounded on the field. But at this, the moment of his greatest triumph, Henry indulges in a seemingly frivolous trick. Williams enters, wearing Henry's glove in his cap, and reveals that he has a grievance against the man displaying his own in like manner. When he leaves, Henry asks Fluellen to wear his glove and "apprehend" anyone who challenges him. It seems a cruel joke to play on two loyal soldiers.

4.8 Fluellen and Williams come to blows as the king and his noblemen enter to separate them. Henry reveals his identity and asks "satisfaction" from Williams for challenging a king. The soldier defends himself stoutly, and the king, satisfied, returns his glove, now filled with crowns. All that can be said for the incident is that Henry's prankish wit extricates him from a potentially embarrassing situation. He had challenged a common soldier in a sudden and quite human flash of anger, but it would have been entirely inappropriate for a king to answer to one of his subjects. Henry therefore resorts to a trick, in a glimpse perhaps of Falstaff's rough humor still alive in the king.

The battle over, casualties are counted. While Shakespeare's numbers for the French—about ten thousand—are quite accurate according to historians, he errs considerable on the English side, where the loss was an estimated sixteen hundred rather than "but five and twenty." It is nonetheless an impressive victory, and Henry gives the credit to God, ordering that hymns be sung, the "Non Nobis" (not us) and "Te Deum" (to God).

The difference in treatment of this scene by the two film versions is striking. In the Olivier production of 1944, the king leads a triumphal march toward Agincourt Castle, illuminated in the distance by the setting sun, while the hymn rises in intensity—a celebration of the kind of victory that the actor's wartime audience fervently hoped would soon be· theirs. Forty years later, Branagh used the same "Non Nobis," but it is more a dirge than an anthem as the note of celebration is muted by the scene it is sung to. The king enters the smoldering camp and, lifting the body of the murdered Boy, carries him across the battlefield to a cart loaded with the dead. It is a long interval, and as the hymn rises in volume, we are witness to the carnage of the battle scene—dead men and horses strewn about in grotesque postures, battlefield scavengers cutting the purses of the dead, injured soldiers struggling to stand, others, glaze-eyed, wandering aimlessly among the corpses, and a procession of walking wounded slogging painfully across the muddy field. As the music fades, Henry is seen with his eyes closed and his mud-spattered head bowed. The scene is not in Shakespeare's play, to be sure, but it dramatically reflects the mixed feelings with which a later generation contemplates the spectacle of war.

5.Cho.   The chorus fills us in on subsequent events: the march to Calais, Henry's triumphal procession to London, and his return to France to pursue his campaign, which actually continued for another four years.

5.1   The fifth act opens on the comic figures, though the humor it contains is rough indeed. The Welsh minority of England has its day as Fluellen manhandles Pistol, forcing him to eat a leek, the national emblem of Wales, while beating him with a cudgel. After a tongue-lashing by Gower, Pistol is finally left to himself. He laments the death of his wife but quickly recovers and determines to turn "bawd." "To England will I steal," he says, "and there I'll steal." He will claim, moreover, that the injuries he suffered from Fluellen's beating are war wounds. As a comic figure, Pistol is no Falstaff, whom we grow to love for all his faults. This English "ancient" is despicable—a braggart, a coward, and an insolent posturer, a figure that Shakespeare uses to describe the false soldiers familiar to all the armies of the world.

5.2   The long final scene of the play depicts the treaty between the victorious Henry and his defeated French counterpart. It opens with a moving plea by the Duke of Burgundy on behalf of "the naked, poor, and mangled Peace." Shakespeare completes his many-dimensional image of war with a passage of inspired poetry deploring its destructive effects upon the land and its innocent people. The neglected fields of France, Burgundy pleads, are now choked with weeds; and as "our vineyards, fallows, meads, and hedges, / Defective in their natures, grow to wildness," so too the children "grow like savages." The image calls to mind pictures in our own time of ten-year-old boys armed with rifles in Beirut, Bosnia, and Africa.

Henry is perhaps moved by the speech, but he is single-mindedly determined that, having won a difficult war, he will not lose the peace. He has submitted his "just demands," he announces, and the choice between war and peace is now up to the French. As the parties leave to confer, Henry asks that Katharine be left behind. In this delightful scene he woos his future wife, and it is worth noting that he does not really have to, since marriage to her is one of his chief demands. But he does so anyway, all the while claiming that he is inept at it. Using skills that perhaps served him well during his madcap days in Eastcheap, he declares himself a simple soldier, lacking the social graces of a courtier but possessed of "a good heart." He tries some halting French but soon discards it, and though Katharine may not fully understand everything he says, she cannot help but be impressed by his intensity. He finally asks, "wilt thou have me?" and when she accepts on the condition that it please her father, he remarks with ironic assurance: "Nay, it will please him well, Kate; it shall please him, Kate."

The provisions of the treaty are agreed to and peace prevails, with the hope that the two nations, "whose very shores look pale / With envy of each other's happiness / May cease their hatred."

Epil. Alas, it was not to be, for as the chorus tells us in closing, "this star of England" was to rule for but a short time, leaving an infant son to inherit the two crowns. Sadly, he concludes, during the child's minority "so many had the managing" of the kingdoms "that they lost France, and made his England bleed," a tale "which oft our stage hath shown"—that is, in Shakespeare's *Henry VI* plays.

This, then, is Shakespeare's vision of war in all its glory and brutality. He shows us its heroes and villains, the brave and cowardly, the loyal and treacherous, the noble and foolish. He evokes the deep sense of brotherhood bonding those who face its dangers together, and the awful solitude of those who must contemplate their end alone.

And in Shakespeare's image of the soldier-king, sketched in epic proportions for a mere two hours on the stage, he offers Henry V, a figure so contradictory in character as to bring pride to the breasts of some and disgust to the minds of others, one who combines the clear-eyed purpose of an inspiring leader with the wily skill of the most divisive of Machiavellian princes, who knows that in the "play for kingdom, the gentlest gamester is the soonest winner," but is prepared to unleash the terrors of the sack upon a helpless city, a king whose tongue can weave a web of diplomatic intrigue and woo a maiden with ardent simplicity, can sway an assembly of noblemen and speak of the soul with the common man.

It is no wonder that the play is both applauded and reviled—Henry combines much of the best and the worst in us all.

HENRY VI, PARTS 1, 2, 3

THE THREE PARTS of *Henry VI* were Shakespeare's earliest plays and apparently proved quite popular in their time. They are seldom, if ever, staged today, however, except in severely abbreviated form. The involved account of the origin and conduct of the War of the Roses, with its long list of characters and shifting alliances, can leave a modern audience confused as to who is on which side and why. The central conflict is a struggle between two noble families, those of York and Lancaster, for the throne of England, occupied at the time by an ineffectual king, Henry VI, whose efforts to achieve peace among his contentious lords prove futile. In the end he loses his crown, and his life, in civil wars that lay bare the remorseless brutality of both sides.

This brief survey will attempt to clarify the issues and alliances as Shakespeare dramatized them. He compressed fifty years of English history, from 1422 to 1471, into six hours on the stage, a formidable feat in itself, and he may be forgiven whatever liberties he took with that history.* Our emphasis will be on those events and figures that bear on the brilliant play to follow, *Richard III*.

HENRY VI, PART I

On the death of Henry V his brother, the Duke of Bedford, is left as regent of his conquests in France, with the noble Lord Talbot as commander of the English armies. While they labor to maintain English control

---

*Roughly, *Part 1* chronicles English history from 1422 to 1445, *Part 2* from 1445 to 1455, and *Part 3* from 1455 to 1471.

there, back in England the powerful nobility fall to squabbling. The death of the king leaves a nine-month-old baby, Henry VI, as heir to the throne, and the ensuing power vacuum during his minority encourages ambitious factions to contend for advantage. Fatal animosities that would have been held in check by a forceful monarch arise to trouble the kingdom, chief among them the hatred between the Duke of Gloucester, the young king's uncle and official Protector, and the ambitious Henry Beaufort, Bishop of Winchester. Of more importance, however, is the rivalry between Richard Plantagenet of York and the Lancastrian Earl of Somerset. The two appear before the Earl of Warwick, who undertakes futilely to resolve their differences. In a gesture intended to emphasize his intransigence, Richard plucks a white rose from a nearby bush, and in reply Somerset picks a red one. The roses become a symbol of their enmity.

Somerset taunts Richard about his disgraced father, the Earl of Cambridge, who was executed for treason by the former king.* Disturbed by the allusions, Richard seeks the full story from his aged uncle, Edmund Mortimer, the Earl of March, who has been held prisoner in the Tower for years. Mortimer reveals that when Richard II left to campaign in Ireland, the king had named him rightful heir to the throne, and Richard's father, of York ancestry, had espoused his claim, leading a rebellion against the Lancaster king, Henry V. The old man, preparing for his death, declares Richard his heir.

King Henry attempts unsuccessfully to arrange a truce between the Duke of Gloucester and the Bishop of Winchester. At the urging of Gloucester and Warwick, the king restores Richard to his title and lands. He is now the Duke of York.

While these animosities are brewing in England, Talbot has to contend with rising French resistance, inspired by the charismatic Joan of Arc. She persuades the Duke of Burgundy to abandon his English allies and support the cause of France. Combining their armies, they lay siege to Talbot in Bourdeaux, and when Somerset refuses to come to his aid, he is defeated and dies, lamenting the death of his son. The English restore their forces, however, and return to capture and execute Joan. The French king agrees to end the fighting, and Henry appoints him his viceroy in the reconquered land.

*See *Henry V*, though the crime is somewhat different there.

Meanwhile the Earl of Suffolk recommends a marriage between Henry and the French Margaret of Anjou, with whom he has developed a romantic liaison himself. The king agrees and Suffolk exults, scheming to exercise power through her: "I will rule both her, the King, and realm."

HENRY VI, PART 2

The principal figures in *Part 2* are King Henry and his queen, Margaret of Anjou, who is carrying on an adulterous affair with the Earl of Suffolk; the earl himself, who is elevated to duke as the play opens; the Duke of Gloucester, who still serves as Protector, though the king has reached maturity; and, increasingly, Richard, Duke of York, who harbors ambitions to be king.

Suffolk returns from France as escort to Margaret, and the terms of the marriage contract are revealed. The French provinces of Maine and Anjou, then under English control, are ceded to Margaret, but they are immediately transferred to her father, effectively returning them to France. The Duke of Gloucester and the Earl of Warwick lament that the two provinces, which they have all sacrificed so much to conquer, should be so easily surrendered. The Bishop of Winchester, Gloucester's habitual enemy and now a cardinal, reprimands him for raising objections to the king's will and, when the duke leaves, warns that Gloucester must be watched. The scene effectively draws the line between the contentious parties. Allied with Gloucester are the Earl of Salisbury, the Earl of Warwick, and Richard, Duke of York; with the Bishop are Suffolk, the Duke of Buckingham, and the Duke of Somerset. In a *soliloquy* at the end of the scene, York renews his determination to secure the throne, but he is content, he says, to bide his time until he can force his claim upon the house of Lancaster.

The campaign to unseat Gloucester begins, and York is perfectly willing to ally himself with the opposition to bring about the downfall of his patron. He and Buckingham join forces to arrest Eleanor, the Duchess of Gloucester, for consorting with a witch. When the king hears of her offense, he dismisses her husband from his post as Protector and banishes her to the Isle of Man. Meanwhile York argues his claim to the throne to Warwick and Salisbury, who embrace his cause: "Long live our sovereign Richard, England's king!" York then joins the bishop's allies in condemning Gloucester, who is arrested. They decide that he must die, and Suffolk agrees to do the deed.

News arrives of a rebellion in Ireland, and York is selected to suppress it, an appointment that pleases him as an opportunity to conscript an army. He has stirred up further discord to trouble the kingdom during his absence, deluding a Kentish commoner, John Cade, into believing that he is a Mortimer, hence heir to the throne. He raises a rebellion of the discontented common people of England, whose welfare has been neglected while the nobles struggle among themselves for power.

In a separate uprising entirely, the commoners, having heard that Suffolk is responsible for the death of the popular Gloucester, riot against the court. The king banishes Suffolk, and he and the queen bid each other a tearful farewell. Meanwhile the Bishop of Winchester is grievously ill and with his last breath confesses to the king his complicity in Gloucester's murder. On his voyage into exile, Suffolk is killed.

John Cade leads a mob of commoners on London, taking vengeance along the way on anyone who appears to be a gentleman—one indiscreetly speaks Latin, another admits that he can write his name.* The mob is met by Buckingham and old Clifford, who persuade the commoners to remain loyal to the king. Deserted by his followers, Cade takes refuge in a gentleman's garden, where he is killed.

At this point the most influential nobles in the kingdom—Gloucester, Winchester, and Suffolk—are dead; and York, returning from Ireland, marches at the head of an army into the power vacuum they leave. Buckingham challenges him at St. Alban's, outside London, and York declares that his only intent is to remove his enemy, Somerset, from the king's council. Buckingham assures him that the man is already a prisoner in the Tower. When the king enters with Somerset by his side, obviously still in favor, York is furious. He asserts publicly his claim to the throne, raging that Henry is unworthy of the crown, and demands that the king abdicate in his favor. Somerset attempts to arrest him for treason, but Warwick and Salisbury enter with armed soldiers to prevent it. The contention between the houses of York and Lancaster is now openly

---

*One of Cade's rebels has the famous line: "The first thing we do, let's kill all the lawyers."

proclaimed. Henceforth their differences will be played out on the field of battle.

The armies clash at St. Alban's, the first battle of the War of the Roses. York kills old Clifford, and the slain man's son vows to be avenged on the house of York, even if it means slaughtering their children. In these final scenes we are introduced to York's son Richard, who will figure prominently in the next play and the one to follow. He dispatches Somerset, and the king and queen flee to London, pursued by York and his allies, Warwick and Salisbury.

HENRY VI, PART 3

Part 3 takes up where *Part 2* left off, as the Yorks celebrate their victory at St. Alban's, and Richard enters proudly displaying Somerset's head. This is Richard "Crook-back," who was born with a hump on his back and a withered arm, a handicap he compensates for with burning ambition and a fierce courage in battle. The strife in England has already taken a heavy toll on the country's nobility, with more deaths to come. But a new generation is rising to take their place, typified by York's four sons (in order of birth): Edward, later Duke of York and Edward IV; George, later Duke of Clarence; Richard, later Duke of Gloucester and Richard III; and young Rutland.

The victorious York forces occupy the Parliament building, and the duke seats himself on the throne, claiming his right to the crown. Henry VI enters demanding that he step down, but York, backed by his soldiers, refuses. A compromise is reached, allowing Henry to remain on the throne with York to be designated as his heir if he agrees to end the fighting. The pact infuriates Queen Margaret, who rages at her husband for disinheriting their son Edward, the Prince of Wales.

Sometime later Richard persuades his father to break his oath to Henry, and news arrives that Margaret has raised an army and is advancing on them. The Lancastrians triumph in the Battle of Wakefield, where Lord Clifford, to avenge his father's death, cruelly murders York's son, the schoolboy Rutland. York himself is taken prisoner, and after a scene in which his captors taunt him, he is stabbed to death by the vindictive Margaret and her ally, Lord Clifford. The Lancastrian forces are then defeated in the Battle of Towton. Clifford is killed, Henry flees to Scotland,

and Margaret to France. Edward, now Duke of York, assumes the crown, and Warwick undertakes a mission to France to arrange for the marriage between Edward and the king's sister-in-law, a Lady Bona. The new king names his brother George the Duke of Clarence, and Richard the Duke of Gloucester.*

Henry is taken prisoner when he ventures out of Scotland into English territory. Edward becomes captivated by an attractive widow, Lady Elizabeth Grey, and decides to make her his queen, much to the consternation of his brothers. In a long, revealing *soliloquy*, Gloucester ponders his ambition, calculating the number of figures, both York and Lancaster, who stand between him and the throne. Comparing his path to the crown to a "thorny wood," he vows to "hew my way out with a bloody axe." He can "smile, and murder whiles I smile," he says, and scheme so cunningly that he will "set the murderous Machiavel to school."

While her husband languishes in the Tower, Queen Margaret appeals to the French King Lewis for aid. Warwick arrives to propose the marriage of Edward and Lady Bona, and the king agrees, setting aside Margaret's violent objections. Even as the agreement is reached, however, word arrives from London of Edward's marriage to Lady Grey. Warwick is furious at what he considers a blatant betrayal of trust and joins forces with Margaret and King Lewis to "uncrown" Edward. Clarence, also incensed by the marriage, deserts his brothers and joins Warwick, while Gloucester decides it is in his best interest to remain with Edward.

Warwick and Clarence lead an army to England, capture Edward, free Henry, and restore the house of Lancaster to the throne.† Gloucester manages to rescue his brother, however, and they flee to Burgundy. Henry appoints Warwick and Clarence to serve jointly as "Protectors" of England, while he characteristically retires to a life of religious devotion. Edward and Gloucester return with help from Burgundy, enter the city of York on a ruse, and once more claim the throne. They advance on London, seize Henry, and lay siege to Warwick's castle in Coventry. Several Lancaster allies come to Warwick's aid, but Clarence refuses to fight against his brothers and switches back to the York cause.

---

*The reading text refers to them henceforth by their titles—and so shall we.
†The powerful Earl of Warwick was called the "kingmaker" because he engineered Edward's rise to the throne and then replaced him with Henry.

In the ensuing Battle of Barnet, Warwick's army is routed and he suffers a mortal wound; but a new threat looms as word arrives that Queen Margaret has landed with a large army from France and is marching toward Tewkesbury. She suffers defeat in the battle, however, and the victorious Yorks take her prisoner along with her son Edward, Prince of Wales. He is defiant and infuriates his captors, scorning them as "lascivious Edward," "purgur'd George," and "misshapen Dick." In response they stab him as his mother looks on in anguish and begs them to kill her too. They refuse and banish her to France.

Gloucester hurries to London to perform the final act of the War of the Roses—he murders Henry in the Tower. So Edward IV sits securely on the throne again and foresees a time of peace and "lasting joy." He catalogues, with some satisfaction, the losses suffered by the Lancaster nobility, and in the list Shakespeare draws attention to the terrible cost of the war. Aside from King Henry and his son, the casualties include "three Dukes of Somerset," "two Cliffords," "two Northumberlands," Warwick, and his brother Montague.

RICHARD III

RICHARD III, according to Shakespeare, is an unscrupulous villain. Motivated by a single-minded ambition to mount the throne of England, he ruthlessly eliminates all those who stand between him and his goal, among them two innocent boys. He is heartless, repulsive, vicious, callously unrepentant—and enormously entertaining. The stage, otherwise occupied by relatively uninteresting historical figures, lights up at his entrance, so that we become impatient for his appearance, wondering what outrageous devilry he will be up to next.

These figures are historical, however, and a glance at their history, to which there are frequent references in the dialogue, will read us into the action and enhance enjoyment of the play. The War of the Roses, chronicled in Shakespeare's *Henry VI, Parts 1, 2, and 3,* was a devastating civil conflict between two noble houses vying for the throne of England—Lancaster, whose emblem was the red rose, and York, the white. The Lancastrian Henry VI, son of the great Henry V, proved an ineffectual king, his cause largely championed by his resolute French queen, Margaret of Anjou. The York faction finally prevailed at the battle of Tewkesbury in 1471, where the king was captured and his son, Edward, the Prince of Wales, slain. Henry was murdered shortly thereafter, and both deaths, according to Shakespeare, were at the hand of Richard, Duke of Gloucester. Richard's elder brother assumed the throne as Edward IV and ruled until his death in 1483, an event dramatized early in the action.

The play itself opens on Richard's *soliloquy* in which he declares himself a villain and discloses a scheme to do away with his brother, Clarence. That accomplished, on the death of the king he arranges for the murder of his two young sons, Edward, the Prince of Wales and heir apparent, and the Duke of York, the famous "Princes in the Tower." He then assumes the crown and inaugurates a reign of terror that unites all factions against him behind the claim of Henry Tudor, Earl of Richmond. The English, tiring of Richard's despotism, rally to Richmond's cause and triumph over the king's forces at Bosworth Field, killing him in the process and putting an end to the internecine warfare that had plagued the country for thirty years. Richmond marries Edward IV's daughter, Elizabeth, thus uniting the houses of Lancaster and York, and mounts the throne as Henry VII, restoring peace to the kingdom, according to Shakespeare, and establishing the rule of the Tudor monarchs.*

The phrase "according to Shakespeare" appears with annoying frequency because the poet is in some respects singularly unhistorical in his chronicle of English kings. In *Richard III* he includes scenes that could not have happened. The final illness and death of Edward IV establishes the time frame of the action as 1483 to 1485. In the opening episodes, however, we discover that Anne, who was betrothed to the Lancastrian Edward, Prince of Wales, is escorting the corpse of his father, Henry VI, to his grave, though both father and son had been dead for some twelve years. Further, Richard's brother Clarence, who appears in the first scene, had been executed five years earlier; and Henry's queen, Margaret of Anjou, who died in exile in 1482, appears very much alive and still spitting venom at the Yorks. Shakespeare was surely aware of the anachronisms and is simply adapting history to his purpose, creating encounters in which Richard has scope to demonstrate his devious skills.

But Shakespeare was apparently unaware that the historical Richard III may not have been the monster he placed before us on the stage. The principal sources for this image were composed by staunch supporters of the Tudor monarchs, including the highly regarded Sir Thomas More. Early in the reign of Henry VIII, More ingratiated himself with the young king by composing *The History of King Richard the Third*, which describes Richard as a despotic villain, responsible for the murder of the princes. Historians under the reign of the later Tudors accepted More's version, firmly establishing the image of Richard as a figure of evil in the minds of Shakespeare's audience—and, it seems, in the imagination of the poet as well. But twentieth-century historians question whether this

*See the introduction to "The Histories."

is an accurate picture, suggesting that the stamp of criminal and usurper was imposed upon Richard by Tudor apologists to discredit his reign and legitimize the tenuous claim to the crown of the Earl of Richmond, who became Henry VII.*

These matters need not distract us, however, from Shakespeare's portrayal of a consummate and thoroughly entertaining villain.

1.1 The play opens on a soliloquy by Richard, Duke of Gloucester, who confides in the audience that he is discontented with "this weak piping time of peace." He is happier in a time of war, he says, since because of his physical deformity he cuts an inelegant figure in a social setting. Tradition had it that he was a hunchback with a withered arm, and since he cannot thrive in a peaceful society, he concludes, he is "determined to prove a villain." Shakespeare does not explore the forces that create a "villain"—we should consult *Macbeth* for that—but he leaves the distinct impression that Richard's twisted nature is somehow associated with the fact that he was "deform'd, unfinish'd" at birth, "scarce half made up," as he himself complains. A person becomes evil, Shakespeare is content to say, for any number of reasons, perhaps even because he is ugly.

Richard has already set in motion a plot to discredit his brother George, Duke of Clarence, in the king's eyes by spreading rumors of a mysterious prophecy that someone whose name begins with "G" will murder the royal heirs. The *dramatic irony* is a bit obvious here, since the Elizabethan audience was well aware that the eventual murderer will be the Duke of Gloucester. At this point there is no indication of Richard's motive for planting the rumor, an act that just seems to flow naturally from his professed villainy, but our knowledge of the scheme sets up his encounter with Clarence, who is being escorted to confinement in the Tower of London. Richard is all concern and commiseration, blaming his brother's disgrace on the queen, "my Lady Grey," who was also responsible, he claims, for the imprisonment of Hastings, the lord

---

*The disappearance of the princes nonetheless remains a mystery. During renovations of the Tower in 1674, workers found the remains of two boys, a discovery interpreted as further evidence of Richard's villainy. He has received kinder treatment in modern popular literature. Two works among many more sympathetic to him are Josephine Tey's intriguing mystery *The Daughter of Time* and Sharon Kay Penman's comprehensive historical novel *The Sunne in Splendour*.

chamberlain.* He promises to plead for his brother's release, but as Clarence leaves, Richard gloats over his success: "Go, tred the path that thou shalt ne'er return."

Richard then encounters the newly released Hastings and is again ingratiatingly sympathetic. They exchange remarks about revenge against the queen and the health of the king, who has taken to his sick bed. Hastings passes on, and in a continuation of his soliloquy Richard tells more of his schemes. He is the youngest of the three brothers, and he is determined to do away with Clarence before King Edward dies so that, as the only surviving male York, he will be in a powerful position in the kingdom. It is, he says gleefully, a "world for me to bustle in." To further enhance his prospects he plans to marry "Warwick's youngest daughter," forming an alliance with one of England's most powerful noble families.† This is Anne, widow of the Prince of Wales, Henry VI's son, whom Richard also killed, according to Shakespeare.** He is so devious as to be almost unwilling to voice to himself the purpose of all this intrigue—it is "for another secret close intent . . . which I must reach unto."

1.2   In the following scene we find Anne accompanying the body of her father-in-law, Henry VI, for burial. She laments the loss of both the father and the son, Edward, her late husband, and condemns their murderer:

> O, cursed be the hand that made these holes;
> Cursed the heart that had the heart to do it;
> Cursed the blood that let this blood from hence.

We encounter a great deal of this parallel structure and repetition in the play, most frequently in the form of curses, laments, and prophecies. Such passages are admittedly far removed from the cadence or substance of

---

*The chamberlain was an important court official entrusted with the management of the royal household.

†Richard Neville, Earl of Warwick, called the "kingmaker," was instrumental in securing the crown for Edward IV in 1461. Then, feeling himself betrayed by the king, he returned in 1470 to defeat the York forces and briefly restore Henry VI to the throne. He was killed in battle in 1471.

**The poet here again adapts history to his purpose. Anne was betrothed, not married, to the Prince of Wales, and many others had a hand in killing him at the battle of Tewkesbury. Shakespeare attributes the murder of Henry VI to Richard, though he actually died in the Tower of causes unknown.

common speech, but the style adds an ominous tone of ritual incantation, loading the words with significance.

Anne continues her lament, calling down further curses on Richard, wishing him father to an abortive child as misshapen as he, and a wife made miserable by the loss. Richard comes upon the procession suddenly, orders the bearers to set the casket down, and then embarks upon what must be the most outrageous wooing scene in stage history. Anne is repelled by his appearance and hurls curses at him. Pointing to the corpse, she rages: "O God! which this blood mad'st, revenge his death; / O earth! which this blood drink'st, revenge his death." She continues in this vein as Richard cleverly deflects her curses with compliments, finally professing that he killed her husband and father-in-law only because he was overcome by her beauty—she "did haunt me in my sleep" he claims, "to undertake the death of all the world." And it gets better! In reply Anne spits on him, but he is undeterred, launching into a long speech declaring his passion. In a final dramatic gesture he hands her his sword, kneels, bares his breast, and urges her to avenge the deaths by killing him. And when she refuses, he daringly urges her further, "then bid me kill myself."

It works! She relents, accepts his ring, and leaves, observing that "much it joys me too, / To see you are become so penitent." Richard is exultant—and scornful: "Was ever woman in this manner woo'd? / Was ever woman in this manner won?" "I'll have her," he goes on, "but I will not keep her long." He then toys ironically with the thought that if he can win a woman with such ease, he must indeed be "a marvelously proper man" and not the disfigured cripple he had thought. He promises himself gleefully to consult a mirror and "study fashions to adorn my body" so as to take advantage of this surprising revelation.

1.3 The next scene introduces Edward IV's queen, Elizabeth, or "my Lady Grey," as Richard calls her. The widow of a Lord Grey when Edward married her, she brought to the court two grown sons from her former marriage, the Marquess of Dorset and Lord Grey, as well as a brother, Earl Rivers. They represent a significant faction in the shifting allegiances of court politics, one standing in opposition to the group of counselors who surround the king, hence an obstacle to Richard's ambitions. She has also borne a younger generation of children to the king, among them Edward, heir to the throne, then twelve years old; Richard, Duke of York, age nine; and a daughter, Elizabeth of York.

The scene opens with the queen's son and brother attempting to relieve her distress over the king's illness. The Duke of Buckingham and Lord Hastings enter with encouraging words about his health and the message that he wishes to heal the animosities that have grown among the factions in the royal household. Richard enters, complaining angrily about those who have sought to discredit him with the king, and accusations begin to fly. The queen denounces him for hating her and her relations. He claims she is responsible for the imprisonment of Clarence. She denies it. He accuses her of turning the king against Hastings, the lord chamberlain, and goes on to remind her of his staunch loyalty to Edward at a time when her family was allied with their enemy, the Lancastrian Henry VI. It is not a pretty scene as the lines of conflict are clearly defined. Meanwhile Henry's widow, Margaret of Anjou, has entered unseen. In a series of *asides* she undercuts each of Richard's claims with her own grievances. The mutual recriminations grow more heated until Margaret bursts upon the group, demanding, "hear me, you wrangling pirates, that fall out / In sharing that which you have pill'd [pillaged] from me!"

Margaret has an important role in the play. First, she hates them all and succeeds in uniting them, only moments before at each other's throats, against her. Second, and more significantly, she acts as a prophetess, a "foul wrinkled witch," as Richard calls her, who foretells the downfall of everyone present, predicting that their sorrows will mirror her own, in just retribution for her losses. Elizabeth's son Edward, the Prince of Wales, will, she rages, "for Edward, my son, which was Prince of Wales, / Die in his youth by like untimely violence," and further the queen, like herself, will "die neither mother, wife, nor England's queen." She prays that the others present—Rivers, Dorset, and Hastings—will be "by some unlook'd accident cut off," but she saves her most vitriolic curses for Richard, "thou elvish-mark'd, abortive, rooting hog." * Margaret intones her predictions with those parallels and repetitions of speech that give them an aura of inevitability. The hatred, cruelty, and

---

*The Duke of Gloucester's emblem was the wild boar, which explains this and later references to him as a "hog."

thirst for vengeance that marked the war years, the treacherous switching of loyalties and ruthless murders that brought the Yorks to the throne, she foretells, will now be visited upon the victors, who will suffer the same fate as the vanquished—none will escape. And the instrument of retribution stands among them, the malicious Richard, that "bottled spider" and "poisonous bunch-back'd toad." She urges Buckingham to be wary of him, "take heed of yonder dog! / Look when he fawns, he bites," and then leaves them with a final prediction that on some future day they will remember her warnings and "say poor Margaret was a prophetess."

Word arrives that the king desires their attendance, and the court retires to his bedchamber, leaving Richard alone on stage. He is quite pleased with his performance and congratulates himself for turning the court against the queen's faction while covering his own "naked villainy / With odd old ends stol'n forth of Holy Writ, / And seem a saint when most I play the devil." He then confers with two shadowy figures, whom he sends off to the Tower to murder Clarence.

1.4   In the Tower, Clarence offers an anguished account of his nightmare in which Richard knocks him overboard from a ship at sea and he drowns. In the dream he approaches Hell where he encounters the shades of the Earl of Warwick and Margaret's son, the Prince of Wales. In truth, he is not exactly the innocent, "simple, plain Clarence" that his brother makes him out to be. He aided Edward in gaining the crown and then joined Warwick in deposing him to reestablish Henry VI on the throne briefly, only to switch sides once again in the ensuing conflict, rejoin Edward, and participate in the murder of the Prince of Wales. Hence he is to Warwick "false Clarence," and to the prince "false, fleeting, perjur'd Clarence." In a sense he represents the worst of those whose duplicity and treachery marked the War of the Roses, qualities that now seem embodied in the person of Richard, Duke of Gloucester.

The murderers carry a warrant for the death of Clarence. In a long scene he pleads eloquently for his life, to no avail. They stab him and for good measure drown him in a "malmsey butt [barrel of wine]." * One of the murderers has an attack of conscience and refuses to accept the fee for the deed.

---

*So it is recorded in contemporary accounts, though he was executed in 1478, not 1483.

The first act, then, presents us with a court torn by contending factions. The divisions are no less severe than those that precipitated the War of the Roses and seem in a sense to have been inherited from those turbulent years. Time has not healed the wounds of the war. New animosities build on the old ones as the royal family prepares for the power struggle to follow the death of the ailing king. It is an atmosphere of intrigue and mistrust that the ever-resourceful Richard can indeed "bustle in."

2.1   The sickly Edward attempts to reconcile the queen's family and the old York advocates represented by Hastings and Buckingham. With stiff formality they obediently pledge undying love for one another, all convinced that the vows they receive are as hollow as the ones they give. Richard comes upon this counterfeit scene and, catching the spirit of the occasion, outdoes them all in his commitment to amity, declaring grandly, "I do not know that Englishman alive / With whom my soul is any jot at odds" and concluding, "I thank my God for my humility." It is an outrageous performance, to be sure, but he is no more or less fraudulent than any of the others—he is just better at it.

Edward is dumbfounded to hear that Clarence has been executed. He had indeed ordered his death but sent a later message countermanding the earlier one. Richard had secretly seen to it that the first order was carried out before the second arrived. The king grieves at the news, recalling his brother's care and service during the wars, and he chastises all present for their failure to plead for Clarence's life. The royal couple leave, and Richard mutters to those remaining that the queen is responsible for his brother's death. But he concludes piously, "God will revenge it." This scene adheres to a pattern we have already witnessed and will again as the play progresses. It opens with minor figures enacting a rather dreary ritual and comes alive only when Richard enters. We grow to anticipate his appearance, expecting that he will somehow outshine them in whatever charade they are engaged.

2.2   The next scene finds the Duchess of York, Richard's mother, attempting to console Clarence's two children, while she herself grieves over his death and the illness of her other son, Edward. The boy reveals that Richard confided in him that the king is responsible for his father's death, "provok'd to't by the Queen," and that his uncle wept as he spoke.

The duchess marvels at the level of deceit to which Richard will stoop. She knows her son!

The queen enters, sorrowing at the death of the king; and all engage in a ritualistic lament at their losses—the children for their father, the duchess for her two sons, Clarence and Edward, and the queen for her husband. Rivers alertly advises her to send for the prince so that he may be quickly crowned, urging her to "drown desperate sorrow in dead Edward's grave, / And plant your joys in living Edward's throne." Richard enters, accompanied by the Yorkish faction, and we are eager to see what he will make of the occasion. He is all ostentatious sympathy, comforting the queen—"all of us have cause / To wail the dimming of our shining star"—and kneeling meekly to ask his mother's blessing.

It is all show. The two factions glare at each other across the bowed figures of the grieving women and spar over the issue that concerns them most, control of the future king. Buckingham sanctimoniously reminds all of the peace the late king had pledged them to and counsels that the young prince be escorted to London by a modest train so as not to unduly upset the populace. It is so agreed; but when the others leave, Buckingham advises Richard that they should make haste to reach the prince before "the Queen's proud kindred." Richard praises the wisdom of the duke, who has become his closest ally: "My other self, my counsel's consistory, / My oracle, my prophet, my dear cousin."

2.3 The following scene is characteristic of a number that Shakespeare inserts from time to time in his plays. It records the response of the ordinary citizens of the kingdom to the power struggles of the mighty, which have all too often resulted in misery for their subjects. In this sense they act in the capacity of a *chorus* to the action. Here the "3 Cit.," who seems the most perceptive of them, questions whether the new king will be able to settle the kingdom, for "woe to that land that's governed by a child." He is reminded of the troubles that followed the succession of the nine-month-old Henry VI to the throne. The common people are anxious, he says, knowing that "full of danger is the Duke of Gloucester, / And the Queen's sons and brothers, haught and proud," presaging a power struggle that will subject the already "sickly land" to more desolation. "If God sort it out," he concludes fatalistically, "'tis more than we deserve, or I expect."

2.4 In the next short scene the queen learns that Richard and

Buckingham have imprisoned her brother Rivers and her son Grey. The
struggle has begun, and, sensing danger, she seeks sanctuary for herself
and her young son, the Duke of York. In medieval custom the church offered its protection to any and all who appeared at their doors; the state,
it was said, had no authority to apprehend those who found sanctuary on
ecclesiastical lands. The Archbishop of York agrees to protect them.

3.1 The third act opens with an extended exchange between
Richard and the two young princes. This the only opportunity we have to
become acquainted with the boys, and Shakespeare is obviously intent on
arousing pity for them. This he does with dramatic irony, playing on the
audience's awareness of their fate as he portrays the scheming villain toying with his intended victims. As the only surviving brother of the dead
king, Richard has been appointed regent, or "Lord Protector," as the
prince calls him, entrusted with the management of the kingdom during
the minority of Edward V. In this we see the importance of doing away
with Clarence, who, had he survived, as the older brother would have assumed the position on the king's death.

Richard and Buckingham welcome the young prince to London. He
is uneasy, however, and complains, "I want more uncles to welcome me."
Richard replies that his other uncles (such as Rivers) are dangerous to
him, not to be trusted. The prince is unconvinced, however, and asks anxiously why his mother and brother are not also there to greet him. Hastings enters with the news that they have taken sanctuary, prompting a
scornful outburst from Buckingham, who directs the Cardinal Archbishop of Canterbury to secure the boy. The cardinal objects to any violation of sanctuary, but Buckingham imperiously interprets canon law for
him, claiming that the Duke of York is too young to claim such protection, hence no privilege is broken by bringing him out. The cardinal submits meekly and departs with Hastings to do as Buckingham has
directed.

Richard counsels the prince that he and his brother will be housed in
the Tower until his coronation, a prospect that increases the boy's anxiety:
"I do not like the Tower, of any place." Hastings and the cardinal return
with young York, and in a touching scene the two brothers, recently so
close, contemplate the new distance between them now that Edward is to
become king. York is a precocious child and engages in a witty exchange

with Richard, who plays the role of a smiling, indulgent uncle until the boy makes the unfortunate suggestion that he carry him on his shoulders, a taunting reference to the deformity of the hunchback. The banter ends abruptly, and we can imagine that Richard's mask of good humor slips for a moment as he glares at the boy with barely concealed hatred. The princes leave for the Tower—from which, we know, they will not emerge alive—and Shakespeare loads the moment with dramatic irony. York expresses his fear of meeting the ghost of his uncle Clarence, setting up a tense exchange:

> PRINCE. I fear no uncles dead.
> RICH. Nor any that live, I hope?
> PRINCE. And if they live, I hope I need not fear.

Once the princes have left, Buckingham directs Catesby to confer with Hastings and sound out his response to a proposal that Richard assume "the seat royal of this famous isle." Although it has been no secret to us, this is the first overt reference in the play to Richard's ambition, and it is of interest that Buckingham is the first to utter it. The duke, it will be noted, has assumed an assertive role as Richard's chief supporter and close adviser. He makes the unpleasant decisions, such as that to deny York sanctuary, thus allowing Richard to conceal his intent behind a public display of avuncular affection and concern. Here again it is Buckingham who sends Catesby on his mission. Buckingham is the essential stage manager of Richard's rise to the throne, and for his labors he is promised the earldom of Hereford, a rich prize, once that goal is achieved.

Buckingham asks Richard what is to be done if Hastings objects to the proposal. "Chop off his head, man" is the spontaneous response, and the duke hardly blinks an eye.

3.2 We move to Hastings's house, where a messenger from Lord Stanley, the Earl of Derby, arrives with an account of his master's dream in which "the boar had razed [cut] off his helm" and his proposal that they hastily make their escape. Hastings scoffs at Stanley's fears and dismisses the messenger, who leaves as Catesby enters. He sounds out the lord chamberlain, asking if he will support Richard's claim to the throne, and receives in reply an unequivocal rebuff. Even the news that his enemies, "the kindred of the Queen," are to be executed at Pomfret Castle fails to move Hastings from his position; and curiously he perceives no danger to himself, so secure is he that he is "dear / To princely Richard and to Buckingham." Several others enter, and to each Hastings expresses his satisfaction at the defeat of the queen's party. He is a well-meaning but bumbling innocent compared to the sharks he has the misfortune to cross, a pathetic victim who for some reason believes that Catesby is his man and that he has the absolute trust of the scheming Richard. He is a ripe fruit ready to be plucked, and the intriguing question is how the resourceful villain will manage it.

3.3–4   At Pomfret Castle the queen's kinsmen are escorted to their execution, which will confirm, they lament, Margaret's curse upon them "for standing by when Richard stabb'd her son." Meanwhile at the Tower the Council meets, as Hastings blithely announces, to decide on a date for the coronation of Edward V. Richard is absent, as is the pattern in such scenes, but the lord chamberlain confidently declares that the two of them are so close that he can cast a vote for both. Richard enters, acknowledging archly that "his lordship knows me well, and loves me well." He unexpectedly sends Morton, the Bishop of Ely, out to secure strawberries for him, a gesture, more than anything else, that demonstrates his authority over the assembly. Richard and Buckingham draw aside as Hastings once again expresses his innocent confidence in the lord protector: "I think there's never a man in Christendom / Can lesser hide his love or hate than he."

Richard returns and unexpectedly launches into a tirade against those who have caused his deformity. Baring his arm, "like a blasted sapling wither'd up," he blames his disability on "Edward's wife, that monstrous witch" and asks what should be done to those guilty of such a crime. Hastings, taken aback, acknowledges that "if they have done this deed"—but he is cut off. The "if" is enough for Richard, who rages that he is a traitor for even questioning the accusation. Storming off, he commands, "Off with his head!" Hastings regrets that he, "too fond, might have prevented this," and laments that Margaret's "heavy curse / Is lighted on poor Hastings' wretched head." As he is led off, he voices a prophecy of his own that for England this will be "the fearfull'st time to thee / That ever wretched age hath look'd upon."

3.5   The two conspirators now set in motion a plan to secure the approval of the people of London for Richard's assumption of the throne.

First they must justify the execution of Hastings. They array themselves "in rotten armor, marvelous ill-favored," as if to protect the Tower from assault. As Catesby enters with the lord mayor, Richard dashes about, shouting orders to alert the garrison for an impending attack. Lovell and Ratcliffe appear bearing Hastings's head, and Richard explains that much to his sorrow the lord chamberlain had proved a traitor who, Buckingham explains, plotted "to murder me and my good lord of Gloucester." * The mayor is duly impressed and leaves to inform "our duteous citizens" that justice has been done.

Richard sends Buckingham to follow him and seize the opportunity to spread slander against those who stand in the line of succession to the throne. Buckingham is to claim that the children of Edward IV are bastards and that the late king himself was not a legitimate son of the Duke of York. He is then to lead the people to Baynard's Castle, one of Richard's residences in the city, where, he promises, they will find him "well accompanied / With reverend fathers and well-learned bishops."

3.6–7   The response of the people to these fabrications is recorded in the Scrivener's short speech and in Buckingham's report to Richard on the public meeting at London's Guildhall. The citizens, it would appear, see through the deception and know Richard for the impostor he is. Buckingham reports that he declared the bastardy of Edward and his children, went on to praise the only legitimate claimant to the throne, and concluded with the cry, "God save Richard, England's royal King!"—only to be greeted by "a wilful silence" from the assembly. He had taken the precaution of planting a cache of his followers in the crowd, however, and on cue they raised a cheer, "God save King Richard!" Richard is incensed at the lack of response, but Buckingham calms him and describes the next step in the charade. In the presence of the citizens, now approaching, he will urge Richard to accept the crown, but he is to pretend reluctance and "play the maid's part," as the duke puts it, "still answer nay, and take it." Richard leaves to prepare for his act as the lord mayor and citizens enter.

The episode that follows is truly outrageous, but it is rare entertain-

---

*Catesby, Ratcliffe, and Lovell, minor figures in the play, were loyal followers of Richard, remembered chiefly in a piece of doggerel verse popular in Tudor times: "The Cat, the Rat, and Lovell Our Dog / Rule all England under the Hog."

ment. Richard gains the throne, Shakespeare makes evident, by means of a shameless charade, acting "the maid's part" with a show of sanctimonious reluctance to abandon his supposed contemplative life and accept the burden of office. He is sent for but returns word that he is engaged in prayer and meditation "with two right reverend fathers," providing a cue for Buckingham to praise his virtue. He is sent for again and is again reluctant. Finally he appears "aloft" on the balcony above the stage. It is a comically ludicrous picture, with Richard, a prayer book in hand, flanked by two bishops, "props of virtue for a Christian Prince," as Buckingham calls them. The duke launches into a long speech urging him to accept the crown. Richard replies at even more length, pleading his unworthiness for such a high office and reminding his listeners that "the royal tree hath left us royal fruit" in the two princes. Buckingham then repeats the evidence of their bastardy and urges Richard once more to accept the crown, only to be rejected yet again: "Alas, why would you heap this care on me? / I am unfit for state and majesty." Buckingham in mock exasperation abandons the argument and stalks out: "Come, citizens; zounds, I'll entreat no more." Catesby, on cue, urges Richard to call them back; as they return, he agrees, with an air of pained resignation, to assume the throne, adding piously, "God doth know, and you may partly see / How far I am from desire of this." It is agreed that he will be crowned the following day. Although he is an unscrupulous scoundrel, it is difficult not to delight in his performance.

4.1   While all this is going on, the three women, Elizabeth, now the dowager queen; the elderly Duchess of York, Richard's mother; and Anne, his wife, seek entrance to the Tower to see the princes. They are prevented by Brakenbury, who in a slip of the tongue informs them that "the King" forbids it—but quickly corrects himself. Stanley arrives to escort Anne to Westminster for Richard's coronation; and Elizabeth, shocked at the news, urges her son, Dorset, to flee England and join the Earl of Richmond in France (the first mention of him in the play). Anne laments her marriage to Richard, observing ruefully that the curse she had laid on him earlier has now returned to plague her. She reveals that she cannot sleep in his bed because he is afflicted nightly by "timorous dreams," the first hint in the play that all is not well with him. They depart as Elizabeth, looking back at the Tower, pleads, "pity, you ancient stones, those tender babes / Whom envy hath immur'd within your walls."

4.2   Richard is king now and appears in state. He engages Buckingham in private conversation and asks obliquely for his agreement to the murder of the princes. The duke, either failing to grasp his meaning or not wishing to, avoids the question until Richard blurts out impatiently, "shall I be plain? I wish the bastards dead," and demands a reply. Buckingham is evasive, requesting "some pause" to consider the matter, and then leaves. The king, who had perhaps counted on him to arrange for the deaths, now finds he must do it himself, and he sends for Tyrrel. The duke's hesitation, however, is enough to discredit him with Richard: "The deep-revolving, witty Buckingham / No more shall be neighbor to my counsels." He is king now, to be sure, but, having achieved his goal, he grows uneasy, suspicious of his closest confidant at the first slight sign of disloyalty. He must take steps to secure himself in the throne and so plans to do away with the princes and neutralize the children of Clarence. He instructs Catesby to spread rumors that his wife Anne "is sick and like to die" so that he can eliminate her, leaving him free to marry Elizabeth of York, the princes's sister. These are drastic measures, he admits, but, as he observes, "I am in / So far in blood that sin will pluck on sin." Readers will hear in these lines an echo of Macbeth's "I am in blood / Stepped in so far that, should I wade no more, / Returning were as tedious as go o'er"—and indeed the parallels between the two figures invite comparison.

Richard instructs Tyrrel to murder the princes. As he leaves, Buckingham returns. He alludes to the question at first, but the king dismisses the subject. Buckingham then reminds Richard of his promise of the earldom of Hereford, but the king evades the matter. The duke presses his claim while Richard pretends not to hear, preoccupied, it seems, with another matter entirely: the prophecies that Richmond will be king. He finally turns sharply on Buckingham and dismisses his suit with a contemptuous, "I am not in the giving vein today." He then stalks out to leave the duke alone contemplating his status. "Made I him king for this?" he asks, and decides that he had better make his escape "while my fearful head is on."

4.3   Shakespeare does not dramatize the murder of the princes. He may have considered two episodes of violent death in the Tower one too many for the play. So he places before us the well-deserved death of Clarence rather than the cruel murder of two innocent young boys, a scene he perhaps felt too traumatic for the stage. We hear of their deaths from Tyrrel, who has employed two men to carry it out. His words strike a note of regret at "the most arch deed of piteous massacre / That yet this land was guilty of," and he reveals that the murderers themselves, though "flesh'd villains, bloody dogs," wept at the telling of it, stricken with "conscience and remorse." Two elements of this brief speech deserve attention. The first is Tyrrel's allusion to the guilt of "the land"—not Richard, it will be noted, but England itself, which reminds us of the theme so prominently defined in Margaret's curses. The kingdom carries the weight of a host of murders and must be purged of crimes if it is to be restored to health. The second reference of interest is Tyrrel's allusion to the murderers' "remorse and conscience." It will be recalled that one of Clarence's murderers is so conscience-stricken that he refuses payment for the crime; and, confessing his many treacheries, the doomed duke himself fears that God will "be aveng'd on my misdeeds." In raising the issue of conscience, Shakespeare poses the question about Richard: does he display any remorse or drop of guilt about his "misdeeds"?

The king concludes the scene, noting that he has effectively nullified the position of Clarence's children and somehow effected the death of his wife, Anne. He is now free, he celebrates gleefully, to seek the hand of Edward's daughter Elizabeth, and so "to her I go, a jolly thriving wooer." He certainly has reason to be pleased with himself, for everything seems to be going his way. But at the very moment he assumes this air of smug satisfaction, cracks begin to appear in his crown. John Morton, the influential Bishop of Ely, has fled abroad to join Richmond, and Buckingham has assembled a rebellious army. Richard reacts to these reports with characteristic vigor, observing that "fearful commenting [anxious debate] / Is leaden servitor to dull delay." He takes to the field, his natural element, with the command: "Go muster men. My counsel is my shield."

4.4–5 The following scene takes the form of a ritual recital of the griefs of the kingdom as well as an impassioned evocation of the theme of just retribution. It is a reprise of an earlier episode in which three women appear to mourn their losses. Here two ex-queens and a royal mother lament the past and the condition to which they have been reduced. The first to appear is Margaret, who conceals herself to overhear the grieving of the others. Queen Elizabeth enters, mourning the death of the princes, and the Duchess of York echoes her in a regret that Edward had to die. The two women sink to the ground in grief as Margaret comes forward, chanting an indictment of the whole history of internecine warfare:

> I had an Edward, till a Richard kill'd him:
> I had a husband, till a Richard kill'd him:
> Thou hadst an Edward, till a Richard kill'd him;
> Thou hadst a Richard, till a Richard kill'd him.

The incantation of the names imbeds the impression that there is a form of divine justice at work here, lives rightfully forfeited for the lives of others, and the repetition of "Richard" leaves little doubt as to who is the instrument of that justice (the victim of the final line is the young Duke of York). Shakespeare implies that Richard III, as wicked as he is, has been visited upon the kingdom, a "Scourge of God" sent to punish all those guilty of earlier crimes. He is not to be exonerated for his acts, nor is he any the less entertaining for this allegorical role, but these poetic repetitions lend him the air of a divine nemesis sent to exact retribution for ancient wrongs. The scene continues in this vein, with Margaret relishing a harsh satisfaction at the suffering of the other women and delighting in the fulfillment of her dire prophecies. She leaves, content now that their woes "pierce like mine."

The king appears, leading an army to oppose Buckingham. He is confronted by the two women, who condemn him in the most vindictive terms. Most telling are the curses of his mother: "Bloody thou art: bloody will be thy end. / Shame serves thy life and doth thy death attend." On her departure, Richard pauses to speak with Elizabeth in a reprise of his earlier wooing scene with Anne. He appeals to the queen to intercede with her daughter for him, using some of the same arguments that had proved successful on the earlier occasion. Accused of murdering her brothers, he responds, "say that I did it for love of her"—it worked before, so why not now? His chief appeal, however, is to Elizabeth's self-interest. "I did take the kingdom from your sons," he admits, so "to make amends I'll give it to your daughter," and in consequence she will be once more "mother to a king." Richard continues to appeal his cause, even to adopting the pose of a penitent—"plead what I will be, not what I have been"—another approach that was effective with Anne, until it seems he has once more had his way. "Write to me very shortly," Elizabeth concludes, "and you shall understand from me my mind." Again, as in the earlier scene, privately he has nothing but scorn for her: "Relenting fool, and shallow, changing woman!" Elizabeth's words may imply agreement, but we are left with the impression that she is made of sterner stuff than simple Anne, and that Richard's scorn may be sadly misplaced this time.

Ratcliffe brings reports of the approach of Richmond's fleet and Buckingham's march to join forces with him. Richard loses his composure momentarily, ordering Catesby to carry a message to the Duke of Norfolk and then berating him for not being gone. Catesby responds patiently that he has yet to be told what message to deliver. A disconcerted Richard replies, "O, true, good Catesby," but then countermands a like order to Ratcliffe. He is clearly rattled but soon recovers his composure. Stanley arrives with further news of Richmond's moves. The king, distrusting the earl as he now does all about him, orders him to muster men but to leave his son George behind as hostage to his loyalty. A quick succession of messengers bring more bad news, including a report that Richmond has finally landed at Milford in Wales, and Richard promptly orders a march toward Salisbury to rally forces in opposition. Shakespeare takes nothing away from Richard as a warrior and commander in battle. It is his relentless aspiration for power and his alienation from those who are repelled by his method of gaining it that leads to his destruction. In describing the arch-villain, Shakespeare gives the devil his due.

In a conference with one of Richmond's allies, Stanley, who is the earl's stepfather, shows himself a traitor to the king—afraid to change sides, however, for fear of retaliation against his son. Richard, it appears, has good reason to mistrust him.

5.1–2 In the opening scene of the animated fifth act, we find that Buckingham has been defeated and captured. He is led to his execution, fulfilling Margaret's prophecy that he will regret his alliance with Richard. In the short scene that follows we first meet Richmond, who professes that England is "bruis'd underneath the yoke of tyranny" by "the wretched, bloody, and usurping boar," and predicts that Richard's defeat will "reap the harvest of perpetual peace." Here and later, Richmond excites little dramatic interest. He is a one-dimensional figure who cannot even be called a *foil* to the more engaging and complex villain.

The future Henry VII is a spokesman for the Tudor party line, and Shakespeare makes no effort to depict him as other than a stilted mouthpiece.

5.3   The setting of the next long, busy scene is Bosworth Field on the night before battle. Rather than alternate between the two armies in a series of scenes as he does later in *Henry V*, Shakespeare chose to present both camps on the stage at the same time. We are asked to imagine the opposing forces in close proximity, with Richard's tent to one side and Richmond's to the other, separated by but a few yards, though in fact they are obviously at a much greater distance.

The first to appear is Richard, who orders his tent to be raised at, let us say, stage left, and expresses confidence in the numerical superiority of his army. Next arrive Richmond and his followers, at stage right, and he in turn expresses confidence in the anticipated defection of Stanley's forces, which are a part of Richard's line of battle but at some distance from it. Richard then speaks of his doubts about Stanley's loyalty, and to confirm his suspicions, the earl appears at Richmond's tent, declaring his allegiance but a reluctance to make an overt move for fear of endangering his son's life. As he departs, Richmond kneels and prays to God, "whose captain I account myself," for victory in the battle. This episode is not repeated in Richard's camp, his earlier mockery of religion having evidently rendered an image of him in prayer inappropriate.

Both leaders then retire to sleep, only to be visited by the ghosts of Richard's victims. They float on stage, each condemning Richard's crimes with the curse, "despair and die," and encouraging Richmond, "live and flourish." Richard wakens abruptly from the dream and in a complex *soliloquy* examines its meaning. He assumes that it is an affliction of "coward conscience," and he wrestles with his thoughts: "Is there a murderer here? No. Yes, I am!" and "I am a villain—yet I lie, I am not!" He contemplates his many crimes and in a moment of despair regrets that "there is no creature loves me, / And if I die, no soul will pity me." But he quickly recovers with the resolute thought that since he has no pity for himself, he expects none from others. And yet the appearance of the ghosts is an ominous sign, so he sets out to test the loyalty of his followers: "I'll play the eavesdropper, / To see if any mean to shrink from me." He trusts no one.

This attack of conscience marks Richard's lowest moment in the play, but Shakespeare does not make much of it. The figure has been portrayed as a man without conscience throughout, and to show him now suffering from guilt would create an inconsistency in his character. He is obviously shaken, but anyone visited by the ghosts of his victims might be expected to lapse into momentary fear. Conscience has been a theme of the play, in which Shakespeare portrays even the most hardened criminals, the murderers of Clarence and the princes, subject to remorse for their deeds. But these figures are largely foils to Richard, who shows no regret as he moves from one plot to another even more vicious with an air of carefree abandon, delighting in his own ingenuity. We would be disappointed if he were to fall victim to "coward conscience" at this late stage, and it comes as a relief that he does not.*

Richmond wakens, refreshed by a sound night's sleep, the dream not unexpectedly having heartened him. He addresses his soldiers in the stage tradition of the oration before battle. He speaks of the justice of the cause and the assurance that God is on their side against the wicked foe: "Then, if you fight against God's enemy, / God will, in justice, ward [protect] you as his soldiers." There is a great deal of talk before battle in these plays and precious little of the battle itself—indeed, Bosworth Field is portrayed in only one short scene and part of another. The limitations of the Elizabethan *stage*, or for that matter any stage, do not permit the dramatic spectacle of combat with a cast of thousands seen in modern films. Richard arms for battle, apparently recovered from his fit—"Conscience is but a word cowards use, / Devis'd at first to keep the strong in awe"—and addresses his army as well. There is no talk of God here, only disparagement of this "scum of Bretons and base lackey peasants" who if not defeated will "lie with our wives" and "ravish our daughters." † Defying orders, Stanley fails to bring his forces on the line of battle, and the king does not hesitate: "Off with his son George's head!" He sets his army in motion.

5.4 The battle rages as Catesby rushes in with an account of the king's prowess in combat. He has been seeking out his opponent in the enemy ranks and complains that there are "six Richmonds in the field,"

---

*Shakespeare was fond of this theme, as in Hamlet's "conscience does make cowards of us all."

†Richmond has been in exile in Brittany (Bretagne), and Richard makes much of the fact that his army contains more French conscripts than English yeomen.

five of whom he has killed. Medieval monarchs, when they led forces in battle, often arranged for others to wear the royal armor. The practice was a form of insurance for the king and served to encourage his soldiers who were inclined to fight more vigorously if they thought themselves in his presence.* In the heat of combat Richard has lost his mount, occasion for what is the best-known line in the play: "A horse! A horse! My kingdom for a horse!"

5.5   Richmond comes upon him, the two fight, and Richard is slain. This is the climactic moment of the play, though neither character has lines during the encounter, leaving it entirely to the staging to convey the excitement of the action. Richmond announces the victory— "The day is ours; the bloody dog is dead"—as Stanley retrieves the crown from the dead king and places it on Richmond's head. The new monarch, now Henry VII, proclaims his intention to marry Elizabeth of York, thus uniting "the white [York] rose and the red [Lancaster]" and ending the long conflict between the two noble houses. "England," he laments, "hath long been mad, and scarr'd herself." The union gives promise of a future "smooth-fac'd peace, / With smiling plenty, and fair prosperous days."

Thus Richard is dead, bringing to an end the kingdom's long nightmare. But Richmond's closing remark that "England hath long been mad, and scarr'd herself" calls for further thought. In the end it seems the dead king is all but forgotten—no parading of his head on the end of a pike as in *Macbeth*. He was in a sense a consequence, rather than a cause, of his country's madness, and the land is to be healed not so much by his death as by the union of the warring houses that have "scarr'd" it. Richard may be seen in several different lights. As a dramatic character he is quintessentially evil, showing no sense of remorse, no sting of conscience for his crimes. But he is endlessly fascinating as he treads his bloody path to the throne. In another sense he is but the final burden placed upon this torn kingdom, a form of punishment imposed on England for a crime committed three generations earlier—the killing of an anointed king, Richard II. The tyrannical reign of Richard III, it is implied, was but a brief time of terror and anguish for England; but now

---

*In *Henry IV, Part 1*, Douglas complains bitterly about the practice.

that he is dead the land's long penance is over, and its people can again look forward to peace and plenty.

Seen thus, Richard III is a kind of scapegoat. Thirty years of hatred and treachery during the War of the Roses are embodied in his figure, his humpbacked shoulders made to bear the weight of all that cruelty. In killing him Richmond exorcises the malignancy, purging the land of its sickness, and initiates a reign that promises to lead it back to health. Then again, Richard assumes the role of the "Scourge of God," sent to punish the offending houses. He is responsible for deaths on both sides— the Lancastrian king, Henry VI, and his son, and then the surviving Yorks. Both houses have been guilty of perjury, hatred, treachery, and heartless slaughter, creating an atmosphere of mistrust and nurtured grievances in which unprincipled malice can thrive—it is "a world" for Richard "to bustle in."

The death of Richard III is not tragic, as Aristotle defines the term.[*] He is irredeemably evil, a figure empty of conscience or remorse, who suffers a well-deserved death, hence beyond our sympathy. Unlike Macbeth, who at the outset at least is "too full o'th milk of human kindness," Richard is consistently wicked from beginning to end. And yet we regret his passing. We were able to check our sense of moral outrage in the cloakroom and settle back for an enjoyable evening, entertained by an ingenious villain who outthinks, outtalks, and outwits a group of characters who are only moderately less disagreeable and certainly less interesting than he is. It is difficult to develop empathy for a parade of mourning women, a household full of contentious, scheming relatives, and on such short acquaintance even a pair of sadly doomed children. And the triumphant Richmond is such a stick! We shall miss the demonic splendor of Richard III—the villain we love to hate.

*See "Tragedy," pp. 7–8.

KING JOHN

❧

ON HIS DEATH in 1189, Henry II of England left two sons by his tempestuous wife, Eleanor of Aquitaine (here "Elinor"). Richard *Coeur de Lion* (the Lion Hearted) succeeded his father, and when he died, his brother John assumed the throne. His right to reign was contested, however, by Constance, the widow of a third son, Geoffrey, who claimed the rightful heir was her son Arthur, then a boy in his teens. John is best known to modern audiences as the English king who was forced by his nobles to sign the Magna Carta, which limited the arbitrary power of the monarchy—but that event goes unmentioned in the play.

Act One   King Philip of France, prodded by Constance, claims the English crown for young Arthur. In England, King John decides that the issue can be decided only by war, but first he has a domestic matter to attend to. Philip Faulconbridge, the bastard son of Robert (referred to in the reading text as the "Bastard"), contests his legitimate half-brother's inheritance of their father's lands and title. Both John and his mother, Elinor, remark on the Bastard's resemblance to the dead King Richard. Intrigued by his appearance, the king offers to take him into his service if he will drop his suit against his brother. The Bastard readily agrees and is knighted. Later he confronts his mother, who confirms that he was indeed sired by Richard *Coeur de Lion* while her husband was abroad.

Act Two   King Philip and his ally, the Duke of Austria, lay siege to the French city of Angiers, then under English control, demanding that its citizens acknowledge Arthur's claim to the English throne. They are interrupted by the approach of a large English army under King John, who has come to ensure the continued allegiance of the city. After a long exchange of claims and counterclaims by the two monarchs, they address a citizen of Angiers, who acts as spokesman for the city. Philip demands that he surrender in the name of Arthur, and John counters with his own claim. But the citizen refuses, protesting that the city can open its gates only to the one who proves himself the rightful king of England. At the Bastard's urging, the contentious kings set their differences aside for the moment and agree to join forces and reduce Angiers, leaving until later the issue of the succession.

The citizen proposes that they consider a measure that will avoid bloodshed: Let King John's niece, Blanche of Castile, marry the French royal heir, Lewis the Dauphin, thus healing the breach between the two kingdoms. They agree, much to the Bastard's disgust. He is eager for battle and complains in a long *soliloquy* that "commodity"—that is, expediency or commercial self-interest—has dissuaded them to favor "a most base and sick-concluded peace" rather than "a resolved and honorable war."

Act Three   Constance laments the unexpected amity between France and England, since the match leaves Prince Arthur without a champion. She rages against the agreement. The peace in fact is short-lived and the agent of discord is Cardinal Pandulph, the papal legate. John had rejected the pope's choice for Archbishop of Canterbury, and Pandulph threatens him with excommunication if he does not reverse his decision. The king resolutely defies the pope's authority—"No Italian priest / Shall tithe or toll in our dominions"—and is promptly declared "cursed and excommunicate," a decree that absolves any of his subjects or allies from allegiance to him.

Pandulph then turns to Philip and in a lengthy legal argument persuades him to break his pact with the reprobate John. Urged on by Lewis and Constance, and ignoring the pleas of Elinor and the newly married Blanche, Philip submits to papal authority, and the two armies prepare for combat. The Bastard distinguishes himself in the battle, killing Austria and rescuing Elinor from the French, and Arthur is captured. John entrusts the prince to his loyal servant Hubert, with orders to put him to death.

In the French camp Philip despairs over his defeat, and Constance laments the capture of Arthur. The wily Pandulph counsels that all will be well and urges Philip to make preparations for an invasion of England.

Act Four   Later in England, Hubert prepares to put out the eyes of young Arthur, but the prince pleads with him so eloquently that he relents and promises to protect the boy. Meanwhile at the palace, two of King John's powerful nobles advise him to release Arthur, whose imprisonment has caused discontent among the English people. The king agrees, but Hubert, in an effort to shield the prince, reports that Arthur is already dead. The nobles leave to recover the body as John receives notice that the French are preparing to invade and that the ladies Elinor and Constance have died. The Bastard comes in to inform the king that the people are fearful and the lords resentful, and John sends him back to do what he can to ensure their loyalty. Hubert confesses that Arthur still lives, and John hurries him out to inform the lords.

Arthur attempts to escape but kills himself as he jumps from the castle walls. The lords approach the castle as the Bastard meets them, and together they find Arthur's body, immediately attributing his death to Hubert, acting on the king's orders. Hubert enters, announcing that Arthur lives, only to be confronted with his body. He denies the crime, and the Bastard has to defend him against the enraged lords. Thoroughly disgusted with John now, they leave to join forces with the invading French, and the Bastard returns to the palace.

Act Five   In the face of adversity, John is forced to endure a symbolic ceremony—surrendering his crown to Pandulph, who accepts it in the name of the pope and then in his name again returns it to the now submissive king. Having achieved his purpose, the cardinal hurries out to head off the French invasion. The Bastard comes upon an inconsolable John and urges him to rouse himself, rally his subjects, and repel the invasion: "Let us, my liege, to arms!" The king revives momentarily and appoints the Bastard commander of his armies. In the French camp the Dauphin Lewis greets the English nobles gratefully, only to be urged by Pandulph to end the war. The dauphin refuses with a show of resolve—"Am I Rome's slave?"—as the Bastard enters to defy them. The armies prepare for battle.

King John is sick and retires to Swinstead Abbey while the Bastard holds his own in the field. Melun, a fatally wounded French lord, informs the English lords that the dauphin intends to behead them once he has conquered the country, and they decide to renew their loyalty to John. The Bastard and Hubert make their way to Swinstead to find that the king has been poisoned and the English lords have deserted the French. A monk, it seems, has administered the poison, which proves fatal to the king. The Bastard pledges himself to his successor, Prince Henry, as Pandulph arrives with offers of peace from the French. Shakespeare ends the play on a patriotic note as the Bastard declares that "England never did, nor ever shall, / Lie at the proud feet of a conqueror" as long as her nobles remain loyal.

It is not a pretty picture that Shakespeare paints of the imperious Pandulph lording it over submissive kings, fomenting wars to assert the sway of papal power, while those same monarchs squabble over succession to a throne. But it was not a pretty time, this era when ambitious nobles easily switched loyalties to advance what the Bastard scorns as "commodity." Indeed, he is the only figure who seems to emerge from this spectacle of medieval anarchy with any dignity.

HENRY VIII

❧

HENRY VIII, it is generally agreed, was Shakespeare's last play, and he is said by some to have composed it in collaboration with John Fletcher, another playwright of the time. The focus of the plot is the king's divorce of his wife of twenty years, Katherine of Aragon, and his marriage to Anne Boleyn ("Bullen" here). It is an account of the rise and fall in the king's pleasure of various lords and ladies—Buckingham down, Wolsey up; Katherine down, Anne up; Wolsey down, Cranmer up—dramatized in a series of trial scenes.

Act One   The play opens on a trio of English lords engaged in court gossip, exchanging views on the recently concluded meeting between King Henry and Francis I of France. The two young kings competed to outdazzle each other with the splendor of their courts at the Field of the Cloth of Gold. The Duke of Norfolk describes the event in glowing terms, but the Duke of Buckingham complains of the fruitless extravagance to achieve a treaty that France has already violated. Cardinal Wolsey was responsible for the ostentatious display, he charges, designing it at great expense solely to enhance his influence with the king. Norfolk warns Buckingham to be careful because of Wolsey's influence over the king. Similar conversations take place throughout the play, where minor figures perform the function of a *chorus*, commenting on the action and filling us in on intervening events.

The cardinal enters briefly, glowers at Buckingham, and passes on to interrogate the duke's "surveyor," the overseer of his estates. Buckingham knows Wolsey is corrupt and he intends to inform the king that the cardinal "does buy and sell his honor"—but before he can do so he is arrested for treason. He suspects that his surveyor has falsely betrayed him.

In the king's council chamber, Queen Katherine pleads the cause of subjects heavily taxed by Wolsey, who denies knowledge of the matter. Henry orders a pardon for those who have refused to pay and then interrogates Buckingham's surveyor, who at the instigation of Wolsey accuses the duke of treason. Buckingham will have a trial, but it is clear that Henry has already decided he is guilty.

After more court chitchat between a pair of nobles, this time about the king's order suppressing French customs that have crept into English speech and dress, they depart for a ball hosted by Cardinal Wolsey. The arrival of Henry and the royal party is announced by the boom of cannon,* but they enter masked and playfully dressed as shepherds. The king singles out Anne Boleyn, one of his wife's ladies-in-waiting, for special attention.

Act Two Buckingham is tried, condemned, and led off to execution. Two gentlemen of the court discuss the latest events: Henry is separated from his wife, Katherine, and a Cardinal Campeius has arrived from Rome to hear the king's appeal for a divorce. Conversation among the lord chamberlain and the dukes of Suffolk and Norfolk confirms their distrust of Wolsey, who they say favors a divorce so that Henry may marry the French king's sister. Henry is troubled by his decision to divorce his wife but agrees that the case will be heard before the two cardinals. Anne expresses pity for the queen in a scene that establishes her innocence in the affair. The chamberlain enters to inform her that she has been appointed Marchioness of Pembroke with an allowance of a thousand pounds a year.

In a public trial, Katherine pleads her case to the king, refuses to be heard by the cardinals, appeals to the pope, and departs. Henry acknowledges her virtue and asks for a divorce, but Campeius counsels that in the absence of the queen the court be adjourned.

---

*In all probability it was wadding from the blanks fired in these cannon that set fire to the thatched roof of the Globe in 1613 during a performance of the play and burned the theater to the ground.

Act Three   An interview between Katherine and the two cardinals emphasizes her virtue and their duplicity. Wolsey's plan to marry Henry to the French king's Catholic sister has been defeated by the king's infatuation with Protestant Anne, so Wolsey writes to the pope advising him to refuse the divorce. His scheme is uncovered when Henry comes into possession of Wolsey's letter. The king in fact has already married Anne secretly and is preparing for her coronation. He has also found an inventory of the cardinal's great wealth, accumulated over the years by misuse of the powers of his office. He dismisses Wolsey.

Act Four   Gentlemen of the court watch the passage of the coronation procession and hear a glowing account of the new queen. Katherine hears that Wolsey is dead. She writes to the king, asking him to treat their daughter Mary kindly and then exits to prepare for her own death.

Act Five   Anne is in labor. Thomas Cranmer, Archbishop of Canterbury, has replaced Wolsey as Henry's closest adviser, and several high nobles plot to discredit him in the king's eyes. Henry informs the archbishop that he will have to answer their charges in a trial, but he gives him a ring to display, authorizing a direct appeal to the king should the decision go against him. Anne is delivered of a baby girl, the princess Elizabeth, and Henry hurries off to be at her bedside.

Cranmer is brought to trial and accused of spreading "new opinions / Divers and dangerous; which are heresies"; but when the archbishop asks that his accusers "stand forth face to face" and state their charges, he is refused.* It is decided rather that he will be confined in the Tower to await the king's pleasure, but Cranmer produces the ring, forestalling the arrest. Henry, who has been listening from behind a curtain, emerges and roundly scolds the accusers, expressing his full confidence in the archbishop. He honors Cranmer by asking him to stand as godfather to his newborn child and requires all those present to accept him as a friend. At the christening Cranmer turns prophet in a long speech foretelling that Elizabeth "now promises / Upon this land a thousand thousand blessings" and will in time "create another heir . . . as great in fame

---

*Cranmer was one of the driving forces of the English Reformation.

as she was," an allusion to King James I, who doubtless attended a performance or two of the play.

Shakespeare's Henry VIII is not the monster that later historians describe. He is rather a sympathetic figure who agonizes over the divorce and seems to be genuinely in love with Anne. He is loyal to his followers, dismissing Wolsey only because of damning evidence against him, and defending Cranmer against his accusers. Shakespeare avoids mention of the executions of Anne and Sir Thomas More, or of the king's later wives, as well he might in a play about Queen Elizabeth's father and the great uncle of King James I. In 1613 it was better to remain silent about such matters.

Appendix: Words and Phrases

Arranged Marriage Modern audiences may be uncomfortable with the image of an overly submissive daughter bowing meekly to the demands of a father who peremptorily chooses a husband for her with no concern for her sentiments in the matter. But such was the custom among the upper classes in Shakespeare's patristic society. In keeping with the belief in universal order, the father was considered the absolute head of the family, and as such he had the prerogative, indeed the obligation, to provide suitable mates for his daughters. On a more practical note, a young woman of marriageable age was looked upon as a valuable asset to a family, a means of cementing commercial or political alliances, of merging the fortunes of powerful merchant houses or bonding uneasy treaties between hostile nations. The daughter, whatever her affections, was obliged to submit to the higher good of social order in the fragile political and economic structure of the time. The practice reached absurd proportions at times, as when Charles VI of France, in hopes of securing peace with England, gave his seven-year-old daughter Isabelle in marriage to the mature Richard II (a discrepancy in ages that Shakespeare ignores).

The tension within a young woman, torn between the desires of her heart and devotion to her family—that is, between love and duty—is a frequent theme in Shakespeare's plays, and he explores it in both its comic and its tragic effects. He uses the custom to complicate the plots of his comedies, sometimes carrying the device to extremes, as in *The Merchant of Venice* where Portia is faithful to her father's wishes even though he is long dead, and in *Much Ado About Nothing* where the groom agrees to the elder Leonato's choice of a bride he has never laid eyes on. Shakespeare exploits the comic possibilities of young lovers devising ingenious schemes to evade the paternal designs, as in *The Taming of the Shrew, The Merchant of Venice*, and *A Midsummer Night's Dream*. The tragedies repeat the pattern but more often to the misfortune of the lovers: Desdemona defies her father in choosing Othello, as does Juliet in marrying Romeo. The paternal prerogative reappears in various forms, as in Lear's design to barter off Cordelia to the highest bidder, and Ophelia's submission to her father's command to sever her liaison with Hamlet.

Aside   When an actor delivers his lines in such a way that it is obvious some or all of the other characters on stage are not intended to hear him, he is said to be speaking an aside. When spoken to another character, the player will indicate by gesture or demeanor that the words are meant for that person's ears alone. In this instance we are asked to suspend our disbelief that, though the lines can be heard clearly in the last row of the balcony, a character three feet away is deaf to them.

The effect of an aside, as with a soliloquy, is to introduce dramatic irony into the action, since the audience now knows of plots and sentiments that some or all the characters in the play are unaware of. In comedies an aside will often conceal a clever remark that comments satirically on the behavior of another character, as in the exchange between Sebastian and Antonio mocking Gonzalo in *The Tempest*, or the witty responses of the sophisticated court to the ridiculous performance of *Pyramus and Thisby* in *A Midsummer Night's Dream*. Although a soliloquy achieves the same effect as an aside, it is generally much longer and is more often spoken by a character on an empty stage.

Chain of Being   The medieval and Renaissance mind struggled to construct an essential order out of the social and political chaos that marked the age. It longed to find a divinely designed structure to all existence. To that end it conceived of a great Chain of Being, an image of universal order that ordained a place for everything and everything in its place. This metaphysical construct imagined all existence as a giant chain stretching from the throne of God down to its lowest link in the lifeless, immobile stone. From the deity on down descended an intricate hierarchy of spiritual beings, from lordly archangels to the subordinate spirits of sea and land. From the stone upward rose the realm of vegetation and then the animal world. Humankind occupied a unique position at the center of the chain, a link that shared the qualities of the visible and the invisible worlds, both material in its mortal body and spiritual in its immortal soul. An elaborate set of beliefs grew up around the image, all of which confirmed the presence of the divine will at all levels of existence.

Chorus, Choric   In ancient Greek drama the chorus was a group of men or women who added music and dance to the plays, singing or chanting their lines as they moved about the stage. They were often a group of ordinary people—elder citizens, ladies of the court, or simple townsmen—who commented on the action as might anyone who does not have knowledge of the outcome of events. In this respect an audience could relate to them as people like themselves but lacking any special insights into the motives or intentions of the several characters or of future developments. Without that knowledge, which creates dramatic irony in the play, they were at times wrong in their judgment, but they always spoke with common sense.

In Shakespeare's time that role was more frequently assumed by a single figure. Sometimes he was an integral part of the plot, like Enobarbus, who comments knowingly on the characters in *Antony and Cleopatra*. But it was as often a jester who moved about on the edge of the action, like Feste in *Twelfth Night*, who adds wit and song to the comic atmosphere but is only marginally involved in the plot. Lear's Fool is a choric figure in his often biting appraisals of his master's condition, as to a lesser degree is Touchstone in *As You Like It*. On some occasions, notably in *Henry V*, *Romeo and Juliet*, and *Pericles*, Shakespeare employs a chorus who is outside the plot entirely, a figure who appears before each act and speaks directly to the audience, setting the scene and filling in gaps in the historical narrative.

Courtly Love   The code of courtly love evolved in twelfth-century France, where wandering troubadours entertained with songs of a knight's undying devotion to his "lady." It grew out of the Christian code of chivalry, which held that women occupied a special place in society. It was a knight's solemn obligation to protect, cherish, and "serve" them, a tradition perhaps best known to us from the tales of King Arthur and the knights of his Round Table. Life in medieval times was brutish, but somehow the ladies of the manor were able to persuade their rough husbands, whose idea of a spring fling was to ride out and raid their neighbors' villages, that they should stay by the fireside and talk of love, a practice that led to an elaborate code defining the proper behavior of a lover toward his lady.

The elements of this code are best illustrated by a popular story of the day, "The Knight's Tale" from Geoffrey Chaucer's *Canterbury Tales*, which Shakespeare and John Fletcher later dramatized in *The Two Noble Kinsmen*.

According to this tale, in a war between Athens and Thebes the victorious Athenians under Theseus capture two Theban nobles, the cousins Palamon and Arcite. They are imprisoned for life in a high tower overlooking a spacious garden, where one day they see the king's sister Emily, who has come to gather flowers. The two fall immediately in love with her and squabble over who saw her first. Arcite is liberated, but under pain of death if he is ever seen in Athens again. He returns to Thebes, where he pines away for Emily, envying Palamon who though still imprisoned can catch sight of her during her daily visits to the garden. Arcite's sorrows so change his appearance that he returns to Athens in disguise, where he manages to enter the service of Emily.

There is more to the story, of course, but this bare outline includes a number of elements of the courtly love code that appear frequently in Shakespeare's imagery and plots. First, the two cousins fall in love with Emily at first sight. Next, they contentedly worship her from afar. It was not necessary in the tradition that the lovers consummate the relationship—indeed it would not do at all if the lady is a queen or a married noblewoman. The knight is perfectly happy just to be in her presence; and if she acknowledges him with an occasional smile, his joy is complete. His only thought is to "serve" her, that is, to prove himself worthy of her regard, which he often does by feats of arms, fighting her enemies, riding off on Crusades to slay the Turk, championing the weak, and righting wrongs. Thus Arcite is entirely content just to enter Emily's service, even though he can never reveal his identity or hope to be anything more than her servant.

Of more importance to our understanding of Shakespeare's imagery, however, is Arcite's pitiable condition once he is set free and deprived of the sight of Emily. He is afflicted with what was called "the love disease," whose symptoms have been best described by the distinguished scholar Maurice Valency:

> In the initial stages the symptoms were not unbecoming—sleeplessness, loss of appetite, loss of flesh, and the characteristic pallor of the lover, together with love of solitude, and a tendency to weep, particularly when music was played. But we are told, unless the disease was cured, it became dangerous—the lover might pass into a melancholy, waste away, and die.

And, further:

> The lover sighed incessantly. Since each sigh came from the heart and
> cost him a drop of blood, his face grew pale, betraying his anemia. For
> lack of spirit, his bodily members failed. He froze and burned with
> love's fever, trembling constantly, consumed inwardly with excessive
> heat, outwardly chilled. In addition he suffered psychic tortures beyond
> description—jealousy, doubt, and fear, and incessant inner debate. He
> cut indeed a pitiable figure in the eyes of the world.*

While the courtly lover's condition may seem somewhat bizarre to modern taste, it must be admitted that, stripped of its excesses, it might be
said to describe the suffering of a similarly afflicted young man of our
own, or of any, day.

Shakespeare employs several other features of the tradition: If the lady
rejects the lover, he will die. It was said that if she were to look upon him
with disdain, her eyes would wound him, and mortally unless she saved
him by showing "pity." In Chaucer's tale the last plea of the dying Arcite
is "Pity, Emily!" The words have more earthy connotations, however,
since in the poetry of the day "to die" also meant sexual consummation,
and the lover's cry for "pity" was a plea for the lady's favors, that is, relief
from the terrible pain of his desire.

Readers and theatergoers will at times encounter imagery based on
this tradition in the tragedies—*Hamlet* and *Romeo and Juliet* come to
mind—but more extensively in the comedies, where Shakespeare employs the symptoms of the "love disease" more often than not to make
sport of the distraught lover. Like his modern counterpart, he is a figure
of fun, the butt of many jokes by well-meaning friends who, while sympathetic and perhaps even envious, will not let slip an opportunity to
comment wittily on his distracted state. Anyone who has attended a
prenuptial bachelor party will be familiar with the custom.

Deus ex machina   Ancient Greek dramas often concluded with a
god descending from Mount Olympus to remedy impossibly tangled
predicaments created by muddled humans, or to enact justice on the
wicked. The god entered from above, dangling at the end of a rope sus-

*Maurice Valency, *In Praise of Love* (New York: Macmillan, 1958), pp. 154–155.

pended from a derricklike mechanism that slowly lowered the deity from the imaginary skies—literally "the god out of the machine." In modern commentary the phrase is used to criticize a play whose plot is so contrived that the author must introduce some artificially manufactured factor, not necessarily supernatural, to resolve the action—a rich uncle who dies, leaving a tidy sum to an orphan on the verge of starvation, for example, or the sudden conversion of a hitherto ruthless villain. Such devices are acceptable in comedy—see *As You Like It* for sudden conversions—but not in serious drama, where the ending is expected to evolve reasonably out of the motives and actions of recognizable characters. Shakespeare does occasionally include gods in the cast, such as Hymen in *As You Like It*, Jupiter in *Cymbeline*, and Diana in *Pericles*; but, except for the last, they do not influence the course of events.

Dramatic Irony   This is an essential element of any successful stage production. Briefly, it is present when the audience knows more about what is going on than do any number of the characters in the play. Irony can be introduced in a variety of forms, directly with asides, as in *King Lear*, when Cordelia tells us that she cannot speak before refusing to, or in Hamlet's soliloquies, when he reveals his inner thoughts and intentions. It can be introduced artificially, as when at the beginning of Act Two of *Henry V* the chorus informs the audience of the plot against the king. Irony creates a heightened level of expectation in the audience as we await the impact of anticipated events on unsuspecting characters. We are drawn emotionally into the action of the play, reacting to situations in such a way as to become participants in the unfolding events, which is what every drama strives for. On a less weighty level, it is a necessary condition for comic effect as well. If we know that there is a figure lurking behind the door with a lemon meringue pie in hand, our anticipation adds to the hilarity when it ends up in the face of the unsuspecting victim.

On another level, irony is engaged when we know how a play or film will end, because we see events in a different light when we are aware of their consequences, either because the play is an account of familiar historical events (the North won the American Civil War, the *Titanic* sank) or because we are seeing it for a second time. Only good plays can tempt us back to the theater for another viewing, and, indeed, audiences attend performances of Shakespeare's works time and time again. One may see dozens of Macbeths and Hamlets in a lifetime, but obviously we do not return to discover what happens at the end. These plays have a rich texture of ironies, revealing the follies and nobilities of human nature, and we see them again and again, always discovering some new and surprising insight that had earlier escaped our notice. On first seeing Lear banish his only loving daughter and reward the unloving pair for their hollow words, we may well respond with the detached observation that he is a foolish old man. But when we know that his impulsive act will result in the death of almost all the major figures in that scene, himself included, our level of engagement in the action is heightened and our response to his folly more complex.

Foil In the theater a foil is often a minor character whose presence serves to emphasize certain traits in the chief figure, throwing light on them by contrast. We come to know that figure better when he is paired with another so different in some respects as to draw attention to his uniqueness. The most famous of Shakespeare's foils is Horatio, whose even-tempered composure lends emphasis to Hamlet's mercurial temperament. Indeed, it may be said that most of the characters in that play act in some way as foils to the central figure: Claudius, in his decisive action and swiftly hatched plots; Laertes, in his open, forceful challenge to those he believes murdered his father; Ophelia, who is truly mad, casting doubt on the degree of Hamlet's distraction; and Fortinbras, who in his brief appearances exemplifies the man of action in contrast to the man of thought. They all help define Hamlet's contradictory nature and puzzle us the more. A foil, therefore, does not necessarily stand in sharp contrast to the main figure—an evil character, for instance, who emphasizes another's virtue—Iago, in brief, is not a foil to Othello. In most cases the two figures have a great deal in common, as do Prince Hal and Hotspur in *Henry IV, Part 1*, where the similarities between the men, their youth and martial valor, lend emphasis to their differences.

Malaprop One of Shakespeare's comic devices is the mangling of the language. Characters such as the Gobbos in *The Merchant of Venice* and Dogberry in *Much Ado About Nothing* attempt elaborate words and get them wrong, even contrary to their intent, as when Dogberry proclaims that a criminal he has arrested will "be condemned to everlasting redemption." *The Merry Wives of Windsor* is particularly rich in characters who voice like absurdities. These comic misuses are referred to as "malaprops," though the word was unknown to Shakespeare, being derived from Sheridan's *The Rivals*, a mid-eighteenth-century play in which a character by that name excels in the practice. This form of wit is a bit cruel, based as it is so often on the inept efforts of marginally educated members of a certain class who aspire above their station and make a shambles of it. But all humor, in a sense, is cruel. The laughter is always at someone's expense, and frequently enough at the expense of people trying to be something they are not. Shakespeare's comedies are crowded with overblown egos just begging to be punctured.

Masque   An alternate form of dramatic entertainment in Shakespeare's time was the masque, performed not in the public theater but in private or semi-private locations such as large manor houses or the royal court. These were highly formal and ritualistic productions, with long set speeches and little action, composed especially for some important occasion—to celebrate a birth, a wedding, a military victory, or a feast day. The theme tended to be highly moral, in praise of virtue and censure of vice, with a plot—what there was of it—in which mythological gods and goddesses abound. Parts were frequently composed for performance by members of the host's family. The poetry is carefully balanced and heavily rhymed, perhaps to ease memorization by untrained actors, and recited or sung to the accompaniment of music and stately dance. The settings for court performances became increasingly elaborate. A contemporary of Shakespeare's, the gifted architect Inigo Jones, who designed and built the gracious Banqueting Hall in Westminster, wasted his considerable talents creating scenery for these costly productions, which was often destroyed after one performance.

Shakespeare wrote no masques that we know of, but on occasion he introduced episodes that imitate the studied ceremony and ritual decorum of the form, with its artful merging of poetry, music, and dance, as in *The Tempest* and *As You Like It*.

Pastoral   The pastoral tradition has been called "a universal impulse of the human mind." This judgment arises from the common perception that those who are close to nature—the farmer, shepherd, or woodsman—are somehow more genuine than are those in courts and cities. They are thought to be more honest, more sincere, less complicated, less artificial than the men and women who must assume the many façades and adapt to the mannered codes of a sophisticated culture. The simple herdsman, it is said, is closer to reality and, significantly in Shake-speare, more capable of true love and friendship than are those touched by the corrupting influence of a more advanced society.

This is a highly romantic notion. Nature can be cruel, particularly to those creatures lower in the food chain—it is "red in tooth and claw," in Tennyson's words. But like all such fanciful ideals the pastoral has an ele-ment of truth to it. Human beings are as much a part of nature as any eagle, eel, or sunflower. Our species emerged from caves and forests a short ten thousand years ago, a mere blink of the eye in the three-billion-year history of life on this planet; and we carry within us yet the genes of that long forest stay. How many city dwellers, tiring of the ceaseless bus-tle of the streets, long for the stillness of a forest glade or mountain meadow? And how many search for renewal on the shore of an ocean or by a placid pond?

So there is something to be said for this "universe impulse," and it has fired the imagination of poets since Homer first sang. The earliest of these poets formalized the concept into a literary tradition upon which succeeding generations have drawn for inspiration. These poets, Greeks from the island of Sicily, fixed upon the shepherd as the most apt example of "natural man," but any reference to shepherds is complex indeed. He is close to nature because he spends his days watching over his flock in meadows watered by mountain streams. Poets identified themselves with the figure because, having a great deal of time on his hands, he was said to fashion "pipes," or simple flutes, from reeds growing wild by those streams—hence, like the poet, he was a maker of music. In time he be-came a religious figure as well. Jesus was the "good shepherd," the local priest is still called a "pastor," and the bishop carries a shepherd's hook as a mark of his office. Each of these figures—the shepherd, the poet, and the priest—is said to have a gifted insight, an ability to see clearly and interpret movingly the truth of our nature.

Shakespeare employs the pastoral tradition in a variety of ways, at times in gentle satire, at others with serious intent. He often sets up a contrast between court and country, as in *As You Like It*, or city and coun-try, as in *The Merchant of Venice*. In *Richard II* it is the dutiful gardeners who see the king's shortcomings most clearly and most compassionately, and Henry V regrets momentarily his life of superficial ceremony, almost envying the simple peasant who rises and retires with the passage of the sun. In brief, those close to the soil have an honesty and integrity that the mighty have lost somewhere along the way.

Place   Quite often in Shakespeare's plays the location of the action has a significance of its own, particularly when he sets up a strong contrast between settings. In the pastoral tradition, honesty and integrity prevail and true love prospers in a country or forest setting, while greed, duplicity, hatred, and treachery mark life in a city or court, as in *As You Like It* and *The Merchant of Venice*. In *Antony and Cleopatra*, Rome symbolizes civic responsibility and the play for political power, and Egypt irresponsible self-indulgence, the one devoted to the forging of empire, the other to the pursuit of individual pleasure. The same place can take on a different character, however, in separate plays. In *The Merchant of Venice*, for example, the city is obsessed with commercial gain, its people given to racial intolerance and a desire for vengeance. In *Othello*, on the other hand, it is a place where the rule of law prevails over these same passions, where disputes are heard and resolved in court, in contrast to the almost frontier anarchy of Cyprus.

Soliloquy   This is a speech in which the character reveals to the audience his reaction to what is going on. It is sometimes addressed directly to the audience, the character seemingly taking us into his confidence, as in the opening lines of *Richard III*. Alternately it may take the form of inner musings, the character contemplating his condition or his choices, as with Hamlet on several occasions, Richard II in his prison cell, or Henry V deep in thought about "ceremony." A soliloquy differs from an aside in that the latter may be spoken at times to another figure in the play, but the effect is the same. We learn of feelings and intentions that other characters in the play have no knowledge of, thus introducing dramatic irony into the action.

Stage   The Elizabethan theater was a multisided structure some three stories high. How many sides it had is in dispute—the reconstructed Globe in London has twenty. The stage jutted out into the space within, called the "pit," where playgoers could stand during a performance for the box office price of a penny. A higher fee entitled them to sit on hard benches in the circles of covered balconies that rose on all sides. Despite holding an audience of two or three thousand, it was an intimate theater, with patrons in the pit crowding about the stage, at times quite literally within spitting distance of the actors.

Of more importance to our appreciation of the plays, however, is the fact that the theater was open to the elements. In the absence of adequate lighting, it could offer performances only during daylight hours. This limitation accounts for frequent references in the lines to the time of day or to ominous changes in the weather. Modern stage devices and cinematography can duplicate darkness or a storm, but Shakespeare had to convey the condition of the elements through his poetry, since his audience stood or sat in broad daylight. Lear's famous storm scene had to be evoked without benefit of lightning, rain, swirling wind, or a sound track of rolling thunder. Indeed, some of Shakespeare's most memorable lines identify the dawn or darker hours: Horatio's "but look, the morn in russet mantle clad / Walks o'er the dew of yon high eastward hill," or Macbeth's "now o'er the one half world / Nature seems dead, and wicked dreams abuse / The curtain'd sleep." The latter play is especially rich in such lines, since most of its scenes seem to take place during the hours of darkness. It was not until late in his career that Shakespeare's company secured the use of an indoor theater, Blackfriars in London, where he was relieved of the threat of an afternoon shower and could devise lighting to distinguish night from day.

Props were scanty in the Globe—an elaborate chair for a throne, or a single four-poster for a bedchamber, and vast armies locked in battle were represented by half a dozen extras in white uniforms at stage right and a similar number in red rushing in from the left. The chorus in *Henry V* entreats his audience to "piece out our imperfections with your thoughts," a task made easier, again, by Shakespeare's compelling poetry. Above the backdrop was a balcony, the setting for episodes in *Romeo and Juliet*, *Richard II*, and *Richard III*, among others. At some point a trapdoor was constructed in the floor at stage center, which enhanced the dramatic effect of the ghostly procession of Banquo's heirs in *Macbeth* and served as Ophelia's grave in *Hamlet*. For a reasonably accurate representation of the theater of the time, readers will enjoy the opening scenes of Laurence Olivier's film version of *Henry V* (1944).

Suspension of Disbelief This phrase is used to describe the audience's unspoken agreement to accept as reality whatever actors and playwrights present on the stage, though all are aware it is fiction. We know that Hamlet is a figment of Shakespeare's imagination, but we embrace the illusion that he is real so as to enter into the play and share his dilemmas. Many of the comedies derive their fun from disguises which result in mistaken identities, and our enjoyment of the action depends upon a willingness to accept the proposition, for example, that a brother and sister, both dressed as a young man, could be mistaken for each other (*Twelfth Night*), or that a daughter in the guise of a young man would go unrecognized by either her father or her lover (*As You Like It*). The phrase is useful in explaining the failure of works in which the playwright oversteps the bounds of that unspoken agreement by devising situations so contrived that they exhaust our willingness to suspend our disbelief. Some of Shakespeare's plays strain that willingness to its limits, *The Comedy of Errors* for example, but while we may shake our heads at improbable coincidences, we do so indulgently because of the fun the poet creates of them.

Theme   The theme of a work touches on a common human experience. It is the means whereby an author engages the reader, or in the case of a play draws the audience into the action, by indicating that it is about events or thoughts with which they are familiar. All have been children and many are fathers, and in *King Lear*, for example, Shakespeare announces early in the play that it will throw some light on the challenging and often troubled relationship between them. We encounter many themes in these works: love, dying, loss of innocence, coming of age, the intoxicating exercise of power, the role of spiritual or supernatural powers in human affairs—as well as a number that reflect the contradictions and conflicts of our condition: the desires of the individual versus the demands of society, appearance versus reality, reason versus passion, and good versus evil. Of course a writer cannot just throw themes into a work to give it weight. Success is measured by how well the experience is portrayed, by how often an audience will respond, "Oh, yes, that's how it is with us."

Universal Order*   It was a general belief in medieval and Renaissance times that since God had created everything on earth and in the heavens, all existence was united in a grand design. Since God was "one,"

---

*A reader curious for further information about this system of beliefs should consult E. M. W. Tillyard's *The Elizabethan World Picture* (London: Chatto & Windus, 1943). It is a short book, some one hundred pages, but endlessly fascinating.

it was said, so the universe too was "one." The concept was imaginatively portrayed as a great Chain of Being linking all created things from the lordly angels to the lowly stone. This unity manifested itself in a variety of ways: (1) In the repetition of numbers up and down the chain, as well as their multiples and additions. The number seven, for example, is important in Christian belief, and to the Renaissance mind it was of no small significance that the figure could be found at every level of existence, in the seven days of the week, seven heavenly bodies circling the Earth, seven Holy Sacraments, and seven openings in the head. (2) In the reappearance of certain geometric forms in the heavens and on earth—the triangle, square, quincunx, and especially the circle, a mysterious image of perfection. (3) In social and political resemblances between different levels of existence. It was believed that each link contained all the elements of the entire chain. Put otherwise, each link—a stone, a flower, a human being, a city, or a nation—was a microcosm of the whole universe, or macrocosm. Of perhaps even more importance, as a consequence each resembled all the others. Therefore if a poet compared a beehive to a kingdom, a monarch to the sun, a man's body to an island, or the human race to a continent, the image was something more than an inventive figure of speech; it arose from an article of belief.

Shakespeare employs certain aspects of this unity of existence in his imagery and plots, significantly the concept that since all levels were joined in this great chain, events at one point either reflect or foretell events at another. The storm in *King Lear*, for example, mirrors the disruption of order in the king's mind, in the royal family, and in the country as well, and when Macbeth murders Duncan, both nature and the heavens are in disarray. The parallel most frequently cited in Shakespeare's plays is the presence of a head or ruler at each level of existence. As God reigns over the universe, it was said, so does the sun rule the heavens, the father his family, the lion all beasts, the eagle all birds, the whale all fish, and, of special interest in the plays, the king his subjects. Of equal significance, particularly in the history plays, is the concept that those who presume to disrupt this cosmic design risk the displeasure of the great designer. Defy the divinely ordained order, it was believed, and you do so at your peril—and you may jeopardize the welfare of future generations as well. Shakespeare's imagery of a universal order should therefore not be dismissed as mere poetic decoration. In such images he reflected the beliefs of his fellow Englishmen, and perhaps himself as well, hence they evoked the insubstantial fears of an audience who shuddered at the thought of challenging the will of an omnipotent deity.

Index

If a character is pervasive in the lines, by presence or allusion, inclusive page numbers so indicate. Boldface numbers indicate where the entry is featured in the text.